Wagner and Wagnerism in Nineteenth-Century Sweden, Finland, and the Baltic Provinces

Eastman Studies in Music

Ralph P. Locke, Senior Editor
Eastman School of Music

(ISSN 1071–9989)

Additional Titles on Nineteenth- and Early Twentieth-Century Music

Analyzing Wagner's Operas: Alfred Lorenz and German Nationalist Ideology
Stephen McClatchie

Berlioz: Past, Present, Future
Edited by Peter Bloom

Berlioz's Semi-Operas: Roméo et Juliette *and* La damnation de Faust
Daniel Albright

"Claude Debussy As I Knew Him" and Other Writings of Arthur Hartmann
Edited by Samuel Hsu, Sidney Grolnic, and Mark Peters
Foreword by David Grayson

Debussy's Letters to Inghelbrecht: The Story of a Musical Friendship
Annotated by Margaret G. Cobb

French Organ Music from the Revolution to Franck and Widor
Edited by Lawrence Archbold and William J. Peterson

Historical Musicology: Sources, Methods, Interpretations
Edited by Stephen A. Crist and Roberta Montemorra Marvin

The Musical Madhouse (Les Grotesques de la musique)
Hector Berlioz
Translated and edited by Alastair Bruce
Introduction by Hugh Macdonald

Music's Modern Muse: A Life of Winnaretta Singer, Princesse de Polignac
Sylvia Kahan

The Pleasure of Modernist Music: Listening, Meaning, Intention, Ideology
Edited by Arved Ashby

The Poetic Debussy: A Collection of His Song Texts and Selected Letters
(Revised Second Edition)
Edited by Margaret G. Cobb

Portrait of Percy Grainger
Malcolm Gillies and David Pear

Schumann's Piano Cycles and the Novels of Jean Paul
Erika Reiman

"Wanderjahre of a Revolutionist" and Other Essays on American Music
Arthur Farwell, edited by Thomas Stoner

A complete list of titles in the Eastman Studies in Music Series, in order of publication, may be found at the end of this book.

Wagner and Wagnerism in Nineteenth-Century Sweden, Finland, and the Baltic Provinces

Reception, Enthusiasm, Cult

Hannu Salmi

University of Rochester Press

First published 2005

University of Rochester Press
668 Mt. Hope Avenue, Rochester, NY 14620, USA
www.urpress.com
and Boydell & Brewer Limited
PO Box 9, Woodbridge, Suffolk IP12 3DF, UK
www.boydellandbrewer.com

ISBN: 1–58046–207–3

Library of Congress Cataloging-in-Publication Data

Salmi, Hannu.
  Wagner and Wagnerism in nineteenth-century Sweden, Finland, and the Baltic
Provinces : reception, enthusiasm, cult / Hannu Salmi.
      p. cm. – (Eastman studies in music, ISSN 1071-9989 ; v. 34)
  Includes bibliographical references and index.
  ISBN 1-58046-207-3 (hardcover : alk. paper)
  1. Wagner, Richard, 1813-1883–Performances–Sweden. 2. Wagner, Richard,
1813-1883–Performances–Finland. 3. Wagner, Richard,
1813-1883–Performances–Baltic Provinces (Russia) 4. Operas–19th
century–Performances. I. Title. II. Series.
  ML410.W12S87 2005
  782.1′092–dc22
                          2005020431

A catalogue record for this title is available from the British Library
Designed and Typeset by Mizpah Publishing Services Private Limited

This publication is printed on acid-free paper.
Printed in the United States of America.

Contents

Illustrations

Maps

Figures

Tables

Acknowledgments

It has taken almost ten years to complete this book. In the early 1990s, I decided to delve into the history of Wagnerism, which, at that time, was still a rather unmapped territory. The main idea was not to restrict myself to a single national perspective but to emphasize a more comprehensive, comparative view of the theme. My research for the book led me to read German, Swedish, Finnish, Estonian, Latvian, and even Russian sources and took me into libraries and archives all around the Baltic Sea.

I have many people to thank for their kind assistance and support while I was engaged in this project. I owe a debt of gratitude especially to Mr. Stewart Spencer (London), who believed in my vision, encouraged me to go further, and even helped me with my language problems. At the beginning of my work I also received support from Professor Kalervo Hovi (University of Turku), whose expertise on Baltic history has been valuable. I am also grateful to Professor Livija Akuratere (University of Latvia), Dr. Inese Bula (University of Latvia), Dr. Sven Friedrich (National Archive of the Richard Wagner Foundation, Bayreuth), Professor Sven Hirn (Helsinki), Dr. Marjo Kaartinen (University of Turku), Professor Laurence Kitching (Simon Fraser University), Dr. Kari Kotkavaara (Åbo Akademi University), Dr. Marko Lehti (University of Turku), Professor Vita Lindenberg (Latvian Academy of Music), Dr. Kristel Pappel (Estonian Academy of Music), Mrs. Ieva Rubina (Theater Museum, Riga), Angelo Tajani (Sweden), and Professor Lavern Wagner (Quincy University). I would like to give special thanks to a few of the many librarians and archivists who made my work possible: Anne Ainz (National Library of Estonia); Mika Jantunen, Leo Mononen, and Tuulikki Väänänen (Library of the Sibelius Academy, Helsinki); Bergljot Krohn Bucht, Inger Mattsson and Helena Iggander (Archives of the Royal Theaters, Stockholm); Günter Fischer, Gudrun Föttinger, and Kristina Unger (National Archive of the Richard Wagner Foundation, Bayreuth); Marie Persson and Anna Wolodarski (Royal Library, Stockholm); Veslemöy Heintz and Birgitte Horne Jensen (Music Library of Sweden); and Dagmar Kjellström Thullberg (Stockholm City Archive).

The final editing of my English manuscript has taken place over the last three years. I would like, in particular, to acknowledge the advice and criticism provided by Mr. Uolevi Karrakoski and Professor Anthony Johnson. Dr. Keith Battarbee made an excellent job of translating a number of Swedish and German quotations for the book. I would also like to thank Professor Ralph P. Locke, the editor of Eastman Studies in Music, and Dr. Louise Goldberg, my copy editor at the University of Rochester Press, for their commitment and support.

Finally, I would like to thank the Academy of Finland, the Emil Aaltonen Foundation, and the Niilo Helander Foundation for their financial support.

Hannu Salmi
Turku, August 2005

Notes to the Reader

Around the Baltic Sea, the names of many cities and regions have changed during the nineteenth and twentieth centuries. This is especially problematic in the case of what we think of today as the three Baltic countries: Estonia, Latvia, and Lithuania. The area of present-day Estonia and Latvia was divided into three provinces, Estonia, Livonia, and Courland, which were called the Baltic provinces of the Russian Empire. Present-day Estonia includes both nineteenth-century Estonia and the northern part of Livonia. In Wagner's time, the city of Tartu, which is now situated in Estonia, was in northern Livonia. Present-day Latvia includes Courland and the southern part of Livonia.

In the case of Baltic city names, present-day names are used, but the German equivalents (which were used by Wagner and the Baltic-German population) can be found by consulting the geographical glossary. Estonian, Latvian, and Lithuanian names are preferred because they were also official names at the time and they make it easier for the reader to geographically situate the events described. In the case of East Prussia the situation is somewhat different. Those Prussian cities that are relevant to this study belong to Poland and Russia today, but they were known by their German names, which are therefore preferred in the present book. For example, Kaliningrad is here given as Königsberg and Gdansk is given as Danzig. These names can also be found in the glossary.

I have transliterated all titles of Russian books and articles from the Cyrillic alphabet. Quotations from the nineteenth-century Swedish and German sources have been translated by Dr. Keith Battarbee. All other translations, unless otherwise indicated, are my own.

Prelude

When *Der fliegende Holländer* was premiered in Stockholm in January 1872, the local music critic described Wagner's music as a "chaos of shrieks and signals."[1] To another critic, Wilhelm Bauck, Wagner represented an otherness that led him as far afield as Chinese music in his search for comparisons. Wagner's music was known in Sweden, as it was in the other countries and provinces around the Baltic Sea, by the 1850s. But while several of his early operas had already been staged by this time in countries on the eastern side of the Baltic—especially in Riga, Tallinn,[2] and Helsinki— Sweden had to be content with concert highlights until 1865, when *Rienzi* became the first of Wagner's operas to be performed at the Royal Opera in Stockholm.

Despite the voluminous literature on Wagner, there have been few insights into the reception of his works and the culture of Wagnerism. Wagner's psychological makeup far exceeds scholarly interest in his operatic legacy. This is due to the inevitable complexity of Wagner's historical influence, which reached far beyond the field of music. Wagner had participated in the Dresden Uprising in May 1849 and was known as a political figure throughout the nineteenth century. His theories on art and opera were also widely discussed in Europe as early as the 1850s. The fact that he emphasized the importance not only of music but also of drama, and of art in general, meant that his ideas interested not only musicians and composers but also novelists, dramatists, and poets. Numerous studies point to Wagner's literary influence. John Louis DiGaetani has investigated Wagnerian patterns in the fiction of Joseph Conrad, D. H. Lawrence, Virginia Woolf, and James Joyce.[3] Elwood Hartman has written on French literary Wagnerism,[4] Erwin Koppen on the impact of decadent Wagnerism on *fin-de-siècle* European literature,[5] and Raymond Furness on Wagner's influence on literature in general.[6]

Wagner's legacy has also been studied in the context of national-cultural influences, including, for example, the reception of his music and ideas in Austria, Brazil, Catalonia, England, France, Holland, Italy, Russia, and the United States.[7] *Wagnerism in European Culture and Politics* (1984) offered a valuable discussion of Wagner's influence in various countries.[8] Despite the fact that the Baltic Sea region was of central importance to Wagner, a history of Wagner in present-day Sweden, Finland, Estonia, and Latvia remains unwritten. This may seem all the more surprising when it is remembered that Wagner held appointments in Königsberg in East Prussia (present-day Kaliningrad in Russia) in 1836–37 and at Riga in Livonia from 1837 to 1839. Indeed, Riga later became one of the most important centers of Wagner's music in Europe.

The present volume concentrates on Sweden, Finland, and the Baltic provinces of the Russian Empire during the nineteenth century, analyzing the ways in which Wagner's music and ideas gradually became known there. The reception of Wagner is explored in a broad sense, not only encompassing the way in which his works were received by local audiences, but also taking into account the way in which his ideas were understood and interpreted. According to this definition, Wagnerism is a part of "the Wagnerian reception"; it implies an enthusiastic devotion to Wagner's music and ideas, a devotion that often assumed social forms and was channeled into societies and social activities. The conclusion of this book devotes attention to this organized enthusiasm.

There are three ways of defining Wagnerism. First, Wagnerism can be characterized—although not perhaps exclusively so—as an extramusical aspect of the Wagnerian reception. Wagner was an exceptional composer because of his extensive influence on literature, artistic theory, the theater, and political thought. This extramusical dimension was typical of French, British, and Italian Wagnerism. Second, Wagnerism can be distinguished from *Wagner-Begeisterung* or simple admiration and idolization. Wagnerism is by this definition an intellectual exercise or tool used to study Wagner's art. Third, Wagnerism can be seen as a historical concept describing a phenomenon that no longer exists. According to this interpretation, it is an-*ism* that can be compared to other intellectual movements of the nineteenth century. Wagnerism began during the 1850s and blossomed throughout the following decades before effectively coming to an end with the First World War.[9]

As there are so many different aspects of the Wagnerian reception and Wagnerism, it is hoped that a regional comparison will provide instructive insights into the process as a whole. Preliminary findings suggest that in Sweden Wagnerism assumed more extramusical forms than on the eastern side of the Baltic Sea. As a result, a focus on the influence of Wagner in individual countries has been eschewed in favor of an international/-regional and cross-cultural analysis. There are many other reasons for this decision. First and foremost, nationality is not a relevant basis for a study of musical life during the nineteenth century. At least, the perspective should not be restricted to one single national reception. On the eastern coast of the Baltic Sea, Finland, Estonia, Livonia, and Courland were part of the Russian Empire.[10] Estonia, Livonia, and Courland had been seized by Russia from Sweden in the eighteenth century and were called the Baltic provinces. (Present-day Estonia also includes northern Livonia, while southern Livonia and Courland make up present-day Latvia). After another war between Sweden and Russia, Finland was brought under Russian rule in 1809 (see map 1). The tsar declared Finland an autonomous grand duchy. Finland's position was thus different from that of the Baltic provinces, but the Russian hegemony strengthened connections on the eastern side of the Baltic. The

Map 1: The Baltic World in 1850. Shows the states (largest font), provinces, and cities (smallest font) relevant to this study. Between 1814 and 1905, the kingdoms of Norway and Sweden were united under one monarch in a personal union. After it was conquered by the Russian Empire in 1809, Finland became an autonomous Russian Grand Duchy. It became independent in 1917. Estonia, Livonia, and Courland were called the Baltic provinces of the Russian Empire.

end of the nineteenth century ushered in a period of nationalistic aspirations both in Finland and in the Baltic provinces, but there still remained strong international ties that transcended borders. An illuminating example of this is the fact that before 1882 there was no academy of music in Finland. Those who were interested in a professional career as musicians had to travel to conservatories abroad. Musically inclined Finns very seldom went to St. Petersburg: their favorite destination was Leipzig, which recruited students not only from Finland but from the other Nordic countries as well.

A broad geographical analysis is also justified by the fact that musical as well as political and economic culture had long been manifest on both sides of the *mare balticum*. The Baltic Sea was important for facilitating commercial contacts and also for transmitting cultural influences. In 1949 the French historian Fernand Braudel published an epoch-making study, *La Méditerranée et le monde méditerranéen à l'époque de Philippe II*, in which he examined the Mediterranean from a historical point of view. For Braudel, the Mediterranean was influential as a connective link and as a route for the transmission of ideas and goods, but it also exercised a restrictive influence; the resultant cultural flow depended to a large extent on the cycle of the seasons.[11] For present purposes, we could regard the Baltic Sea as playing a similar role, and acting as both an enabling and a limiting force. The Baltic Sea has been an essential element in the socioeconomic infrastructure of the region as a whole, as David Kirby has noted in his two-volume survey—inspired by Braudel—of the history of the area that he calls "the Baltic world."[12] Kirby points out that the general perception of the two seas has been strikingly different. "The Mediterranean is regarded as the cradle of civilization, the teeming meeting-ground of cultures from time immemorial," he writes; "the Baltic by contrast is usually seen as a chilly, peripheral backwater on the very edge of the civilized world." Kirby goes on to argue that the Baltic world has been more of a cultural recipient than an active "creator of civilization."[13] This hypothesis might not be accepted easily by those who live on that "periphery" and are thus reduced to the level of passive objects watching the process of civilization from afar. There are obvious problems in the dichotomy between "center" and "periphery," although it might be argued that the traffic between the musical cultures of Central Europe and the Baltic was mostly unidirectional. In the case of Wagner, however, there exists ample evidence that his music and ideas were received in terms more of creative adaptation than of passive absorption. It must be stressed that for Wagner himself, Livonia, where he lived, was extremely important, and Riga was to become a center for Wagnerian performances, exerting an influence that extended as far afield as Finland and Estonia. By the end of the nineteenth century, the Wagner Society of Riga was one of the most active in Europe. Moreover, the most influential of all Wagner's biographers, Carl Friedrich Glasenapp, lived in Livonia until his death in 1915.

The present study is a contribution to cultural history, a commentary not only on the reception of Wagner but also on a broader question: how has the Baltic Sea created opportunities for and limitations on cultural interaction? Similarities between musical cultures, as well as disparities, exist. Many of them are not necessarily due to regional attributes but, rather, depend on political and social considerations that can be better articulated by means of this larger geographical perspective.

A number of scholars have already examined the history of music in the Baltic world. The "Östersjöområdet som musiklandskap" (The Baltic Sea Region as a Musical Landscape) project has concentrated on the musical culture of the early modern period, particularly the seventeenth and eighteenth centuries,[14] and has produced, among other things, a number of studies of the movements of musicians around the Baltic Sea. Throughout this period, town musicians, organists, and church musicians were able to circulate freely in the region since working conditions and institutions were quite similar throughout the Baltic world. A composer like Valentin Meder could move from one place to another without any problems, irrespective of the political regime. After leaving Kassel, Germany, in 1672, he worked in Hamburg in 1673, in Lübeck and Copenhagen in 1674, in Tallinn in 1679, in Riga in 1685–86, in Danzig (now Gdansk in Poland) from 1686 to 1698, in Braunsberg (Braniewo, also in today's Poland), in Königsberg in 1700, and again in Riga until his death in 1719.[15] Meder's case is in no way exceptional, for such movements were relatively common.

The German musicologist Heinrich W. Schwab has considered the concept of the Baltic Sea region from the perspective of music history, pointing out that it is difficult to decide what counts as the center and what counts as a periphery within the region.[16] The centers have changed over the course of time, depending on various economic, political, and cultural developments. If we define the Baltic world from a simple geographical standpoint, the *mare balticum* is today surrounded by Finland, Russia, Estonia, Latvia, Lithuania, Poland, Germany, Denmark, and Sweden. Over the centuries, there has never been a single center of the area but many, including the towns belonging to the Hanseatic League in northern Germany, to say nothing of Stockholm and St. Petersburg.

One of the problems in studying the reception of Wagner's works and ideas in the Baltic world is the fact that this world is made up of so many different cultures. The focus here is restricted mainly to German, Swedish, Finnish, Estonian, and Latvian sources and pays only passing attention to Russia, Lithuania, Poland, and Denmark, although the perspectives of those latter countries, too, would undoubtedly be of great interest (for the countries of the Baltic world at the present day, see map 2). Russia, for instance, is an important actor in music history around the region. An excellent study by Rosamund Bartlett has already dealt with the reception of Wagner in Russia up to 1995.[17] The Lithuanian elite, on the other hand, had strong ties with Poland, which for its part was more culturally oriented toward France than Germany, and it is entirely symptomatic of this dependence that there were no Wagner performances in Vilnius during the nineteenth century. Such a state of affairs could hardly be more different from the situation in Riga, where Wagner's operas were performed almost continuously from 1843 onward.[18]

The Wagnerian reception should also be related to the development of his career and should pay attention to his personal influence in the area. Wagner was born in 1813 and died in 1883. A crucial turning point in his life was his Dresden period, from 1842 to 1849. *Der fliegende Holländer* was premiered there in 1843 and *Tannhäuser* in 1845. During the 1850s, *Tannhäuser* was taken up by many German opera houses. It even reached the shores of the Baltic and was performed in Riga and Tallinn in 1853 and in Helsinki in 1857. The 1850s introduced Wagner's name to audiences all

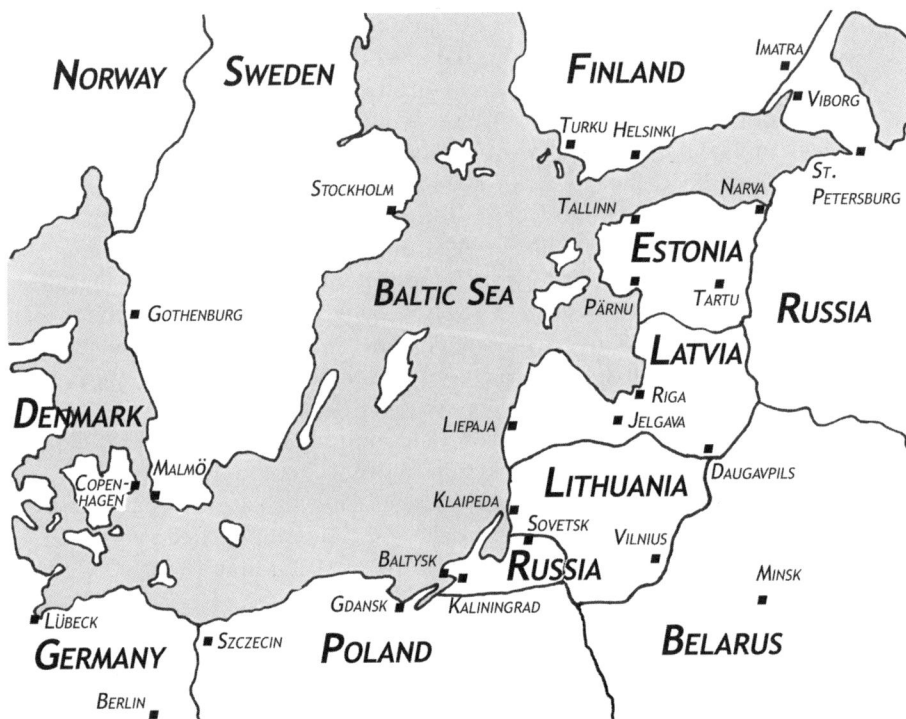

Map 2: The Baltic World in 2005. In 1995, Sweden and Finland joined Denmark, which had been a member of the European Union since 1973. In 2004, Estonia, Latvia, Lithuania, and Poland also became members.

over Europe. The study begins with these early stages in Wagner's burgeoning reputation, including his personal contribution to the musical life of Königsberg and Riga between 1836 and 1839. From the 1850s onward, Wagnerism emerged as a cultural phenomenon, although it peaked only after Wagner's death. The post-Wagner nineteenth century is also included here, in order to analyze the way in which Wagnerism was organized and transformed under the reign of Cosima Wagner. Political developments during this period provide essential background to the analysis as a whole. Toward the end of the nineteenth century, Sweden, unlike its eastern counterparts, remained a stable kingdom. Finland had been part of Sweden until 1809, when it came under Russia, although it enjoyed relative independence. The Russification of Finland began in the 1890s—much later than in the Baltic provinces where, after the Polish Uprising of 1863, Russia rapidly consolidated its stranglehold.

Within this political context, Wagner's art became a complex and potentially divisive issue. Whereas in Livonia he could be associated with the role of the Baltic-German minority and its cultural position, in Sweden he could be regarded as merely an apolitical "artist of the future." Four aspects of all this should be emphasized in the attempt to shed light on Wagner's complex image and its reception on the shores of the Baltic: his personal influence in the area; the spread of his music and the divergent ideas evoked by his compositions; the institutionalization of his position in local understanding; and, finally, organized Wagnerism, including social activities and visits to Bayreuth.

Reception is always a multidimensional question and, as everyone who has ever investigated culture knows, remains a constant and irreducible challenge for the scholar. In my view, the reception of a cultural product invariably involves a dialogue between text and context. Meanings articulated in relation to Wagner cannot be reduced to his works or their internal structure, nor can they be understood as constructs that are wholly driven by context. Meanings emanate from a process of dialogue between Wagner's works and their recipients.[19] Inevitably, this process is influenced by many contextual factors, including traditions of interpretation, local practices of viewing and listening, information received beforehand from the local press or German music journals, and so on. In the case of Wagner, it is essential to remember that he was not a coherent, monolithic phenomenon. His music was not restricted to opera houses: it was heard at soirées and in salons as well. Furthermore, his writings became known all over Europe during the 1850s, either as original texts or as quoted by the musical press. An interesting question is how these different traditions intertwine. In Sweden, for example, one could read Wagner's theoretical writings by the early 1850s, whereas the first of his operas did not reach Stockholm until 1865; in Livonia his operas had been staged since 1843, a difference of circumstance that must have placed Wagner's theoretical achievements in a totally different light.

From the perspective of a historian, an important question concerns the kinds of sources that are available for any consideration of this dialogic process. Of course, there is ample material concerning the stage productions themselves to offer clear indications as to how they were organized and the elements they incorporated. The archives of the Swedish Royal Opera, for example, contain documents that reveal the circumstances in which particular productions were staged and each of their constituent parts. But the material available in Finland, Estonia, and Latvia is quite different. This makes comparisons difficult. There is, of course, no lack of sources illustrating Wagner's own experiences. I have used archival material, newspapers and journals, contemporary literature, letters and diaries, posters, and catalogs. Needless to say, it has been impossible to cover everything and to give a comprehensive account of what remains of this bygone age in the history of music.

My analysis of the reception—and popularization—of Wagner's works and ideas is grounded in a cross-reading of different kinds of sources rather than on a complete examination of those sources. Traditionally, reception historians have based their arguments on a very special type of reception, namely, concert reviews written by professional recipients. Newspaper articles and reviews are essential raw material for this research, but they are only part of the story. First, I will consider Wagner's personal influence on the Baltic world, his years in Königsberg and Riga (chapter 1), as well as his concert tour of Russia in 1863 (chapter 4). Wagner had a great personal impact on the dissemination of his works and ideas in these areas. This aspect of my work is clarified by reference to his letters and memoirs, to contemporary accounts in newspapers, and to Latvian and Russian archival material. Second, in chapters 3, 5, and 6, I focus on the spread of Wagner's music. In this effort, I have been inspired by the study of popular culture. A figure like Wagner has often been presented as an embodiment of highbrow culture, but his music also spread in popular forms, perhaps more than Wagnerians and Wagner scholars have been willing to admit. This popular aspect of Wagner should be acknowledged. I begin by analyzing the way in which his music was arranged for domestic consumption and how excerpts from his works were performed outside the opera house (chapter 2). In particular, I have drawn here on the sales catalogs of music dealers in Sweden and Livonia. Additionally, I refer to newspaper advertisements, concert announcements, and collections of scores. The role of domestic and salon music has all too often been neglected in the study of music history. Paradoxical though it may sound, Wagner's music was widely marketed in the form of solos, duets, and arrangements for all manner of ensembles. Opera performances themselves will, of course, be analyzed on the basis of both archival and printed sources. Newspapers not only reported on what happened on stage but also participated in a wider debate on Wagner's theoretical and political role. Wagner provoked a lively discussion all over the Baltic world, and the analysis of this debate, conducted in newspapers, journals, and contemporary literature, forms the third part of the present study. It is interesting that Wagner also influenced early music historians. The Finnish musicologist and composer Martin Wegelius, in particular, was fascinated by Wagner, whereas his Swedish counterpart Wilhelm Bauck tried to avoid evaluating Wagner for as long as possible (chapter 6). Historiography thus made an essential contribution to the institutionalization of Wagner.

Chapters 7 and 8 concentrate on those Wagnerites whose enthusiasms and activities assumed militant forms from the 1870s onward. After the birth of the Bayreuth Festival in 1876, visitors from Sweden, Finland, and the Baltic provinces also headed off to Germany. It is possible to identify a number of these travelers from the *Fremdenlisten* published by the festival organizers. I have drawn in particular on the lists preserved in the Wagner Archives at Bayreuth and at the Royal Library of Sweden at Stockholm, where they can be found in the Wagner Collection of Fredrik Vult von

Steijern. These lists give not only the names of the visitors and their places of origin but also their social statuses or professions. It is thus possible to define the social as well as the geographical boundaries of Wagnerism. In his study of the reception of Wagner in America, Joseph Horowitz interestingly points out that Wagner's music appealed especially to female members of the audience.[20] I shall, accordingly, undertake a gender analysis of the Bayreuth visitors. Finally, chapter 8 focuses on Wagner societies, whose activities are analyzed on the strength of archival and printed sources. Wagner himself gave an impetus to the establishment of Wagner societies, which soon became meeting places for the most active Wagnerians. These "fan clubs" are another, still largely unexplored, connection between Wagner and popular culture. The final chapter concentrates on the spread of organized Wagnerism in the Baltic world. There is ample surviving evidence relating to the Wagner Society of Riga in particular, a society whose membership profile can be examined from the perspective of both social standing and gender.

Among the most active campaigners for Wagner in the Baltic world were Fredrik Vult von Steijern in Sweden, Martin Wegelius and Richard Faltin in Finland, and Carl Friedrich Glasenapp in Livonia. As the godfathers of Wagnerism, these eminent individuals influenced the reception of Wagner within their own national cultures, while Glasenapp, through his close relations with the Bayreuth Circle, influenced the understanding of Wagner's music and ideas throughout the Western hemisphere.

1

Richard Wagner, the Wandering Musician

Around the Baltic Sea

Even though a discussion of Wagner's life is not normally required for an analysis of the influence and spread of his works, it is nonetheless necessary to examine his relationship with the Baltic world. This is particularly important as Wagner's travels had an impact on the reception of his works. It is by no means a coincidence that Riga, where he lived from 1837 to 1839, was later to become a leading center for the performance of his works (see figure 1.1).

Wagner's own travels reflect the fact that the Baltic world was a potential working environment for many German artists in the nineteenth century. Since the seventeenth century, artists had made extended visits to East Prussia and to the Baltic provinces of the Russian Empire, Estonia, Livonia, and Courland. German actors and musicians planned their tours to include the Baltic provinces, sometimes returning via Finland and Sweden, thus encompassing the whole of the Baltic Sea. Riga, St. Petersburg, and Stockholm formed a triangle whose wealthy population had attracted troupes of traveling players since the seventeenth century.

Besides touring, performing artists also found long-term employment in the region. The role of the Germans became conspicuous in Estonia, Livonia, and Courland, the area of present-day Estonia and Latvia, where the German minority played a prominent role in the nineteenth century. But the contacts made by German musicians were not limited to the areas where the Baltic Germans lived; their influence extended around the Baltic Sea and to Finland and Sweden. For example, Johann Gottlieb Naumann (1741–1801), composer of the opera *Gustaf Wasa* (later hailed as a Swedish national opera), moved from Dresden to Stockholm at the invitation of the king of Sweden.[1] Similarly, Fredrik Pacius (1809–91), who became known as the father of Finnish music, was born in Hamburg, and Richard Faltin (1835–1918), one of the leading figures of Finnish Wagnerism and also a German, was born in Danzig, which is today the city of Gdansk in Poland.[2] Franz Thomé, who conducted the first performance of *Tannhäuser* in Riga, came from Graz, Austria, in 1853.[3] And Friedrich Brenner (1815–98), who

Figure 1.1. The young Richard Wagner. Daguerreotype of a drawing by E. B. Kietz, Paris 1850. National Archive of the Richard Wagner Foundation, Bayreuth.

worked as a teacher of music and organist at the University of Tartu, was a native of Eisleben.[4]

A good impression of visits by German musicians is given by the *Rigasche Stadtblätter*, which recorded artists' arrivals in the city with meticulous care. In 1857, the Riga German theater, for instance, was visited by the actors Mr. Duschnitz from Vienna, Ms. Schubert from Berlin, Ms. Walseck from Bremen, and Mr. Osten from Mainz.[5] Riga's place in the world of German theater and music is well illustrated by Wagner's interest in the city. German artists were also employed, of course, further to the north. In July 1855, the *Rigasche Stadtblätter* reported that the Tallinn theater had recently employed Pauline Zschiesche from Danzig and Ms. Baders from Cologne.[6]

The links with Germany were extremely strong in the Baltic provinces of Estonia, Courland, and Livonia. Lithuania's links were, for historical reasons, mainly with Poland and, hence, with French culture. Yet we know that German emigrants such as Johann David Holland (1746–1827) were active in Vilnius,[7] where a German opera company was founded in 1835 under the direction of Wilhelm Schmiedkopf. Performances were given in Polish, however, as the city's Polish-speaking audiences boycotted cultural events in other languages. Vilnius's Polish associations were further underlined by the fact that one of Poland's leading composers, Stanisław Moniuszko, lived there from 1839 to 1857.[8] By the middle of the nineteenth century, concerts were a regular feature of Vilnius's cultural life, with frequent performances of works by Beethoven, Mozart, Haydn, and Mendelssohn, but with virtually no place for music by composers of the New German School such as Wagner. None of Wagner's operas was staged in the town before the twentieth century.

As early as the seventeenth and eighteenth centuries, the Baltic Sea formed the basis for a cultural entity. Particularly important in this context was the period of Swedish rule, when Swedish dominion extended not only to Finland but also to the Baltic provinces of Estonia, Livonia, and Courland, as well as to northern Germany. According to the Finnish music historian Fabian Dahlström, the reasons for this cultural uniformity were the efficiency of maritime connections, the cohesive force of Protestantism, and a social pattern characterized by the north German view of justice and law that dates back to the period when these regions were under the dominion of the Hanseatic League.[9] The administration of the coastal towns was in the hands of local mayors, town councils, the church, and the merchant guilds, whose German-speaking members were often in the majority. Within this system, the pursuit of various professions, including music, was regulated by an arrangement based on privilege. Since conditions were similar throughout the area, it was easy for musicians to move from place to place. The network of towns included not only Lubeck, Wismar, Rostock, Elbing (Elblag), Stettin (Szczecin), and Danzig (Gdansk), but also Riga in Livonia, Tallinn in Estonia, and Turku and Viborg in Finland. In any consideration of the music culture around the Baltic Sea in general, we should also take into account the music cultivated at the royal courts of St. Petersburg, Copenhagen, Stockholm, and Jelgava (Mitau), where opera was strongly emphasized. Yet it is worth remembering that these cities, too, shared the same musical infrastructure as the other coastal towns of the Baltic Sea.[10]

Despite changes in political conditions in the course of the seventeenth and eighteenth centuries, musical links between the coastal towns of the Baltic Sea remained close, and it was not until the middle of the nineteenth century that the vocational contacts of the town musicians began to dwindle. The early decades of the century saw rapid and influential changes in the way in which music was cultivated in Central Europe. The gradual grafting of Romantic features on to Classical music coincided with the political and economic rise of the bourgeoisie. This, in turn, had an impact on the demand for music. The great breach came with the birth of the concert as an institution, the appearance of traveling virtuosos, the emergence of music criticism as a permanent feature of the press, and the founding of music periodicals.[11] These changes did not take place instantly or simultaneously. Rather, they were part of a process that unfolded over a long period of time and came to influence the spread of Wagner's innovative ideas.

Travel in the Baltic world was inevitably conditioned by the facilities available, notably by the growth of steamboat traffic and the railroads. The introduction of steamboat traffic offered significantly better and more regular connections between the area's various centers than sailing ships. In his treatise on steam power, a Finnish printer, K. E. Eurén, wrote that "Steam has caused an unprecedented change among nations in peacetime, so that traffic between them has grown and bound them together with innumerable ties that earlier were hardly known."[12] It was not until the 1840s and 1850s, however, that the influence of the steam engine began to affect travel in the Baltic world. Wagner arrived in the region in 1836, before these revolutionary changes took place.

"The Siberia of Prussia"

During Wagner's Baltic visits in the 1830s, traveling conditions were still virtually the same as in the previous century, but despite this, travel was perfectly possible, particularly between Germany and the Baltic provinces of the Russian Empire. It must be remembered that, at that time, East Prussia extended as far as parts of what are now Poland and Russia: East Prussia's westernmost town was Danzig (Gdansk) and its northernmost was Tilsit (after 1946 called Sovetsk). The most important town in the region was Königsberg (present-day Kaliningrad; see figure 1.2)—the home of Immanuel Kant—a lively center of music and drama, exerting an influence that extended as far as Memel (now Klaipeda in Lithuania). For Wagner, the town's significance may have lain in the fact that it was the birthplace of no less a person than E. T. A. Hoffmann, who had studied at the local university and attended the lectures of Immanuel Kant while Kant was at the height of his career.[13] Hoffmann was later to become one of the central influences on Wagner.

Figure 1.2. Königsberg in the 1930s. Postcard by Kunstanstalt Stengel & Co., Dresden. Author's postcard collection.

Wagner's arrival in Königsberg was, in fact, occasioned by the circum-stances in which Wagner found himself. At the end of July 1834 he was offered a post as conductor with Heinrich Bethmann's opera company in Magdeburg. The company was currently performing at Bad Läuchstadt, where Wagner made his conducting *début* with *Don Giovanni* on 2 August. Here, too, he made the acquaintance of the actress Minna Planer, his future wife. His work with the company changed the direction of his life: he abandoned his work on what would have been his Second Symphony in E Major and concentrated on a plan to write an opera, *Das Liebesverbot*, based on Shakespeare's *Measure for Measure*.[14] In addition to Shakespeare, another of the influences discernible in *Das Liebesverbot* is that of *Das junge Europa*, a novel written in epistolary form by his friend and idol at the time, Heinrich Laube. In his book, Laube had fictionalized a universal republic that would transcend the boundaries of nation-states.[15] The libretto of *Das Liebesverbot* was completed by the end of 1834, and the music was com-pleted by March 1836. The work received its disastrous first performance on 29 March 1836,[16] and a second performance was prevented from taking place by fighting among the cast. *Das Liebesverbot* was not staged again in Wagner's lifetime.

Bethmann's company had long been on the point of breaking up and was not even able to pay the wages of its singers and musicians. This was disastrous for Wagner, who had increasingly become saddled with debts. When Minna was offered the chance to go to Königsberg, she seized the opportunity, believing that she would be able to arrange employment for her beloved.[17] In the meantime, Richard had also left Magdeburg and moved temporarily to Berlin in the hope of having *Das Liebesverbot* staged at the Königstädtisches theater, which was currently being run by Karl Friedrich Cerf.[18] Wagner's first surviving letter from Berlin is an outburst of despair addressed to Minna on 21 May. The last is dated 22 June and strikes a similar note.[19] From the vantage point of Berlin, the east Prussian town of Königsberg was "so far away, alas, so far."[20] Even though Königsberg had an active cultural life of its own, in comparison with the cultural centers of Europe it seemed very much on the periphery. At the end of 1836, long after he had moved to Königsberg, Wagner shamefacedly described his feelings to Robert Schumann, who was then in Leipzig: "I'm still alive, even though I'm a hundred miles from cultivated Germany."[21] In the same letter he describes himself as having been "exiled to Siberia."[22]

In Berlin it became apparent that Cerf's interest in Wagner's work was limited to mere words, and no concrete results were achieved during the negotiations, which lasted an entire month. In Berlin, the most significant influence on Wagner was a performance of *Fernand Cortez, ou La conquête du Mexique*, which Gaspare Spontini had written nearly three decades earlier in homage to Napoleon.[23] Wagner admired the rhythmic tautness of the work and felt that, as an opera, it had lasting historical significance.[24] The solutions adopted by Spontini specifically affected Wagner's plans when he came to write *Rienzi*.[25]

During his time in Berlin, Wagner kept up a one-sided correspondence with Minna. It is clear from his letter of 22 May that he even toyed with the idea of applying for Franz Gläser's post as conductor at the Königstädtisches theater, but he soon abandoned this plan.[26] It now became more important than ever for him to obtain a job in Königsberg. Minna used her position as a leading actress and tried to arrange for him to be appointed conductor at the theater. She was one of the key figures at the Königsberg theater, and the director, Anton Hübsch, was unwilling to lose his star attraction. This was Minna's last trump card, and Wagner pressed her to use it:

> Arrange it, my dear, that I may soon count on coming to Königsberg; overcome all bashfulness and warn your director that you will leave in the autumn in case he doesn't engage me; so much is clear in any case: if I can't come to Königsberg we must go somewhere else, for we remain separated no longer. Well—courage and steadfastness, we must conquer![27]

Wagner's letter of 6–21 June 1836 is hardly more than a hysterical outpouring of emotions that had been building up in him. He had heard of

Figure 1.3. Deutsche Strasse, "the German Street," in the city of Tilsit. Postcard by Verlag Julius Simonsen, Oldenburg. Author's postcard collection.

the company's tour to Tilsit (see figure 1.3) and Memel, causing him to write in his despair: "Minna, I am inconsolable that you have joined such a traveling company."[28]

By 7 July, Wagner's patience was exhausted, and he left by coach for Königsberg, where the conductor was Louis Schubert. Schubert's family was in fact living in Riga, but he had become embroiled in a passionate love affair in Königsberg and was reluctant to return to Riga, particularly since the theater there was closed. As a result, the conductor's post was not immediately vacant. At the moment when Wagner arrived in this "Prussian Siberia," the company was about to leave for Memel, where it was to stay until September. Wagner continued his journey to Memel by sea. The weather was atrocious, and steamboat service had not yet been introduced: "One of the most melancholy crossings I have ever experienced," Wagner later wrote in his autobiography.[29] His gloom was compounded by the scenery, which brought E. T. A. Hoffmann to his mind:

> As we passed the thin strip of sand that divides this bay from the Baltic Sea, the castle of Runsitten, where Hoffmann laid the scene of one of his most gruesome tales (*Das Majorat*), was pointed out to me. The fact that in this desolate neighborhood, of all places in the world, I should after so long a lapse of time be once more brought into contact with the fantastic impressions of my youth had a singular and depressing effect on my mind.[30]

During his trip to Memel, Wagner, on the advice of his friend Heinrich Laube, read Heinrich Koenig's novel *Die hohe Braut.*[31] He later drafted a scenario for an opera based on the novel and sent it to Eugène Scribe, the regular librettist of Auber, Meyerbeer, and others.[32]

In Memel, Wagner was unavoidably driven into competition with Schubert, who fell ill before a performance of Weber's *Euryanthe,* with the result that Wagner was asked to take the rehearsal, even though he did not know the work. The rehearsal went so well that Schubert staged a miraculous recovery in time to conduct the performance. The situation was so difficult that after returning to Königsberg, Wagner and Minna began to think of moving to Danzig. A supporter of the Königsberg theater, Abraham Möller, took Anton Hübsch to one side and suggested not only that Wagner should be made the new conductor, but also that he should be given a benefit performance to celebrate his forthcoming marriage to Minna.[33]

The plan succeeded. Wagner and Minna were married on 24 November 1836. The benefit performance was Auber's *La muette de Portici,* with Minna as the silent woman of the title.[34] But Wagner had to wait until the spring of 1837 for the post of conductor to fall vacant. Little of his leisure time was devoted to creative work. Among the few pieces that he completed at this time is his overture *Rule Britannia,*[35] while the unfinished works from this period include an extremely interesting draft made in Königsberg in February 1837, the sketches for which were jotted down on the blank pages of the first draft of *Rule Britannia* and published by Wilhelm Tappert in the *Musikalisches Wochenblatt* in 1887. The surviving sketches comprise three numbers: the Introduction, Chorus of Priests, and Chorus of Youths. The names of three Baltic deities are mentioned in the text: Picullos, Percunos, and Potrimpos. The introduction is marked "Marcia, moderato," its rhythms marked out by trumpets and trombones, and is followed by the Chorus of Priests, which includes the following lines:

> Hört der Götter Spruch! Fühlet ihren Fluch!
> Auf blut'gem Throne herrscht Pikullos,
> die Feuerkrone trägt Perkunos,
> doch Glück zum Lohne schenkt Potrimpos.

> [Heed the gods' decree! Feel their curse! / Picullos reigns on a blood-stained throne, / Percunos wears the crown of fire, / but Potrimpos rewards you with happiness.]

Underscored by chords in the wind instruments, the unison Chorus of Priests is followed by the Chorus of Youths: "Perkunos! Perkunos! Nimm auf blutigem Altar unser Opfer gnänig wahr! Leih' uns Deiner Schrecken Macht, stärke uns in wilder Schlacht!" (Percunos! Percunos! Accept our sacrifice on the blood-soaked altar! Lend us your terrors' power, strengthen us in wild battle!) The melodic line is strikingly similar to that of the "Frage-verbot" (forbidden question) in the later *Lohengrin*. The Chorus of Maidens transposes the same melody to F major as the maidens sing: "Potrimpos! Potrimpos! Nimm auf Deinem Weihaltar unsres Opfers gnädig wahr! Sende Deines Segens Macht, strahle Licht in unsre Nacht!" (Potrimpos! Potrimpos! Deign to accept our sacrifice on your consecrated altar! Send your blessing's might, shed light upon our night!) Then all the voices unite to hymn the sacrifice: "Für die Opfer, die wir bringen, steht mit eurer Macht uns bei, daß im Kampfe wir bezwingen Feindes Macht und Tyrannei!" (For the sacrifices that we offer up, support us with your might, so that in battle we may overcome the enemy's might and tyranny!) The sketches end with the priests asking Percunos to tell them whom they should sacrifice in order to obtain the gods' help:

> Die Flamme sprüht, der Holzstoß glüht!
> Perkunos, Blutgott, gib ein Zeichen,
> Wer Dir als Opfer soll erbleichen![36]

> [The flame spits forth, the kindling glows! / Percunos, blood-god, give us a sign / and say who shall perish as your victim!]

These sketches make it clear that, while he was living in East Prussia, Wagner was conscious of his local cultural surroundings and was acquainted with Baltic mythology. The Latvian musicologist Vita Lindenberg has drawn attention to the fact that during the 1830s folklore was already the subject of widespread study, and this was no doubt the case not only in Königsberg but, especially, in Wagner's next place of residence, Riga, where organizations such as the Gesellschaft für Geschichte und Altertumskunde der Ostseeprovinzen (the Society for History and Archaeology in the Baltic Provinces) and the Kurländische Gesellschaft für Literatur und Kunst (the Society for Literature and Art in Courland) arranged lectures and advertised their events widely.[37] Although Wagner's sketches contain a number of hints of *Lohengrin*, he had no plans to write a Baltic opera: his interest, instead, was already in the dramatic possibility of myth.

It is believed that Wagner wrote these sketches as incidental music for Singer's historical drama *Die letzte Heidenverschwörung in Preußen, oder Der Deutsche Ritterorden in Königsberg*, which opened on 17 February 1837. The play has not survived, and neither has Wagner's score—assuming that he wrote anything more than the sketches preserved on the blank sheets of the *Rule Britannia* draft. In the historical drama, Minna played the role of the young heathen Prussian woman, Marga. Wagner, it will be recalled, had no permanent appointment at the theater in February 1837, and it is therefore possible that he wanted to strengthen his hand by writing incidental music for the piece. Wagner's name was not mentioned in the announcement in

Figure 1.4. Königsberg city theater, 1902. Postcard by Dr. Trenkler Co., Leipzig. Author's postcard collection.

the Königsberg *Hartungsche Zeitung*, however, and he himself never at a later date referred to the play or his musical sketches.[38] According to the editors of the *Wagner Werk-Verzeichnis*, Wagner's music was presumably played at the premiere on 17 February,[39] but this remains no more than a hypothesis. It is more likely that Wagner wrote only the sketches and never worked them up into a finished piece. Even so, the sketches remain fascinating in their own right and provide evidence of Wagner's interest in Baltic culture.

Wagner's musical output at this time would no doubt have been greater if he had obtained a position at the theater earlier than he actually did: it was not until 1 April 1837 that he was finally appointed conductor at the Königsberg theater (see figure 1.4). Musically, the theater had made considerable progress since the late 1820s, when Heinrich Dorn had reorganized the company along the lines of the Berlin Hofkapelle, but the theater, which had been run by the energetic Anton Hübsch since 1834, had been in almost continuous financial trouble.

From the perspective of an outsider, such as Wagner, the Königsberg theater was probably not very tempting, least of all in winter. The building was poorly heated, although the local audience was used to the freezing conditions. Moreover, the stage and auditorium suffered from inadequate lighting. (Gas lamps were not installed until 1852). Nonetheless, the company prided itself on performing the latest works, and even before

Wagner arrived there, the people of Königsberg had already been regaled with the local premieres of Donizetti's *L'elisir d'amore* (1833), Meyerbeer's *Robert le diable* (1835), Halévy's *La Juive* (1836), and Bellini's *I Puritani* (1837).[40]

It seems that the Wagners' married life in East Prussia was turbulent in the extreme. Although Wagner describes this difficult period in glowing colors in his autobiography, *Mein Leben*, we have an alternative account left by Minna's eleven-year-old daughter, Natalie, whom Minna passed off as her younger sister. Natalie's presence placed a severe strain on the Wagners' relationship, and Wagner himself is known to have had a violent streak. Through much of this period, Minna was the household's only breadwinner. Finally, on 31 May 1837, she apparently had had enough and ran off with a merchant named Dietrich, taking Natalie with her. Wagner returned from a rehearsal to find that she had disappeared. He tried to follow her but ran short of money and had to return to Königsberg to raise more funds. On 3 June he left Königsberg again. This time he traced Minna to her parents' home in Dresden and asked her to return with him.[41]

In his autobiography, Wagner writes that at this juncture he had already received an offer from the newly opened theater in Riga, where the post of conductor was vacant. In Riga, Minna would not have to act and could devote herself to housework, a move that, if we can believe *Mein Leben*, was more welcome to Wagner than to his wife.[42] Wagner's activities in Königsberg and later in Riga were characterized by a continuous striving to advance his career. He longed for his plans to be accepted and was convinced that a success in Prussia or the Baltic would open the gates to the wider world.

Louis Schindelmeisser, who acted as Wagner's agent in Berlin, had already entered into negotiations with the director of the Riga theater, the poet Karl von Holtei.[43] According to Wagner, it was unnecessary to take any account of Minna in this agreement:

> My dear, dear friend, may I once again ask you to do everything in your power and send me the contract with Holtei as soon as possible. It is of the utmost importance to me. Once again: absolutely no account need be taken of my wife in this—1000 silver rubles for a 2- or 3-year contract.[44]

In Dresden, Wagner stayed at the home of his sister Ottilie and her husband Hermann Brockhaus. From there he traveled to Berlin to sign an agreement with Holtei concerning his move to Riga. To Minna he wrote a repentant letter, asking her to abandon the idea of a separation.[45] After returning to Dresden, Wagner managed to persuade his wife to accept his plans, but within weeks Minna had again decamped with Dietrich. Wagner returned alone to Berlin to prepare for his trip to Riga.

The Riga Years

In the early nineteenth century, Riga could look back on a glorious past: prior to the Napoleonic Wars, Livonia had enjoyed a period of lasting peace and had applied itself to trade and culture. In the eighteenth century the town had been an important center of the German Enlightenment and was noted not only for its printing presses but for its unique philosophical heritage. For example, the Riga publisher Johann Friedrich Hartknoch was the first to print Kant's works.[46] One of the key figures in the town's intellectual history was Johann Gottlieb Herder, who taught at the Domschule, proved to be a popular preacher at the Gertrudenkirche, and served as municipal librarian from 1764 to 1769. He later wrote: "In Livonia I lived, taught, and acted as freely and as uninhibitedly as I shall probably never again be in a position to live, teach, and act."[47]

By the late eighteenth century, there was also a flourishing theater in Riga. The first viceroy of the city, Duke Otto von Vietinghoff, was a German baron and government official who generously and unstintingly supported the theater and was willing to participate personally in the planning of various projects.[48] It was thanks mainly to him that a permanent theater was built in Riga in 1782. For its official opening on 15 September, it chose Lessing's acclaimed tragedy *Emilia Galotti*. From the outset, the theater also functioned as an opera house, and by 19 September, local audiences had already had a chance to see Monsigny's opera *La belle Arsène*.[49] Other operas and musical comedies performed during the company's first fall season were Grétry's *Zémire et Azor* and Johann Adam Hiller's *Die Jagd*, as well as Georg Benda's *Ariadne auf Naxos* and *Der Dorfjahrmarkt*.[50] At the same time, opera was cultivated in other parts of the Baltic provinces. Earlier—especially during the Baroque period—opera had been almost exclusively a form of entertainment for royal courts, designed to bolster the power of local patrons of the arts.[51] In Courland, Duke Peter Biron[52] had founded an opera company at Jelgava (see figure 1.5), and it was under Biron's patronage that Franz Adam Veichter wrote his three *Singspiels* for the company. Johann Adam Hiller—often hailed as the father of the German *Singspiel*—worked briefly as conductor at Jelgava during the 1780s. Although there is no evidence that Hiller had any direct influence on the performance of his *Singspiel, Die Jagd*, in Riga in 1782,[53] the ties between Jelgava and Riga were close, and the two towns together played a prominent role in the history of Baltic opera.

The Napoleonic Wars put an abrupt end to Riga's peaceful existence, and both the Moscow and St. Petersburg quarters of the town were razed to the ground in anticipation of the arrival of French troops.[54] It did not take long, however, for life to return to normal and for the cultural life of the community, especially music, to flourish again. The town's German theater soon became the leading opera house in the Baltic provinces. High points

Figure 1.5. Castle of Jelgava in 1916. Postcard by Verlag Nicolai Hübner, Mitau. Author's postcard collection.

in its subsequent career were performances of *Fidelio* in 1818 and *Der Freis-chütz* in 1822.[55] This renewal of interest in opera encouraged a revival of music and the performing arts in general, with the conductor, composer, and pianist Heinrich Dorn making a particularly important contribution to this development. Like Wagner, Dorn moved to Riga from Königsberg, where he had lived from 1828 to 1833. Dorn retained his position of influence in Riga until 1843, organizing symphony concerts at the German theater and conducting Beethoven's Third and Fifth Symphonies, among others. He also helped to form the first Liedertafel[56] and from 1834 onward served as director of the local Singakademie. He had close contacts with musical life in Germany, with the result that his name appears frequently in the columns of Schumann's *Neue Zeitschrift für Musik*. In order to revive Riga's musical fortunes, Dorn also established the Dvina Music Festival in 1836 and made a significant contribution to the local operatic scene by giving the local premiere of Meyerbeer's *Robert le diable*.[57]

Although histories of music in Riga invariably stress Wagner's contribution to local musical life, the town had a well-established German-oriented tradition long before his arrival in 1837. It is difficult to say exactly what persuaded him to go to Livonia. He was ambitious by nature and constantly sought to advance his career, continuously moving around and attempting to rouse interest in his goals among his audiences and patrons. There is little doubt that, in the 1830s, Riga was a challenging environment. Moreover, as already pointed out, Wagner also had personal reasons for shaking the dust of Königsberg from his feet. His most obvious reason for leaving was bound up with his severe financial problems. Debt had become a chronic feature of his lifestyle and led to serious difficulties in Königsberg. His financial problems made it impossible for him to remain in East Prussia. However, his troubles followed him to Riga: his Königsberg creditors tried to obtain their money through the courts, a development that Holtei, the director of the Riga theater, found tiresome in the extreme. In his memoirs of 1870, Dorn recalled that "poor Holtei had already had to put up with a great deal, namely that proceedings were constantly being instituted against his conductor by the courts in Königsberg, Wagner's former place of residence."[58] Virtually all the Wagnerian documents preserved in the Latvian State Historical Archives are bound up with these proceedings. For example, an invoice written in Königsberg and dated 6 November 1838 shows that Wagner had raised fifty-seven small loans between October and December 1836.[59] Later, when Wagner summed up his life in his *Autobiographische Skizze*, he intentionally omitted all mention of his lawsuits over debt.[60] *Mein Leben* is equally silent on the subject.[61]

Wagner set out for Riga in August 1837. He traveled first to Lübeck and continued his journey from there in a merchant vessel. As a result of adverse winds, the boat had to wait for a whole week at Travemünde for the weather to improve. Travel connections on the Baltic were not as good as they were to become in the 1840s when steamboat services became regularly available. In *Mein Leben*, Wagner writes that he used this period of enforced idleness to read *Till Eulenspiegel*, an experience which gave him the idea for "a real German comic opera." Finally he was able to continue his journey and, after four days at sea, the vessel docked at Bolderaja (Bolderaa) on 21 August. From there Wagner continued to Riga. While his reception at Bolderaja had been cool (in *Mein Leben* he attributes this to his youthful enthusiasm for the Polish Uprising and attendant hatred of Russian officialdom), he was all the more pleased to find himself welcome in Riga, where there was an influential German minority.[62]

From the outset, Wagner was gratified to note the degree of interest taken in the theater by the local population. Most of the Germans in Riga were members of the wealthy merchant class that patronized the theater. In his *Autobiographische Skizze*, Wagner states: "There I found outstanding forces assembled for opera and I set to work employing them with great gusto."[63] But the theater had no leading soprano for the forthcoming season, and so Bellini's *Norma*, which had been planned as the first new production of the season, was replaced on 15 September[64] by Boieldieu's *La dame blanche*.[65] All attempts to find a new prima donna having come to nothing, Wagner proposed to Holtei that Minna's sister, Amalie, should be taken on, and Holtei agreed. An invitation was duly sent to Amalie, who was

then living in Dresden, and the latter replied in the affirmative, adding that
Minna was seriously ill. In his autobiographical account of these episodes,
Wagner states that he received this last piece of news "very coolly," as he
had long since realized that she had been unfaithful to him.[66] Finally,
Minna herself wrote to Wagner at length, admitting to her infidelity and
promising to return to the straight and narrow path.[67] She arrived in Riga
with her sister on 19 October and, as she was still unwell, "we both [Richard
and Amalie] firmly determined not to let Minna go on the stage again."[68]

In his autobiography, Wagner sets out to convince his reader that after
these events he attempted to be a good husband, but he also hints at the
suffering caused him by his wife's childlessness. The couple first tried to
replace the missing child with a dog, then with a wolf, but in the end the
best solution proved to be the "good-natured and homely" Amalie, who
moved in with them. Their meals consisted of "Russian salad, salt salmon"
from the Dvina, and "fresh Russian caviar." Even though they were "far
away in [their] northern home," life was not too unpleasant.[69]

During the autumn of 1837, Wagner enthusiastically conducted performances of some of the best-known operas of his time: Hérold's *Zampa*
(29 September), Weber's *Der Freischütz* (13 October), Mozart's *Don Giovanni*
(5 November), Auber's *La muette de Portici* (30 November), and finally a
benefit performance of Bellini's *Norma* (11 December).[70] Wagner had been
taken on because of what Holtei perceived as his interest in the modern
French and Italian repertoire and was now expected to concentrate on
such works. As he put it in his autobiography:

> As far as I myself was concerned, it was enough for [Holtei] to know that I
> belonged to a family which he knew and liked, and hearing, moreover, of
> my fervent devotion to modern Italian and French music in particular,
> he decided that I was the very man for him. He had the whole shoal of
> Bellini's, Donizetti's, Adam's, and Auber's operatic scores copied out, and
> I was to give the good people of Riga the benefit of them with all possible
> speed.[71]

When Wagner subsequently met his old acquaintance Heinrich Dorn, the
latter was surprised to find that "the eccentric worshiper of Beethoven" had
become an "ardent champion of Bellini and Adam."[72]

On the whole, Wagner had an excellent ensemble at his disposal,
including such fine singers as the soprano Karoline Pollert, who had
recently left Vienna, and the tenor Johann Hoffmann. The orchestra was
not particularly large: two first violins, two second violins, two violas, one
cello, one double bass, a double wind section, and cymbals. These were the
basic forces, but the orchestra was often "strengthened by additional forces
of amateur musicians."[73] Wagner himself praised the orchestra fulsomely,
but difficulties were only to be expected. His rehearsals were considered

too long, and some of the musicians complained that his tempos were too quick.[74] Not only was the orchestra small in size, but the theater itself was extremely modestly equipped. Architecturally, however, it influenced Wagner's views on the ideal theater of the future. The pit was deep beneath the stage, and the auditorium was dark and steeply inclined in the manner of an amphitheater.[75] These features are believed to have influenced Wagner's later plans for his theater at Bayreuth.

The Riga company gave guest performances in the neighboring area during the summer. In Jelgava they performed in the town's large opera house, where among the works that Wagner conducted were *La dame blanche* and *Der Freischütz*. According to the music critic for the *Zuschauer*, the latter performance in the summer of 1838 was almost perfect, better than any heard in Riga.[76]

Public attitudes to Wagner were mainly positive. Surprisingly perhaps, it was his old friend Heinrich Dorn who reviewed a concert on 19 March 1838 with unusual severity and who became his most malicious critic. At this concert, Wagner conducted his *Columbus* and *Rule Britannia* overtures, together with his anthem for the birthday of Tsar Nicholas.[77] Although Dorn seems to have been irritated by Wagner's openly insincere tribute to the tsar, his criticism, in the main, concentrated on Wagner's eclectic style: "to try to unite every possible style and fashion in one's own compositions with a view to having everyone on one's own side is the surest way of upsetting everyone."[78]

From an artistic point of view, the period in Riga was extremely important to Wagner. He had the chance to conduct a large number of operas and, at the same time, he could concentrate on his own creative work. In the peaceful setting of Livonia he found time to devote himself once again to Edward Bulwer-Lytton's novel, *Rienzi, the Last of the Roman Tribunes* (1835), and to draft a French-style *grand opéra* on the basis of it. It is firmly grounded in events that took place in the 1340s. In 1343 the people of Rome sent Rienzi as ambassador to the Holy See at Avignon. On Petrarch's recommendation, the pope chose Rienzi as a notary of Rome, but in May 1347, supported by the Roman people, Rienzi rose up against the nobles and senators and became leader of a popular rebellion.[79] These events were very suitable as the subject of a *grand opéra*, offering, as they did, opportunities for magnificent large-scale choral and ensemble scenes culminating in the sort of total catastrophe that was a feature of French *grand opéra* in the first half of the nineteenth century. Usually in the closing scene of the fifth act, the earth shook, volcanoes erupted, lightning flashed, and buildings collapsed. This may be seen in the operas of that master of the genre, Giacomo Meyerbeer. In *Robert le diable* (1831), the earth opens to the accompaniment of a clap of thunder and swallows the evil Bertram.[80] In *Le prophète* (1849), the leader of the Anabaptists' Uprising, John of Leyden, blows himself up, with his mother, the enemy soldiers, and the rebels themselves, singing: "Ah! viens, divine flamme, / Vers Dieu qui nous réclame."[81]

Wagner clearly aimed to replicate this style, concluding *Rienzi* with an equally impressive catastrophe. As in *Le prophète*, the people forsake their leader. Finally the raging crowds set fire to the Capitol and stone Rienzi and his sister. Adriano, Irene's beloved, rushes to help them, but all three perish in the flames.

Le prophète, whose librettist was Scribe, could not have influenced *Rienzi*, of course, as the former work was not premiered until seven years after the latter, but Scribe's librettos certainly left their mark on Wagner and his views. *Les Huguenots*, also with a libretto by Scribe, had been premiered in Paris in 1836. It ends with a harrowing execution scene.[82] Politics and religion are interlinked, and there is no doubt that Wagner, like Meyerbeer, regarded rebellion as a suitable subject for operatic treatment. In fact, he had already tried to make contact with both Scribe and Meyerbeer. Two of Wagner's letters to Scribe have survived, but Wagner is also known to have written to the French librettist on at least two other occasions, as he refers to these letters in his correspondence with Schumann in December 1836 and with August Lewald in November 1838.[83] He had also written to Meyerbeer before his arrival in Riga in February 1837. In this letter, too, he mentions that he has sent Scribe his draft for an opera, *Die hohe Braut*.[84] (Wagner's libretto was later set to music by Jan Bedřich Kittl).

It is clear, therefore, that in planning *Rienzi*, Wagner was expressly following in the footsteps of Meyerbeer and Scribe. He seems, however, to have been unaware of the fact that the story of Rienzi's destiny has an interesting parallel in the Baltic world, a parallel that has encouraged Harry Herbert Tobies to call *Rienzi* "almost an Estonian national opera."[85] In 1343, while Rienzi was being sent to Avignon by the people of Rome, a rebellion against the nobility was breaking out in Estonia. The uprising began on the eve of St. George's Day (Juriöö, 23 April) at Harjumaa. The tenants on the estates there took up arms and attacked the landed gentry: the rebels then broke into the manor houses of the gentry, razed them to the ground, and killed all the Germans they caught. Tallinn was encircled, and the men of Läänemaa joined the rebellious troops, before laying siege to Haapsalu. The rebels then asked the bailiffs of Turku and Viborg for assistance, but their help arrived too late. The knights of the Teutonic Order had in the meantime defeated the Estonians and captured the castle at Tallinn on 15 May.[86]

It would have been possible to construct a *Rienzi*-style opera from this Baltic subject, but Wagner seems to have been unaware of any such opportunity. Although, in theory, the action of *Rienzi* could have been interpreted as a symbolic representation and a precursor of Baltic nationalism, there is no evidence that such an interpretation was ever intended by Wagner. In 1806, E. T. A. Hoffmann had written incidental music for Zacharias Werner's stage play *Das Kreuz an der Ostsee*, which describes the Baltic tribes' struggle against the Crusaders.[87] The connection with Hoffmann makes it very likely that Wagner knew Werner's play and was aware of its historical analogies, but we must dismiss any idea that contemporary audiences saw *Das Kreuz an der Ostsee*—still less *Rienzi*—as calls for the independence of the Baltic peoples, for it was not until the 1870s that such interpretations arose. Moreover, *Rienzi* in fact constitutes a critique of the struggle for social change: even though the despotism of the nobility is criticized, the people of Rome are unable to arrogate political power to themselves and finally turn on Rienzi. In much the same way, the pursuit of power in the *Ring* ultimately proves to be a destructive activity.

Rienzi did not have national-political undertones. It was, above all, a *grand opéra* aimed at international audiences. It dealt with a political subject, but such a choice of theme was not atypical of French *grand opéra* at the time. *Grand opéra* has often been presented as mere spectacle, but it often dealt with political issues. For example, Meyerbeer's *Le prophète*, first staged in 1849, drew parallels between the Anabaptists' Uprising of the 1530s and the July Revolution of 1830, while *Les Huguenots* (1836) was thematically linked with the long-standing antagonism between Catholics and Protestants. So Wagner's theme was not chosen in response to local Baltic national aspirations; it was based on his interpretation of modern opera.

There is little surviving evidence that would throw light on the depth of Wagner's knowledge of the social and political conditions in the Baltic provinces, although his Königsberg sketches invoking Baltic deities indicate that he had a genuine interest in Baltic history and mythology. His enthusiasm for the subject continued in Riga, although he drew up no further plans for an opera based on Baltic mythology. Vita Lindenberg, however, argues that traces of Livonian folklore are recognizable in a number of Wagner's other works: the final scene of *Die Walküre* is said to contain reminiscences of the local midsummer tradition of Lihgo, while *Die Meistersinger* even includes a direct reference to the "Lihgo melody" in Hans Sachs's Flieder Monologue, in the words "Der Flieder war's: Johannisnacht."[88]

Wagner did not return to his Königsberg sketches, although it has been argued that their underlying conflict between Christianity and a more barbaric natural religion later found expression in *Lohengrin*.[89] In Riga, Wagner remained loyal to his *Rienzi* project. The libretto was completed during June and July in Jelgava and Riga, and he began work on the music in August 1838.[90] It was not long, however, before he realized that Riga did not offer the right conditions for so spectacular an opera, even though he himself had conducted works of a similar kind at the local theater. In his *Autobiographische Skizze*, he claims that "From the very beginning, I planned it on such a grand scale that it would be impossible to perform it in a small theater—at least for its première."[91] In the same text Wagner denies having been influenced by any other works, although the influences on *Rienzi* are in fact obvious. He also states that the first two acts were completed by the spring of 1839.[92]

By now, Wagner's agreement with Holtei was on the point of expiring, and he found no reason to remain in Livonia. In his *Autobiographische Skizze*, he says he had been planning to move to Paris for two years,[93] a statement corroborated by his letters to Meyerbeer and Scribe as well as by the fact that he began to take French lessons while he was in Riga.[94] In the spring, he also produced a French translation of the *Rienzi* libretto, hoping to be able to use it as a visiting card in Paris. This translation was checked and revised in June 1839.[95] At the same time, Wagner had slowly but surely burnt his bridges in Riga. He had suggested innovations in the musical life of the town that were of no interest whatsoever to Holtei. Moreover, Holtei had tried to persuade Minna to return to the stage, thus altering Wagner's relations with his employer. As a result, battle lines were now drawn up. Only when Holtei resigned and was replaced by Johann Hoffmann did the situation show signs of improving. But the theater management appointed Dorn as the new conductor, Wagner being too great a risk to take in view of his mounting debts and Parisian delusions. Wagner now had no alternative but to leave, and to leave, moreover, by stealth, so as to avoid the creditors who were now close on his heels.[96] The prospects for leaving were by no means favorable, as Wagner's passport had been impounded, and to acquire a new one would have drawn attention to his plans. The only solution was to slip away over the border illegally.[97]

After conducting the last of the summer's performances, including *Fidelio* and Weber's *Oberon*, Wagner set off without delay, accompanied by Minna and a merchant from Königsberg, Abraham Möller, who had in fact planned the whole escapade. July was at its hottest, and the journey was far from pleasant. According to *Mein Leben*, however, most of the problems were caused by the composer's dog, Robber. When Wagner had gone to Jelgava, he had left Robber behind in Riga, but the dog had continuously howled for its master, and the neighbors had sent it to Jelgava by mail coach. As there was no room for the dog in the coach that took the refugees through Courland, poor Robber was left to run along beside it.

On the evening of the second day the travelers reached the Russian border, where they met a friend of Möller's who was to escort them to an illegal crossing place.[98] The Wagners waited for nightfall in a tavern "which gradually became filled to suffocation with Polish Jews of most forbidding aspect."[99] As darkness fell they were asked to follow their guide:

> A few hundred feet away, on the slope of a hill, lay the ditch which runs the whole length of the Russian frontier, watched continually and at very narrow intervals by Cossacks. Our chance was to utilize the few moments after the relief of the watch, during which the sentinels were elsewhere engaged. We had, therefore, to run at full speed down the hill, scramble through the ditch, and then hurry along until we were beyond the range of

Figure 1.6. Port of Pillau in the 1930s. Postcard by Eduard Nachtrab, Königsberg. Author's postcard collection.

the soldiers' guns; for the Cossacks were bound in case of discovery to fire upon us even on the other side of the ditch.[100]

Möller's friend was waiting with his coach and took the Wagners to Arnau, only a few kilometers from Königsberg. Here they met Möller, who had used the legal route and who now helped them on their way, for without his financial and other support the whole journey would have been impossible. Wagner had decided to travel first to London, as the journey by coach to Paris would have been too long and difficult for a passenger with neither passport nor funds. Accordingly, the Wagners made for the Prussian port of Pillau (now Baltysk in Russia; see figure 1.6), from which a sailing ship, the *Thetis*, was due to leave for London. They had to hide in the hold, as customs officers inspected the vessel before it set sail. Not until the boat had cast off could they heave a sigh of relief.[101]

Thus ended Wagner's period in the Baltic world: ahead of him lay the most arduous years of his life, in Paris from 1839 to 1842 and in Dresden from 1842 to 1849. His farewell to the Baltic was not without its surprises. There was little wind and it took seven days for the *Thetis* to reach Copenhagen. Here the Wagners remained on board. "In good spirits we sailed past the beautiful castle of Elsinore, the sight of which brought me into immediate touch with my youthful impressions of *Hamlet*."[102] But in the Skagerrak the boat was caught in a violent storm, in which the ship's figurehead was dislodged and Minna's trunk was washed overboard. Finally, the captain had to make for the Norwegian coast but, being impatient, was reluctant to linger too long, and so the hazardous journey continued. It was not until 12 August that the *Thetis* reached London.[103] For Wagner, at least in retrospect, the voyage was an unforgettable experience, later to be crystallized in the atmosphere of *Der fliegende Holländer*.

Wagner's Baltic years have undeservedly been regarded as a kind of prehistory to his life. Arriving in Paris in September 1839, he felt he had come to the very center of the musical world. In Paris he longed desperately for success, a success that ultimately eluded him. And so he returned to Germany in 1842, becoming Kapellmeister to the Royal Court of Dresden in the following year. The Dresden period has often been seen as a turning point in his development, for it was here that Wagner found his voice as a composer. Here, too, *Rienzi* was premiered on 20 October 1842, followed by *Der fliegende Holländer* on 2 January 1843 and *Tannhäuser* on 19 October 1845. The pioneer of Finnish Wagnerism, Martin Wegelius, commented that the innovations Wagner brought to opera produced a reaction that, in turn, led to the emergence of "an ever-growing band of antagonists, something already clearly discernible at the premiere of *Tannhäuser*."[104]

For Wagner, the Dresden period was also a time of political adventure: he took part in the activities of the Vaterlandsverein and, together with August Röckel, Mikhail Bakunin, and Gottfried Semper, mounted the barricades during the Dresden Uprising of 1849. Röckel and Bakunin were apprehended, but Wagner succeeded in fleeing to Switzerland. This was the beginning of his years of exile, a period that was to last until the early 1860s.

2

Wagner as an Orchestral and Drawing Room Composer

Musical Networks

Wagner's music had been heard in Königsberg and in Riga since the 1830s, with Riga soon to become a Wagner center. Even after Wagner's personal influence in the Baltic world declined, and although—unlike many other German musicians at the time—he did not continue his travels to St. Petersburg and the other centers of the Baltic world, a considerable amount of information on the composer's activities, thoughts, and works can be gleaned from contemporary newspapers and musical periodicals, particularly from the 1850s onward. After taking part in the Dresden Uprising in May 1849, Wagner wrote several texts on the theory of art including *Die Kunst und die Revolution, Das Kunstwerk der Zukunft*, and *Oper und Drama*; the sentiments expressed in these books were soon widely quoted in the press, coinciding with a growing interest in Wagner's music.

The purpose of this chapter is to begin a discourse on the initial spread of Wagner's music. Wagner had focused on the composition of music dramas, which—to a certain degree—made his works difficult to export and less suitable for popularization than, for instance, Chopin's piano music. In addition to this, Wagner planned his works to be performed by huge ensembles, thus creating economic and practical hindrances to the spread of productions of his works.

I will address the question of how Wagner's music became better known, the methods by which extracts, separated from the operas, appeared in concert programs, and how Wagner's works were arranged for use in homes and salons. This process of musical distribution was an important factor in the reception of Wagner's work. Reception, after all, was not only a matter of circulating music: it entailed a movement and exchange of people and ideas as well. Here, it was not just through printed sheet music, concerts, music periodicals, and books that Richard Wagner's music became familiar: social interaction also played its part. The reciprocal movement of composers, musicians, singers, and music scholars between Germany and the world of the *mare balticum* created a network through which musical innovations spread rapidly. This musical network not only influenced the spread of music but also affected the formation of the infrastructure on which music was based.

The nineteenth-century Baltic world witnessed the development of a modern bourgeois concert music culture (which took its cue from the latest innovations in Germany). The creation of this culture is revealed in the educational development of musicians, who were directed to German conservatories and music centers. Composers and musicians from Sweden, Finland, and the Baltic provinces often went to study in Germany. In Sweden, however, there had been the Royal Academy of Music since the late-eighteenth century, but Finland got its first conservatory in 1882[1] and Estonia as late as 1919;[2] previously, education had to be sought at foreign institutions like the Leipzig Conservatory, founded by Felix Mendelssohn in 1843.[3] As a multicultural seat of learning where musicians from different parts of Europe could meet, giving rise to cultural contacts that transcended national borders, Leipzig had an international atmosphere.[4]

As for Estonia and the other Baltic provinces, the most significant competitor deserving attention was the St. Petersburg Conservatory. Many of its teachers were of German origin, but the most influential personalities from the artistic point of view were Nicolai Rimsky-Korsakov, Anton Rubinstein, and Alexander Glazunov.[5] The rivalry between the Leipzig and St. Petersburg conservatories was obvious, but other excellent centers of education existed. Alexander Läte, for example, one of the key figures in the Estonian symphony orchestra movement, studied under the guidance of F. A. Draeseke at the Dresden Conservatory from 1895 to 1897.[6]

German music culture exerted a remarkable influence on musical education until at least the latter part of the nineteenth century and was still heavily significant up to the First World War. Studying in Germany allowed the participants to become acquainted with the existing German infrastructure, that is, the concert and opera institutions, the publishers, and the musical press.

Other forms of communication were important in the spread of musical and operatic innovations. Ensembles and individual artists circulated the Baltic Sea, largely following a tradition dating from the eighteenth century. The Austrian pianist Anton Door, for instance, completed a long tour in which he gave concerts in Sweden, Finland, and Russia. In Stockholm, in addition to giving a solo performance, Door played together with the violinist Ferdinand Laub. The program included the Spinning Song from Wagner's opera *Der fliegende Holländer*.[7] Artists did not necessarily restrict themselves to circulating around the Baltic Sea: they could travel through East Prussia and the Baltic provinces to St. Petersburg. In 1853, George Stigelli, a singer from the Covent Garden Opera, performed both in Germany and the Baltic provinces, finally ending his concert tour in "the city of the Neva."[8] Some artists traveled far and wide in the Baltic world, including the London dancer

Figure 2.1. Baltic Sea coast at Memel, present-day Klaipeda. Postcard by Verlag Joseph Cohn, Memel, 1916. Author's postcard collection.

Lydia Thompson, who performed in Riga in October 1856,[9] in Helsinki in July 1857,[10] and in Stockholm in November 1857.[11]

Travel connections also improved. The advent of regular steamship services was, in this respect, of primary importance. Sailing ships did not, at the time, offer precise schedules for voyages, and this made it difficult to plan concert tours. Steamship traffic changed the situation dramatically. As early as the 1820s, an experiment with steamship connections was undertaken when the steam schooner *Stockholm* navigated a route from the Swedish capital via Turku to Helsinki and back.[12] In the summer of 1836, the paddle steamer *Alexander Nicolajewitsch* sailed regularly on the Riga-Tallinn-Helsinki-Turku-Stockholm route, but the venture proved to be economically unprofitable. The following summer, in Finland, the acquisition of two seagoing paddle steamers, the *Storfursten* and the *Furst Menschikof,* made it possible to start a weekly steamship service linking Stockholm, Turku, Helsinki, Tallinn, and Kronstadt.[13] By the 1850s, traffic connections were surprisingly lively, creating a dense network around the coasts of the Baltic Sea (see figure 2.1). Musicians and printed music could now circulate more efficiently than ever, though the volume of steamship traffic was greatest between February and November. In 1853 the steamers *Neva* and *Trave* sailed regularly between St. Petersburg and Lübeck, carrying both passengers and cargo. The route was via both Tallinn and Riga.[14] The steamship *Düna* was also sailing at this time between Riga and the east Prussian city of Stettin (now Szczecin in Poland).[15]

Toward the end of the nineteenth century, the railroad became the most important mode of transportation. Able to cover long distances in any type of weather, the railroads launched a remarkable economic boom, making commercial connections quicker and more reliable. A significant railroad line ran between Riga and Daugavpils, commencing service in 1861. This connected Riga to the St. Petersburg-Warsaw railroad.[16] The building of the Helsinki-St. Petersburg line began in 1867, and it soon became possible to travel by train from Germany through the Baltic provinces to Finland. The line between Tallinn and St. Petersburg went into service in 1870.[17] Through these facilities, newspapers, music periodicals, and sheet music could now be transported more efficiently. As of the 1850s, long-distance communication had also been improved through the introduction of the telegraph.[18]

The new means of transportation were part of a social infrastructure that offered new possibilities for musical communication. The steamships and railroads not only transported musicians and composers but also sheet music and instruments. These transport facilities guaranteed the circulation of the products and ideas of most nineteenth-century composers, but with regard to Wagner the situation was far more complex. Complete operas were not easy to transport. On the coasts of the Baltic Sea, opera flourished under the Swedish and Danish monarchies and the Russian czars. Operatic activities were also very much in evidence in Riga, where the theater was patronized by the trading bourgeoisie. Wagner's compositions also appeared in transportable form through the published sheet music oriented toward home musicmaking. In addition, Wagner's music can be found in the repertoire of local ensembles and traveling artists. Concerts and home music were essential parts of the European musical and social infrastructure, and it is therefore essential to pay attention to this often neglected dimension of Wagner's reception.

Commodifying Wagner's Innovations

In the nineteenth century, in addition to opera houses and concert halls, music was practiced in almost any place where people gathered: at home, or in salons, restaurants, and clubrooms. Before the advent of the phonograph and the gramophone, some mechanized instruments, such as player pianos and music boxes, did exist,[19] but most musical activity in the home took the form of personal performance. Easy arrangements of well-known pieces, songs, overtures, arias, marches, waltzes, and polkas were produced to be played at home. Arrangements of the same pieces could also be made for ensembles of different sizes: from piano transcriptions for two or four hands to the scores used by salon orchestras performing in restaurants.

Andreas Ballstaedt and Tobias Widmaier share the view that the phenomenon of salon music originated in France in the 1830s and 1840s, at a time when the salons of French high society became venues for piano virtuosos.[20] Short piano pieces, of which Chopin's nocturnes, waltzes, and mazurkas are excellent examples, were composed for salon use. However, salon music only really began to take off in the 1850s, when it expanded beyond aristocratic circles to bourgeois families to become widely practiced in the home. Simultaneously, the production of pianos rapidly increased.[21] Home and salon music may well have been the largest field in the music business.[22] This development can also be scrutinized in the light of the gradual "industrialization" and "commodification" processes that took place during the course of the nineteenth century. In this respect, the recording methods that were invented at the end of the nineteenth century were not the most radical forms of change.[23] The key development, instead, was the principle of commodification, now extended to cultural products of various kinds, including music.

Though Richard Wagner first became known in the Baltic world through his ideas and writings (it was not until later that his music became available in its original form), it is extremely important to keep in mind that arrangements of Wagner's music were also produced for performance in salons and homes. It is probable that many of Wagner's tunes were heard for the first time in this form. Symphony concerts and opera performances reached only very limited social circles and geographical areas. On the other hand, popular musical arrangements spread through bookshop networks even to the remotest towns.

Music performed at home was a significant aspect of bourgeois leisure culture in the nineteenth century. Wagner's music was arranged for domestic use, although this does not sit comfortably with his operatic aesthetics, which worked to erode the centralizing features of operas based around set pieces and contemptuously criticized publishing activities. The music publishing business was, however, so lively and generated such large sums of money that not even Wagner could afford to forbid the arrangement of his work. Wagner was, in fact, more concerned with piano transcriptions of entire operas than with smaller-scale arrangements of his music. Hence, although he regularly corresponded with his publisher Breitkopf & Härtel, his letters were not oriented toward music in the home. Generally speaking, it was only when arrangements of entire operas were at stake that Wagner became interested. However, after the publisher produced a piano transcription for four hands of the *Faust* Overture without Wagner's permission in spring 1855, Wagner wrote in reaction on the 6th of June:

> You will be most vexed with me, when I tell you that the arrangement à 4 m. of the Faust Overture, which was sent to me for perusal, pleases me little. I had not suspected that you intended to publish an arrangement such as this; had I known, I would have begged you to allow me to choose who should do the arrangement, and I almost wish it were even now not

too late. The piano arrangements do not reflect the current understanding of the pianoforte, and the score appears to me in general to respect the letter, but not the spirit. Patching up would achieve nothing; Herr Klindworth, on the other hand—to whom I had loaned my original score—would at any rate deliver an excellent arrangement, should it please you to permit me to commission this from him.[24]

The publisher replied laconically to this request: "We are unable to follow the author's wishes in every regard"[25]—the arrangements were made for players with mediocre abilities, and thus should not include scores demanding exceptional pianistic skills. In some of his letters, Wagner proposed that Karl Klindworth, Franz Liszt, and Hans von Bülow should be employed for the production of transcriptions.[26]

The publishers' and agents' sales catalogs are excellent sources of information, indicating the full range of available musical transcriptions, compared to the literary artifacts left by composers. The problem with using the sales catalogs as historical records is that they give information only on availability, not on sales. Even though arrangements of Wagner's work are listed in the catalogs of publishers and agents, this is no guarantee that they were bought. It is probable, however, that they *were* in demand: if it were not so, the agents would not have released a succession of new arrangements on to the market. The culture of arrangements proved to be international. Most of the sheet music came from Central Europe; in Wagner's case, from Germany. Although there were some local and international differences in terms of the transcriptions stocked by suppliers, these were not particularly significant. Although a great deal of the sheet music in the market was imported, as noted above, in the Baltic world as a whole, local publishing activities had existed since the 1830s. In Finland, for instance, some printing presses and book publishers began to publish sheet music—mainly of local solo songs—as early as the 1830s. The real pioneer in the field of music publishing was, however, German-born Ludwig Beuermann, who founded a music shop and a lending library for sheet music in Helsinki in 1850. Beuermann began his own publishing operation two years later. As of 1877, Beuermann's firm was under the ownership of A. E. Lindgren. In many cases, however, only the covers were printed in Finland, and the rest was imported from Germany.[27]

At the time of the spread of Wagner's music in Europe in the 1850s, there were music shops, music libraries, and music publishers on both sides of the Baltic Sea. It was therefore possible to gain some acquaintance with Wagner's music, but novelties like published sheet music generated a significant level of interest only in cultures that had a social affinity with Wagner's Germany. In the Baltic provinces, Estonia, Livonia, and Courland the connections with Germany had been close for centuries and the role of the German-speaking minority was still significant. For this reason, the publishing business in these provinces was also far more active than, say, in the more remote areas of Finland.

In Stockholm and Riga, the publishing business was exceedingly active. In Finland and Estonia, the number of publishers was lower, and they probably did not make many of their own arrangements of international themes. The musical material exploited in the Estonian region apparently came straight from Germany or through Riga and St. Petersburg. A great deal of the sheet music sold in Finland came from Sweden and Germany. Finland was, after all, an important market for the businessmen of Stockholm. Abraham Hirsch supplied sheet music via bookshops throughout Sweden, Norway, Denmark, and Finland.[28] Hirsch had a strong position in Sweden and in Finland, but not in Denmark where there were many large music publishers. In the Swedish market, Abraham Lundquist and Elkan & Schildknecht competed with Hirsch on an equal basis, as did (possibly) Julius Bagge and Carl Gehrman.[29] Sheet music publishers from Riga, having a long tradition behind them, were also influential in the Baltic world. During the 1850s, J. Deubner, Edm. Götschel, and Müller & Zimmermann supplied sheet music in Riga. In the 1870s, Wilhelm Betz, A. Harff, and G. Engelmann came into the market. Other suppliers in the Baltic provinces were H. Dohnberg and G. Zimmermann of Liepaja (Libau in German) and Fr. Lucas of Jelgava.[30] The commission services offered by the shops in Riga also operated in the other Baltic provinces: in 1857, J. Deubner advertised that his company would act as an agency to supply sheet music to bookshops in Tartu, Tallinn, and Jelgava.[31]

The intensification of music publishing and commissioning took place alongside the development of a library network that increased the availability of books and facilitated the acquisition of sheet music. The oldest lending library in the Baltic provinces, founded by Karl Hartwig Müller in 1800, was located in Riga. Müller acquired 7,000 copies of works in sheet music form for the library collection, beginning the lending library system for sheet music. By December 1871, the collection comprised 80,000 book volumes and 50,000 sheet music titles. The capacity of all the lending libraries in Riga increased during the 1860s and 1870s, and this led to an improvement in the availability of music.[32]

In Sweden, in addition to public libraries, many music shops maintained their own collections of scores and arrangements. For instance, in the 1840s, N. J. Gumpert of Gothenburg published a catalog listing the contents of his lending library.[33] In Gothenburg, sheet music could also be borrowed from J. E. Sundberg's office.[34] In Malmö, Clara Öhrström's music shop also served as a library.[35] Hirsch, Josephson, Lundquist, and Rylander of Stockholm advertised that they were prepared to lend sheet music to their customers.[36] The merchants strove to develop their lending services, because this was seen as encouraging the sale of music. If customers were pleased with the sheet music they borrowed, they might buy copies for themselves. Therefore, the network of bookshops guaranteed the efficient marketing of music for performance in the home.

The catalogs of sheet music preserved at the Swedish and Latvian archives reveal that the number of available Wagner arrangements was comparatively low in the 1840s, although, over the following decade, Wagner arrangements were marketed in abundance. N. J. Gumpert of Gothenburg published a catalog of the transcripts available in his music library in the 1840s and 1850s. The 1846 and 1848 catalogs did not yet include any music by Wagner. The first Wagner arrangement is found in the fourth catalog, which was published in 1850; the arrangement concerned was a piano four-hands setting of the *Tannhäuser* Overture.[37] In the following year, Rylander advertised a transcription of a romance from the same opera.[38] The catalog section titled "Oratorios and Operas for Solo Piano" also included the music for Wagner's *Rienzi*.[39] In 1853, A. B. Heinzelmann from Lund, for his part, advertised that an arrangement for piano of Wagner's *Rienzi* Overture was available in his library.[40]

The size of the Wagner repertoire seems to have increased annually in the 1850s. In 1852, Abraham Hirsch started to market compositions that could be classified as marginal in terms of Wagner's output but were, however, suitable for home music. Through Hirsch's agency, it became possible to acquire "Les deux Grénadiers" and the Carnival Song from the opera *Das Liebesverbot*.[41]

Abraham Hirsch's sales catalogs of the 1850s, featuring an increasing list of arrangements of Wagner's music, shows that *Tannhäuser* and *Lohengrin* had gradually gained popularity. In December 1855, Hirsch's latest offering was a solo voice arrangement with piano accompaniment of "Lyrische Stücke" from the opera *Lohengrin*. The catalog does not, however, indicate which extracts were included in the collection.[42] Also in 1855, N. J. Gumpert's library acquired a "Potpourri sur Tannhäuser de R. Wagner, Op. 155," a piano transcription for four hands by G. W. Marks.[43] In 1857, Gumpert's catalog also included a transcription of the *Tannhäuser* Overture for four hands.[44]

Franz Liszt's and Hans von Bülow's arrangements of Wagner were soon listed in the above catalogs. Although Wagner's attitude toward this music industry was decidedly mixed, the arrangements made by Liszt and von Bülow, friends of Wagner and part of his inner circle, can be regarded as authorized versions.[45] The Gumpert catalogs, published in Gothenburg in 1857, also included piano transcriptions of *Tannhäuser* and *Lohengrin*[46] but do not give detailed information on them, although it is thought that they are exactly the same as the pieces published by Breitkopf & Härtel in Leipzig in 1853 under the title *Zwei Stücke aus R. Wagner's Tannhäuser und Lohengrin: für das Pianoforte von Franz Liszt*. The first part of the 1853 edition consisted of "The Arrival of the Guests at Wartburg" (the March) from *Tannhäuser* and "Elsa's Bridal Procession" from *Lohengrin*.[47] The arrangements by Hans von Bülow did not appear in Abraham Hirsch's catalogs until 1857. The Bülow transcriptions included numbers 1 (Introduction), 5 ("Elizabeth's Aria"), and 10 ("Wolfram's Romance"). In addition to these, the catalogs also listed an arrangement of the famous March from *Tannhäuser*.[48]

It was not until the 1850s that *Tannhäuser* and *Lohengrin*, in particular, became widely known as salon pieces. *Rienzi* and *Der fliegende Holländer* remained mere curiosities in the popular repertoire. In the Baltic provinces, the prominence of *Tannhäuser* and *Lohengrin* arrangements can to a certain extent be explained by the fact that Riga had already hosted Wagner's operas: *Der fliegende Holländer* had been performed in June 1843, *Tannhäuser* in January 1853, and *Lohengrin* in February 1855.[49] By contrast, the first Swedish Wagner production took place in 1865, when *Rienzi* was performed at the Royal Opera House. The initial success of *Tannhäuser* in Riga meant that it was also staged on the east side of the Baltic Sea. Due to its reception in Riga, *Tannhäuser* played in Tallinn in 1853 as well as in Helsinki in 1857 (in the latter case, however, only as a guest performance by the visiting German theater of Riga).[50] Nevertheless, the influence of these performances can be seen in the repertoire of salon music. Publishers in Riga made use of the operas performed in the region, and strove to market small pieces connected with the latest operatic novelties.

After the first performance of *Lohengrin* in Riga on 5 February 1855, a piano piece by Josef Harzer was quickly introduced into the market. This arrangement was supplied by the music shops of both Deubner and Götschel and was one of the oddest contributions to the history of Wagner arrangements: the tunes of *Lohengrin* had been arranged in the rhythms of the most fashionable dance of the period: the polka.[51]

A proliferation of *Lohengrin* arrangements appeared on the market during the spring of 1855. As the polka version had gained popularity, Harzer took advantage of the situation, making a *française* (popular French dance) from the *Lohengrin* motifs in March and a "Swan Song" in April. Both of these were piano pieces for two hands.[52] In addition to being available from Deubner and Götschel, the arrangements could also be obtained from H. Dohnberg's bookshop in Liepaja (for a view of Liepaja, see figure 2.2).[53] That *Lohengrin* could inspire someone to make a *française* from its themes seems odd to the modern observer, considering that Wagner himself often criticized French culture and expressed his belief in a struggle between "German spirit" and "French civilization."[54] But Wagner's reputation as an anti-French thinker was outweighed by his international appeal.

Josef Harzer, a music teacher who had worked in Riga from the 1830s until the 1860s, was responsible for the symbiosis of Wagner and popular music. He was known in Riga as a dance music composer with a fluent pen, frequently exploiting material based on operatic novelties. Harzer's Wagner arrangements astonished his contemporaries, as is revealed by the fact

Figure 2.2. Street view in Liepaja. Postcard by Georg Stilke, Berlin. Author's post-card collection.

that Harzer was one of the few composers of dance music who was accepted by Moritz Rudolph for inclusion in the *Rigaer Theater- und Tonkünstler-Lexikon*, published in 1890. In particular, Rudolph mentions Harzer's arrangements of Wagner, claiming that he had even produced a galop based on the Venus motif in *Tannhäuser*. In addition to this, Harzer had completed a *française* based on *Tannhäuser*.[55] These arrangements can be ascribed in part, at least, to Harzer's sense of humor, but he certainly realized the commercial possibilities offered by a combination of opera and dance music.

In comparison with Wagner's other operas, in the case of *Lohengrin* there was an exceptionally strong desire to take advantage of its success on the stage, but signs of a similar phenomenon can also be distinguished later in musical history. When, for instance, *Die Meistersinger* was performed in Riga in 1871, Deubner marketed not only the whole piano score of the opera but a number of pot-pourris for both two and four hands.[56]

Not only operatic performances but also concert performances were exploited for profit in the home music markets. Such performances included concerts given by military bands and other orchestras, especially after the gradual increase in performances of Wagner's works. Elkan & Schildknecht in Stockholm were successful in selling the *Tannhäuser* March during the years 1863–64. The 1864 catalog indicates that this piece in particular was "a favorite number at Herr Filip von Schantz`s concerts."[57] The conductor Filip von Schantz had worked as a director of the first professional orchestra in Finland during 1860–63, but when the New Helsinki theater was badly damaged by fire in May 1863, he moved to Stockholm.[58] The *Tannhäuser* March, a popular piece, was already in his repertoire when he was working in Helsinki.

Even though Wagnerian productions did not reach theaters on the western coast of the Baltic Sea until the 1860s, *Tannhäuser* and *Lohengrin* dominated the market and the formation of Wagner's image. *Tannhäuser*, in particular, was successful throughout Europe, and the opera was quickly acknowledged as the key work in the favorable international reception of Wagner. However, the Finnish music historian Martin Wegelius stated in his *Hufvuddragen af den västerländska musikens historia* (*History of Western Music, 1891–93*) that the innovations Wagner brought to opera gave rise to the birth of a "continuously growing opposition party, which was clearly perceivable at the first performance of *Tannhäuser*."[59] Wegelius also reported that

> From *Tannhäuser* onward, one can speak of a Wagnerian party, and of an organized opposition, although this opposition did not become fashionable until the Year of Revolutions in 1848, and only in the fifties, following the publication of "Das Judenthum in der Musik," did it take on the character of a spiteful and merciless persecution. There are two features here that stand out from the beginning as distinctive. First and foremost, the criticism of Wagner was based on the most dissimilar, indeed contradictory, points of view, and was based, similarly, on extremely diverse motives. It may sound like a joke, but is fully true, that whereas the director of the Berlin Opera (Herr v. Küstner) found *Tannhäuser* to be far too *epic*, the Dresden critics saw it as far too *dramatic*, and a voice was raised in Leipzig asserting that it was far too *lyrical*. . . . The reasons for this astonishing phenomenon are today relatively clear: both in Wagner's orientation, and in his poetic-musical individuality, there was something so original that it was totally alien to the then prevailing aesthetic taste, and could therefore not be comprehended.[60]

Martin Wegelius saw *Tannhäuser*, therefore, as the turning point in the history of the production of Wagner's operas, as a sort of threshold in the development of Wagnerism. The reputation of *Tannhäuser* was accentuated by the Paris performance (1861), which Baudelaire described in his famous essay, "Richard Wagner et Tannhäuser à Paris."[61] It is no wonder that *Tannhäuser* was to play a central role in the field of arrangement music as well.

Tannhäuser and *Lohengrin* had already gained popularity in the 1850s, but the range of salon music arrangements broadened in the following decades. During the 1850s and 1860s, the most significant arrangers were Ferdinand Beyer (1803–63), Henri Cramer (1818–77), and Theodor Oesten (1813–70), who diligently condensed operas into enjoyable pot-pourris.

Cramer published a pot-pourri cycle, "Les fleurs des opéras," with Beyer releasing the series "Répertoire des jeunes pianistes" as well as "Bouquet des mélodies." By 1852, Cramer, Oesten, and Beyer had not yet accepted Wagner's music.[62] In 1859, Cramer's "Les fleurs des opéras" was a highly popular series with extracts from forty-five operas, including, among others, such popular works as Flotow's *Alessandro Stradella*, Verdi's *Ernani* and *Il trovatore*, Donizetti's *La fille du régiment*, and Meyerbeer's *Les Huguenots* and *Le prophète*. *Tannhäuser* was published as number thirty-six in the series. In fact, "The Flowers of Opera" appeared in several parallel series. Piano transcriptions for two or four hands were among the standard requirements of the time, but in the 1859 catalog, Elkan & Schildknecht also included arrangements for violin and piano as well as for flute and piano.[63] The same catalog included Wagnerian products in abundance. There was a *Lohengrin* pot-pourri for four hands by Cramer and a *Tannhäuser* for four hands arranged by Marks. There were also arrangements for two hands from *Der fliegende Holländer*. Furthermore, Cramer had incorporated a pot-pourri of the operas *Indra*, *Tannhäuser*, and *Giralda* (Op. 102) in his "Amusemens brill. sur des mot. d'opéras." Theodor Oesten's "Portefeuille de l'opéra" included pieces from both *Lohengrin* and *Tannhäuser* (nos. 1–2, Op. 141). It is notable that the number of Wagner arrangements increased at a dramatic pace.[64] It is also notable that in 1859 the availability of Wagner's works was not limited to arrangements for instruments but also included vocal arrangements. The Battle Hymn from *Rienzi*, the Pilgrims' Chorus from *Tannhäuser*, and *Das Liebesmahl der Apostel*—representing a very different side of Wagner's output—could be obtained for the use of male choirs. In the arrangements for solo voice, Wagner's name occurs only once: the song "Die beiden Grenadieren" was included.[65]

Wagner's music was thus obtainable in the form of arrangements from the late 1850s onward. Compared to the situation in 1870, there does not appear to have been a great deal of variety in terms of the music sold. Most of the material is from *Tannhäuser*, *Der fliegende Holländer*, or *Lohengrin*. In the Elkan & Schildknecht catalog, *Rienzi*—which appeared not only in arrangements for the piano but also for flute and violin—seems to have joined the other favorites.[66] This may have been due to the fact that in 1865 it was the first opera by Wagner to be included in the repertoire of the Royal Opera in Stockholm. It enjoyed considerable success, and as a result the home music market experienced an increased demand for arrangements.

The gradual change in Wagner's image can be clearly seen in the Elkan & Schildknecht 1870 catalog: by that time the list included a piano transcription of *Tristan und Isolde* for four hands as well as the *Tristan* and *Die Meistersinger* overtures. Both of these were internationally known items. The complete piano scores of *Das Rheingold* and *Die Walküre* had also become available.[67] *Tristan und Isolde* had been premiered in Munich in 1865, *Die Meistersinger* in 1868, *Das Rheingold* in 1869, and *Die Walküre* in 1870. Until 1870 the

Stockholm Royal Opera had performed only *Rienzi*, but one could become acquainted with the new works through the piano scores. The audience that was reached through these larger-scale arrangements was, of course, limited in size. The smaller pieces penned by arrangers like Cramer and Beyer had a larger circulation and dominated the popular Wagner market.

The increasing popularity of Wagner's works can also be seen in the fact that the arrangements gradually covered a much broader selection of instruments. Certain pieces had become so popular that musicians who played various instruments felt compelled to play them. Elkan & Schildknecht's 1870 catalog, for instance, included a transcription of the *Tannhäuser* themes for two guitars.[68] In addition to the violin and flute arrangements, transcriptions of Wagner were also marketed for cellists.[69] In 1876, Abraham Lundquist's catalog broadened the selection even further. That same year, Wagner had succeeded in arranging the first opera festival in Bayreuth, finally ensuring the performance of *Der Ring des Nibelungen*. Lundquist sold pieces from the *Ring* as piano arrangements for two hands as well as the *Kaisermarsch* quickly composed by Wagner in homage to the realization of the dream of German unification in 1871.[70] The best material for arrangements still, however, consisted of the older, popular tunes. The *Tannhäuser* Overture can be found in an arrangement for two violins. Extracts from *Lohengrin*, *Rienzi*, and *Tannhäuser* appeared as variations to be played on the melodica (the physharmonica or orgelmelodium).[71]

Developments with regard to sheet music catalogs in the Baltic provinces follow the same lines, with the exception of the total exclusion of *Rienzi*. In Sweden, after its premiere at the Royal Opera House, *Rienzi* became a sensation, and this was reflected in the market for decades to come. On the eastern side of the Baltic Sea, *Rienzi* did not secure a similar position. It was not performed in Riga until 1878, and not in Tallinn until 1902. In St. Petersburg, *Rienzi* had been staged only in 1879.[72] Wagner's early work did not gain the popularity and significance that it did in Sweden, nor did those who preferred home music show any interest in *Rienzi* (even in the 1880s).

Except for the absence of *Rienzi*, the repertoire of arrangements in the sheet music catalogs of Riga broadened as it did in Sweden, but it appears that an even larger selection of instruments was involved. Carl Blosfeld's music shop was selling, in addition to the usual violin and cello arrangements, sheet music for cornet solo, for cornet duo, and for cornet and piano. Wolfram's "Song to the Evening Star" (*Tannhäuser*) and Siegmund's "Love Song" (*Die Walküre*) were also sold with piano accompaniment.[73] In another catalog, Blosfeld advertised the Bridal Chorus and the Pilgrims' Chorus arranged by Otto Menzel for four instruments (cornet, tenor horn, althorn, or waldhorn, that is, the German forest horn). A real curiosity was the *Rigaer Zither-Album*, edited by H. Bundschau, which included a zither arrangement of Wolfram's "Song to the Evening Star."[74]

Wagner's music achieved its first major breakthrough in the field of home and salon music during the latter part of the 1850s. In 1855–59, above all, the themes from *Tannhäuser* and *Lohengrin* became well known on both sides of the Baltic Sea. These popular arrangements were still prominently placed in the sales catalogs as late as the 1870s and 1880s, even though by this time Wagner's more modern works had gradually begun to appear in the catalogs. It must also be remembered that the salon-worthy melodies suitable for pot-pourris actually offered a rather narrow view of Wagner's works. One could not acquire a deep understanding of the composer's artistic tendencies merely by means of piano arrangements for two or four hands. It is also evident that in the "culture of arrangement," the more traditional works—particularly those of Wagner's early period—were more successful than those, such as *Tristan und Isolde,* that belong to the composer's far more mature later period.

Drawing room music, even though it was only one aspect of the multifaceted international music culture, still revealed regional differences. Home music was regularly inspired by other forms of music, in particular concerts and opera performances, and served to elevate certain works to greater popularity. The success of *Rienzi* in Swedish salon culture was unique in the broad range of its appeal and can be attributed to the fact that it was performed by the Swedish Royal Opera.

Entering the Concert Scene

In Europe in 1850s, *Tannhäuser* was well known as an experimental work. It aroused interest in the Baltic world—though the facilities necessary for its performance were almost nonexistent. The opera had a controversial reputation, and news of its notoriety spread. The natural conclusion was that the public should be acquainted with it—even if they could not see the opera as a whole performed.

The musical infrastructure in place varied from country to country. The possibilities for the performance of "concert music" were considerably better in Sweden than in Finland or in the Baltic provinces, mainly due to the fact that the royal court had patronized both concert music and opera since the eighteenth century. The Royal Orchestra (Hofkapelle), maintained for the opera, also served as a venue for symphony concerts, giving the audience the opportunity to hear the works of such composers as Haydn, Mozart, and Beethoven as well as those of newer, less famous composers. According to Gösta Percy, the first piece by Wagner to be performed in Sweden was the *Tannhäuser* Overture, played under the baton of Jacopo Foroni (see figure 2.3) in concert at Hofkapelle on 9 February 1856. The same concert provided the audience with the opportunity to hear Liszt's paraphrase, *Illustration du Prophète*, which was played by the

Figure 2.3. Jacopo Foroni (1825–58). Reproduced by Marie Persson, the Royal Library, National Library of Sweden.

German pianist Franz Bendel. The *Tannhäuser* Overture was repeated at a vocal concert by Guglielmi during the same month. In 1861, Jacob Axel Josephson (1818–80) conducted the Pilgrims' Chorus from *Tannhäuser* in Uppsala. Three extracts from *Tannhäuser* were performed at a concert by the singer W. D. Richard in the same year. Among those singing in the performance were Fritz Arlberg, Oscar Arnoldson, and Anders Willman.[75] Fritz Arlberg (1830–96) later became known as an influential participant, as a singer and translator of *libretti* in the first Swedish productions of Wagner.[76]

Gösta Percy has analyzed concert programs in Sweden during the years 1857–84. In these years, 135 samples of Wagner's work were performed in Sweden, at approximately five pieces per year. Wagner's repertoire of works performed peaked in the 1870s and 1880s, when Swedish opera productions had already aroused a Wagner fever. Of the Wagnerian "numbers" performed in 1857–84, seventy-five pieces—approximately 60 percent— were extracts from *Tannhäuser*, a statistic illustrating the central position *Tannhäuser* occupied in the early exposure of Wagner's music in the Baltic world. Of the other Wagner operas, the performance figures for *Lohengrin*—comprising approximately 20 percent of the total number of Wagner concert pieces performed—held the second largest share. At the head of the list of *Lohengrin* pieces were the Introduction to Act III, the Overture, and the Bridal Chorus. The Overture was conducted by Andreas Hallén[77] at the concerts of the Gothenburg Music Society (Göteborg Musikförening). According to Percy, *Lohengrin* achieved significant popularity in concert repertoire form only at a much later date—lending even more support to the idea of the uniqueness of *Tannhäuser* in the earlier repertoire.[78] *Tannhäuser* can be seen as a favorite work by Wagner performed in concerts; one may conclude that knowledge of Wagner's music during that time was largely limited to highlights from *Tannhäuser*.

The development of the Swedish Wagner repertoire is well illustrated by the so-called Edberg collection of concert programs (Edbergska programsamlingen), found in the Music Library of Sweden, listing the pieces performed, by composer, at concerts in Stockholm from the 1890s to the 1930s. The collection shows that, up to the end of the nineteenth century, the size of the Wagner repertoire increased, eventually covering Wagner's later works, including favorites from the *Ring*, highlights from *Die Walküre* ("The Ride of the Valkyries," "The Magic Fire Music") and the Good Friday music from *Parsifal*. The repertoire also, of course, featured less popular pieces; it is a little surprising to find that the *Kaisermarsch* was played on three occasions, in 1896, 1904, and 1906.[79]

The most significant music centers in the area around the Baltic Sea were Copenhagen, Stockholm, St. Petersburg, Riga, and perhaps Helsinki as well; activity in Liepaja, Pärnu, Malmö, Tallinn, Turku, and Viborg was more modest. There were regional differences in the position of the concert as a social and artistic institution. In Estonia, Courland, and Livonia, the Baltic-German minority maintained a German-style music culture, and the movement of musicians through East Prussia to Germany was active. Central European orchestral music could be heard in the larger towns such as Tallinn, Tartu, and Riga much earlier than the late nineteenth century, but regular orchestral activities in Finland and Estonia did not begin until then.

In Finland, an interest in amateur orchestral music was already prominent in Turku during the eighteenth century, at a time when the town was
the capital and the largest cultural and political center in the country. The
rich florescence of culture in Turku, however, ended at the beginning of
the nineteenth century, when Finland was separated from Sweden and
came under Russian rule: Helsinki, being closer to St. Petersburg, was chosen to be the new capital. The Royal Academy of Turku, founded in 1640,
was moved to Helsinki, and in addition, Turku suffered a major fire in
1827. In Helsinki, orchestral life was promoted by amateurs and German
emigrant professionals. Karl Ganzauge, Fredrik Pacius, and Filip von
Schantz maintained an orchestra, but its development was spasmodic, and
it often came close to being disbanded. The German-born Pacius, composer of the first Finnish opera, *Kung Karls jagd* (*King Charles's Hunt*, 1852),
founded a symphonic society in Helsinki in 1844. Supported by an orchestra of twelve musicians from the Ganzauge Spa Ensemble, it arranged symphony concerts. In theory, a Wagner repertoire might have been possible
even then, but it was not until the second half of the 1850s that Wagner
achieved any sort of publicity in Helsinki, a point that is corroborated by
the information found in sheet music catalogs. In his diary, Pacius
describes how, during a visit to Germany in August 1857, he met his teacher
and mentor Louis Spohr (1784–1859). Questions concerning the music of
the future (*Zukunftsmusik*) were discussed in his conversations with Spohr,
and it is possible that Wagner was also mentioned in these conversations,
although later, Pacius could only recall discussing Liszt and Berlioz:

> Soon the conversation turned to himself, to his compositions, his playing,
> and to music in general; and I wish I could recall and recount all that I
> heard at that time from the lips of the great Spohr. The "music of the
> future" he totally rejects. Above all, he holds Beethoven—the *great*
> Beethoven, as he explicitly stated—whose final compositions, in his deaf-
> ness, he himself never heard—responsible for making people's heads spin;
> who, in their Beethoven-mania, take everything at its face value, no matter
> how crazy, so long as it be by Beethoven. This may be illustrated in particu-
> lar by his Ninth Symphony, for it is difficult to hear anything more abom-
> inable than its finale, with the hymn "An die Freude." Liszt and Berlioz,
> too, have corrupted good taste, and Paganini has trampled underfoot all
> the principles of good violin playing. It is a pleasure, however, that the
> older music is now being taken up again, such as Bach, for example![80]

Zukunftsmusik was seen as little more than erratic noise, and one should
avoid it by directing oneself toward the old masters. Pacius had a real influence on concert life in Helsinki during the 1850s. His low opinion of
Wagner's contemporaries, such as Berlioz, is illustrative of the reputation
of these composers in Finland at the time. The possibilities for the

performance of Wagner's music did not improve until Filip von Schanz entered the arena in the 1860s.

After 1853, concerts were only occasionally arranged in Helsinki.[81] The situation changed when Tsar Alexander II granted an annual allowance of 3,000 rubles for the foundation of a theater orchestra. Because there were not enough qualified musicians in the country, a scholarship for studies at the Leipzig Conservatory was established by the state for Filip von Schantz and six other musicians. The orchestra began to function in 1860, and during the following concert season Schantz arranged ten symphony concerts. In addition to the symphonies of Beethoven and Mozart, modern music by, among others, Liszt, Offenbach, Verdi, and—for the first time in Finland— Wagner was also performed. However, this favorable development was halted when the new theater of Helsinki suffered a fire in May 1863. During the hiatus caused by the fire, Schantz decided to move to Stockholm and, under these conditions, Pacius was obliged to assemble his own orchestra in 1866.[82]

Yet even by this time, Pacius was no advocate of Wagner. On 18 December 1867, during a visit to Germany, he wrote in his diary:

> Today, at 2 o'clock, the dress rehearsal for the Philharmonic concert tomorrow: the Overture to Coriolan by Beethoven. What a gigantic, impressive composition! True greatness and an unparalleled wealth of ideas! Not to be compared with the current spectacular displays by Wagner *et consortes*, with nothing behind them.[83]

Pacius's negative attitude did not, however, prevent him from listening to Wagner's operas in their entirety when the opportunity arose. In 1870, Pacius attended three Wagner performances in Germany, and wrote to Karl Collan in his native country:

> Of Wagner, we have heard *Der fliegende Holländer*, *Tannhäuser*, and *Lohengrin*, performed by Niemann. No matter how little the music has to say, consisting for the most part merely of instrumental effects, yet the final movements, with their characteristically modern celebrations to high heaven, often carry one along irresistibly. Delicate finesse, or true characterization, such as one finds in Mozart's operas—of these, there is no trace. The music for *Lohengrin* would be equally well suited to *Tannhäuser*, just as that for *Der fliegende Holländer* would fit *Lohengrin*! Were it not for the outstanding performance of Niemann, the famous tenor, these operas would not arouse half the interest.[84]

Despite his disparaging statements, Pacius began to develop an interest in Wagner's works, though he publicly denied this. In Pacius's last opera, *Die Loreley* (1887), Wagner's musical influence is clearly distinguishable.[85]

Nevertheless, the consolidation of the concert as an institution in Finland was a slow and sometimes sporadic process. The situation did not radically change until 1882, when the theater ensemble was replaced by a permanent orchestra of professional musicians, the establishment of which was strongly supported by the conductor, Robert Kajanus. The orchestra required an educational basis, and the Helsinki Conservatory—the precursor of the present Sibelius Academy—was founded under the leadership of Martin Wegelius in 1882.

There are no catalogs on the orchestral repertoire played in Finland in the 1850s and 1860s, but it seems that the programs emphasized the Classical Viennese style. In this respect, Pacius's influence alone must have been considerable. The name Wagner appeared for a while in the repertoire of August Meissner,[86] who had moved from Gothenburg to Helsinki and acted as conductor of the theater orchestra. In a concert in May 1865, the program, besides Weber, Beethoven, and Dalayrac (d'Alayrac), included Wolfram's "Song to the Evening Star" from *Tannhäuser.* Hermann Paul reviewed the concert in *Hufvudstadsbladet,* a Helsinki newspaper, on 1 June:

> Last Monday, Herr Meissner gave his last symphony concert for this season. Weber's Jubel Overture, which opened the concert, cannot, despite its beautiful middle movement, be considered one of the composer's classic works. . . . The overture was followed by an enchanting little duet from an older operetta by d'Alayrac, which was performed by Messrs. Hafgren and Raa, with accomplished routine and in good voice; both of these gentlemen have excellent singing voices, which Mr. Raa later put to outstanding effect in the romance from *Tannhäuser,* "To the Evening Star."[87]

Essentially, the modernization of the repertoire in Helsinki began in 1870–78, when German-born Nathan B. Emanuel was the conductor of the theater orchestra. The Helsinki audience could then hear, for the first time, the overtures to Wagner's *Lohengrin* and *Die Meistersinger.*[88]

In Estonia, the introduction of Central European music culture was equally slow, and it manifested itself in a variety of different forms. In Finland, the struggle to establish concertgoing as an institution can be interpreted as being due to a strong desire to present an image of itself as a nation culturally similar to other European countries in all fields of artistic endeavor. In Estonia there was also a need to create and demonstrate nationality through music and musical infrastructures, in relation both to Russians and to the Baltic-German nobility

In the 1860s, 1870s, and 1880s, Estonia witnessed a boom in singing and orchestral music, centering on the birth of a tradition of popular singing and brass music. The first Estonian brass bands came into being in the 1820s and 1830s.[89] In 1863, there were five brass bands in Estonia. By 1901 the total number stood at 224.[90] There were many reasons for this speedy expansion. In the schools, the teaching of polyphonic music had improved, and at the same time socioeconomic shifts had increased

people's leisure time, allowing them to pursue their interests more enthusiastically. A significant underlying factor was the Estonians' relationship
with the Baltic-German minority, which had traditionally attended to the
cultivation of the arts. Song festivals and brass bands became a symbol of
the rising Estonian national movement. This self-sustaining culture was
further reinforced when the policy of Russification began in the 1880s.[91]

The proliferation of brass bands was a remarkable phenomenon from
the viewpoint of Estonian national music development, but in considering
the reception of Wagner, the most important factor was the increase in the
size of the orchestra. The tradition of European concert music was deeply
rooted in town orchestras, which were founded mainly in the 1880s and
1890s. Industrialization led to the rapid growth of urbanization. Social
activities were energized in cities, and societies began to arrange musical
evenings (soirées musicales) as well as concerts. In 1876, only five town
orchestras were known to exist in Estonia: two in Tartu as well as one each
in Tallinn, Narva, and Viljandi.[92] Of course, not all of these were symphony
orchestras. According to Kasemaa, a decisive change in the tradition of
symphony orchestras occurred when Alexander Läte (1860–1948) gathered amateur musicians together and founded a symphony orchestra in
Tartu.[93] Its first concert was held on 19 November 1900. The program
included Joseph Haydn's "Oxford" Symphony, the "Unfinished" Symphony
and the *Rosamunde* Overture by Franz Schubert, and Luigi Cherubini's
Overture to the opera *Lodoïska*.[94] The orchestra had much in common with
the Helsinki Philharmonia, which was founded by Kajanus and featured
indigenous symphonic music.

Prior to this development, European concert music was already being
performed in Estonian towns—above all, in Tallinn and Tartu—during the
1850s, 1860s, and 1870s (see figure 2.4). In festivities arranged by the University of Tartu in December 1852, for instance, the audience was able to listen to
Haydn, Hummel, Lortzing, Schulhoff, and Mendelssohn under the direction
of Friedrich Brenner. The climax of the concert was "Die Himmel erzählen
die Ehre Gottes" from Haydn's oratorio *Die Schöpfung* (*The Creation*).[95]

Over the course of time, fragments of Wagner's music could also be
heard. Extracts from *Lohengrin* were performed in Tallinn in the soirées
arranged by Krüger, the director of music, during the winter season of
1859–60. When the newspaper critic Oscar von Riesemann summed up the
achievements of the concert season, he focused especially on *Lohengrin*:

> The impression made upon the members of the audience by Wagner's
> music, with which they were previously almost entirely unfamiliar, was
> astonishing. According to Wagner's principles, it is possible to understand
> and to honor his operas only if they are performed for the public upon the
> stage, in such a way as to present the compound effect of an organic whole.
> The maestro accords his own principles so little significance, however, that

Figure 2.4. Open-air concert in Kuressare, Estonia. Author's postcard collection (no publisher or photographer mentioned).

he has not scorned to present his operas to the Paris public in the form of extracts performed in the concert hall. In this manner, our public was therefore entitled to allow itself to be overwhelmed by the orchestral arrangement of the finale from *Lohengrin*. And so it fell out. There is a most wonderful attraction in these musical images of deepest seriousness and true nobility. The composer does not seduce his listener's ear with mellifluous melodies, but rather brings his intentions to expression through the use of harmony, which, with its wealth of new, surprising, and in many cases extremely daring combinations, assaults the heart of the audience with mysterious enchantment.[96]

The series of concerts conducted by Krüger included, apart from symphonies, a number of shorter pieces by, for example, Mendelssohn, Marschner, and Wagner. The Wagner section of the program for one concert was listed as "The First Finale from Richard Wagner's opera *Lohengrin*, arranged by von Wittmann."[97] The Wagner themes were thus heard as arrangements, but this did not prevent Riesemann from referring to "the magic" of this difficult music. Riesemann also stated that Wagnerian music was "almost entirely unfamiliar," an observation that, for all its truth in general terms, is contradicted by the depth of knowledge Riesemann demonstrates regarding Wagner's works.

On 19 October 1860, after the publication of Riesemann's review, the *Tannhäuser* Overture was performed at a concert arranged in the Hall of the Great Guild. In the same concert, the audience also heard Beethoven's "sublime work," the Symphony in C Minor, as well as Mikhail Glinka's Overture to the opera *Ivan Susanin* (*A Life for the Tsar*). The critic for the local *Revalsche Zeitung*, also Oscar von Riesemann, wrote three days after the concert:

> With regard to Wagner's work, there was no applause in the true sense of the word, yet it made a visible impression. It is a fact that many of the composer's declared theoretical opponents, when they hear his works, are converted—the fairest revelation of the power of genius. The often shocking musical fabric is the clothing for thoughts before whose incomprehensible majesty all true human hearts must bow in instinctive admiration. Reserving a more detailed analysis of the overture (wherein the composer introduces the entire proceedings of his opera) for the full premiere of *Tannhäuser*, we note that notwithstanding the enormous difficulties encountered, the performance was moving. Regrettably, the wind instruments, not least the bass tuba and second bassoon, with their excessively low register, rendered it extremely difficult for the strings to make their due effect. As an example, we could point to the combination of the counter-motif with the chorale at the end of the overture.[98]

Wagner's reputation was already well established in 1860. Riesemann refers to him as a "master" and a "genius." Riesemann also refers to *Tannhäuser* in terms of the complete opera. Baltic Germans such as Riesemann did not merely have close contacts with Riga: they were also familiar with German music centers where they became acquainted with the musical innovations of the moment. The same "internationalism" also characterized the Finnish and Swedish intellectuals who traveled to culturally influential France, Germany, and Italy.

In the case of Estonia, samples of Wagner's music were occasionally performed, especially during the 1880s and 1890s, when there was an increase in the number of orchestras. During these decades, Wagner's themes probably reached only the most active towns, such as Tallinn and Tartu. It is also likely that, if Wagner was played, the pieces performed must have been mostly from *Tannhäuser* and *Lohengrin*. But Wagner pieces seem to have been rare. This gains support from the fact that not a single piece of Wagner was performed in Pärnu in 1881, even though its musical life was extremely active, and local and visiting orchestras (such as the Stadt-Capelle and Dilettanten-Orchester) performed several times a month. Among other composers, Reinecke, Haydn, and Mendelssohn were heard at the concerts of the Stadt-Capelle.[99] One of the large-scale projects of the season was Franz Schubert's *Die Allmacht* for tenor, chorus, and orchestra, performed by an amateur ensemble under the baton of E. Maczewsky, with the assistance of the choir and quartet of the male choral society. The same concert also contained a few brief preliminary pieces, including Pacius's *Laulu Suomelle* (*The Song of Finland*) under the name *Suomi's Sang.*[100] The interest in Pacius is not the only indication of external contacts in the Baltic world. In 1881, in addition to many German guests, Pärnu was visited by the "Swedish national singers"—Erikson, Stenfelt, Smedberg, Fischer, and Rydling. According to a newspaper announcement, the audience could also hear, in addition to Rikard Nordraak's song, *Zum Vaterland* (*To the Fatherland*), music by Carl Michael Bellman and August Söderman.[101] Söderman was one of the most famous Swedish Wagnerians, who in his Leipzig years (1856–57) had familiarized himself with Wagner's music and was aiming to achieve the style of his paragon, particularly in his songs (for instance, *Der schwarze Ritter, The Black Knight*).[102] In May, the orchestra of the Haapsalu Spa visited the town and performed in open-air concerts,[103] and in June a quartet and quintet of cornets from the orchestra of the Riga Town theater also came to Pärnu.[104] Reciprocally, the quartet of the Pärnu Male Chorus Society achieved great success in Riga.[105]

In a situation in which the establishment of concert music as an institution had not yet been finalized, nonpermanent ensembles, amateur orchestras, and theater orchestras were of great significance in the Baltic provinces. Equally important were military bands, which influenced the music of their region. In Finland and Sweden, for instance, these ensembles performed popular concert pieces arranged for military band throughout the nineteenth century.

The Swedish Military Archives catalog band parts and provide essential information on the spread of Wagner's music. The archives are not, however, unproblematic. Often the publication or performance date was not mentioned or has not survived. The dates that are given must be looked at critically. It is possible that pieces were performed much later than the date given in the archives suggests. But when we take the material as a whole, the dates given correspond in general with the home music catalogs. The dates given are at least an indication of the time at which an interest was taken in Wagner, and, in combination with the home music catalogs, catalogs demonstrate that Wagner had established his position as a composer of popular music before his works were staged in opera houses.

For the purpose of this analysis, I have examined the number of Wagner pieces performed by five military bands: the Dragoons of the Guard Regiment,[106] the Norrland Artillery Regiment,[107] the Regiment of Southern Scania,[108] the Regiment of the Guard of Grenadiers,[109] and the Jönköping Regiment.[110] In total, the Swedish Military Archives contain 99 pieces. Out of these, as many as 45 pieces came from *Tannhäuser*, 22 from *Lohengrin*, and 11 from *Der fliegende Holländer*. The rest are extracts from *Die Meistersinger* (7), *Rienzi* (6), *Tristan und Isolde* (3), *Die Walküre* (3), and *Parsifal* (2). Much of the archival material is undated, but the dates that have

been preserved give indications of the chronological order of the performances of the pieces as included in the repertoire. The earliest date is associated with the brass band arrangement of the Pilgrims' Chorus from
Tannhäuser, the manuscript of which was dated 1860.[111] The latest arrangement appears to be the Overture to *Der fliegende Holländer*, which was in the
repertoire of the Regiment of Southern Scania and has been preserved as a
transcription made by Graham T. Overgard in 1940.[112] In fact, the band
music collection of the Regiment of Southern Scania—as well as the first
volume of the Regiment of the Guard of Grenadiers—seems to contain
arrangements that date only from the twentieth century. If these and the
arrangements that may clearly be dated to the twentieth century are
excluded, and the focus is switched exclusively to nineteenth-century material, the emphasis on *Tannhäuser* and *Lohengrin* becomes even clearer. The
share of the former is as much as 50 percent of the total, while the share of
the latter is 19 percent. The range of Wagner arrangements represented is
also reduced: *Parsifal* and *Die Walküre* are totally excluded, and *Tristan* and
Rienzi are limited to one arrangement each.

The repertoire of the military bands therefore corroborates the image
of the spread of Wagner's music that is provided by home and salon music.
In the public repertoire, the arrangements concentrate even more clearly
on the popular works. For example, there are no extant complete arrangements of the *Tannhäuser* and *Lohengrin* overtures among the sheet music of
the military bands: the weight is even more clearly on popular pieces than
in the sales catalogs for sheet music. Furthermore, the *Tannhäuser* arrangements consist, in practice, of only three pieces: the March ("The Arrival of
the Guests at Wartburg"), the Pilgrims' Chorus, and Wolfram's "Song to the
Evening Star." The March was particularly suitable for arrangements. Wolfram's "Song to the Evening Star" was certainly a favorite, but, unlike the
March or the Pilgrims' Chorus, it was not suitable for wind instruments.
Wolfram's "Romance," however, was already established in the 1860s in the
repertoire of baritones and also appeared in soirée programs.

Despite some regional differences, Richard Wagner's music spread in
the Baltic world in a uniform and consistent manner from the 1850s
onward. It is illuminating to discover that Wagner was heard, for the first
time, almost at the same instant both in Sweden and in Russia. While
Jacopo Foroni conducted the *Tannhäuser* Overture in Stockholm on 9
February 1856, the St. Petersburg Philharmonic Society performed it on
15 March.[113] It is difficult to evaluate the significance of a single area
(concerts, home music, and so on) in the distribution of Wagner's works:
changes in specific areas can, rather, be regarded as cumulative phenomena. Wagner's music entered the public arena and thus became an object
of evaluation and criticism through concert halls, but simultaneously
Wagner's works were heard, and consequently judged, by a much larger audience through music in the home. Even though melody-based arrangements

were central to home music, the selection was much wider than in concert repertoires. The significance of home and drawing room music is illustrated by the fact that, by the beginning of the 1860s, the highlights of *Tannhäuser* were already familiar to audiences. When Wilhelm Bauck reviewed Herr Richard's concert in March 1861, he stated that Wolfram's "Romance" was "famous" and the *Tannhäuser* March "well known"—even though these pieces had not yet been played frequently at concerts.[114]

The public consumption of music was thus unavoidably entwined with its private consumption. The social developments of the late nineteenth century, however, began to lead to a situation in which public concert activities gradually began to push aside the private practice of music. The final structural change did not take place until the following century during the period of mechanical music, the time of the phonograph and gramophone. Even though home music was bound more to the past than to the present, publishers still accepted modern music as material for the home music market. Wagner's music was, after all, material that could be made suitable for this sector of the music industry, but in fact the process that led to a deeper split between art music and popular music had begun—at least in part—with Wagner himself.

In addition to the circulation of music, the constant movement of people and ideologies is of major importance in the reception of Wagner. Even though the eastern and western shores of the Baltic Sea belonged to different states, surface contact existed in the cultural arena. The Swedish newspapers reported on the first song festival in Estonia. The German Opera of Riga visited Helsinki. Meissner, the violinist from Gothenburg, also exerted an influence in Finland. There are numerous examples of such interaction.

In evaluating the reception to Wagner's music there are, however, two significant and distinctive additional details—the fact that Wagner himself had lived in Riga and the fact that in the 1860s, he made a commercially driven visit to Russia (which will be described in detail in chapter 4). The Baltic relationship with Wagner's works and thoughts was for this reason probably much stronger than it would otherwise have been. And, in the course of time, this familiarity may have been reflected in the fact that entire Wagner operas could also be heard in the form in which the composer had wanted them to be performed.

3

The First Steps in the Cultural Struggle

Riga as a Wagner Center

A remarkable difference between the western and eastern sides of the Baltic Sea is that operatic productions appeared in Scandinavia much later than in the Baltic provinces of the Russian Empire, especially in Livonia. Prior to the 1870s, Wagner's music was mainly heard at home, in restaurants, and in concerts, not in opera houses. This is exemplified by the fact that *Tannhäuser*, which proved to be crucial to the success of the Wagnerian reception, was not performed as a total work in Copenhagen until as late as 1875 (and a year later in Stockholm and Christiania), whereas the same opera had already been heard in Riga, Tallinn, and Helsinki in the 1850s.[1]

The lively operatic activity in Riga made it the most significant center on the eastern side of the Baltic Sea (for a view of Riga, see figure 3.1). Paradoxically, Wagner himself had estimated that Riga would never be a performance place for his works, and had, therefore, left Riga, with great expectations, for Paris. However, the Riga German theater was one of the first playhouses to become interested in Wagner's works. Riga was an active business center with a rising population, and its German bourgeoisie willingly supported the arts. At the beginning of the 1840s, the Riga German theater's director was Johann Hoffmann (1805–65), who had been a singer in the house (1837–39), during Wagner's residence.[2] In 1839, he was chosen as acting director or manager, and continued to hold the post until 1843. Harsh criticism of the theater's board of directors appeared in the town during the spring of the same year. The *Rigasche Stadtblätter* stated that Riga had perhaps been in the vanguard of German theaters, but that period was now in the distant past.[3] It is possible that this remark provoked the board of directors into looking for new music.

After his desperate Paris years, Richard Wagner returned to Germany in 1842, having been engaged as conductor of the Royal Dresden theater in Saxony. Wagner succeeded in having his new work, *Der fliegende Holländer*, included in the theater's repertoire; the opera was premiered in Dresden on 2 January 1843. The post of court conductor to the king of Saxony was a remarkably conspicuous position, and the new work certainly did not go

Figure 3.1. Riga and the Dvina River. Author's postcard colletion (no publisher or photographer mentioned).

unnoticed. The opera also gained attention in Riga, as can be seen in a news item in the *Rigasche Zeitung* on 19 January 1843:

> A new light has arisen in the German theater. A young poet, previously unknown, by the name of Richard Wagner, has composed both the libretto and the score for a number of operas, which have been taken up with an enthusiasm like that which greeted Weber's *Freischütz*. His latest composition, *Der fliegende Holländer,* has caused great pleasure in Dresden.[4]

Even though it has often been stated that it was *Tannhäuser* that aroused greater attention, *Der fliegende Holländer* had already primed the press for the coming of "a new light" in the German theater. The reporter for the *Rigasche Zeitung* does not seem to have remembered that Wagner was already familiar to the Riga public, for he refers to the composer as "previously unknown." The reporter does state, with good reason, that Wagner had composed "both the libretto and the score for a number of operas." *Rienzi* had been premiered in Dresden on 20 October 1842, and *Tannhäuser* would in turn be premiered on 19 October 1845. During a period of just a few years, Wagner had thus brought three lengthy works into the limelight.

In the other regions around the Baltic Sea, Wagner's new works did not arouse such spontaneous excitement, but the Baltic-German press, particularly in Riga, followed events in the German art world intensely. In fact, the *Rigasche Zeitung*, in which the news item on Wagner appeared, was mainly directed toward foreign countries. It had been founded in 1778 under the name *Rigische Politische Zeitung*, and its purpose was to convey news from abroad, thus counterbalancing the *Rigische Anzeigen* newspaper, which concentrated on domestic affairs.[5]

When Wagner was publicized as "a new light" in Riga, Hoffmann seized this opportunity to improve his reputation and contacted Wagner directly. One factor that might have encouraged the town to be receptive to Wagner was the fact that he had been known to the Riga population a few years previously. This is exploited in a poster advertising *Der fliegende Holländer* that was to be seen throughout the town a couple of days prior to the premiere:

On Saturday the 22nd day of May 1843, premiere performance: *Der fliegende Holländer*. A major Romantic opera, in Three Acts. Libretto and music by Richard Wagner, Court Composer to the Royal Court of Saxony.

The astonishingly favorable reception that this opera has received in Dresden has caused me to lose no time in arranging for a performance here, since I am convinced that this will meet with the approval of the respected public, especially since the composer formerly worked with our stage here, and the memory of his enthusiasm and effort will not yet be dimmed among our local connoisseurs and friends of art. Although this opera has already been accepted by the greatest opera houses in Germany, and is even now being rehearsed for the Royal Court Theater in Berlin, Riga will nonetheless be the second stage where it will be performed, to which I have the greatest pleasure in inviting you to attend.

The Box Office is open from today for ticket bookings; for those with season tickets, however, their seats have, as usual, been reserved.

Riga, 20th May, 1843
J. Hoffmann.[6]

It is apparently no coincidence that Hoffmann in his advertisement echoes the *Rigasche Zeitung* in stating that the success of *Der fliegende Holländer* in Dresden was "ungemein" (unusual). The advertisement also contains references to the wishes of the "respected public"; this was intended to correct the misconception, introduced by the *Rigasche Zeitung* reporter, that Wagner was previously unknown. Hoffmann also intends to remind the public that Wagner, a former inhabitant of Riga, had achieved such success that his works were already being presented not only in Dresden but also in Berlin. Hoffmann also states with pride that, after Dresden, Riga would immediately become the next location for the performance of *Der fliegende Holländer*, and that the German theater of Riga was keeping abreast of the times.

According to the local Julian calendar, the premiere of *Der fliegende Holländer* began at 6 p.m. on 22 May 1843. The part of Daland was performed by Mr. Schreiber, Senta by Ms. A. Köhler, Erick by Mr. Schunk, Mary by Mrs. Lafrenz, the Dutchman by Mr. Günther, and the Helmsman by Johann Hoffmann himself. The crew of *Der fliegende Holländer* consisted of six singers, and the number of the Norwegian sailors was thirteen.[7] Originally, Mr. Sammt should have performed the role of the Helmsman, but he fell ill just before the first night, and Hoffmann decided to take the role.[8] The advertisement for the premiere does not mention the size of the orchestra, which therefore probably remained at its usual size, approximately twenty musicians. The orchestra was certainly not, even at its best, able to reach any grandiose *Wagner-Klang.*

Unfortunately, information on the premiere is sparse. The press commented only briefly on it. The *Rigasche Zeitung* was generally sparing in words with respect to events in its hometown. Not much column space was allotted to music. In spring 1843, a far greater celebrity than Wagner was an individual by the name of Bosco, who traveled throughout Europe performing Egyptian magic.[9] It was only later that Wagner was noticed. When the theater made a routine visit to Jelgava after the end of the season, the *Rigasche Zeitung* reported on the performances of *Der fliegende Holländer* in that town in June and July 1843.[10]

The only review of *Der fliegende Holländer* that I have discovered was in the *Zuschauer.* On 25 May, according to the Julian calendar, the writer (who remains anonymous) states that he has already heard of Wagner's works, and also mentions his knowledge of Wagner's "genius" and "professional skills." Expectations were high but, even so, the work was of such high quality as to surprise the listener. The critic focuses attention on the exceptional fact that both the text and the music are from the same pen. During this phase of his development, Wagner had not yet formulated his theory of a total work of art in which the artist was to aim for a fusion of the skills of Shakespeare and Beethoven, the skills of a dramatist and a musician. In 1843, such a fusion was a rarity, as the critic for the *Zuschauer* emphasizes. The author heaps praise on the work: as early as the overture, the work was already revealed as "an impressive tonal painting," and the singing was clear, simple, and melodic "in a noble sense." In particular, the critic stresses Wagner's excellence as an orchestrator and mentions that, in this respect, the composer has apparently assimilated influences from Paris, although the work is very different from the fashionable operas of the period. Finally, the critic focuses his attention on the interpretation: Heinrich Dorn had rehearsed the orchestra in an excellent fashion and the soloists performed their roles faultlessly.[11]

Der fliegende Holländer broke the ice for the Wagner performances in Riga. Immediately after the first two performances on 22 and 25 May, Hoffmann wrote to Wagner that the performances had gained popular acclaim.

Wagner was so delighted that he quoted Hoffmann's letter in his own letters both to Robert Schumann and to Minna. He mentioned to Schumann
that *Der fliegende Holländer* had been received "with enthusiastic applause."[12]
To Minna he sent a more lengthy quotation:

> A letter from J. Hoffmann in Riga, where he writes: "I consider it my duty
> to inform you that your brilliant tone poem Der fliegende Holländer was
> presented, to great applause, on the 22nd May of this year". . ."this was
> repeated, again to great applause, on the 25th, and the next performance
> will be in Jelgava"—etc.
>
> He has enclosed not only the theater bill but also a review printed in the
> *Zuschauer* magazine, which I shall immediately send to the *Theater-Chronik*,
> wherein my work is adjudged to be brilliant, "impressive," and enchanting,
> and the performance is also highly praised.—You shall also read all of
> these at a later date, but for the present I have other uses for them![13]

Wagner was not only delighted with the success but also, in a way, shocked by
it. In December 1843, he wrote to Franz Löbmann, who had been playing in
the Riga theater orchestra, that previously he had believed more in the possibility of success for *Rienzi* than for *Der fliegende Holländer*. "The warm reception of my *fliegende Holländer* among you arouses my deepest amazement: for
you must yourselves admit, this opera is not suitable for all audiences. With
regard to *Rienzi*, I was more confident that this would please its audiences."[14]
This comment is interesting because Wagner seems to have been vacillating
between different operatic styles. *Rienzi*, which could be likened to French
grand opéra, might well gain financial success, whereas *Der fliegende Holländer*,
which was musically more difficult, was not "for all audiences." Apparently,
the success of the latter in Riga may have convinced Wagner that the style of
Der fliegende Holländer was worth following. Could the Riga German theater
have indirectly influenced the clarification of Wagner's style, or, at least, contributed to his choice of stylistic features? Whatever the case, the situation
certainly seemed to elicit a conscious choice from the composer. Before the
Riga premiere of *Der fliegende Holländer*, Wagner wrote to Samuel Lehrs in
Paris: "We opera composers cannot be Europeans, which means we are
either French or German."[15] Encouraged perhaps by his Riga experiences,
Wagner decided to be more clearly "deutsch" (German) when he began to
compose *Tannhäuser* in July 1843.[16] In the literature relating to Wagner, the
role of this Livonian—or Baltic-German—response has not been taken into
account in considering the means by which Wagner's nationalistic emphases
actually came into being. Wagner's German orientation is revealed in his
open letter to Ferdinand Heine, written at the beginning of August and published in a Leipzig paper, the *Illustrierte Zeitung*, on 7 October 1843:

> The fact that this opera [*Der fliegende Holländer*] has won so many friends,
> including friends among the wider public, not only in Dresden, but also in

Riga and Kassel,[17] seems to me a striking indication that I should indeed write as the inherent sense of German poetry requires, without giving way to foreign fashions; and I must quite simply select my material and treat it in such a way as to be most confident that it will please my countrymen. In this manner, we can once again achieve an original German opera, and all those who betray this idea, and adopt foreign fashions, may turn to the *Holländer* (which is certainly conceived in a way no Frenchman or Italian could have done) as an example.[18]

This text demonstrates that there are connections between the success of *Der fliegende Holländer,* Wagner's rising nationalism, and the clarification of his stylistic goals.

After the event, it is, of course, impossible to estimate the amount of enthusiasm among the first audience in Riga, but in any case the opera's success was not great enough for the directors of the theater to immediately include *Rienzi* or *Tannhäuser* in the repertoire. Such inclusion could have been feasible, but the decision may well have been influenced by the reception of *Tannhäuser* in Dresden. *Tannhäuser* was staged in that city in 1845, but, in contrast to *Der fliegende Holländer*, it aroused controversy. *Tannhäuser* sharply divided opinions and thus laid the foundation for the antagonism between the Wagnerians and the anti-Wagnerians that in the following decades would influence the entire reception of Wagner, as well as other areas in which musical and aesthetic innovation was taking place.

One obvious reason for Riga's decision was the fact that Johann Hoffmann was forced to resign in autumn 1843. His successor was to be Louis Schubert. In December 1843, Wagner mentioned to Franz Löbmann that Schubert was one of his adversaries: "Now, he will not be sympathetic with me, as in general wherever I look, I will see only enemies; that means those who envy me."[19] This change in personnel at the theater was one of the factors that prevented the Riga public from seeing a new Wagner opera immediately after the performance of *Der fliegende Holländer.*

The performance of *Der fliegende Holländer* did not provoke a Wagner boom in Riga; nor did it create an audience that would willingly have received other new works. Apparently, Hoffmann had been too hasty in his attempts to improve his reputation by including a new work in the repertoire at the very end of the season. After a few performances, the summer break began, and therefore it was not possible to create a dedicated audience for the work, not to mention a long-lasting success.

From another point of view, it was not surprising that *Tannhäuser* did not immediately appear in Riga. From an international perspective, the triumph of *Tannhäuser* did not begin until the 1850s, and only in 1852–53 did the Riga board of directors see that there was reason to attempt another Wagner premiere. Wagner himself had conducted the premiere of *Tannhäuser* in Dresden on 19 October 1845. Wilhelmine Schröder-Devrient appeared as Venus and Joseph Tichatschek as Tannhäuser. In 1848, Wagner revised the end of the opera, and *Tannhäuser* fever began to take off in the 1850s. The 1852–53 period was decisive: the opera was performed in Schwerin on 26 January 1852, in Breslau (now Wroclaw, Poland) on 6 October 1852, in Wiesbaden on 13 November 1852, in Leipzig on 31 January 1853, in Frankfurt am Main on 15 February 1853, in Kassel on 15 May 1853 (under the baton of Louis Spohr), and in Posen (Poznan) on 22 May 1853. In Dresden the opera was again performed on 26 October 1852.[20] Apparently, the board of directors of the Riga German theater had already become interested in the work in August and September 1852, for in a letter to Theodor Uhlig on 27 September, Wagner mentioned that Riga might possibly take the work.[21] The agreement was finally confirmed in October, for on 1 November, Wagner asked Uhlig to send the score to Riga through his Berlin agent Hermann Michaelson.[22]

Over a period of ten years, conditions at the opera house had greatly improved. The playhouse itself was still the same as in Wagner's time, but the orchestra had increased in size to twenty-six musicians. The *Rigaer Theater-Almanach* for the year 1853 indicates that the orchestra consisted of five violins, two violas, one cello, two double basses, two flutes, two oboes, two bassoons, four French horns, one trombone, two trumpets, and timpani. The chorus consisted of ten men and ten women. Ferdinand Roeder acted as the director of the theater, and Schràmek and Genée as conductors.[23]

According to the local Julian calendar, *Tannhäuser* was premiered on 6 January 1853.[24] A great deal had been invested in the performance, as is revealed by the remarks on the new stage decor and additional forces in the orchestra that were included in the poster advertising the premiere. Three different sets were promised to the audience: "the interior of the grotto of the Venus mountain," "the hall of the singers," and "a valley in the background of Wartburg Castle." The scenery was mentioned as having been designed by Mr. Bredow. The size of the orchestra had been increased "through many distinguished amateurs" and "through the music produced by the Hauptboisten-Corps of the Neapolitan Regiments." The costumes were partly new, and Mr. Schwarz was responsible for them.[25] The *Tannhäuser* poster was an obvious attempt to appeal to the audience's interest in spectacle. The emphasis on special effects, the exceptionally large orchestra, and the striking scenery was notable even in comparison with later Wagner productions. In a way, it is no wonder that many contemporaries, who admired Beethoven's early works—such as the German-born Fredrik Pacius (who eventually became a Finn)—were shocked at Wagner and regarded him as a composer of spectacular displays![26]

In the course of ten years, the ensemble of soloists at the Riga German theater had changed several times. In the premiere of *Tannhäuser*, the part of Landgrave Hermann was sung by Mr. Breuer, Tannhäuser by Mr. Baumann, Wolfram by Mr. Kunz, Walther von der Vogelweide by Mr. Leszinsky,

Biterolf by Mr. Weiss, Heinrich by Mr. Dill, Elizabeth by Ms. Zschiesche, and Venus by Ms. Schröder.[27]

Even though the performance of *Der fliegende Holländer* had excited Wagner's interest, *Tannhäuser* in Riga was a far more conspicuous media and music event. At the beginning of the year 1853, offers from German theaters came pouring in, which required Wagner to spend a long time on negotiations and also on calculations concerning prices. In his correspondence, however, Wagner commented on the success of *Tannhäuser* in Riga only very infrequently. At the end of his letter to Franz Liszt on 19 February 1853, he penned only a short, hasty line: "The performance has taken place in Riga, in Russia."[28] The most important reason for this silence was, in all probability, his busy life. The composer's next opera, *Lohengrin*, had already been premiered in Weimar on 28 August 1850 and was conducted by Franz Liszt himself.[29]

The most significant comment on *Tannhäuser* in Wagner's correspondence is found in his letter to Franz Löbmann. Again Wagner expresses his astonishment at the success of the evening: "Your success with *Tannhäuser* is most amazing; I can scarcely imagine how your small stage and limited resources were adequate to the task. Yet I also know that an enthusiastic spirit can achieve wonders, and this, it seems, you have among you."[30] Wagner had scored *Tannhäuser* for a far more complex ensemble than his earlier work. Therefore, the theater had to augment its twenty-six-member ensemble with amateurs and members of military bands. The recruiting of military musicians was really necessary, for in the opera there was a particular need for additional brass and woodwinds.

Even before he composed *Tannhäuser*, Wagner had decided to choose the German rather than the French style; this did not mean minimizing the size of the orchestra. French *grand opéra* has often been criticized for its abnormal orchestral effects and pompous scenery. In all probability, Wagner's *grand opéra* period influenced his interest in orchestral effects, leading them in a direction that would later cause problems for small opera houses and, hence, hinder the spread of his operas. Wagner's development as a composer was clearly oriented toward the use of larger resources, which finally caused him to dream of his own operatic theater. On the other hand, this tendency made it difficult to perform his new works in small playhouses with small orchestras. The enormous need for space in Wagner's later works would have made it impossible to perform them in the Riga German theater of the 1840s and 1850s. Wagner even considered it impossible to perform *Tannhäuser* at the Riga theater.

Among the press in Riga, *Tannhäuser* aroused much more attention than *Der fliegende Holländer*. Even though the opera had also provoked some strong antagonism in Germany, the work was favorably received in Riga. Media critique, of course, does not provide much evidence as to the attitudes of the public. The media had an inclination to exaggerate, particularly where a critic or reporter felt a need to prove the excellence of

Wagner's music. On 26 February 1853, the *Rigasche Stadtblätter* published an interesting news item quoting a description of Wagner's reception in Riga from the Leipzig *Illustrierte Zeitung*: "Report in *Die Illustrierte Zeitung*, number 103: 'In Riga, Richard Wagner's *Tannhäuser*, despite tickets at twice the normal price, has been the most powerful attraction in the history of the local opera. The public is ecstatic, and the opera house is virtually besieged at each performance.'—A good example of reliable reporting in the press!"[31] Apparently, the editor of the *Stadtblätter* wanted to make it clear that the reception of *Tannhäuser*, after all, was not as favorable as was claimed by the *Illustrierte Zeitung*. In any case, the audience did show an interest in the work, for it was a real box office hit in spring 1853. If the work had not attracted audiences, it would certainly have been shelved.

The Rigan Wagner researcher Carl Friedrich Glasenapp, who later became court historian of the Bayreuth Circle, is responsible for the earliest materials on the performance history of *Tannhäuser* in Riga from 1853 to 1875. According to the handwritten catalogs included in Glasenapp's literary *Nachlass*, *Tannhäuser* was performed on fourteen occasions in Riga and on three occasions in Jelgava, the center of Courland, during spring and summer 1853. During the period 1853–75, the work reached the stage in Riga on fifty-two occasions.[32] These figures reveal its great popularity.

Shortly after the premiere of *Tannhäuser*, a critic for the *Rigasche Zeitung*, using the initials C. A., published a two-part review on 10 and 14 January 1853. Behind the pen-name was Carl Alt, who was born in the east Prussian town of Breslau (Wroclaw) in 1807. In 1834–37, he had worked as a private tutor in Pärnu in Estonia, and he had moved from there to Riga in order to teach in the cathedral school. In 1842, he was an organist and worked diligently both as a composer and as a writer. Among other works, he wrote the libretto for Heinrich Dorn's opera *Das Banner von England* (*The Banner of England*). During his later years, in 1846–58, Alt was a reporter and music critic for the *Rigasche Zeitung*.[33]

Carl Alt considered *Tannhäuser* to be an opera with which it was well worth familiarizing oneself. In the first lines of his review he reveals that he already knew Wagner, both as a composer and as an author:

> The first performance of the music drama *Tannhäuser, oder der Sängerkrieg auf der Wartburg*, by R. Wagner, took place on Thursday 6th January. Given our conditions, this performance was overwhelmingly successful, and the overall impression this work made was in any case significant. We considered it our duty to offer our readers in our earlier articles at least some indication of Wagner's new aims and directions, insofar as this can be detected through a reading of his three-volume book, *Oper und Drama*.[34]

The viewpoint presented above is interesting, because it claims that, in order to understand *Tannhäuser*, the reader—and, thus, to a certain extent, the members of the audience as well—should know Wagner's thoughts on music and art. In relation to the performance of *Der fliegende Holländer* an important change had taken place in attitudes. Wagner was now understood to be a reformer of opera, even a revolutionary. A theoretical framework, which the audience should comprehend, underlay the work. This view was certainly associated with information on Wagner's participation in the Dresden Uprising in May 1849, even though the reviews made no mention of it. In his Dresden period, Wagner had been interested in democratic ideals and participated in the activity of the patriotic Vaterlandsverein, and, through this, he had become acquainted with the Russian anarchist Mikhail Bakunin. When the waves of the 1848 Revolutions in Europe reached Dresden in spring 1849, Wagner was ready to rise to the barricades together with his friends Bakunin, August Röckel, and Gottfried Semper. The uprising was eventually suppressed: Röckel and Bakunin were apprehended, but Wagner quickly fled across the border. He finally found asylum in Zürich and was not allowed to return to German soil until the year 1861, when his fears about recriminations had been allayed. Political defeat did not, however, abolish the idea of revolution: the political mission was channeled into art-theoretical texts, the best known of which are *Die Kunst und die Revolution* (1849), *Das Kunstwerk der Zukunft* (1850), and *Oper und Drama* (1851). These created the foundations of an art-theoretical framework through which Wagner's works would be listened to during the following years. These texts (or, at least, a certain amount of knowledge about their central content) spread rapidly and—as is revealed by the critique in the *Rigasche Zeitung*—Wagner's main tenets were also rapidly assimilated within the music circles of Riga.

Further, Carl Alt stated that although *Oper und Drama* was far from being a clearly written work, it was impossible to completely ignore Wagner's ideas any longer. According to Alt, there were three ways of scrutinizing Wagner: first, by analyzing the performance and the work itself; second, by discussing Wagner's theories; and third, by discovering how *Tannhäuser* was related to these theories (that is, by finding out whether the new work really was the type of work called for by Wagner in *Oper und Drama*).[35]

In his two-part review, Alt comments on all these perspectives. First, he gives a survey of Wagner's theory, above all, in light of *Oper und Drama*. Central to this introduction is Wagner's idea that drama is most significant in opera; in relation to drama, music is only a means to an end. In modern opera, the musical means had tended to become the end, and the dramatic end a means. Wagner had already begun to approach this question in a letter to Ferdinand Heine in August 1843, in which the central argument of *Oper und Drama* is found in embryonic form. Wagner stated that in *Der fliegende Holländer* he had already wanted to relinquish "the modern division of opera into arias, duettos, finales etc.," for the most important purpose of opera is simply to tell a story.[36] In the case of *Der fliegende Holländer*, this radical feature was not generally stressed, because neither the average audience member nor the critics had any knowledge of Wagner's operatic aesthetics. Through the triumph of *Tannhäuser* in the 1850s, this knowledge was widely spread in the public's mind. Thus, the critic for the *Rigasche Zeitung* could state: "Wagner has shown us a way to another continent, which is not lying beyond the sea, but just *amidst* us, in the *depths*."[37] Wagner had shown a direction that would lead to something new and unknown; no one could, however, define the directions of the future development of opera. An interesting feature is that Alt describes the content and its treatment of *Tannhäuser* using words that resemble Wagner's own, as if Wagner had created a specific language through which his works should be evaluated:

> Wagner's aim is to reduce material to truth, and to accord this its maximum potency. . . . Through his highly successful excursions into the stuff of legend, Wagner has shown how and where poets should search for the material for their drama—cleansed in advance of the accidental, the historical, the political—material whose plot can adequately be concentrated, to enable it to be perceived through the feelings, without a great admixture of ratiocination and thought.[38]

In this passage, the critic closely approaches the idea of *Gefühlsverständnis* (emotional intelligence),[39] which is very clearly advanced in Wagner's *Oper und Drama*. On the whole, Alt appears to emphasize the idea that *Tannhäuser* parallels the theories of its creator, and he refrains from an examination of the differences between the theories and the work. The analogy between the theory and the artwork is not, however, presented openly, although the semblance of an analogy appears to exist where the critic describes the influence of the work by adopting Wagner's views on the subject.

After a thorough examination of the history of Finnish music criticism, Jukka Sarjala has concluded that criticism makes taste normative through two means; in the first, it generates constitutive norms that are related to the definition of music, and in the second, it generates regulative norms.[40] The criticism of *Tannhäuser* is mostly constitutive in the sense that it makes judgments on our comprehension of music, particularly that of opera. Simultaneously, the criticism creates a new basis for the establishment of standardized norms for taste by seeking a theoretical justification in the composer's literary texts. A regulative dimension is, however, also included in this criticism. Wagner is likened to an explorer who is seeking a new continent and whose explorations are worthy of support. The discoveries made in the course of these explorations deserve to be observed, even though they will not please everyone.[41]

As is common in opera reviews, Carl Alt not only described the work but also evaluated the interpretation. The Riga theater Orchestra succeeded in the performance of the work, even though the music was "overwhelmingly difficult." The first strings were particularly praised. Of the singers, Alt paid special attention to Mr. Baumann, who sang the role of Tannhäuser. The part had required several months' study, the result of which was "inspiring, generally appealing." In particular, Baumann had succeeded in the performance of "The Story of the Pilgrimage to Rome," which was impressive. Ms. Zschiesche, who performed the part of Elizabeth and whose voice was "faultlessly beautiful like the tolling of the bells" and "full of inner expression," was also showered with praise. On the other hand, Ms. Schröder, who sang the role of Venus, was criticized because, particularly in the first act, her voice was strained. Similarly, the performance of the song contest and the relationship between Tannhäuser and Elizabeth, as far as Alt was concerned, needed a more careful interpretation.[42]

On the whole, *Tannhäuser* was regarded as a significant new work. On 17 January the *Rigasche Zeitung* even published a third article dealing with the opera; this referred to the general significance of Wagner's oeuvre. It is impossible to decide whether, once again, the writer was Alt, because the text was not signed or initialed. This time the author states that the work is mostly successful: "Two thirds or three quarters of the whole is impressive, appealing," but it appears to be too early to see where Wagner's project will lead in the future: "The true value of Wagnerian musical drama will be determined in the decades to come. Until such time, the polemicists, be they for or against, could set their argument aside. Nothing of true classical value has ever been totally lost."[43] This comment clearly illustrates how widespread an awareness already existed concerning the passions excited by the composer in 1853. Wagner was a controversial person who aroused emotions for and against him. The reporter for the *Rigasche Zeitung* tries to compromise by stating that time will reveal the works that have genuine classical power. From the viewpoint of 1853, it was impossible to see over the "for and against." It is, indeed, surprising how soon this juxtaposition of two contrasting forces came into existence. In a way, the situation was caused by Wagner himself, because he presented his works as parts of a larger musical, ideological, and political change. If the listener did not accept this, he or she would certainly meet with difficulties in relation to the works themselves. It is probable that many listeners, at least in Germany, knew Wagner's thoughts in advance through the press before they had heard any of his music in an opera house. Such information was not necessarily available in Livonia at that time; therefore, Carl Alt felt it necessary to cite *Oper und Drama*. On the other hand, such reviews and news items surely created opinions that influenced the interpretation of forthcoming performances and the new works themselves. In addition, Riga was an important regional center, and its newspapers were read throughout the Baltic world.

In 1854, the German composer Joachim Raff published *Die Wagner-frage*, which was one of many pamphlets dealing with Wagner. The message of the pamphlet spread quickly through bookshops and newspaper reviews. To begin with, Raff states that there exists a *Wagner-Bewegung* (Wagner movement): this did not concern merely an individual, a composer, and his intentions; the question was one of a phenomenon with a broader impact on the world of music. In the same breath, he gave evidence of a principle that was already perceivable in the *Tannhäuser* criticism by the *Rigasche Zeitung*: namely, that one should distinguish the practical side of the move-ment from the theoretical one.[44] Besides *Oper und Drama*, Raff also pays attention to *Das Kunstwerk der Zukunft*:

> This *Kunstwerk der Zukunft* . . . contains the first draft of a theory that the author then partly expanded and expounded two or three years later in his *Oper und Drama*—As it chanced, the public already had these books in their hands before they heard the operas *Tannhäuser* and *Lohengrin*; the press is always more accessible to producers than the stage is. But who is con-cerned with dates?[45]

According to Raff's interpretation, it was a mere coincidence that Wagner's literary works reached the public before his operas, but in fact, it was hardly a coincidence. Without doubt, Wagner himself was intuitively conscious of the significance of his theories, and he also believed in their necessary influence on the reception of his operas. He did not, however, realize how quickly his thoughts and reputation would spread. In this process, the press, which was also mentioned by Raff, had an important role, much more immediately pervasive than that of the salon and home music cul-ture, which has already been mentioned. The first Wagner pieces, which were excerpted from the operas, were not heard in the Baltic world until the latter half of the 1850s. Similarly, the sheet music catalogs made *Tannhäuser* and *Lohengrin* familiar only after the middle of the decade. We might say that, in the long run, salon pieces made Wagner known in wider circles, but this came somewhat later. The press had already begun to write on Wagner at the beginning of the 1850s.

Raff refers both to coincidence and to the role of the press without mentioning the fact that he himself participated in the creation of public knowledge of Wagner's theories shortly before the Riga premiere of *Tannhäuser*. In 1852–53, an extremely lively discourse on Wagner's theory of art took place in the German newspapers: in addition to the *Neue Zeitschrift für Musik* edited by Franz Brendel, the *Reinische Musikzeitung* under the leadership of Ludwig Bischoff and the *Neue Berliner Musikzeitung* edited by Gustav Bock also participated. The two last-mentioned music papers (as well as the *Signale für die musikalische Welt*) published several crit-ical comments on Wagner, whereas Brendel's *Neue Zeitschrift für Musik* took a more positive attitude toward the reformer. Brendel (1811–68) had become editor in chief of the journal upon the death of Robert Schumann in 1844. Wagner's relationship with Brendel was very cordial, and Brendel had published Wagner's controversial two-part article, "Das Judenthum in der Musik," in September 1850. Wagner was extremely worried about Raff's ideas, which also appeared in the columns of Brendel's journal. During February and March 1853, Wagner wrote aggressive letters to the editor in chief through which he clearly strove to influence the views through which his art would be scrutinized in the journal. Sometimes Wagner completely lost his sense of proportion:

> It really is not necessary that you should go to such trouble over me; we shall simply need to wait for an understanding of the *content* of my works— of what it is that I aim at—until such time as the form that I use can be brought to a clear exposition. This I can never expect from *our singers, directors*, and theaters—or—God knows when. But—in my opinion—you should hold to the point more, to the critique and to the creation of form, when this finally becomes possible. (The productions, too, for our purposes, need to be criticized more sharply).—That is why—and I will tell you this quite plainly—I hold *Raff's* demarche (in the form advertised) to be untimely; so leave me out of it, and concentrate on the *point*; but does Raff understand anything about the point? Although he launches out with the "specific German spirit," in truth this is no more than a new confusion of totally abstract generalizations! And what can come of that?— Furthermore, I consider Raff to be extremely limited, unproductive, cold, mannered, and incapable of true understanding. Let him show if he can really understand anything: give him the themes set out above!— But—as God wills; I merely told you my opinion—since you requested it!
>
> But once more: do not dispute about myself, but about the *technical point* in question. Any other proceeding brings only confusion; this is the only way to achieve clarity. To offer an immediate approach: begin from the totality, rather than from the details, of what I have argued in *Oper und Drama*: (i) from my criticism of absolute melody (end of the First Part); (ii) from my criticism of absolute poetry; (iii) from my criticism of the prevailing combination of the two (both at the beginning of the Third Part). If this is done well, then the paper will have an entire year, or more, of highly productive life. *Over these things*, you should engage in battle again and again, even to the smallest details—do not fear weariness: it is necessary! But where is the benefit of arguing over things that no one can as yet understand, since they do not yet exist in the appropriate form (by means of fully appropriate performances)—
>
> Protest once more against the stupidity, or maliciousness, of attributing to me the statement that *Tannhäuser*, for instance, is the art of the future!—How ghastly! Do you want *Raff* to come out with more of these tasteless misunderstandings?[46]

As is revealed in this letter, Wagner was not only concerned with the fact that too much attention was focused on his personality; he also worried about the continuous comparison of his theories to his works. The *Neue Zeitschrift für Musik* was one of the most significant German music papers and was read throughout Europe. Through this discourse, "the question of Wagner" spread with rapidity, but not quite in the form the maestro himself would have liked. In any case, the debate made Wagner famous and aroused greater interest in him. His accomplishments were now followed very closely.

The press in Riga also exercised a significant influence on the creation of a detailed account of "the question of Wagner." The newspapers followed Wagner's accomplishments with care. The *Rigasche Stadtblätter* reported that Wagner, "our former citizen," had been invited to London to conduct his music during the forthcoming concert season. This was regarded as a manifestation of respect with which only real masters such as Mendelssohn and Spohr had been honored.[47] A lot of discussion of the pamphlets and analyzes of Wagner that had been published in Germany also appeared in the papers. The *Rigasche Stadtblätter,* which did not generally focus its attention on literature, analyzed Friedrich Hinrich's work, *Richard Wagner und die neuere Musik* (1854), in January 1855.[48] The author comes to the conclusion that Hinrich "is not an uncompromising worshiper of Wagner; nor is he an enemy to him, but places his views on the middle ground."[49] It seems that the author takes the role of a mediator: it was possible to be interested in Wagner's music but to belong neither to the camp of the Wagner fanatics nor to that of his enemies. This kind of mediatory viewpoint appeared to be quite common among the people of Riga: the German cultural struggle was felt to be a distant phenomenon to the extent that strong emotional outbursts were usually avoided.

Lohengrin in Livonia

Joachim Raff, the author of *Die Wagnerfrage,* was particularly inspired by *Lohengrin*, which, after its initial difficulties, began to spread among German opera houses in 1854. The work had been premiered in 1850, and had been performed in, among other places, Wiesbaden on 2 July 1853, Leipzig on 7 January 1854, Schwerin on 15 January of the same year, Frankfurt am Main on 12 April, and Breslau (Wroclaw) on 31 October.[50] As with *Tannhäuser,* this innovative work led to a great deal of polemical writing, but it seems that it was *Lohengrin* that became the main focus of discussion in Riga, arousing unusually strong emotions. A partial cause of this was the fact that Wagner had consciously begun to develop an operatic style that created difficulties for small opera houses. In fact, Wagner seriously questioned whether Riga was a suitable place for his new work at all. In the spring of 1853, Wagner had heard from his Berlin agent Hermann Michaelson that Franz Thomé, the new director of the Riga theater, was interested in producing *Lohengrin* in the very near future. The Riga public had enthused about *Tannhäuser* to such a degree that the new director believed that a policy of performing Wagner would lead to success. Thomé, who had functioned as a theater director in Graz, had been chosen in March 1853 to be the director at the Riga German theater for a period of three years from the following September.[51] Not until the end of July did he take up his post,[52] but in Graz he had already started the preliminary negotiations and plans for his forthcoming season. In fact, Wagner was surprised at the fact that Thomé had contacted Berlin and not the composer himself. On 1 June 1853 he wrote to Franz Löbmann:

> I have been informed by a theater agent in Berlin that the new director in Riga, Thomé, wishes to have my *Lohengrin*. But why does the man not turn to me himself? This opera is a heavy undertaking, and how you are to manage it, even for the orchestra alone, remains a mystery for me. In any case, I adjudge *Lohengrin* as above *Tannhäuser*, also in its impact; but the musical director should look at the piano version very carefully first, and ponder how he is to implement the production. For the full score, one must turn to Breitkopf & Härtel in Leipzig, who have brought it out in print, and will supply it to theater managements for 15 taler; this sum does not include the royalties, of course, which should be sent me immediately when the score is purchased. Herr Thomé should pay me fifteen friedrichs d'or; if this is not distasteful for you, you might tell him so.[53]

Wagner was thus suspicious about the resources available at the Riga Opera House but was not skeptical enough to refuse to accept money. In any case, the letter not only reveals Thomé's willingness to start the season with a controversial new work: it also notes the enthusiasm of the Riga public after the *Tannhäuser* performances (an enthusiasm about which Thomé, apparently, was well aware). Finally, it appeared that the preparations for a performance of *Lohengrin* required a lot of time: it was "eine schwere Sache," "a difficult matter." The premiere did not take place in 1853, or even in 1854. The score had been ordered by Thomé from Breitkopf & Härtel in March 1854,[54] but the work was not premiered, according to the Julian calendar, until 24 January 1855.

The poster advertising the premiere of *Lohengrin* once again reveals that the opera was to be spectacular (although the point was not made with a verbosity comparable to that of the *Tannhäuser* poster):

On Monday the 24th of January 1855, the First Time
Lohengrin

The orchestra is enlarged with additional forces. Totally new stage decor by Mr. Bredow—Costumes new. Stage direction by Director Thomé. The Cast

Heinrich the Fowler	Mr. Strobel
Lohengrin	Mr. Weiss
Elsa	Ms. Wollrabe
Duke Gottfried	Mr. Hübsch
Friedrich von Telramund	Mr. Leithner
Ortrud	Ms. Schnabel
The King's Herald	Mr. Hurst[55]

The opera was reviewed in the *Rigasche Zeitung* on 29 January: "On 24 January, we have finally heard *Lohengrin* for the first time on the stage in Riga."[56] The review, by Carl Alt, reveals that the work had been long anticipated. Apparently, by the beginning of his period of leadership in autumn 1853, Thomé had already promised to stage *Lohengrin* at the theater, but the production had required more time than had been foreseen. At the beginning of his review, Alt stated that the new work was far from being easy; on the contrary, it had created real challenges for the singers, the chorus, the orchestra, and the conductor. At the same time, he thanked the performers for their hard work. On the whole, the performance had gone well, but it had also encountered problems, particularly, in the two central roles, since the parts of Lohengrin and Ortrud had been too difficult for the performers. Weiss as the Swan Prince had sung beautifully but with inadequate volume: his voice was apparently unsuitable for Wagnerian singing. Mr. Weiss's voice had started to fade toward the end of Act I, but in the third act it had again been in good condition. Ms. Schnabel, who sang the part of Ortrud, had also been in trouble. The critic described the role as extremely difficult, for the singer has to wander "almost all the way through labyrinthine musical cliffs in the darkness of the night, only seldom illuminated by a few harmonious thunderbolts."[57] The basic problem was the fact that Ms. Schnabel had a very high soprano voice, which noticeably lost volume in the lower registers. She seemed to succeed only at a high pitch, a failing that, of course, undermined her performance of this dramatic role. In the critic's opinion, the interpretation of the other roles also met with difficulties: Ms. Wollrabe's Elsa had been satisfactory, but her dramatic expression had remained incomplete; there had been much good in Mr. Strobel's interpretation of the role of Heinrich, but the role was difficult. These problems occasioned a general comment from Alt:

> The excuses that they will produce in reply are already familiar in Riga, and we will therefore pass over them. If it was a mistake by the management to put on *Lohengrin* at all in such circumstances, then it is they who will suffer most terribly; at any rate, the public has had the opportunity to

experience the most significant composition in contemporary dramatic music, at least in its main outlines. That constitutes an advantage that any other opera would have difficulties in surpassing."[58]

The Riga German theater was apparently compelled to struggle with local conditions and the changing world of music. In the new music, performers and those responsible for stage facilities were confronted with requirements whose fulfillment was beyond the capacity of small theaters. In the case of Wagner, particularly, the strangeness of the vocal parts puzzled the singers. The large orchestra that was required caused difficulties, but these do not seem to have been the most crucial problems. The size of the local orchestra could be increased, as it was in the case of *Lohengrin*: one harp, two violins, one cello, and a double bass being added to the ranks. The use of additional forces to meet the composer's wishes was not possible in all cases, but such forces could be provided in situations where there was a lack of the instruments necessary to produce a particular effect. As for *Lohengrin*, such reinforcements were apparently not used. Alt claims that "Wagner requires far more wind instruments than are available in the normal orchestra. This necessitated certain simplifications in the harmony, which Herr Ott has carried out with taste. In consequence, through the reduction of twelve trumpets to four, we have in fact lost nothing essential."[59] The idea that twelve trumpets would originally have been needed for *Lohengrin* must have been based on a misunderstanding. In *Lohengrin*, according to the score, there are only three trumpets in the orchestra, and another three behind the stage. It is true, however, that in *Tannhäuser* Wagner had used twelve trumpets, which must have had a shocking effect on his contemporaries.[60] To facilitate these special effects, a military band was used to augment the orchestra in the *Tannhäuser* performance in Riga. Apparently, not even then did the number of trumpets match Wagner's requirements, but the conductor must have used creative freedom and arranged the passages concerned for a smaller ensemble. It is difficult to decide why the question of arrangement was included in the criticism of *Lohengrin*. Could it have been that conductor Ott, in discussions with Alt, had commented on the difficulties connected with Wagner's works in general, and the operas could then have become mixed up in Alt's mind? The director of the theater, Franz Thomé, was also planning to restage *Tannhäuser* at the time of the *Lohengrin* premiere. It is probable that the score of *Tannhäuser* was rearranged, and the critic mistakenly associated the twelve trumpets with *Lohengrin*.

The size of the orchestra of the Riga German theater was, however, considerably increased; the *Rigaer Theater-Almanach* for the year 1856, published in the fall, indicated that it consisted of twenty-nine players.[61] Normally, the orchestra had only two trumpets, and additional forces were, accordingly, also needed for *Lohengrin*. There has been a great deal of

Figure 3.2. Riga German theater. Built 1860–63. Author's postcard collection (no publisher or photographer mentioned).

discussion about the so-called Wagner orchestra in the study of music, but, in practice, the sizes of orchestras used in Wagner performances varied remarkably. If problems emerged, the conductor could discreetly simplify the score in order to make the performance feasible. Opera scores were not considered as so sacred that they could not be altered. As a critic, Carl Alt, at least, seems to claim that nothing essential had been taken away. He does not discuss the strings at all, but the Riga performance of *Lohengrin* must have had a different sound from present-day interpretations, as, for instance, the lyrically ethereal overture was performed by an ensemble that was about the size of a chamber orchestra.

Limitations were also caused by the small size of the playhouse of the Riga German theater (for a view of the new theater, see figure 3.2). Compared to *Der fliegende Holländer* and *Tannhäuser, Lohengrin* was much more of a historical spectacle, impressively staged. Alt mentions that the scenery designed by Mr. Bredow attracted the audience, but the truth was that sometimes there was simply not enough room for the spectacle. When the swan appeared, for example, the singers, as a group, had to step aside to make it possible to fit the swan on the already crowded stage.[62]

At the end of his article, Alt reveals that the Riga audience was not enthusiastic about the work:

> The performance was greeted with but little applause; this we consider partly to be due to the choice of performers for the leading parts, but in equal measure to the novelty of the effect achieved by this difficult composition. Even for those who surrender to the music without prejudice, this effect is in part too overwhelming, in part too internal and profound, for the expression of applause not to be forgotten. Moreover, the music for *Lohengrin* offers far fewer moments of immediately striking beauty than does that for *Tannhäuser*; and the somber theme associated with Ortrud and Friedrich, which takes up at least one third of the opera, is presented in such a dismal, indeed in such a grim and depressing manner, that we do not find the response to the premiere to be in any way surprising.[63]

The problems associated with the performance were apparently among the reasons for the negative attitude of the audience, but, in fact, Alt may have been correct when he said that the incomprehensibility of the work made demands not only upon the abilities of the singers but also upon the audience. In *Lohengrin*, Wagner had striven to a much lesser degree to please the audience with superficial beauty than he had in *Tannhäuser*. It is possible that the incomprehensibility of *Lohengrin* aroused a reserved or restrained attitude among the audience. No signs of hostility were, however, distinguishable. In this respect, the 1861 Paris performance of *Tannhäuser*, which ended with catcalls, could be taken as an object for comparison. No such a reaction was seen at the premiere in Riga, or even subsequently. Wagner was experienced as an interesting and innovatory composer whose works deserved attention, but, as for *Lohengrin*, it appears that the audience was confronted with a barrier to its understanding.

In Riga, Wagner, of course, also had supporters who were shocked at the critical attitude of the press. On 27 January 1855, the *Rigasche Stadtblätter* published a piece in the readers' column that emphasized the value of Wagner's works specifically as German art: "Wagner is a German through and through. Only a German could create *Lohengrin*, this depiction in such glowing colors of the Middle Ages, whose spirit Germany truly was."[64] With the exception of the text quoted above, no national perspective is perceivable in the press reports on *Lohengrin*. It is possible that nationalistic emotions were broadly shared, but they were not apparent in the press. *Lohengrin* was actually the most nationalistic work in Wagner's output thus far. In a way, it was a reply to the nationalistic challenge that had been announced by the composer in *Das Kunstwerk der Zukunft* and *Oper und Drama*. German opera should address the public. A composer should also, as Wagner had stated in his letter to Ferdinand Heine, choose whether to be "deutsch oder französisch" (German or French). In *Tannhäuser*, Wagner had already made a clear choice on behalf of the Germanic sphere. This line of interest continued in *Lohengrin*. *Tannhäuser* was based on German history, but in the opera, in fact, very little attention was paid to Germany or Germanness. In contrast to *Tannhäuser*, the patriotic rhetoric is striking in *Lohengrin*. In the third act King Heinrich sings:

> Proudly I see you gathered round
> Would that throughout this glorious land
> such valiant men as you were found!
> Now let the empire's foes attack,
> we are prepared to drive them back.
> Out from the east they will ride in vain:
> we will defeat them once again!
> Protect your country with your sword!
> Triumph will be your just reward![65]

The king's warriors join in the last verses, which are full of an overflowing feeling of German strength. In the opera, the threat to German culture comes from the east. This is also emphasized in Lohengrin's words a little later: "Nach Deutschland sollen noch in fernsten Tagen des Osten Horden siegreich niemals ziehn!" (And due to that victory the eastern hordes won't ever threaten you again).[66]

It is probable that the Baltic-German minority sympathized with Wagner's project owing to its nationalism, especially as in *Lohengrin* German culture is juxtaposed against that of the east. Readers of the *Rigasche Zeitung* seem to have been forerunners of those Wagnerians who, in the 1870s and 1880s, retained the strength to blow the trumpet on behalf of the master. Apparently, as early as the 1850s Wagner's works were already apt to excite national emotions in the Baltic-German minority, but a truly opportune time would come only after decades had passed: when, for one thing, nationalist movements began to raise their profile in the Baltic provinces and, for another when a stricter tsarist policy of Russification was gradually enforced upon larger areas. As early as the 1850s, Wagner could thus be seen as a symbol and forerunner of Germanness, even though the nationalistic ideal was not to reach fruition until the 1870s and 1880s.

Lohengrin, however, was unable to raise itself to a level at which it could generate a feeling of togetherness among the Germans in Riga, even though it had all the elements required for the birth of nationalistic pride. Owing to its incomprehensibility, the work aroused conflicting emotions and, in addition, it proved to be too difficult to perform successfully on the small stage of the playhouse. The opera's performances on the Riga stage were, however, finally ended only in the spring of 1855, when Tsar Nicholas I suddenly died, and owing to the mourning period all entertainments were forbidden. Along with other operas, *Lohengrin* was shelved.

Tannhäuser, however, remained a favorite of the audiences in Riga. It was restaged immediately after the premiere of *Lohengrin*, but it was performed only once, on 19 February 1855, before the death of the tsar. The popularity of the work is mirrored in the fact that, before the performance, the *Rigasche Zeitung* published a long article (an exception to normal practice in the prevailing conditions). The article had been initialed by Fr. v. R., and it seems that the poet Friedrich von Riekhoff—who was born in Riga in 1809 and had studied theology and law in Tartu—was the author. In the 1840s and 1850s, he became known in Riga both as a dramatist and as a librettist. He wrote the librettos for a number of Johann Schràmek's operas including *Die Testamentsbraut* (*A Bride According to the Testament*) and *Der schwarze Pirat* (*The Black Pirate*). Strongly Wagnerian themes are found in Friedrich von Riekhoff's literary output. He penned a five-act tragedy *Rienzi, der letzte Tribun* (on the same theme as Bulwer-Lytton's novel, and Wagner's opera). Among Riekhoff's works, a libretto, "Sangeskrieg, oder: Deutsche und italienische Schule" ("The Song Contest or the German and Italian School")—which, at least, in light of its name, seems to have been influenced by *Tannhäuser*—remained in his drawer.[67]

The article in the *Rigasche Zeitung* begins by mythologizing Wagner:

> Richard Wagner—how much discussion has he provoked; how much has been written; what opinions, judgments, and arguments have his compositions aroused; what statements, refutations, and rattling of shields has his new style of opera occasioned; what intellectual stimulation, what spirited exchange of thoughts, and what exhilaration his music has provoked;—this Niagara of notes, which calls forth more admiration than affection, more exhaustion and saturation than satisfaction and true enjoyment.[68]

The number of *Tannhäuser* performances, as we have noted, was reduced to just one, which may help to explain the fact that it is missing from Carl Friedrich Glasenapp's catalog.[69] However, the work was again included in the repertoire during 1856–57 and continuously attracted the public who were greatly interested in the work.

The author behind the initials "Fr. v. R." stated that Wagner's music excited "more admiration than affection." Perhaps the author himself was one of those admirers who were impressed by "the Niagara of notes," but who, despite this, did not experience this style as being his own. In any case, Wagner had come to stay both as a composer and as a controversial issue. His name constantly cropped up in the newspapers. Information was willingly given about his forthcoming projects: attention was not only focused on the works he had already created but also on those that would be completed in the course of time. Wagner himself was willing to discuss his plans and probably also wanted information oriented toward the future to become public. On 19 February 1855, the *Rigasche Zeitung* reported that

Wagner was preparing a comic opera. According to the paper, the adversaries of Wagner did not believe that the composer was able to create a comic opera, but *Die Meistersinger* was to repudiate these rumors. The paper even quotes the Monologue of Hans Sachs: "Zerging das heil'ge Römische Reich in Dunst, Uns blieb doch die heil'ge Deutsche Kunst" (Even if the Holy Roman Empire should vanish in mist, For us Holy German Art would still remain).[70] The opera was completed much later, in 1867, and it was premiered in Munich in June 1868, when confidence in German national strength was at its highest. In the final libretto, Hans Sachs's words were changed to "Zerging im Dunst das heil'ge röm'sche Reich, uns bliebe gleich die heil'ge deutsche Kunst."[71] In fact, these verses were among the rare passages that were almost identical in the first sketches (made by Wagner in July 1845) and the final librctto (completed in 1861–62 and 1866–67).[72] *Die Meistersinger* found a favorable response in the ultranationalism of Germany in the process of Reichsgründung, but the roots of its nationalistic tone are the same as those of *Lohengrin*. It is no wonder that the *Rigasche Zeitung* regarded the emphasis on German culture as so important that it directly quoted the sketch of Wagner's libretto. It was *Die Meistersinger* that finally became the hallmark of German nationalism, for which, thanks to its more simple musical language, it was far more suitable than *Lohengrin*.

Wagner was also a newsworthy topic in the forthcoming years. Thus, by January 1854, the *Rigasche Stadtblätter* could already report that Wagner's new opera would be *Die Walkyren*.[73] In February of the following year, the *Rigasche Zeitung*, for its part, reported that Wagner intended to perform a whole opera-tetralogy in Zürich at the earliest in 1859: "Richard Wagner is even now assembling in Zürich suitable singers and musicians in order to put on his great tetralogy *Die Nibelungen* in a theater especially constructed for the purpose. This great composition will not be complete until the summer of 1859."[74] Throughout his life, Wagner constructed scenarios and working projects for his own future use. In 1857, he strongly believed that the *Ring* tetralogy, whose overall plan he had already made at that time, could be completed in the course of a few years. This optimism is revealed in many of the composer's letters. For instance, he wrote to Luise Meyer in Vienna on 26 March 1857:

> Please permit me with utmost devotion to entreat you for the production of my new great composition. I intend to be ready with it within the next year, and in the summer of 1859—if all goes well—to arrange its production, under the most special of circumstances, probably in Weimar (assuming that I may once again enter Germany), at a theater to be especially erected for the purpose, with hand-picked artists, &c., in three festival performances.[75]

Even though this information was given "mit aller Inständigkeit" (with utmost devotion), the same information had already been reported in the newspapers in Riga a month earlier! In all probability, Wagner strove for publicity because the great project, a theater that was specifically designed for his operas, was possible only through the support of the public and his patrons. Wagner wrote that this would be possible "if all goes well." Unfortunately, however, all did not go well. Wagner's chronic shortage of money worsened, and the opera-tetralogy was not performed until 1876, almost two decades later.

The information given in advance, however, exercised an important influence on Wagner's career and reputation. His composing seems to have been connected with intensive expectations for the future: several projects were continuously in progress. At the same time, the publicity reveals the difficulties of his music. Wagner had by no means simplified his musical language; on the contrary, he was now creating works that required a theater and a music festival of their own. The publicity reinforced the "modernistic" aura that had come into existence around Wagner, and was also apt to increase people's interest and curiosity. Contemporaneous with the growth of his project was an intensification of the criticism and antipathy concerning his personality. In Riga, *Lohengrin* was really a turning point: it was a boundary that could not be crossed before performance facilities had been considerably improved. One symptom of the invasiveness of the Wagner debate was the appearance of the first local Wagner parody, which was performed in the summer theater on 3 July 1855. The most important item in the program was Johann Nepomuk Nestroy's farce, *Einen Jux will er sich machen* (*He Will Make a Joke*), which ended with a tableau that parodied Wagner: "Lohengrin und Elsa, oder: Der Einzug in's Brautgemach, bewegliches Bild mit Ouverture, Gesang und bengalischer Beleuchtung" ("Lohengrin and Elsa, or A Bridal Procession, a Moving Picture with an Overture, Singing and Bengal Lights").[76] Two years later, Nestroy parodied Wagner in *Tannhäuser und die Keilerei auf Wartburg. Zukunftsposse mit vergangener Musik und gegenwärtigen Gruppierungen* (*Tannhäuser and the Battle at Wartburg Castle: A Farce of the Future with Archaic Music and Modern Arrangements*). The music for the work was composed by Karl Binder.[77] Nestroy's *Zukunftsposse* was not performed in Riga until 1866, when it achieved great success.[78] The idea of the music of the future was now so well known that it was possible to laugh at it without inhibition.

"Living in the Past": Estonian Responses

Riga cast its influence on knowledge about Wagner along the entire eastern flank of the Baltic, in Estonia, and even in Finland. The Baltic possessions of Russia were well aware of each other's activities: for instance, the Tallinn, Tartu, and Riga papers were followed in Finland, at least, by newspaper editors. In the area constituting the Russian Empire, influences also

Figure 3.3. Tartu University church. Author's postcard collection (no publisher or photographer mentioned).

spread rapidly owing to the relative ease of communication within the empire. The Crimean War (1853–56), which made border crossing more difficult, had a negative impact on communications.

As has already been mentioned, musical activity was lively in the largest Estonian towns in the 1850s. Orchestral activities were particularly pronounced in Tallinn and Tartu. The influence of the University of Tartu (see figure 3.3), which was re-established in 1802, could be seen in the town, and the symphony concerts and soirées were in tune with student life.

From 1839, Friedrich Brenner acted as the music teacher at the university, and exercised an influence on musical life in Tartu until 1893.[79] Operatic activity did not, however, flourish there: better conditions for music theater existed in Tallinn, which had already had strong theater traditions in the eighteenth century. A Weimarian, August von Kotzebue, who founded an amateur theater in Tallinn in 1784, had exercised an influence in the town from the year 1783 onward. The theater's repertoire also included musical plays, among others, *Die väterliche Erwartung* (*Fatherly Expectation*, 1788), which was written by Kotzebue with music by August Hoerschelmann. The Hall of the Great Guild was used as a playhouse before the completion of the theater in 1809. At the turn of the century, Kotzebue had traveled throughout Europe and visited Vienna, Paris, and Berlin. But, in the end, having left Tallinn in 1813, he never returned; and his absence was to have severe repercussions on local theatrical life. During the following decades, activity declined; and a fatal blow was dealt by the burning down of the play-house on 21 October 1855. A new house was built and completed by 1860, after which theatrical activity was revitalized. A new director, Eduard Berent, came from Riga, and he directed the performances from 1869 to 1896.[80]

Even though the operatic repertoire did not grow rapidly until the 1860s, some new operas had, of course, been performed earlier. Surprisingly, Wagner was within the reach of the Tallinn public as early as December 1853, when *Tannhäuser* was performed. The repertoire of the previous season, 1852–53, had included Friedrich Flotow's *Martha*, Carl Maria von Weber's *Freischütz*, Mozart's *Don Giovanni*, François Auber's *Fra Diavolo*, Meyerbeer's *Robert le diable*, Gaetano Donizetti's *Lucia di Lammermoor*, Albert Lortzing's *Undine*, Hérold's *Zampa*, and Giacchino Rossini's *Otello* and *Il barbiere di Siviglia* (*The Barber of Seville*).[81]

The Estonian musicologist Kristel Pappel has studied the first Tallinn production of Wagner and come to the conclusion that Tallinn clearly had contact with the Wagnerian tradition in Riga. The Tallinn *Tannhäuser* was directed by Theophil Fass, who had arrived in the town in March 1853 and who had earlier been a tenor at the Riga German theater.[82] It is evident that Fass was aware of the *Tannhäuser* performed in Riga in 1853, and that he had probably even seen it.

Wagner himself had already heard of Tallinn's interest in *Tannhäuser* by June and July 1853, because he mentions the matter in his letter of 11 July to Wilhelm Fischer.[83] As commission for the Tallinn performance Wagner received ten louis d'ors, whereas the Riga theater had paid him fifteenth.[84] Wagner made no other comment on the Tallinn performance in his letter.

An announcement of the *Tannhäuser* premiere in Tallinn, dated 12 December 1853 (according to the Julian calendar), has survived in the Baltika-Department of the Library of the Estonian Academy of Sciences. In the advertisement Fass states that "I have spared neither time nor expense in order that this magnificent work might be performed in a manner perfectly worthy of it. Both the stage settings and the costumes for each act are all new; furthermore, the orchestra has been enlarged; so that the costs for the opera amount to nearly 1000 silver rubles."[85] The premiere was on 21 December 1853.[86] In Tallinn the stage machinery was markedly smaller than in Riga; the number of performers plus technical personnel was only fifty-four, whereas the team in the Riga German theater was twice as large.[87] The information available on the premiere does not reveal the number of additional forces used in the orchestra. Probably, as in Riga, local military musicians were employed for the performance, as the work contains several parts for brass and woodwinds. Apparently, in this case too, the part written for twelve trumpets must have been arranged for a smaller ensemble, although there is no mention of this modification. Despite the scarcity of resources, Fass stressed the extravagance of the performance by revealing specific sums of money: "a magnificent work," praised as being successful in all respects, was put on at a cost of almost 1000 silver rubles. Like his colleagues in Riga, Fass stressed the visual elements of the work: the stage decorations and costumes were new, and thus the work also offered, in this respect, a spectacle for the audience.

The title role had been given to Carl Marloff, who had come to Tallinn from Darmstadt at the beginning of the fall season and had sung as his first role the part of Raoul in Meyerbeer's *Les Huguenots*. According to Kristel Pappel, it is possible that Marloff had already sung the role of Tannhäuser in Darmstadt. The Darmstadt premiere took place, according to the Gregorian calendar, on 23 October 1853.[88] In Tallinn, the other main roles were performed by Mr. Erdensohn as Wolfram, Mr. Leszinsky as Walter, Ms. Mayerhöfer as Elizabeth, and Ms. Martienssen as Venus.[89] Mr. Leszinsky, who performed as Walter in Riga, also sang in Tallinn.

During the 1853–54 Tallinn season, *Tannhäuser* was performed on six occasions, after which the work was neglected for many years. It probably did not attract an audience to the same degree as the Riga performance, which was received with enthusiasm. In 1853, the music of *Tannhäuser* had not yet made its breakthrough into home and salon music, and, therefore, the audience apparently came to know Wagner's music for the first time at this performance. Even though Fass had boasted of the investment of 1000 silver rubles, the resources of the Tallinn theater were limited, and not comparable to those of the Riga theater. Owing to the scarcity of contemporary sources, it is difficult to say how successful the performances were, but one can conclude with certainty that, at this time, Wagner did not quite manage to find his audience in Tallinn. In Livonia, most of those attending the performances had probably not even heard of Wagner, or, if they had, they had no idea of the kind of theoretical visions that underlay the work. In relation to a Wagner work, knowledge or pre-comprehension was a significant contextual factor in Wagner's reception, as the following years in Estonia were to reveal.

The fact that newspaper comment on the 1853–54 *Tannhäuser* performances cannot be found reflects the prevailing condition of the Estonian press. Music criticism was not yet published. The situation in Riga was different. The infrastructure of bourgeois music life had already reached Livonia and was also embodied in the existence of critics, but in Estonia, as in the more northern area of Finland, such changes had not yet come to pass. In fact, newspapers were virtually nonexistent in Tallinn. The local German newspaper, the *Revalsche Wöchentliche Nachrichten*, founded in 1772, had been suppressed in 1852. The Estonian-language *Maa Walla Kuuluttaja* was founded only in 1856, the *Revalsche Zeitung* in 1860, the *Revaler Beobachter* in 1878, the *Tallinna Sōber* in 1879, and the *Virulane* in 1882. And even though the *Estländische Gouvernements-Zeitung* had been founded as early as 1853, it never commented on opera.[90]

The cool reception of *Tannhäuser* was reinforced by the press after the founding of the *Revalsche Zeitung* in 1860. Oscar von Riesemann, who used the initials O. R., wrote that the Wagner opera, which had been performed many years ago, "was then staged with obscurity, and was soon to be totally forgotten."[91] At that time, Oscar von Riesemann was twenty-seven years old; he had earlier studied law in Tartu and also acquired a knowledge of the arts, apparently, through his studies in Germany.[92] Wagner's newsworthiness in 1860 was due to the fact that the work was being revived for a new performance on the stage of the newly built playhouse in Tallinn: and its premiere, according to the Julian calendar, was to take place on 15 November 1860. The new interpretation was staged by Carl Nielitz, who had earlier performed as an actor in minor roles in Riga. A significant contributor to the performance was the conductor, Louis Saar, who was later influential as a conductor and pianist in Riga, Rotterdam, London, Hamburg, and Strasbourg.[93]

Besides Wagner, the repertoire of the Tallinn theater in the autumn of 1860 included Gaetano Donizetti's *Lucrezia Borgia* and *Lucia di Lammermoor,* Friedrich von Flotow's *Alessandro Stradella,* Giuseppe Verdi's *Ernani,* Carl Maria von Weber's *Freischütz,* and Giacomo Meyerbeer's *Robert le diable.* The *Theatralisches Vergissmeinnicht* (*The Theater Reminder,* 1861), edited by Christian Müller, recorded all the operatic performances throughout the fall and spring season up to March 1861. According to this catalog, *Tannhäuser* was performed only on two occasions during this period, on 15 and 21 November.[94]

The cast had totally changed since the 1853 performance. In the new production, Mr. Dalfi was cast as Tannhäuser, Ms. Hülgerth as Elizabeth, Mr. Massen as Wolfram, and Ms. Jacobsohn as Venus. The role of the Landgrave was performed by Mr. Bartsch, acting director, who was also responsible for the stage direction.[95] Oscar von Riesemann, who was the critic for the *Revalsche Zeitung,* stated in an article of 19 November that the performance was, all in all, successful. Mr. Dalfi had shone in his "Story of the

Pilgrimage to Rome," full of "wild desires and desperation"; Ms. Hülgerth had been "the wonderful Elizabeth" whose personality reflected "saintliness, fidelity, and renunciation." Mr. Massen's voice was characterized by Riesemann as being "a continuously developing metallic voice," but he had not yet become immersed in the role. Ms. Jacobsohn, for her part, had sung "with correct rhythms, but not without strain." The direction and scenery were also praised. In particular, the painted backdrops by Mr. Thompson were deemed to be "highly effective."[96] Finally, Riesemann referred to his experiences in other theaters. He had seen *Tannhäuser* before: "We recall that on many major German stages, when the death of Elizabeth is proclaimed by the male chorus from offstage, her body has not been displayed in its coffin; and having regard to the lack of motivation and the discomfort of the sight, we regard this excision to be entirely justified."[97] As this quotation reveals, Riesemann had seen *Tannhäuser* several times in larger playhouses. He could not help noticing differences caused by the more modest conditions of the local theater. At that time, the Tallinn theater Orchestra comprised only twenty-two musicians.[98] The orchestra had again been augmented, but the Tallinn ensemble could not compete with those of the larger German opera houses.

According to Riesemann, by 1860 Wagner had achieved fame and reputation in Estonia. As for the applause given to the performance, Riesemann states: "There were, it must be conceded, not many hand artillery [pieces] firing their full salvoes of applause; yet the effect of the work on the public was plain enough to see in the expressions of excitation and sympathy of the entire auditorium."[99] The plain truth concerning the reception of *Tannhäuser* is, however, revealed by the performance figures. The work was quickly excluded from the repertoire and returned to the stage only after a very long period of time. It never became a permanent favorite, as it had in Riga, and was not included in the repertoire until 1892.

In 1860, national values were not sufficient to raise the level of interest in *Tannhäuser*, although Riesemann stated that the story of Tannhäuser "is well known to everyone who belongs to our nation."[100] Riesemann already speaks of "our" nation, for although it was not until 1871 that Germany became a *Staatsnation*; the Baltic Germans had already realized that they could belong to the *Kulturnation* of Germany and thought that, despite their distant geographical location, they shared the same cultural capital as other Germans. But in 1860, not to mention 1853, nationalism had not been aroused to such an extent as to elevate Wagner to symbol of Germanness in Estonia. The situation did not change until the 1880s, when the popularity of Wagner blossomed as *Lohengrin* was premiered in Tallinn on 15 March 1883.[101] By the end of the century, it had been performed on thirty-one occasions.[102] Wagner's death, which occurred on 13 February 1883, focused more attention on the work. The third Wagner opera to be performed in Tallinn was *Der fliegende Holländer* on 9 December 1892.[103]

In 1860, Wagner gained a great deal of publicity in Tallinn, thanks, in the main, to Oscar von Riesemann. Besides the opera itself, the Finale of Act I of *Lohengrin* had been performed at a concert during the previous concert season.[104] Immediately before the Tannhäuser premiere, on 14 November, Oscar von Riesemann wrote in the *Revalsche Zeitung* an article titled "Richard Wagner und die Zukunftsmusik," one of the most significant Wagner analyzes in the Baltic world. What is interesting is that it was precisely the concept of "the music of the future"—which during the 1850s had gradually become a fashionable idea, and which has previously been referred to—that the article discussed.

It seems that the further one ventures into the borderlands of Europe, the more anxious the educated classes seem to be about the fact that indigenous local culture has not yet adopted the thoughts and concepts of the center. This concern is also clear in Riesemann's text:

> Although the literature concerning the Music of the Future has, by now, swollen to monstrous proportions, and the debate has expanded from the circle of initiates and has, as it were, become a universal question, yet our musical life in general has been but little affected by this. We are situated far from the field of battle for the future development of mankind and maintain, for the most part, positions already scorned in western Europe. We still live in the times of Haydn, Mozart, Beethoven, Mendelssohn; we are only now making the acquaintance of Schumann.[105]

The nineteenth-century imagination was imbued with the idea of progress. Riesemann's writing shows how progressive views were attached even to music history. The "development of mankind" was seen not only as a temporal but also as a geographical process. Estonia was interpreted as living in the past, while progress in "western Europe" had already gone further. Here, Wagner was clearly characterized as a modernist who represented future development. The Wagner issue, in Riesemann's view, had changed from a question involving the struggle of a small circle into a question regarding the whole of mankind, but the people in Tallinn (for a view of Tallinn, see figure 3.4) were still living in the company of Haydn, Mozart, and other non-modern composers. This was certainly true, in the sense that musical and other innovations moved forward slowly, in phases. A similar situation also apparently prevailed in Finland, accentuated by the Weberian-Spohrian-Beethovenian inclinations of such opinion leaders as Pacius. Riesemann's view brings to mind David Kirby's assessment of the Baltic Sea as a peripheral "backwater," which as a cultural area creates nothing genuine but adopts influences from elsewhere. In Riesemann's perspective, Estonia was also "far from the field of battle for the future development of mankind." The only way to improve this situation was to engage in a rapid study of European intellectual movements and bring them within the reach

Figure 3.4. Port of Tallinn. Author's postcard collection (no publisher or photographer mentioned).

of local people. This was what happened, to a considerable extent, in the field of concert music in the nineteenth century. From this perspective, the relationship between Central Europe and the Baltic world was not based upon mutual reciprocity or upon a negotiable situation. It became reciprocal only with the rise of nationalism, which, with its correspondent focusing of more attention on local cultures, in the course of time, also influenced the field of music. In terms of the reception of Wagner during the 1850s and 1860s, this reciprocal influence was not yet perceivable, except in a sense that the Riga performances influenced Wagner's choice of sketches for his forthcoming works and, thus, had an impact on Wagnerism on a large scale.

The most central goal in Riesemann's writing was to import European discourse to Estonia in order to make it possible to comprehend Wagner in a general fashion. Riesemann saw that it was necessary to inform the audience of Wagner's theories in advance of the 1860 performance, as though comprehension of *Tannhäuser* would have been impossible, or, at least, difficult without a contextual knowledge of the work:

> The pitched battle that has raged on the field of art, and more especially of music, for the past decade, has been of a bitterness unprecedented in the history of art—and the Knights of Noble Art still stand to arms, in their two camps. The Past! The Future!—these are the cries that rise from the battle.

Reckless passion is in command; the furious warriors assault each other with brazen weapons—not arrows, but quills, dipped in gall and venom; on all sides, polarizations and blind partisan hatred;—a barren, unedifying mêlée, which should have been kept far from the noble peace of Art.[106]

Wagner had created what was essentially a party struggle and changed music into politics, or into war. Riesemann was, without doubt, correct in stating that nothing like this had previously happened in the history of music. Wagner had declared that he would show the path to the future, but the change was possible only through a rupture: "Following his political convictions with regard to republicanism, he also called for a colossal revolution in the field of art."[107]

An interesting feature in Wagner's *Das Kunstwerk der Zukunft* is that the ideas of future and history are inseparably combined. Here, Wagner was obviously inspired by Ludwig Feuerbach and his book, *Grundsätze der Philosophie der Zukunft*, published in 1843.[108] Despite this influence, Wagner's own book was groundbreaking in the field of music and emphasized new kinds of thoughts on time and history. In the eighteenth century, the concept of time had been linear, and the individual had not often been seen as an agent of change. Voltaire had written in his *Dictionnaire philosophique* (1764) that history was only a chain of events, a *chaine des événemens*.[109] It was only the Great Revolution of 1789 in France that revealed that it was possible to have an impact on the course of history. The world was not in the Leibnizian way of thinking "the best of all possible worlds": rather, a new direction could, if required, be given to the course of history. This idea made possible the nineteenth-century history of revolution. Wagner was, of course, also interested in political change, as may be seen in his activities in support of the revolutionary movement in Dresden. But, without doubt, Wagner was the first artist who consciously wanted to change the direction of the development of his field (that is, to change art by redefining, in literary form, the qualities it should exhibit). This prescriptive tendency characterizes the texts of his Zürich period.

Of course, prescriptiveness or the employment of musical scenarios certainly existed earlier in the history of art; but what makes Wagner's case exceptional is the fact that he himself strove to act in response to the theoretical challenge and to publicize his thoughts. And in this, as Riesemann's writing reveals, he was successful. On the other hand, Riesemann states that a section of the public interpreted Wagner's writings as "letters of recommendation" for his own works, and that this was apt to arouse suspicion and hatred. Wagner's strategy also therefore sowed the seeds of party hatred.

Riesemann's writing clearly reveals the contents of two of Wagner's books, *Das Kunstwerk der Zukunft* and *Oper und Drama*. Instead of the artwork of the future, Riesemann concentrates upon "the drama of the future." Through his compositions, Wagner strove "to realize his ideals, to allow his theories to exert an influence in practice." This meant that there were no longer any arias and duets in his works: "Every word, every note is an unbroken ring in the chain of the dramatic whole."[110] Riesemann directly quotes the famous sentence from *Oper und Drama* in which Wagner states that in the art of opera, "a means of expression (music) has been made the end, while the end of expression (the drama) has been made a means."[111]

Riesemann continues his analysis of the music of the future. He compares Wagner's projects with absolute music: "Wagner is not completely free from the earlier influences of that which the most charming appearance of the absolute musician in his inner self supports."[112] In his writings, Wagner succeeded in putting forward the idea of rupture so successfully that it was difficult for his contemporaries to see the connection between the admiration of absolute music crystallized in the Beethoven cult and Wagner's operatic reform. But, in fact, Wagner saw that he was continuing the heritage of Beethoven: Beethoven's symphonies had also been dramas, that is, they embodied a struggle between themes and counter-themes. Wagner wanted, in a certain way, to move the symphonic principle to opera, which unavoidably meant rejecting the set pieces in French-Italian opera. Carl Dahlhaus has stated that Wagner, after all, had no other alternative in his attempt to create a "German music." In Germany there was no operatic tradition that could have spread widely in Europe. Carl Maria von Weber's *Freischütz* had been successful in Paris under the title *Robin des bois*, but, according to Dahlhaus, German opera was a national not an international phenomenon. Wagner had earlier already experimented with the Italian style in *Die Feen* (*The Fairies*) and with the French style in *Rienzi*, but his experiments had failed. When, in the 1840s, he began to be more strongly interested in German culture—even though he was not willing to relinquish the opportunity of international success—there was no other alternative than to turn to the symphonic tradition of German music.[113]

Oscar von Riesemann's writing offers interesting contemporary evidence of the use of the concept of *Zukunftsmusik*. This concept, which originated in the controversy caused by *Das Kunstwerk der Zukunft* and *Oper und Drama*, was frequently employed in the 1850s to describe the continuing revolution in music. In 1854, Joachim Raff defined this concept in *Die Wagnerfrage*. According to Raff, Wagner's theory of the artwork of the future led the composer's operas to be called "the operas of the future" and his music "the music of the future."[114] It was no wonder that the master of comedy, Nestroy, could formulate a new concept, *Zukunftsposse* (the farce of the future), in his *Tannhäuser* parody.

A knowledge of the concept is clearly displayed in Fredrik Pacius's and Louis Spohr's critical discussion on the music of the future in August 1857, a discussion in which Spohr also classified Berlioz and Liszt as composers of *Zukunftsmusik*.[115] The term did not necessarily refer, as Raff had stated, to the music of Wagner's operas alone: it had become a more general concept. Writing in the *Revalsche Zeitung*, Oscar von Riesemann seems to agree with Raff's view in the sense that a discussion on the music of the future did not negate the idea of the artwork of the future, even though the concept of *Zukunftsmusik* carried the idea of a preference for music over other forms of art. Wagner himself was more willing to be considered as an artist than as a composer, but despite this, music was regarded as the most central element in his works. In contrast, Spohr used the term to refer to a wider reform of music, which, in addition to Wagner, embraced many other composers. In this case, the concept referred, above all, to a more chromatic music with a vacillating tonal variety that was also represented by Liszt and Berlioz. The music historian Franz Brendel called this group the New German School. Brendel acted as editor in chief of the *Neue Zeitschrift für Musik*, and later also became a teacher of music at the Leipzig Conservatory. Through these positions, he exercised an influence not only on the concept of history developed by his German students but also on that of the students from the shores of the Baltic Sea.[116]

Wagner himself did not use the word *Zukunftsmusik* in the texts from his Zurich period, and we do not know exactly when the word was coined. In his biography of Wagner, Martin Gregor-Dellin claims that it occurs for the first time in a letter of Louis Spohr's in November 1854.[117] This is not precisely true (as an examination of Raff's work may also reveal). The term was already commonly used in 1854, at least, in musical circles; and it occurred, for instance, in Friedrich Wieck's *Clavier und Gesang* (1853).[118] Apparently, *Zukunftsmusik* became a common term during the controversial debate of 1852–53, at which time Wagner himself had become nervous about the innumerable "misunderstandings" that it might create. A different question is whether "the word" also denoted "the concept," for the concept could have existed before it was connected to the word. Gregor-Dellin holds that the expression "the music of the future" (*Musik der Zukunft, musique de l'avenir*) was already used in reference to the music of Chopin, Liszt, and Berlioz, among others, by the 1840s.[119] Even though the original term, *Musik der Zukunft*, is slightly different from its derivative, *Zukunftsmusik*, it seems to be conceptually close to it; at least, it indicates the meaning that Spohr associated with it.

In time, the confusion of words and concepts began to irritate Wagner. He had already been shocked at the discovery that his works had been labeled *Zukunftsmusik*: in September 1860, two months before the appearance of Riesemann's article in the *Revalsche Zeitung*, Wagner wrote *"Zukunftsmusik." An einen französischen Freund (Fr. Villot) als Vorwort zu einer Prosa-Übersetzung meiner Operndichtungen*. The title refers to the French versions of *Der fliegende Holländer, Tannhäuser, Lohengrin*, and *Tristan und Isolde*, published under the name *Quatre poèmes d'opéras* in 1861. In fall 1860, Wagner was in Paris preparing the premiere of *Tannhäuser* and noticed that the concept *Zukunftsmusik* was associated with him. Wagner's text was addressed to Frédéric Villot, who had been working as a curator at the Louvre and was an ardent supporter of Wagner's music.[120]

At the beginning of the text, Wagner acknowledged that his theories had led to a large number of "mistakes and prejudices." Now that *Tannhäuser* had been performed in Paris, he hoped it would not be compared to the theory but would be listened to in the same way as other works of art. Wagner argued that an artist cannot be guided by a theoretical reflection but is guided by an intuitive desire to create.[121] The theoretical texts had been written in a situation in which, according to Wagner, German opera did not exist. The point was not only that composers had imitated Italian and French styles, but that the social conditions for the reform of opera did not exist. In his treatises, Wagner wanted to delineate an ideal art in which music and drama could be in harmony; but as he did not see any possibility of the realization of this ideal in the prevailing situation, he named his ideal "the artwork of the future." At the same time, Wagner opined that the expression "the music of the future," which had become common even in France, was a misunderstanding, a false term; and that its users did not understand the premises upon which the idea of "the artwork of the future" had originally been based.[122] Wagner also made it clear that his completed operas were far from being ideal works produced through theories. Instead, he had wanted to compose modern opera "mit der Symphonie Beethoven's im Herzen" (with the Beethoven symphony at heart). This perspective had led him to think of the unity of drama and music. He had not followed the worship of melody that was so popular in many contemporary operas.[123]

Thus, Wagner at this time did not subscribe to the idea that he was "an artist of the future," nor was this claim made by Oscar von Riesemann. In the publicity connected with Wagner, expectations concerning the future, were, however, conspicuous, as has already been revealed in the examination of the discourse of the press. Wagner seemed to be a precursor of something that was not yet on the horizon. In the Riga press, for example, the references to an explorer and the news items on the preliminary stages of Wagner's operatic projects were connected to this form of rhetoric. Even though Wagner argued that the fulfillment of the ideal that had been formulated in theory was not realizable under the present conditions, he seemed, despite this, to be attempting to change these conditions. The first news of the *Ring* tetralogy surely caused such associations for, by that time, Wagner had embarked upon the creation of a totally new atmosphere in which his operas would be heard and seen.

Alone in the Temple of Thalia: *Tannhäuser* in Helsinki

Helsinki, the capital of Finland, also had contact with Richard Wagner's art in the 1850s. At that time, there was no opera house in Helsinki, and performances were arranged through the employment of amateurs. Inter-national opera companies also visited the city at regular intervals, enliven-ing the opera and theater world in Helsinki. During 1827–34, Arnold Schoultz's company performed fashionable operas, including Carl Maria von Weber's *Freischütz*. In 1839, the Kesteloott Company restricted its performances to opera, although its repertoire usually consisted of musi-cal comedies and other theatrical sub-genres. Among other works, the Kesteloott Company performed Bellini's *Norma* and Rossini's *Il barbiere di Siviglia* in Helsinki. The repertoire also included *Der Freischütz*, which was thus performed again in the capital.[124]

In the mid-19th century, interest in opera and theater grew rapidly. This could be seen in the increase in amateur performances: in 1849 Rossini's *Il barbiere di Siviglia* was staged with an amateur cast on three occa-sions in succession and Donizetti's *L'elisir d'amore* (*The Elixir of Love*) was per-formed in the following spring.[125] Johann Heinrich Wilhelm Gehrmann's opera company from Tallinn increased Helsinki's familiarity with opera by performing a series of twenty operas, including, among others, Mozart's *Le nozze di Figaro* (*The Marriage of Figaro*), *Don Giovanni*, and *Die Zauberflöte* (*The Magic Flute*), Beethoven's *Fidelio*, and Meyerbeer's *Les Huguenots*.[126] The guest performances continued when Theophil Fass brought his opera com-pany from Tallinn to Helsinki for a four-week period in July 1852. Most of the performers were from the Tallinn and Riga theaters, and they gave six-teen performances in all.[127] The Baltic connection continued when Johann Schràmek gathered an opera company consisting of Estonian and Livonian members in 1856. Schràmek arrived in May and stayed almost three months, offering fifty-one performances to Finnish opera lovers, works such as Meyerbeer's *Le prophète*, Auber's *Gustave III, ou Le bal masqué*, Flo-tow's *Martha*, and Donizetti's *Lucia di Lammermoor*. Schràmek promised to return the following summer but later had to cancel the tour.[128]

The enthusiasm for opera was reflected in Finnish music. At that time, the giant in the Finnish music world was Fredrik Pacius, who, as we have seen, had come to Finland in 1835 and taught music at the University of Helsinki. As has already been mentioned, Pacius assembled an orchestra of amateur players, and he also arranged operatic performances, of which the most popular was Pacius's own composition, *Kung Karls jagd*, a work based on Zacharias Topelius's libretto, which was premiered at the Society House on 24 March 1852. Topelius (1818–98) was a writer and newspaperman who later became professor of history at the University of Helsinki. Although, he was especially famous for his historical plays and novels, Topelius was very interested in music and followed musical life in France and Germany. *Kung Karls jagd* tells of a deer-hunting trip to the islands of Åland made by the Swedish King Charles XI when he was only sixteen years old. During the trip, the nobles conspired to assassinate the king, but their plans were thwarted by honest Finnish peasants. Musically, the work follows

Figure 3.5. Final scene of *Kung Karls jagd*, painted by Magnus von Wright, 1852. National Museum of Finland.

the style of Louis Spohr and especially that of Carl Maria von Weber. The *Helsingfors Tidningar* commented on the enthusiasm exhibited on the first night:

> *Kung Karls jagd* played to a full house last Wednesday (six performances have been fully subscribed in advance). The salon was illuminated *en gale*, and presented a beautiful appearance, for it was occupied from floor to ceiling by an educated audience, including many visitors, and both the audience and the orchestra were in evening dress. When Mr. Pacius mounted the podium, with his baton in his hand, tumultuous applause swept through the hall, followed soon afterward by utter silence, as the beautiful overture began. . . . When the performance ended, Mr. Pacius was summoned to the front, and was greeted, crowned with laurel leaves, by the audience in the hall and the surrounding young people with the most lively, delightful applause. The evening came to a dignified end with Vårt land sung from the stage.[129]

The evening ended with *Vårt land* (*Our Land*), which later became the national anthem of Finland and Estonia. *Kung Karls jagd* had all the hallmarks of a national symbol, even though, at that time, there were no signs of a movement for independence. Tsar Nicholas I had, however, been tightening his regime's hold, and censorship had become more strict, so that from a political perspective, the world took on an increasingly gloomy appearance. Seen against such a background, Pacius's bright, optimistic work, which praised Finnishness, became an indisputable success.[130] When he was planning the libretto for the opera in June 1851, Topelius, however, offered a different view of nationalism, for he purposefully strove to parody nationalism in the scene at the beginning of the third act in which two Jewish merchants are arguing about their nationalities:

> . . . after long consideration, I have resolved to do something new, using *two* worn-out characters: two Jews, instead of one; the two of them get into an argument about their nationality—a preposterous altercation—one says, "ich bin ein Schwede," the other, "ich bin ein Finländer,"—and in this manner, they parody the national difference that is profiled in the finale—which gives the whole play some sense. And by the way, what do you say to a Swedish-Finnish double chorus at the end? It would be fun if it could be done.[131]

The Finnish-Swedish double chorus was finally realized on the stage, but not bilingually: the final scene was in Swedish only (see figure 3.5). In all probability, the scene portraying Jewishness was also interpreted as merely presenting a stereotype and not as a parody of nationalism.[132]

Kung Karls jagd was performed at the Society House, as the old playhouse was already in a dilapidated condition. In fact, a collection in aid of the building of a new theater was made during the performance. During the Crimean War (1853–56), the playhouse of the Helsinki theater was used as soldiers' quarters, a circumstance that very probably increased the desire for a new playhouse.[133] The project was not, however, completed until 1860.

In this situation, various operatic performances were offered for the Helsinki public by companies from the Baltic provinces of the Russian Empire, especially from Riga. Schràmek, who had visited Helsinki in summer 1856, had promised to return in the following year, but, as we have noted, this plan fell through. In this situation, the Finnish organizers turned to the director of the Riga German theater, Franz Thomé, who was invited to visit Helsinki.[134] Both Schràmek's and Thomé's visits probably reflected the altered political situation. The Crimean War had ended in the previous year. The Baltic Sea had been one of the central theaters of the war, which had certainly diminished the enthusiasm for touring. Thomé's visit was noticed by the Livonian press. The *Rigasche Stadtblätter* wrote on 11 April: "It is reported from Helsinki that Mr. Director Thomé has received an invitation from the local theater to arrange operatic performances there during July and August, and this flattering request will be complied with."[135] On 22 May, the *Rigasche Zeitung* laconically reported that Thomé's company was to perform in Jelgava from 21 May to the end of June and, after that, would visit Helsinki, where performances were to continue until mid-August.[136] After performing in Jelgava, Thomé and his company traveled to Helsinki at the beginning of July to give guest performances. It is interesting to note that the repertoire now included Wagner, who was played for the first time for a Finnish audience. If the first Wagner performance in Tallinn had (through Fass and Leszinsky) a connection to Riga, the first Wagner performance in Finland had an even more direct connection with the Livonian music center.

In any case, the visit of the Riga German Theater was significant in the Finnish context, as were the other guest performances of the 1850s. At the beginning of the decade, the population of Helsinki was about 20,000; thus, the city offered possibilities equal to those of Tallinn.[137] Thomé's company swiftly provided a remedy for the deficiency in music, offering a total of thirty-three opera performances during a period of six weeks, including Friedrich von Flotow's *Martha, Alessandro Stradella,* and *Indra,* Giuseppe Verdi's *Ernani* and *Rigoletto,* Gaetano Donizetti's *Lucia di Lammermoor* and *Linda di Chamounix*—and Wagner's *Tannhäuser.*[138]

Thomé with his singers and musicians arrived in Helsinki on 7 July 1857. When the guest performances in Jelgava were completed, the company traveled on the steamship *Fulton* from Riga to Tallinn and from there to Helsinki.[139] The group consisted of ten soloists, an eighteen-member chorus, and an orchestra of twenty-four musicians.[140] According to the *Rigaer Theater-Almanach* of the previous year, the orchestra was normally composed of twenty-nine players.[141] When *Tannhäuser* was performed in Riga in 1853, the orchestra had been augmented with amateurs and military musicians; but the sources do not reveal how Thomé's company could cope with, say, the passage written for twelve trumpets.

The arrival of the opera company aroused an interest in many newspapers, even though the summer was at its hottest, and the theater season was officially over. In particular, the Swedish-language papers, the *Helsingfors Tidningar* and the *Finlands Allmänna Tidning,* noted the sudden increase in the opera repertoire, whereas the Finnish paper *Suometar* offered only a brief comment: "During the summer, there have been almost daily amusements in our town. Mr. Thomé with his singing group is performing plays diligently in our playhouse: sounds of music are heard in the Spa Room, that is, in Kaisaniemi and in Töölö almost every evening."[142] The gulf between Finnish and Swedish culture in Finland was so deep at that time that newspapers like the *Suometar* dealt mainly with subjects such as the catechism and lichen bread, not opera. The reporter for the *Suometar* could not even employ the concept of opera: he uses the word "näytelmä" (play), as there was no word for "opera" in the Finnish language at the time.

In studying the Swedish, Finnish, and Baltic provinces reception of Wagner, one should keep in mind that the boundaries of this reception were not only geographical but also social. Thus, in the 1850s Wagner was already being discussed by the German press in Estonia and Livonia and also by the Swedish press in Finland, whereas the press in the Estonian, Latvian, and Finnish languages was silent.

The librettist for *Kung Karls jagd*, Zacharias Topelius, was also a reporter for the Swedish-language *Helsingfors Tidningar*. It is likely that the text concerning Thomé's visit was written by Topelius, and that he was interested in opera. On 12 August, the anonymous author gives an account of his emotions and anxiously notes the lack of interest exhibited by the Helsinki public toward the new works heard during the operatic weeks. In all probability, the public's meager interest was due not only to the fact that the composers were unfamiliar but also to the hot August weather:

> Mr. Thomé has attempted . . . by the production of a number of new, distinguished operas—*Tannhäuser* by Wagner, *Indra* by Flotow, *Linda di Chamounix*—to attract an audience, but has failed to fill more than half the house; at times, indeed, even less. This is all the more to be decried, since the works chosen, in terms of both their intrinsic musical value and their overall very successful performance, would in full measure have merited greater public attention. Insofar as they have aroused so little interest, one might be tempted to suppose that the city's public has become *cold* toward art—were it not that every one of us knows from personal experience that the temple of art, the theater—has in fact become too *hot* for the connoisseur. In such circumstances, both Mr. Thomé and his company deserve every respect, since neither he nor they have allowed the fashion to fall into abeyance but continue to perform, with the greatest enthusiasm and devotion, for the benefit of those few who have persisted in demonstrating better taste for good opera than for promenading in our dusty avenues.[143]

After noting the low attendance, the critic for the *Helsingfors Tidningar* also briefly mentions *Tannhäuser*, which was performed on two occasions during the operatic weeks: "Yesterday was the second performance of *Tannhäuser*. The house was very thinly attended—the performance highly skilled—the members of the orchestra, especially, deserve full praise for the excellent way in which they performed this opera's brilliant but difficult music."[144] *Tannhäuser*, which was performed on 5 and 10 August, was given more space in the *Finlands Allmänna Tidning*. On 12 August, the paper published a lengthy article written by the Swedish-born critic Fredrik Berndtson (1820–81). In addition to being a newspaper columnist, Berndtson was a professor of aesthetics and modern literature at the University of Helsinki.[145] A surprising feature of his review is the fact that it contains more criticism of the interpretation than of the work:

Tannhäuser, which was performed for the first time, has powerful, if somewhat difficult music, and constitutes one of the most famous works in contemporary German music; this composition by Richard Wagner is
distinguished by departing from the usual rules to such an extent that the
orchestra here plays the leading role, to which the singing is subordinated;
most of the sung roles are modeled upon a true declamation in a recitative, which is the most demanding of all forms of singing. Mr. Arnold
(Tannhäuser) strained his voice less than usual, and succeeded rather well,
especially in the third act. Mr. Pettenkofer (Hermann) performed his role
with great dignity, and Dr. Duschnitz (Wolfram) sang exceedingly well.
Mrs. Pettenkofer (Elisabeth) had a very difficult role, but came off well,
with her strong, rich voice, though she did not moderate this enough; in
the dramatic parts of her role, however, she achieved more than one could
have hoped for; in the third act of this opera there is a prayer, which when
well performed is moving in its beauty. Ms. Hofmann was a pretty little
"Venus" and did with her role what she could; she has a clear and rich
albeit not yet fully developed voice, and it is a pleasure to see and hear her
on the stage. The choruses in this opera are beautiful, and were performed
in a creditable manner.[146]

Berndtson saw it as his duty to comment on all the performers of the main
roles, but he did not pay much attention to the orchestra, the chorus, or
the scenery. In fact, the newspaper reviews did not refer to the stage decor
or costumes at all. It is possible that existing Finnish scenery was used in the
operas. It would have been impossible to transport all the necessary items
from Riga. On the other hand, time would not have allowed for the production of new items in Helsinki. This explains why the criticism emphasized the music and not the visual elements: the critics knew that it was
impossible to offer impressive sceneries, and therefore, their evaluation
was excluded from the reviews. The article written by Berndtson on 12
August also seems to refer to earlier experiences, although he is not altogether clear on this point. The author apparently knows the basics of
Tannhäuser. He refers, for instance, to the Prayer of Elizabeth in the third
act, which "when well performed is moving in its beauty." It is, of course,
possible that such views were culled from music papers and literature, and
the critic is simply trying to present an image of himself as an expert.
Berndtson also alludes, through his statement that the orchestra has the
leading role in the work, to Wagner's operatic reform. It is difficult to
estimate the power of the orchestra's performance in the Helsinki performance, bearing in mind that the orchestra consisted of only twenty-four
musicians. In any case, the writer seems to be referring to Wagner's
thoughts in *Oper und Drama*, according to which, in opera, the orchestra
should have a role comparable to that of the chorus in Greek tragedy.
Apparently, he was familiar with Wagner's theoretical texts either as origi-
nals or from quotations in the music periodicals.

Overall, Thomé's performances aroused a great deal of attention in Finland. The press in Turku also covered the performances in short news items.[147] Despite this, the audience does not appear to have been willing to attend all the performances: the repertoire of the company included thirty-three operas, rather too many, given the normal demand for opera; and the situation was worsened by the summer heat, which, as we have noticed, diminished the public's interest in opera. This is revealed by a report in the *Helsingfors Tidningar* on 19 August: "How much influence the weather exercises in such cases was demonstrated last Sunday, when the cool, less pleasant evening contributed to the fact that Donizetti's *Dom Vincente* played to an almost full house, whereas the brilliant creations of Flotow and Wagner, only shortly before, had been performed for the benefit of only a few dozen hearers."[148] If there were in fact no more than "a few dozen" persons in attending the Wagner performance, it is no wonder that the performance did not create any Wagner boom in Finland.

When the doors of the theater were closed, the *Finlands Allmänna Tidning* commented that "When the long, dull, and dark autumn evenings arrive, many audience members will look at the closed doors of the Temple of Thalia with nostalgia."[149] The last performance took place on Sunday 23 August, and on the next day the opera company departed via Tallinn for Riga.[150] The exceptional character of the visit is reflected in the fact that the matter was reported by the press not only in Helsinki and Turku but also in Riga and apparently even in Germany.[151]

It was not, however, only through the Riga German Theatre that Wagner touched the Finnish mentality; for this was the end of the 1850s, the time when news of "the new music" and "the artwork of the future" was landing on the coasts of Finland. It is difficult to assess the degree to which Wagner was examined by the Finnish press during the 1850s without engaging in a systematic scrutiny of the press for the whole decade. But it is fairly clear that the Finnish press did not cover Wagner to the same extent as, for example, the press in Livonia.

Instead, the Finnish newspapers published descriptions of travels to Central Europe in which the name of Wagner would occasionally appear. One of these travelogues was Zacharias Topelius's series of articles, "Söder om Östersjön" ("South of the Baltic Sea"). This series of articles also told of new operas, for instance, Giacomo Meyerbeer's *L'étoile du nord* (*The North Star*), with a libretto by Scribe. The events of the first act of the opera took place near Viborg on the Carelian Isthmus:

In Paris and Dresden I saw Scribe's and Meyerbeer's beautiful if historically monstrous opera, *The North Star*. Not the least interesting circumstance, for a Finnish listener, was the fact that the whole of the first act and the end of the last act are set in Finland, in the vicinity of Viborg, where—so alleges Scribe—Peter the Great made his first acquaintance with Catherine, the

"North Star." The landscape was, it must be admitted, pure imagination: beautiful rocky cliffs, a beach, a village, &c.; but the costumes, especially those of the ladies, were both in Paris and in Dresden evidently copied from the famous costumes of Jääski. In all probability a copy had been obtained of the illustration printed here. The Finns, poor country people, be it said, behaved with good cheer, if not in a very Finnish manner, yet at least not so as to cause embarrassment to our party, and the first chorus, with its outstandingly beautiful music, is a song in honor of Finland: "Buvons pour la Finlande!"—which in Dresden had been translated as "Finnland soll leben!" The elegant society of Paris, and the rougher paws of Saxony, applauded with all their might—at the fine music, I dare say; but I can assure you that these Finnish recollections, however fantastic, made a powerful impression on those present. The Finns are, incidentally, treated favorably throughout the play; all, naturally, for the sake of the North Star.[152]

The articles also aroused the attention of the press in Sweden and some of them, at least, were published in a Stockholm paper, the *Svenska tidningen*, in 1857. This newspaper published the article "Den moderna operan" ("Modern Opera"), which included a reference to Wagner. In this article, Topelius states that he wishes to scrutinize opera "to be able, after that, to judge whether Richard Wagner was right in stating that this genre of art was a mistake."[153] In fact, the article refers to Wagner not as a composer but as a theorist: the composers analyzed were Gluck, Mozart, Cherubini, Boieldieu, Méhul, Weber, Rossini. . . .

The writer of "Söder om Östersjön," Zacharias Topelius (see figure 3.6), had made a trip to France and Germany in 1856. He had kept up with the art scene in Central Europe and had earlier learned of Wagner. Topelius was very interested in opera, even though he did not write very many opera librettos. His libretto writing is, however, tangentially relevant to Wagner's theory of opera.

From the point of view of the Finnish reception of Wagner, one interesting feature is an opera project planned by Topelius in collaboration with the composer Conrad Greve (1820–51)[154] from Turku. Topelius decided to write a libretto based on the stories connected to the church of Raisio, which is near Turku: the opera would deal with the building of the church and the essentials of the conflict between Catholicism and paganism. According to the original plan, the work would be limited to the period around the year 1300, and the opera would consist of three acts.[155] This libretto, *Sancta Maria*, haunted Topelius's correspondence for a long time. The sudden death of Greve halted the project, and Pacius could not be inspired to work on it, because work on *Kung Karls jagd* was already underway. Topelius also offered the libretto to Karl Collan and to the Swedish composer J. A. Josephson. In the end, the work was never composed.[156]

Figure 3.6. Zacharias Topelius (1818–98). National Museum of Finland.

In his discourse with Josephson, Topelius also referred to Wagner, in fact, to the same ideas that are found in "Söder om Östersjön." Topelius and Josephson exchanged letters over a four-year period, 1853–57. In December 1853, the influence of Wagner is not, at least explicitly, distinguishable in his letters: Topelius's more important models are Meyerbeer's religious-minded operas *Le prophète* and *Les Huguenots*:

> I would merely remind you of certain situations in Meyerbeer's *Le prophète* and *Les Huguenots*, passing over the rest in silence. That which there is a dissolving thundercloud, however, has here become a night sky through the thunder of which the stars shine. *Sancta Maria* is a Christian romantic opera—it shows an ancient period, collapsing upon its own gaping emptiness, where Christianity's role—which one might see as passive—has already in large part been fulfilled before the play begins. Slowly but implacably, it has undermined the basis of paganism, until it needs no more than a nudge for it to fall, leaving Christianity standing, as the sun dawns over the departing night, as it is described at the beginning of the third act in a readily understood antithesis.[157]

Despite the references to Meyerbeer in this quotation, the fundamental questions involving Wagner are conceived in relation to his way of viewing the unity of music and drama. Topelius even apologizes to Josephson for the fact that he has approached the territory of music, "but the truth is that, while writing the text, the music has always been in mind." But, finally, Meyerbeerism is clearly discernible: "Great environments generate great ideas: to be a Meyerbeer for Sweden, as he would have been if he had been born Swedish." Topelius does not see any difference between Swedishness and Finnishness, despite the fact that Finland had been under Russian suzerainty since 1809. The ties of kinship to the western side of the Baltic Sea were indisputable.

It was not until April 1854 that Josephson replied to Topelius's letter concerning the libretto, stating that, at that particular time, he was unable to take on the project, and that, in addition, the libretto would require a lot of effort and abridgement as well as a number of additions.[158] The matter was dropped, but emerged again in the correspondence between the two men at the beginning of 1857. In January, Josephson wrote that he had done nothing about the matter. Josephson had heard from Pacius that the text was of importance to Topelius but feared that the work would not function as an opera without dialogue, and suggested that it might be better as a drama enlivened by music.[159] In April 1857, Topelius replied, obviously irritated by Josephson's comments, and appealed to the authorities in the field. Now he no longer paid attention to Meyerbeer but to Wagner. In fact, Topelius relinquished the models he had followed four years previously:

> Dear Mr. Josephson (please excuse me for preferring this simplest title; please do the same yourself);—that *Sancta Maria* upset you does not surprise me; I feared this from soon after the beginning. This play is serious enough for modern standards, but has nothing or little of what modern taste has come to expect of an opera in external glitter—not one single ballet, neither skating nor military parades, but, rather, a dark mysticism.[160]

The remark that *Sancta Maria* does not contain a skating scene refers to Meyerbeer's *Le prophète,* a work earlier mentioned by Topelius as having been his guiding star. In the 1850s, *Le prophète* aroused astonishment due to its skating scene. When the work was performed in Antwerp at the end of 1852 and the beginning of 1853, as far away as St. Petersburg the press reported that "in the skating ballet scene the whole stage was covered with tightly fitted quadrangular ice blocks, and on these quads the skaters were able to perform their figures."[161]

Topelius states that, as a libretto, *Kung Karls jagd* had been better, but that, for musical reasons, it should have been more tightly constructed.

Josephson could have done the same with *Sancta Maria*. Topelius then moves on to Wagner's criticism of opera:

> The experience I have had more recently, which has been strengthened by a closer acquaintance with modern opera, has in retrospect fostered a conviction as to what the future will bring, which has been appositely expressed by Richard Wagner, when he wrote: "*Die Oper ist ein Irrthum, denn in diesem Kunstgenre ist ein Mittel des Ausdruckes (die Musik) zum Zweck gemacht, der Zweck aber (das Drama) zu Mittel.*" This is truly so. I believe that this implies no disrespect for music, but on the contrary, its full recognition, or, in other words, simply the judicious insistence that a genre of art, in order to become what it should be, must needs follow its own laws of development. I have seen in opera how the music, having first tyrannized and subordinated the drama, has itself been displaced by the ballet, and the ballet in its turn often enough by the decor, step by step away from the ideal goal in the direction of sensual temptation;—and I maintain that here we can see a Nemesis that will degrade Art to a powerless degradation. This must be prevented; and if our strength, Mr. Josephson, be not adequate to clear new pathways, then let us not waste this strength upon a doomed genre of art—for sooner or later, modern opera assuredly is doomed—I assure you that the *marriage of the arts* has been one of my most cherished dreams; who would turn aside from such a dream?—but if this task is to be achieved, it must be achieved in such a way as to permit within this marriage each of the arts to retain its autonomy, to continue to be itself, upright, not trampled underfoot by its closest allies. In those genres that are closest, this problem has already been solved, i.e., in music and lyrical poetry. I therefore consider that until this riddle has in the future been solved for the stage—Wagner has attempted it, in *Tannhäuser*, whether with success or not, I cannot judge; opinions are divided—until such time, then, music should uphold this bond, and merely amplify the form, e.g., as in the *Ode-symphony*, or in the purely lyrical accessories of a drama.
>
> Herein, Mr. Josephson, you may discover my unhesitating reply concerning *Sancta Maria*—that I have abandoned any hope of its becoming an opera; just as for my own humble part, I shall probably never again attempt an opera libretto—and in all sincerity, and with all due gratitude for the goodwill that *Kung Karls jagd* has met with in Stockholm, I would add that the next time I write something, if God grant me health, I have the modest hope not to be condemned for faults other than those of my own work.[162]

Topelius had been extremely disappointed with *Kung Karls jagd*, particularly in the spring of 1857, when he had heard from Pacius how poorly the opera had been received in Stockholm. Ernst Ludvig Bjursten had criticized the opera's libretto in particular, and he had wondered how the work could have achieved success in Finland.[163] Topelius was offended by the fact that the dramatic weaknesses that resulted from the collaboration between writer and composer and "to the requirements of the music" were now seen as the fault of the librettist. The only solution to the problem would be for the composer and the librettist to be the same person, as was the case with Wagner. No schism would arise under such conditions. The fusion of the arts would be possible only if the independence and originality of each art could be retained, and in this union one art should not be subordinated to another. In his various writings, Topelius did not quote much from Wagner, but in this passage he seems to have reinforced his own thoughts by reference to Wagner. Modern opera did not correspond to Topelius's expectations as a dramatist. Thus, he appears to accept Wagner's idea that opera as an art form is "a mistake." As a result, Topelius was more interested in concentrating on his historical plays, which did not require him to submit to musical taste. If *Sancta Maria* had been realized, it could have become the first Finnish or Swedish opera influenced by Wagner, but Topelius and Josephson understood that they did not have the strength required "to clear new pathways."[164]

Topelius believed there was no reason to spend time on an effort that could end in complete failure. Prior to the year 1857, Topelius had either read Wagner's *Oper und Drama* or had read about it in a music paper; but he had not taken a stand on the question of whether the combination of music and drama was possible and whether Wagner had succeeded in achieving such a blend in *Tannhäuser*. Before April 1857, Topelius had not yet seen Wagner's controversial opera, for he says he was unable to evaluate it. Not until the following summer did he have an occasion to hear the work, when the Riga German Theater performed it in Helsinki.

Topelius's surviving literary material does not reveal whether *Tannhäuser* had a particular influence on him. If the review of the opera in the *Helsingfors Tidningar* was from Topelius's pen, Wagner's music had then appeared "ingenious," but Topelius was no longer willing to interfere in new operatic projects. There are no indications that Topelius regarded *Tannhäuser* as a realization of the idea of a united artwork (*Gesamtkunstwerk*). Apparently, this view was not widely held in Finland at the time. After all, Wagner would not be heard on the Finnish opera stage until years later.

In the 1850s, no Wagner debate arose in Finland. In 1857, Topelius referred to *Oper und Drama* in his letter to Josephson, as did Berndtson in his review of *Tannhäuser*. The Finnish literary scholar and historian Fredrik Cygnaeus (1807–81) had already quoted *Oper und Drama* by 1853, in his treatise *Det tragiska elementet uti Kalevala* (*The Tragic Element in Kalevala*). This quotation is so direct that Cygnaeus certainly knew Wagner's original work.[165] In all probability, Topelius and Berndtson also knew the original, not only summaries in the musical press. But, in the end, there was no public debate on Wagner in Finland. From the 1860s onward, more and more Wagner pieces were performed at concerts, but no complete productions of Wagner's works were staged. From 1872, regular operatic activity was carried on in the Finnish theater, founded by Kaarlo Bergbom. An opera department was also established within the theater, but Wagner was not included in its repertoire. The department's first production was Donizetti's *Lucia di Lammermoor,* premiered on 21 November 1873.[166] Unusually, the premiere was in Viborg. The opera department was closed in 1879. Yet, before this, many large works had already been performed, including Meyerbeer's *Les Huguenots,* Halévy's *La Juive* (*The Jewess*), and Auber's *Fra Diavolo.* Wagner, however, remained unperformed; for despite the fact that Richard Faltin had proposed the inclusion of *Tannhäuser* in the repertoire, Bergbom did not warm to the idea.[167] In fact, the first Finnish Wagner production was not staged until 1904.[168]

4

Entr'acte: Wagner's Promotional Tour in Russia (1863)

Concerts and Controls

After leaving Riga in 1839, Wagner did not return to Livonia or to any part of northern or eastern Europe. The Baltic world was not to re-enter his life until 1863, when he was invited to give concerts in St. Petersburg and Moscow. This episode requires particular attention, as it marked a turning point in the Russian reception of Wagner. The influence of this visit was reflected in neighboring areas, including Finland.

It was this visit, specifically, that, in Finland and the Baltic provinces, invigorated the reception of Wagner that had begun in the 1850s. That decade had been an extremely lively and productive period, for Wagner had been given the opportunity to travel and conduct concerts in London, Brussels, Paris, Vienna, and Venice. Shortly after the Dresden Uprising, Wagner, now in Zurich, wrote his most significant art-theoretical works. *Rienzi, Der fliegende Holländer*, and *Tannhäuser* were premiered in the 1840s and were followed by *Lohengrin* in 1850. *Tristan und Isolde* was completed during the same decade, but it was not to be premiered until 1865.[1] The most obvious setback to Wagner's career was the Paris premiere of *Tannhäuser* on 13 March 1861, an event that motivated Baudelaire to write his famous essay, "Richard Wagner et Tannhäuser à Paris":[2] a volley of whistling began when the Parisian *jeunesse dorée* (members of the Jockey Club), who had attended the opera only to witness the ballet scene in the second act, were disappointed at the omission of the ballet in its entirety. The rest of the audience remained calm, but—according to the testimony of the Finnish spectator Severin Falkman—the German members of the audience joined in the vocal derision, perhaps in cognizance of the strength of emotion that *Tannhäuser* had evoked at its German premiere.[3] On the other hand, the same opera had been presented in many different localities: in 1849 in Weimar; in 1852 in Schwerin, Breslau (Wroclaw), and Wiesbaden; in 1853, for example, in Riga, Leipzig, Tallinn, Frankfurt am Main, Kassel and Posen (Poznan); in 1854 in Graz; in 1855 in Hanover, Karlsruhe, and Zürich; in 1856 in Munich; and in the following year in

Vienna. The American premiere took place in New York in 1859. The work grew to be so popular that it became a target for parodies. In 1857, Johann Nepomuk Nestroy wrote the musical farce *Tannhäuser und die Keilerei auf Wartburg.*[4]

In the late 1850s and early 1860s, Wagner was already an international celebrity, and the fiasco in Paris only enhanced his reputation. Despite this, he was by no means satisfied with his situation at the time. He still yearned for acceptance and therefore sought a wealthy patron. On receiving an invitation to Russia in November 1862, he simply could not afford to refuse, as the Russians had promised the princely sum of 2,000 silver rubles for two concerts in St. Petersburg.[5]

While traveling to St. Petersburg, Wagner must have recalled his previous visit to the Russian Empire. Conditions in eastern Europe were now much more turbulent than before. In the 1840s, a decisive breakthrough for nationalism had taken place in Russia, where the nationalists had become highly organized and had formed a Slavophile party. The outlook of the Slavophiles was aggressively antagonistic toward western European culture. At the same time, a strong interest in national sovereignty came into existence in the western provinces of the Russian Empire. Its first manifestation was the Polish Rebellion at the beginning of 1863. The Lithuanians joined the resistance, but were unable to salvage the situation. The rebellion was quickly suppressed. All in all, attempts at resistance stirred the zeal of the Slavophiles, who were now aiming for the abolition of the privileged politico-judicial position of the Baltic provinces. From the perspective of the Baltic provinces, the situation was dramatically worsened when the Slavophiles merged to form the largest political party in the Russian Empire.[6]

At the same time, the establishment of the German state was in progress under the leadership of Prussia and Bismarck. The Russians were extremely distrustful of the Germans, though Bismarck had given his assurance that Prussia had no interest in the Baltic Germans.[7] It was therefore no wonder that the Russians became suspicious of Wagner when news of his tour began to spread. Wagner, after all, had fled without a passport from Russia to Prussia and had participated in the rebellion against the King of Saxony in 1849.

Wagner had already heard of the political unrest on his way to St. Petersburg. He spent a night in Königsberg and continued his journey toward the Russian border in the morning:

> With certain uneasy memories of my former illegal passage of this frontier, I carefully scanned the faces of my fellow passengers during the long hours of travel. Among these I was especially struck by one, a Livonian nobleman of German descent, who, in the haughtiest German Tory tone, proclaimed his disgust at the Czar's emancipation of the serfs. He wished

me clearly to understand that any efforts on the part of the Russians to obtain their freedom would receive but scant support from the German nobles settled in their midst. But as we approached St. Petersburg I was genuinely frightened to find our train suddenly stopped and examined by the police. They were apparently searching for various persons suspected of complicity in the latest Polish insurrection, which had just broken out.[8]

Despite the chaotic atmosphere, the train reached its destination on 12 February 1863, according to the local Julian calendar. At the formal reception, orchestral musicians and board members of the Philharmonic Society greeted the guest with words of welcome.[9]

Wagner arrived in St. Petersburg as a much-admired celebrity, but was still remembered as a former revolutionary. Therefore, throughout the visit, he was kept under surveillance by the secret police (that is, the agents of the Third Department of the Ministry of the Interior). An eight-page memorandum on Wagner's movements in Russia has been preserved in the Russian State Archives in Moscow.[10] The two first pages of the memorandum were written in large but illegible handwriting, while the handwriting on the remaining six pages is different and more legible. The first pages are dated 11 February: the police had apparently been waiting for Wagner well before his train arrived.[11] On 12 February, the police stated that Wagner, despite his participation in the 1848 uprisings in Germany, seemed to have settled down.[12] Three days later, a secret observer from the police noted that "Measures have been taken to keep him, as far as is possible, permanently under surveillance."[13]

Apparently, the authorities soon noticed that, with respect to Wagner, there was not much to survey. The reports remained brief, but they do contain detailed, exact descriptions of the first concerts in St. Petersburg. On 20 February the report states:

> Yesterday, during the evening at the House of Nobility, the composer Wagner called, in accordance with the program, both the male and female members of the chorus to the front of the stage and had the National Anthem, "God Save the Tsar," performed: this was rather coolly received by the audience. During the opening chords of the anthem, some members of the audience turned about and left: they were all young men with beards.[14]

"God Save the Tsar" was apparently meant to be a repudiation by Wagner of his reputation as a radical. The genuine revolutionaries expressed their views by leaving. The audience apparently regarded the performance of the anthem as mere flattery, but the rest of the concert was rewarded with stormy applause.

The last report is dated 15 April:

> The well-known composer of music, Richard Wagner, traveled back to his native country. According to the information given by the theater musicians on the day of his departure, Grand Duchess Elena Pavlovna presented Wagner with a contract as a gift, according to which she agreed to buy an estate in the Rhineland for which Wagner had been negotiating. The grand duchess, judging from what has been rumored, paid 10 million gulden for the estate. Last year, Wagner actually lived in Bibrich in the Rhineland, in a house that was built in a park and that he intended to buy.[15]

It is significant that the agents recorded nothing between 20 February and 15 April. Wagner apparently seemed so apolitical that there was nothing to be concerned about, and his behavior at the concerts revealed that he would rather honor the tsar than call for revolution.

From the day of his arrival on 12 February, Wagner was obliged to follow a hectic schedule: ahead of him were three important concerts on 19 and 26 February as well as on 3 March (dates according to the Julian calendar). The concert on 19 February (see figure 4.1) included, in addition to Beethoven's Eroica Symphony, a giant-sized selection of Wagner's works: the Overture and, the Sailors' Chorus from *Der fliegende Holländer*; and the Overture, Pilgrim's Chorus, "Song to the Evening Star," and March from the opera *Tannhäuser*.[16] The program for the other concerts was particularly distinctive, considering that now the St. Petersburg audience could also hear extracts from the forthcoming but yet to be finalized *Ring* tetralogy. Most of these fragments were from *Die Walküre*, but some were from *Siegfried* (the Smelting Song and the Forging Song).[17] The repertoire also contained extracts from *Tristan und Isolde* and *Die Meistersinger*.[18]

After the final concert in St. Petersburg, Wagner immediately departed for Moscow and, amid all the haste, came down with a cold. In Moscow he conducted three concerts and on 19 March returned to St. Petersburg, where he gave another series of three concerts and lectured on his future plans for opera. According to his original schedule, he was to be in St. Petersburg for only a week, but his stay was prolonged until 15 April.

Before his arrival in Russia, Wagner had already provoked discussion and, therefore, the appearance of his music in the repertoire was not surprising. According to Rosamund Bartlett, Wagner's name appeared in the press for the first time in June 1841, when the *Repertuar russkogo teatra* published a translation of Wagner's essay "Über die Overture" ("About the Overture"). The essential breakthrough in his ideas did not, however, take place until the early 1850s, when his writings from the Zürich period became known in Russia.[19] William Weber has pointed out that, initially,

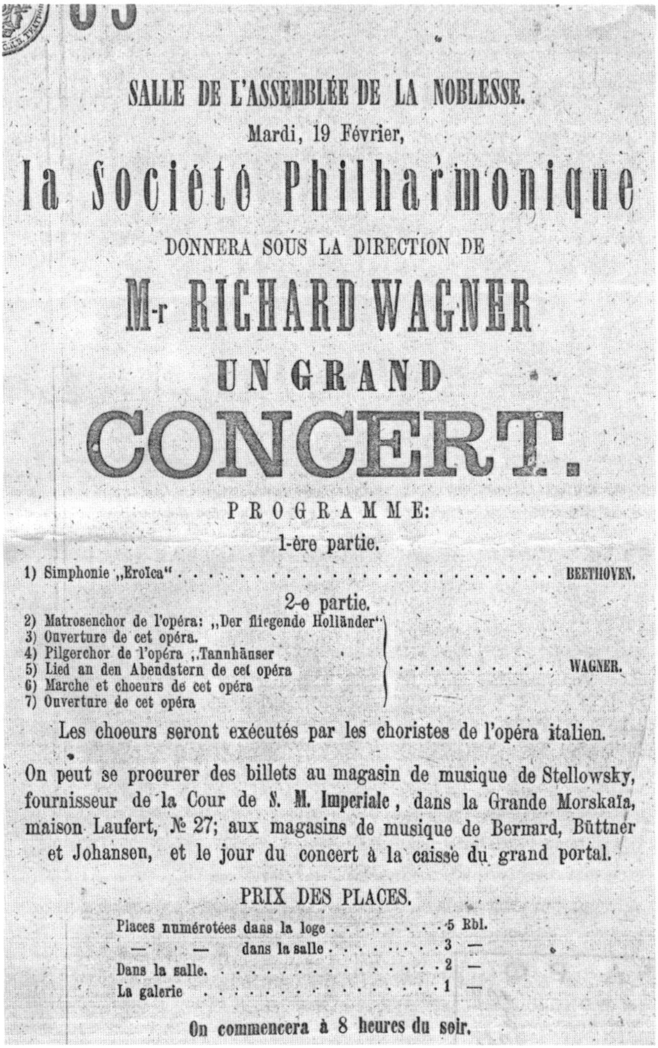

SALLE DE L'ASSEMBLÉE DE LA NOBLESSE.

Mardi, 19 Février,

la Société Philharmonique

DONNERA SOUS LA DIRECTION DE

M-r RICHARD WAGNER

UN GRAND

CONCERT.

PROGRAMME:

1-ère partie.

1) Simphonie „Eroïca" . . . . BEETHOVEN.

2-e partie.

2) Matrosenchor de l'opéra: „Der fliegende Holländer"
3) Ouverture de cet opéra.
4) Pilgerchor de l'opéra „Tannhäuser
5) Lied an den Abendstern de cet opéra . . . . WAGNER.
6) Marche et choeurs de cet opéra
7) Ouverture de cet opéra

Les choeurs seront exécutés par les choristes de l'opéra italien.

On peut se procurer des billets au magasin de musique de Stellowsky, fournisseur de la Cour de S. M. Imperiale, dans la Grande Morskaïa, maison Laufert, № 27; aux magasins de musique de Bernard, Büttner et Johansen, et le jour du concert à la caisse du grand portal.

PRIX DES PLACES.

Places numérotées dans la loge . . . . 5 Rbl.
— — dans la salle . . . . 3 —
Dans la salle. . . . . 2 —
La galerie . . . . 1 —

On commencera à 8 heures du soir.

Figure 4.1. Concert in Russia. Poster advertising Wagner's concert on 19 February 1863. Russian State Archive, Moscow.

Wagner's writings were of greater importance than his music to the spread of his reputation: his theories became known first, and only after that did his music dramas become popular.[20] The same occurred in Russia. As far as is known, Wagner's music was heard for the first time on 15 March 1856 at a concert in which the *Tannhäuser* Overture was performed by the St. Petersburg Philharmonic Society.[21] After this, although Wagner's music was occasionally heard, it was by no means frequently performed.

Wagner's most ardent advocate in Russia during the 1850s and the 1860s was Alexander Serov (1820–71). Like many other Wagnerians, he had come to know his master for the first time through Wagner's literary works; in 1852, he read *Oper und Drama,* but his enthusiasm essentially arose from *Das Kunstwerk der Zukunft,* which he read a year later. In terms of the music, the turning point was his visit to Germany in 1858, during which he heard *Tannhäuser* six times in six days.[22] On 30 July 1858, after the performances in Dresden, he wrote:

> Wagner's work has put me into a naïve astonishment, as though I had never known what theater, drama, or opera were! The brilliant fulfillment of this great undertaking—the fusion of three great forms of art into one single one—is truly astonishing.[23]

This is reminiscent of a religious conversion. To his friends he wrote in expressive words: "I am fascinated by Wagner. I play and rehearse his works, I read about him, talk about him, write about him, preach about him. I am proud to be his apostle in Russia."[24] In the following year, Serov returned to Germany and heard *Lohengrin* in Weimar. He was finally able to meet the composer in Switzerland later.[25] The visit caught Wagner's imagination, and he describes it in his autobiography:

> Alexander Serov from St. Petersburg came to stay some time in the neighborhood. He was a remarkable man, of great intelligence, and openly prepossessed in favor of Liszt and myself. He had heard my *Lohengrin* in Dresden and wanted to know more of me—an ambition I was obliged to satisfy by playing *Tristan* to him in the rough-and-ready fashion peculiar to me.[26]

The interest in Wagner's music was, above all, a question of "party policy." Thanks to Serov's work as a disciple of Wagner, earnest efforts to have Wagner's operas performed in the Russian language soon began in Russia. Serov himself translated the librettos of *Tannhäuser* (1862) and *Lohengrin* (1868).[27] As a result of this, the director of the Imperial theater sought out Wagner in Paris during August 1860, and invited him to come to St. Petersburg to conduct concerts and supervise the finalizing of the Russian production of *Tannhäuser.* Wagner could not agree at that time,, as *Tannhäuser* was being staged in Paris.[28] The visit did not take place until 1863, and the first Russian Wagner production was deferred to 1868, when *Lohengrin* was performed at the Mariinsky theater in St. Petersburg

Serov was a devoted Wagnerian, but many activists in the world of music were critical of the composer. Alexander Dargomyzhsky became acquainted with Wagner for the first time on borrowing a piano transcription of *Tannhäuser* from Serov; he later argued that the employment of the voice in Wagner's work was unnatural. According to Rosamund Bartlett,

Dargomyzhsky was hostile to Wagner because he was afraid that "the music of the future" would have a negative influence on the members of the New Russian Nationalist School—known later as "The Five." The composers of the younger generation, Mili Balakirev, César Cui, Modest Musorgsky, Alexander Borodin, and Nicolai Rimsky-Korsakov, essentially did not see Wagner as a threat and seem to have been totally uninterested in his visit to Russia.[29] (César Cui, however, later participated in the first Bayreuth Festival.[30])

Despite this lack of interest, Wagner's visit caught the attention of the readers of the German and Russian press in St. Petersburg. In the *Severnaya pchela* newspaper, Feofil Tolstoy sharply criticized Wagner's style of conducting. In contrast, Mavriki Rappaport's critique in *Syn otechestva* was full of overwhelming praise. One of the supporters of Wagner was Serov, who wrote for both *Yakor* and *Sankt-Petersburgiskie vedemost*.[31] In many newspaper articles, comprehension of Wagner's music was seen as a victory for Russian culture. Two years earlier, the French had disparaged *Tannhäuser*, but the Russians seemed to be more modern in their attitudes than the French. N. A. Melgugov stated in the *Nashe vremya* that "As a northern people, we Russians are more able than the French (not to mention the Italians) to understand the innovator who has broken all links with routine and boldly thought of re-creating dramatic music on new foundations."[32] The Russian press thus articulated—through Wagner—an appreciation of open sincerity and modernity. The German press in Russia also remembered to emphasize the favorable attitude of the Russian audience toward Wagner in a positive comparison with the attitude of the French. The *St. Petersburger Zeitung* stated that the first concert in St. Petersburg was "a splendid demonstration against French taste."[33] It seems that the taunts in the German press focused on the strong interest in French art that prevailed at the time in St. Petersburg. The critic for the *St. Petersburger Zeitung* was particularly inspired by the fact that the Russians, despite their strong criticism of the German-Russian minority, had acknowledged the power of German art:

> Just as the great and truly educated Russian public keeps its distance from all the petty and malicious attacks against the Germans that are spread by writers in the trivial press, so it is also ready warmly to acknowledge and do homage to the great power of German art.[34]

To the German minority, Wagner's triumph seems to have been a national-political matter: through Wagner's music, the Germans could reinforce their national identity, which was under pressure from the Russian Slavophiles and the French-oriented Russian nobility. It is no wonder that the critic for the *St. Petersburger Zeitung* reminded the readers of the Parisian fiasco, which could be seen as "a mere anti-German demonstration."[35]

In 1863, however, Wagner's music was not, in the main, seen as a musical-political question, though national-political themes were already perceivable in it. Wagner's value as a political symbol became clearer later, when the position of the German minorities in the Baltic provinces of the Russian Empire worsened.

In the spring of 1863, Wagner apparently socialized very little with the Germans of St. Petersburg and Moscow, though he did meet Anton Rubinstein, among others, during the course of his visit. Instead, he had close contact with the music-loving nobility, from whom he expected to obtain considerable and significant financial support. At a dinner arranged at the home of Count Wielhorsky, Wagner met Baron Vietinghoff, whose name later appeared in the lists of visitors to the Bayreuth Festival. On the same occasion, Wagner met the Swedish pianist and composer Ingeborg Stark:

> About the same time, a certain Baron Vietinghoff [Wagner's spelling is Vittinghoff] had also made himself known to me as an enthusiastic lover of music, and honored me with an invitation to his house, where I met once more with Ingeborg Stark, the beautiful Swedish pianist and composer of sonatas, whom I had formerly known in Paris. She amazed me by the impertinent outburst of laughter with which she accompanied the performance of one of the Baron's compositions. On the other hand, she assumed a more serious air when she informed me that she was engaged to Hans von Bronsart.[36]

Without a doubt, Wagner's most significant acquaintance in Russia was Grand Duchess Elena Pavlovna; after the St. Petersburg concert, she presented Wagner with 1,000 rubles and promised to give him a similar sum annually until his economic position improved. In practice, this support never materialized (partly because Wagner was too aggressive in his requests for funds), and he was openly disappointed with the nonpayment of the promised donation at the beginning of 1864.[37] Wagner had intended to return to Russia as soon as possible, but he did not in fact do so, as he suddenly received an invitation to Munich from the king of Bavaria, Ludwig II. After his discovery of the German prince, the assistance of the Russian nobility was no longer required!

"Adieu, charmant pays!"

Interesting—though disputed—traces of Wagner's tour in Russia have survived in an area of Finland close to the Russian border. A heated debate on whether or not Wagner visited the country's eastern border has been going on in Finland since 1863. This debate offers a captivating addition to the Baltic reception of Wagner and therefore deserves a detailed examination

Figure 4.2. Lower pavilion at Imatra rapids. National Museum of Finland.

in this study. As this matter shows, Wagner was a source of speculation perhaps more than any other artist at the time.

During 1809–1917, Finland was part of the Russian Empire. In eastern Finland there was a place of remarkable natural beauty that—particularly at the end of the nineteenth century—became a tourist attraction for the Russian aristocracy: This wonder of nature was the Imatra rapids, close to the present border between Russia and Finland.

It appears that on 2 September 1863, a traveler from Finland, attracted to the rapids, found a penciled note in French among the numerous messages and outbursts of emotion engraved on the roof and columns of the lower pavilion (see figure 4.2) at the waterfall. The inscription, in its entirety, was as follows:

> I am leaving for Germany. Adieu, delightful country! Adieu, my much beloved Russians, a noble and intelligent nation! You alone have known how to appreciate my divine music; you alone have applauded my sublime creations, which were greeted in Paris, that center of ignorance, with whistles! . . . To reward you, my dear Sarmathian music lovers, I swear, before this waterfall, to compose an opera wherein the principal hero shall

be this Imatra; the other roles shall be taken by rocks, by fir trees, by fish, &c. Possibly, it may be worthwhile to insert a man into this scene as well; but that point has not been decided yet.

Richard Wagner.[38]

This inscription was published for the first time in the *Borgå Bladet* newspaper on 3 December 1863 as a Swedish translation. The French original of the inscription was published in the *Åbo Underrättelser* six years later, on 14 August 1869, and on this occasion the editor of the newspaper scrutinized the content of the text.[39] As the 1863 and 1869 texts are identical in their content, there is every reason to suppose that the French text given in the newspaper in 1869 is close to the original text. Unfortunately, the pavilion itself had been destroyed, and, as far as is known, no photograph or any other exact replica of the inscription has survived.

The stories of Wagner's visit to Imatra were revived in 1869 because Wagner was rumored to be sketching an opera titled *Imatra*, that is, the work he had promised to compose in the text penciled on the wall. Many newspapers reported this rumor as fact. According to the Finnish historian Sven Hirn, the rumor appeared for the first time on 24 July 1869 in a Swedish newspaper, *Ny Illustrerad Tidning*, which claimed that "Imatra is the name of Wagner's latest opera."[40] It seems from his correspondence that even Martin Wegelius, the Finnish advocate of Wagner, at this time accepted the story of Wagner's visit to Imatra and the rumor about an opera titled *Imatra*.[41]

Richard Faltin, also known as a Wagnerian, was intrigued to hear of his idol's possible connection with Finland. An envelope, on whose back the content of the inscription of Imatra had been penned, was found inside a copy of Adolf Bernhard Marx's work, *Die Musik des neunzehnten Jahrhunderts* (1855), in Faltin's library. It is impossible to tell whether Faltin had copied it from a newspaper or directly from the pavilion at the Imatra rapids. There is, however, an interesting error in the text. The phrase "Adieu Finlande" has been substituted by Faltin for "Adieu Russes"![42]

The report on the opera *Imatra* and the authenticity of the inscription, found six years earlier went unquestioned in the news items of 1869. This is reflected in the disappointment of the *Åbo Underrättelser*'s editor, as he considered on the egotistic nature of the great artist's thoughts:

Not even in Imatra could he forget his injured pride, and he reacted to one of nature's most sublime landscapes like an opera libretto, good material for one of his own "sublime landscapes," for an opera he promised to compose as repayment for the flattery he was subjected to in St. Petersburg!—An opera created for motives such as these must undoubtedly be called "divine music"![43]

By the end of summer 1869, the news items referring to Wagner's connection with Imatra ceased as mysteriously as they had begun. It is interesting that in the late nineteenth- and early twentieth-century Finnish writings on Wagner, the matter is never discussed. In *Hufvuddragen af den västerländska musikens historia* (1891–93), Martin Wegelius does not even mention Imatra.[44] The matter is also completely neglected by the first Finnish Wagner biographer, Bruno Nurmi.[45]

No information on Wagner's alleged visit to Imatra is to be found in Wagner's literary *Nachlass*, either in his autobiography or in his correspondence. This does not, however, mean that the visit could not have been made. On arriving in St. Petersburg on 12 February, Wagner was in great haste, and he would not have found the time to plan an excursion to Finland. A visit to Imatra would, however, have been possible after his return from Moscow to St. Petersburg. When the concert of 21 March was over, he had a two-week break before his final concerts (2 and 5 April). A letter sent by Wagner to his friend Standhartner is dated St. Petersburg, 27 March. Because the rehearsals for the last concerts took place during the last days of March, the only time when he could possibly have paid a visit to Imatra would have been the period between 22 and 26 March. All in all, however, this is highly improbable, since Wagner intended to devote his last days in St. Petersburg to the search for patrons. Wagner spent his time in the company of the nobility and in the Imperial Court, planning future visits to Russia. These plans, as can be proved, delayed his departure. After the final concert, he remained in St. Petersburg for three days, not leaving until 15 April.

If Wagner had visited Imatra, it would have been between 22 and 26 March. Imatra was one of the greatest tourist attractions of Finland, within reach of St. Petersburg. Imatra was regarded as a remarkable natural wonder, located in the same region as the principal city of Imperial Russia. If one came to St. Petersburg, one would certainly think of making an excursion to the famous tourist site. On the other hand, the rapids were not particularly attractive in March, which was also a poor time for traveling. In his memoirs and other writings, Wagner does not mention any such visit. During his lifetime, Wagner wrote over 10,000 letters, and his correspondence was one of the most voluminous of its time. It would be surprising if, having made the visit, he had never mentioned it, even though—according to the inscription—"he" had been greatly impressed by the scenery.

In Finland, Wagner's purported visit has long posed a serious problem for both scholars and journalists. Tauno Silvonen looked at the news coverage of 1863–69 in the journal *Musiikkitieto* in 1936, but he could not find any easy solution. His article ended with a question: "Did the inscription, faded into the moldering [surface] of the pavilion, come from Wagner's pen—or was it only a misrepresentation of the great artist's human foibles, written by a wicked person?"[46] In 1958, Sven Hirn again raised the problem in his book, *Imatra som natursevärdheten*. He concluded that the inscription was merely a practical joke, basing this on the weather conditions and on the odd choice of French as the language in which it was written.[47] The music critic Seppo Heikinheimo again revived the subject in the columns of the *Helsingin Sanomat* (9 December 1984), putting forward the view of the Bayreuth Museum, that Wagner might have visited Imatra. According to a former curator of the museum, Manfred Eger, Wagner's silence on the matter might have been due to the fact that he visited the place in the company of a duchess from St. Petersburg. Wagner dictated his autobiography to his future wife Cosima, and was not willing to reveal his amorous adventures to her.[48] This seems extremely unlikely, however, for there is no credible reason for Wagner's complete self-censorship of the visit and the possible *Imatra* opera project in his correspondence.

The latest speculation concerning the matter, Petri Sariola's article, "Did Richard Wagner visit Finland?" leans toward Eger's view.[49] No references to the journey to Imatra are found in Richard's literary *Nachlass*, but Sariola focuses attention on a comment found in Cosima's diary that indirectly concerns the matter. In July 1869, Alexander Serov visited the Wagners in Germany. In the entry for Sunday 11 July, Cosima writes: "Serov told me recently that he had found verses carved in the rock near a waterfall in Finland, signed 'Richard Wagner.' But R. has never been there."[50] It is questionable whether Serov himself had seen the inscription, as he claims that it is engraved on a rock. According to Sariola, Cosima could not write about the pavilion, because it would have made readers suspect that Wagner had had a love affair. The year 1869 was a turning point in the relationship between Wagner and Cosima. Cosima, though still married to Hans von Bülow, was living with Wagner, her new amour, and thus it is very likely that neither Wagner nor Cosima were willing to dwell upon anything concerning their past. But in response to Sariola it must be pointed out that in 1863 the situation was altogether different: if Wagner had visited the Imatra rapids, he would certainly have sent a letter from there or commented on his visit in the letters he sent from St. Petersburg. Why should we not take Cosima's remark, "R. has never been there," literally, at its word?

In addition to this, Serov acted as an adviser to Wagner throughout the Russian tour. He had already met Wagner on 12 February, on the composer's arrival in St. Petersburg. Serov would surely have known if Wagner had left the city for several days.

Even if we knew nothing else, the content of the inscription would make us suspect the authenticity of the source. Hirn wondered why the text had been written in French: Wagner was, above all, an advocate of German culture.[51] Even though the writer of the text denigrates the French, one has to keep in mind that aristocrats in St. Petersburg often communicated with each other in that language. In St. Petersburg and Moscow, Wagner conversed, in the main, with aristocrats; thus, it is possible that he chose to write the text in a language that the aristocrats understood.[52] The language by itself is therefore insufficient reason to question the authenticity of the inscription.

In the inscription, the juxtaposition between Paris and Russia is mentioned in a manner similar to that which was employed by the Russian press during Wagner's visit. It is also notable that Wagner, in his autobiography, does not compare his success in Russia to the fiasco in Paris two years earlier.

The inscription was dedicated, in particular, "to the noble and intelligent people" of Russia. The writer appears to regard the Imatra rapids as Russian, though in the nineteenth century many travelers saw them primarily as Finnish (see also the entry in Cosima's diary) and well worth seeing on that basis alone. It is therefore possible that the writer was, if not a Slavophile, at least a patriot from St. Petersburg who was aware that Wagner had visited Russia; the writer may also have heard Wagner's music and, inspired by this, wrote in homage to his own people. In doing this, he may not have been able to resist the temptation to draw attention, ironically, to Wagner's egotism: he makes Wagner emphasize the "nobility" and "divinity" of his own art. Before leaving for Germany, Wagner lectured on his forthcoming opera plans, and he must also have mentioned the *Ring* project, which was now at an advanced level of development: the libretto was being printed and was to be launched later in the spring.[53] Could the writer of the inscription have come across the idea of an opera on the subject of Imatra—having heard that Wagner was planning an opera that would be based on a water course theme (*Das Rheingold*)? A similar misunderstanding may have led to the reports in the Finnish newspapers during July and August 1869. It is probable that the emergence of the *Imatra* opera rumor in the news, six years after the inscription of the text, was due to the fact that the press had received information on an opera that would be premiered in Munich in September of the same year: it was actually *Das Rheingold*, premiered on 22 September 1869.[54] The information on the new opera and the rumors about the Imatra inscription merged. In the fall, when the newspapers confirmed that the name of the opera, after all the consternation over the inscription, was indeed *Das Rheingold*, Finnish newspaper readers and Wagner enthusiasts evidently realized that there was something suspect in the news concerning the Imatra inscription, and therefore Martin Wegelius and Bruno Nurmi refrained from referring to the matter again.

The authenticity of the inscription is, of course, called into question by its ironic tone. The fact that a composer who is famous for his Germanness addresses the Russians as "chers Sarmanthes mélomanes" is mere mockery of Wagner. The Sarmatians were a North Iranian nomadic people, related to the Scythians and living north of the Black Sea. They participated in the

Marcomanni Wars and joined the Germanic tribes during the era of migrations. The name "Sarmatian" was later broadened to encompass a much larger group of people and geographical area. Eastern European (Slavic) peoples in general were called Sarmatians. The roots of this can be dated to 150 A.D. when Ptolemy gave the name Sarmatia to the area that extended from the Vistula River to the Volga. In the north, Sarmatia extended as far as the Gulf of Finland.[55] The Sarmatians are also associated with eastern Europe due to the fact that, as early as the seventeenth century, an ideological movement called Sarmatianism had been spreading in Poland: the movement was based on the belief that the nobility were descended from the Sarmatians. It was connected with the Polish nobility's aspirations for power, and was reflected even in the nobles' mores and attire.[56]

The application of the word "Sarmatian" to Russians is not necessarily value oriented, because the word, generally, at that time, may have been used to mean "Slavic." On the other hand, the word can be interpreted as a metaphor, intended to ridicule Wagner's orientation to the past and his overwhelmingly emphasized Germanness. It must also be remembered that the real Sarmatians finally merged with the Germanic tribes. If one thinks more deeply about the meaning given to the concept of "Sarmatian-ness" in Poland, one could come to the conclusion that the phrase "Sarmanthes mélomanes" could convey a certain irony, as the Sarmatians in Poland were famous for their Spartan lifestyle. To what extent the term Sarmatian was associated with the Poles, the Russians, or, in general, the Slavic people in spring 1863 when the Polish Uprising was crushed remains a riddle. What were the differences between the German and Russian interpretations of the term "Sarmatian" in 1863?

The word "Sarmatian" does not occur in Wagner's literary *Nachlass*. Instead, in the diary entries addressed to Ludwig II and written in September 1865, he frequently employs the term "the Slavic peoples."[57] The general term employed by Wagner for eastern European peoples is "Slavic," not "Sarmatian." It is probable that the term "Slavic peoples" had already become established, and the word "Sarmatian" was used only to give a text an archaic or ironic tone. If Wagner had written the Imatra inscription, he would not have ridiculed the Russians. This seems to be out of the question, given the fact that he was extremely grateful to the Russians for all the understanding he had received during his visit.

Extremely striking in its irony is the claim that Wagner was about to compose an opera in which Nature would be given the leading role, and the human voice would not be heard at all. One should remember that in the 1860s, Wagner represented the most modern idea of art: he intended to remove, totally, from his artistic works, the traditionally singer-centered qualities of the "number opera" and to create a new texture in which the human voice would be only one of many instruments. Is it possible that the idea of an *Imatra* opera in the inscription mocks this modern concept of opera?

Because the inscription attributed to Wagner is, for the time being, the only evidence of a visit to Imatra that has been discovered, and because this inscription appears to be a forgery, there is no reason to believe that the composer visited any other place but St. Petersburg and Moscow during his visit to Russia. The inscription discovered in the lower pavilion at the edge of the Imatra rapids is just one of many literary visiting cards.

It would be important to discover who, in fact, wrote the text, but it is also important to note the facts concerning the reception of Wagner in Russia that are found in the text. The writer was very likely a Russian aristocrat who had read about Wagner's visit. In addition to this, the writer had acquired at least a preliminary knowledge of Wagnerian modernism. The forger must also have been aware of Wagner's Germanness and his anti-Frenchness. The fact that the text was not written by Wagner docs not mean it is without historical value: the text and the news coverage concerning it are part of the history of Wagnerism: after all, they document attitudes toward Wagner's works and personality in the Baltic world.

Cries and Whispers:

Early Swedish Encounters with Wagner

"Oh! Wagner, Wagner! I Must Cry Out!"

When considering Wagner's reception in the Baltic world, it is worth bearing in mind that until the 1860s, Sweden was to some extent isolated from the discourse on Wagner. His music was indeed performed, but mainly as music at home or as concert pieces. Wagner was already being discussed during the 1850s—as is exemplified by the letters J. A. Josephson from Uppsala exchanged with Topelius—but this kind of discourse seldom became public. Nor did it appear in newspapers.

Interest in Wagner's works or ideas could, however, be kindled during travels and vacations in Germany. One of the leading Wagnerians in Sweden was August Söderman (see figure 5.1), whose enthusiasm for Wagner originated in such a journey. Söderman studied at the Leipzig Conservatory in 1856–57.[1] On 18 December 1856, at a concert given by the Leipzig Gewandhaus Orchestra, he heard Wagner's Faust Overture, which greatly influenced him. At this time, he had not yet seen a complete performance of a Wagner opera. Despite this, he was doubtlessly aware of the debate on Wagner through the news. In his letters, he reflected on the question of Wagner with an early Wagner enthusiast, Fritz Arlberg. In February 1857 he wrote to his friend:

> I am willing to put up with Wagner's every defeat, since, I believe, he wins new honors every time that one of his compositions has "durchgefallen." Wagner was condemned, and considered by the public at large, as a crazy visionary, but it is clear today that there are those who understand his music—those who admit it as the product of genius—and the majority of these persons, moreover, are themselves recognized persons of genius too (for instance, Liszt, possibly Wagner's *greatest* admirer in *all* respects). This raises the question: who is in the *right*? the public at large, or the great genius?[2]

The more Wagner was disparaged, the more Söderman's sympathy for him increased. The letter also shows that Söderman's attitude was positive even

Figure 5.1. August Söderman (1832–76). Archives of the Royal Theaters, Sweden.

before he had had the chance to evaluate Wagner's works: could a genius like Franz Liszt be so badly mistaken?

Söderman's interest stemmed essentially from a *Tannhäuser* perform-ance conducted by Liszt in Leipzig on 4 March 1857. In May of that year, he attended another performance, in which the title role was sung by a visiting Bohemian tenor, Tichatschek, whose reputation as a singer of Wagner was unique at the time.[3] After hearing *Tannhäuser* for the second time, Söder-man wrote in his notebook:

The Wagnerian masterpiece made an even greater impression upon me this evening than on the previous occasion when I heard it, although then conducted by Liszt. . . . it went much better than this time; yet a master-piece—be it performed well or badly—is, and remains, a masterpiece. When one hears this music, it is if one were transported to another world—one sits with breath held, as if afraid of falling back to earth.[4]

In the history of music, there is scarcely any figure with the exception of Wagner who has excited such intense, almost religious emotions. The words of August Söderman could be those of an entire generation. The first experience of Wagner's music is characterized as a transcendental, supra-mundane event in which the master revealed "another world" to humankind. In the same way, the *Rigasche Zeitung*'s resident critic wrote in January 1853 that Wagner had shown people the road to "another contin-ent," a place that did not exist beyond the oceans but in the depths of our true self, "in der Tiefe."[5]

The religious tone of the rhetoric employed in Söderman's notebook culminates in ecstatic words: "I cry tears of joy in my heart that this music is written—Oh! Wagner, Wagner! I must cry out!"[6] It is difficult to know whether these "tears of joy" were caused by the feelings that captured Söderman during the performance or whether they were derived from an awareness that Wagner represented a point of entry into areas of dispute. Söderman was thoroughly familiar with Wagner's theories. During his time in Leipzig, he had acquired Wagner's *Das Kunstwerk der Zukunft* and *Oper und Drama*.[7] As may be seen in the letter to Fritz Arlberg, Söderman had adopted an emphatically positive attitude toward his idol even before hear-ing any of Wagner's works. The situation certainly created a feeling that one should, somehow, react to those works. Wagner had put forward views of the future—visionary ideas—and he was ready to accept the role of a prophet. This consciousness of the beginning of an epoch, or rather a consciousness of a real turning point in the history of music, influenced the act of listening which became characterized by features like those of conversion—or at least there was a strong motivation to describe it in conversional terms. An interesting feature here is that conversion under such circumstances also meant a form of submission; this experience could not be resisted. One should allow the music to overwhelm one. The descriptions of conversions to Wagnerism stress the role of overwhelming emotionalism. On the other hand, Wagner became known in the early 1850s for his operatic theories, and it might be suggested that if Wagneri-ans took the theories as their point of departure, their way of listening to the operas would have been expected to be unemotional or based in rea-son. It is possible, instead, that Wagnerians actually took Wagner's concept of *Gefühlsverständis* as a guide, and tried to understand through emotion, rather than reasoning.

Another feature distinguishable in the early experiences of Wagner is addiction. Wagner's music is described as being uncompromisingly irresistible, to the extent that one is "forced" to listen to it as much and as often as possible. Alexander Serov had listened to *Tannhäuser* six times in Dresden. The Finnish composer and conductor Armas Järnefelt later said that he had heard *Tristan und Isolde* on fifteen successive occasions in standing room in Berlin.[8] Even though this took place as late as 1890, it can be compared to Söderman's description of conversion. Armas Järnefelt comments upon his own enthusiasm: "Then Wagner entered my life like a fever that seizes a man in total indiscreet rapture, a state that cannot be compared to any other except that of a passionate enamored infatuation, which also lacks in judgment, hesitation, and the senses of sight and hearing—if one is allowed to use the last—mentioned word in a discussion concerning music."[9] Järnefelt compares his enthusiasm over Wagner to "the passionate infatuation" of youth. Most of the Wagner converts were young people, which makes it possible to interpret the birth of Wagnerism as a conflict between generations: the opponents of Wagner were often members of the older generation.

In any case, signs of Wagnerism are already perceivable in people like August Söderman. This developed into a real "fan" culture, a commitment to an idol and a "cherished personality" cult in Germany and the Baltic world in the 1870s, but those who felt kinship with Söderman were, all things considered, in a key position in this process. Söderman contributed to the staging of the first Wagner productions in Sweden. He served as the chorus master at the Royal Opera from 1860 until March 1875.[10] He was also a composer, cultivating influences from Wagner in his works, though—instead of opera—he concentrated on short pieces of vocal music. A good example is the ballad *Der schwarze Ritter* (*The Black Knight*, 1874), which perfectly summarized his Wagnerian influences.[11]

Another significant figure in the first phase of the Swedish reception of Wagner was singer Fritz Arlberg (see figure 5.2), who accepted the role of an advocate of German influences, regularly visiting Dresden to seek out what was new and fresh in the air.[12] He later became known as a director, singer, and translator of librettos into the Swedish language at the Royal Opera House. Arlberg belonged to that class of opinion leaders who had taken on the role of missionaries and devoted themselves to the importation of Wagner's music into Sweden. As far as Sweden is concerned, the history of the reception of Wagner deviates from developments on the eastern side of the Baltic Sea, inasmuch as production of the operas began considerably later. This generated the idea that Sweden had delayed its reception of Wagner because it had not been able to follow the new, modern trends in music. This inspired Söderman and Arlberg to begin their mission work and to correct the imbalance in regard to the nation's music.

Figure 5.2. Fritz Arlberg (1830–96). Archives of the Royal Theaters, Sweden.

Rienzi as Zukunftsmusik

Sweden differs significantly from Finland, Estonia, and Livonia in that opera had been under royal patronage since the eighteenth century. This difference should not be seen, in keeping with modern views, as a national difference, for the musical influence of royalty was mainly felt in Stockholm and its surrounding area. The question was more one of local, not

national, differences. In Stockholm, the king patronized the operatic theater in the same way as the tsar did in St. Petersburg. On both stages, Wagner appeared relatively late in the 1860s, and the essential breakthrough
did not take place until the 1870s.

Evidently, Wagner was more successful in national than in royal culture, but Russia was an exception. In St. Petersburg, the nobility had
become so interested in Wagner that the composer was personally invited
to the Imperial City. Alexander Serov himself acted as agent for his idol,
and strove to arrange a performance of *Tannhäuser* at the Mariinsky theater. In Serov's opinion, *Tannhäuser* was "the best foreign modern opera."
His plan, however, did not materialize, as the board of directors of the
opera house accepted the proposal of young conductor Eduard Nápravník,
who chose *Lohengrin*. Accordingly, the premiere of *Lohengrin* took place on
4 October 1868: *Tannhäuser* did not appear in the repertoire until six years
later, on 13 December 1874.[13]

In St. Petersburg, the Wagner repertoire was introduced according
to the usual pattern, the opening performances being *Tannhäuser* and
Lohengrin. In Stockholm, the situation was entirely different: the first Wagner production by the Royal Opera was *Rienzi*, a choice that, in terms of the
1860s, was extremely unfashionable. As is shown by the investigations of
Gösta Percy, *Tannhäuser* and *Lohengrin* dominated concert programs in
Stockholm. It might seem likely that concert performances aroused an
interest in performance of these particular operas. The Royal Opera House
was not, however, bound to succumb to market pressures. The operas that
were to enjoy a preferential position in the repertoire could be chosen with
considerable freedom.

The selection of *Rienzi* was a logical consequence of the fact that the
Royal Opera in Stockholm was, traditionally speaking, extremely French
oriented. *Grand opéra* was still—as late as the 1860s—a dominant genre,
and it would, therefore, have been quite natural to want a stage production
of one of Wagner's more French-influenced operas. The Swedish theater
historian Göran Gademan has shown that the most pivotal source of influence in Sweden was Paris: and it was to Paris that August Bournonville,
Ludvig Josephson, and Frans Hedberg journeyed in search of inspiration.[14]
This was reflected in the repertoire of the opera: during the 1860–82 period
(which was the subject of Gademan's research), the largest percentage of
performances consisted of French opera, 52 percent in all. This figure covers not only premieres but all performances, and it also offers some clues as
to the kinds of works that were popular. In the seasons from 1859–60 to
1882–83, there were 3,963 operatic performances in the opera house, of
which 2,052 were French operas (by composers such as Auber, Halévy,
Hérold, and Meyerbeer). There were no more than a hundred Wagner
performances, while there were 392 performances of other German
operas.[15] Even though Wagner was established in the repertoire of the

opera house, Wagner performances made up only a small share of the total. The only opera by Wagner performed in the 1860s was *Rienzi*, which was staged on eleven occasions during 1865–66 and on five occasions during the 1870–71 season.[16]

When the first Wagner production was staged in Stockholm in spring 1865, Eugène von Stedingk acted as the director and Ludvig Norman as the court conductor at the Royal Opera. Norman was more interested in symphonic music and was therefore willing to leave the baton in the hands of Söderman.[17] A significant agent in the choice of *Rienzi*, however, was Fritz Arlberg. During his visits to Dresden, he had become acquainted with the chamber singer of the Royal Court of Saxony, Joseph Tichatschek (1807–86), who had sung in the premiere of *Rienzi*. Due to Arlberg's persuasion, Tichatschek arrived in Stockholm in spring 1863 and gave a guest performance in Meyerbeer's *Le prophète*.[18] Apparently, Arlberg was influential in the selection of *Rienzi* for the repertoire. It is also feasible that the idea of its inclusion originated with Tichatschek. Hence it is possible that the forthcoming performance had already been agreed upon during Tichatschek's 1863 visit to Stockholm and that, at the singer's request, the choice had been *Rienzi*. Arlberg's own enthusiasm for Wagner probably affected the choice. But why did he, as an expert on Wagner, advocate the unfashionable Rienzi, which did not at this time—even in Wagner's opinion—deserve a new series of performances? A probable explanation, as we have seen, is the tradition of the Stockholm Royal Opera, which greatly favored *grand opéra*. Maybe Arlberg believed that this would be a good means of making the public familiar with Wagner's music. Arlberg was therefore willing to offer the leading role to his friend, Tichatschek, who had sung the title role at the *Tannhäuser* premiere in Paris, but it is also possible that the 1861 fiasco in Paris was still fresh in people's minds and therefore *Tannhäuser* would not have been a wise selection. *Rienzi* was a more suitable alternative.

Shortly before the premiere of *Rienzi*, the name Wagner began to appear in Stockholm's newspapers. The *Tannhäuser* catastrophe in Paris and Wagner's miraculous salvation from destruction at the court of the Bavarian king in 1864 were widely reported by the media, and these reports also aroused attention in Stockholm. In March 1865, *Aftonbladet* was quick to report that "Richard Wagner has now fallen into disgrace with his high patron, the reigning king of Bavaria, and he will leave Munich in the near future."[19] This information was based on a claim published in a Munich newspaper, the *Neueste Nachrichten*, on 12 February, insinuating that Wagner had dishonored himself before Ludwig II. The same suggestion was repeated in an Augsburg paper, the *Allgemeine Zeitung*, on 14 February.[20] On the following day, Wagner himself responded by repudiating these claims.[21] Behind these rumors was an incident that had taken place on 5 February, resulting in a situation in which Ludwig refused to give an audience to Wagner.[22] Two days after Wagner's response, the misapprehension was cleared up, but this did not save Wagner from unfavorable publicity. The *Allgemeine Zeitung* published an article, "Richard Wagner und die öffentliche Meinung" ("Richard Wagner and Public Opinion"), that was a direct attack on Wagner. According to the newspaper article, the former "Barricadenmann" (man of the barricades) had unscrupulously exploited the king.[23] A detailed scrutiny of the incident is unnecessary here, but, in fact, the affair mainly concerned the strained relationship between king and press. Public opinion in Bavaria finally gave Wagner no option but to depart in December 1865. Thus, his departure did not take place "in the near future" as *Aftonbladet* had predicted, and the reason for Wagner's departure was not "his high patron, the reigning king" but rather the adverse publicity, in which *Aftonbladet* had itself participated.

All things considered, the newspapers did not provide a fully accurate picture of Wagner's conduct. A good example of misinformation is a news item published by *Aftonbladet* on 9 May 1865 on preparations for *Rienzi*, in which the opera was described as the composer's best-known work:

> Activity at the royal theaters continues unabated. On the lyrical stage, preparations are underway for Richard Wagner's *Rienzi*, possibly his most popular work, and one of the most magnificent operas ever performed. It is expected that the preparations will be complete by the end of the month, when Herr Tichatschek, who is to sing the title role, is expected here.[24]

It is difficult to assess this sort of misinformation concerning the popularity of *Rienzi*; one could perhaps conclude that it was not a misunderstanding at all but a deliberate exaggeration that would attract much larger audiences to attend the performance.

In any case, while Wagner was toiling over the preparations for the Munich premiere of *Tristan und Isolde*, *Rienzi* was staged in Stockholm on 8 June 1865. The timing was unwise, as temperatures were rising, and the heat of the summer was ahead. Apparently Tichatschek's schedule did not allow an earlier date for the premiere, a supposition that is supported by *Aftonbladet*'s report that the heroic tenor would not be coming to the city before the beginning of June. The stage direction of *Rienzi* was by Fritz Arlberg, the ballet scene was choreographed by Théodore Martin, and the scenic designer was Fritz Ahlgrensson. The libretto was translated into Swedish by Arlberg himself.[25] Aside from Tichatschek, the most important roles were sung by Fredrika Stenhammar as Irene, Conrad Behrens as Colonna, and Agnes Jacobsson as Adriano.[26] The newspaper reports constantly reminded readers that a genuine spectacle on a large scale was being prepared. The performance of *Rienzi* was to be one of the costliest productions of the opera, and this helped to generate considerable pressure to raise ticket prices. At the same time, the public was repeatedly reminded that Rienzi had been one of Tichatschek's greatest triumphs.[27]

Immediately after the first night, the *Post-och inrikes tidningar* published a short news item on the occasion:

> Yesterday evening there was the first performance of Richard Wagner's opera *Rienzi*, with Herr Tichatschek in the title role. The performance was superb, and the music imposing. Herr Tichatschek was greeted with applause on his first entrance, and was called back for applause after each act. The audience was excited in the extreme.[28]

The premiere had been sold out and the auditorium was full; this was also reported in the other newspapers.[29] Tichatschek's performance was especially praised. The tenor, the star of the evening, was called to the front of the stage after each act, and after the third act, he delighted the audience by appearing on horseback.[30]

The reception of the work in reviews of the performance was clearly positive. *Aftonbladet* dealt only briefly with the interpretation of the work in the production, noting Tichatschek's "artistic and energetic" performance. The critic at *Aftonbladet* concentrated largely on the opera itself. From the very beginning, the opera seemed to be a trickily constructed mass of sounds, which caused problems for the orchestra. The work was far from being an all-embracing, coherent whole, but the composer had been able to rise to the level of his lofty subject. What was best about *Rienzi*, according to *Aftonbladet*, was that the composer had not been tempted to imitate effects that in recent operas had become so trivialized. These effects had resulted in a stylistic eclecticism of which Wagner could not be accused. On the other hand, only a few impressive set pieces could be distinguished in the work: the opera contained many choral scenes, marches, and other ensemble scenes, but there were very few arias. According to the critic for *Aftonbladet*, Wagner had thus succeeded in creating an idiosyncratic style of his own.[31]

The *Dagens Nyheter* also reviewed the performance. On 9 June, the paper noted that "this is the first of Wagner's operas that has appeared on the Swedish stage."[32] It also mentioned that Wagner was one of those talented composers who wrote both the text and the music for their works. An account of the plot of the opera takes up most of the review. Finally the critic comes to the music itself:

> The opera was performed in an outstanding manner, and the modern public appeared to display a greater affinity for the music of the future than one might have anticipated, at least if one is to judge by the powerful applause that resounded around the chamber. The music also has abundant moments of great beauty; those that appeared to strike the public most were the magnificent choral parts—inter alia one might mention

among the loveliest the church choir in the first act, and the song of the messengers of peace in the second.[33]

An interesting feature of the review is that *Rienzi* is connected to the music of the future; another is the fact that the Swedish audience, according to the critic, had received the new music with more enthusiasm than could have been expected.

The idea of interpreting *Rienzi* as new, reformed music was not confined to the critic for the *Dagens Nyheter*: a similar interpretation can be seen in the review in the *Post-och inrikes tidningar*, apparently written by C. V. A. Strandberg:[34]

> In this opera, one can hear the inception of a new, reshaped music, of which Wagner can still be regarded as the most distinguished representative. Since the aspirations embodied in the "music of the future" cannot as yet be said to have achieved a lasting result, it may perhaps be still too soon to pronounce an overall judgment upon it. With respect to *Rienzi* in particular, what arouses one's unreserved interest is the serious quest for dramatic truth that permeates the entire work, and the energy of feeling and warmth of imagination that support it all; although on the other hand one admittedly feels unable clearly and distinctly to identify the adequate expression of melodic forms—somewhat in the same manner as, in a tropical forest, no wider prospects can be discerned by the eye, since the whole presents an interwoven, luxuriant mass of trunks only half distinguishable, curiously twisted branches, and an all-covering colorful foliage.[35]

The writer stresses the idea that Wagner is still the best-known representative of the reformed music, but it is too early to judge the significance of the new movement. This, after all, would have been premature, when most of the people of Sweden could have no idea of what Wagner's music was like. In addition to *Der fliegende Holländer*, *Tannhäuser*, and *Lohengrin*, *Tristan und Isolde* were already available. *Tristan und Isolde*, in particular, represented a change in Wagner's work. The three preceding works had been described by Wagner as "great romantic operas." In *Tristan*, Wagner began to experiment with entirely new possibilities. In 1854, he had read Arthur Schopenhauer's work, *Die Welt als Wille und Vorstellung*, which greatly influenced his view on art.

In the Sweden of June 1865—or, for that matter, anywhere else—people had no inkling of the revolutionary change that this work of Wagner's would create in music. It also seems apparent, however, that Swedish music critics did not know much about the composer's Romantic period. In the reviews in *Aftonbladet*, the *Dagens Nyheter*, and the *Post-och inrikes tidningar*, there is no mention of Wagner's other works. This seems strange, for *Tannhäuser* had certainly been seen by many students during their journeys to Germany, and descriptions of this opera had appeared in German music periodicals. It is precisely through such publications that Topelius was able to refer to *Tannhäuser* as early as 1857, even though he had not yet seen the work. In addition to this, some of the music from *Tannhäuser* and *Lohengrin* had been performed at concerts. It appears that Wagner was known only in extremely limited circles in Sweden, and the critics for the *Dagens Nyheter* and *Post-och inrikes tidningar* were not members of these circles. The critics had apparently acquired information on the music of the future through publications and music performances, but they were hardly familiar with Wagner's theoretical writings, as they mistakenly classified *Rienzi*—which was composed as a *grand opéra*—as the music of the future ("framtidsmusik").

Neither were the reviewers aware of Wagner's *"Zukunftsmusik,"* written in 1860, in which Wagner denied the entire concept enunciated in the title. Of the larger Stockholm newspapers, only the *Nya Dagligt Allehanda* kept abreast of the situation. During the years 1860–71, its music critic was Wilhelm Bauck (see figure 5.3), who was also a teacher of the history of music and aesthetics at the Royal Academy of Music, a professor at the conservatory and a composer at the same time. Bauck had studied in Berlin from 1856 to 1857, at the same time that Söderman was in Leipzig.[36] It is highly possible that Bauck had already heard *Tannhäuser* by that time, for he gave the impression in his later writings that he had been familiar with the work for some time. Such, for instance, is the impression given by Bauck's 1861 review of Mr. Richard's concert in which fragments from *Tannhäuser* were performed.[37]

Writing about *Rienzi*, Bauck proves to be, in the main, a music historian. He begins by surveying the development of the grand tragic/heroic opera from Lully to Rameau and from Gluck to Spontini, also classifying Naumann's opera, *Gustaf Wasa*, as part of this tradition. Now a controversial composer, Richard Wagner had continued in the spirit of French *grand opéra*.[38] Bauck was clearly aware of the background to *Rienzi*, stating that it had originated in 1839 during Wagner's Riga and Paris periods, and that it had been premiered in Dresden as early as 1842.[39]

Even though many of the Stockholm critics regarded *Rienzi* as a deviation from Giacomo Meyerbeer's style, mainly due to the composer's ingrained personal voice and his avoidance of the standard effects, Bauck sees a clear resemblance between *Rienzi* and Meyerbeer's works. It is possible that the spread of information about the music of the future forced other critics to look in desperation for change in works that had nothing to do with it. According to Bauck, Wagner strove—following Meyerbeer—for grandiose theatrical effects using processions and other massive ensemble scenes. In this respect, Wagner even surpasses Meyerbeer.[40]

According to Bauck, the drama in *Rienzi* was not in harmony with the stylistic devices. Unlike Meyerbeer's works, *Rienzi* did not create an atmosphere of time and place, that is, an impression of historicity. Far more

CARL WILHELM BAUCK.

Figure 5.3 Carl Wilhelm Bauck (1808–77). Reproduced by Marie Persson, the Royal Library, National Library of Sweden.

dominant than the historical atmosphere was the erotic element that Wagner wished to emphasize in his libretto. This was too weak an element to constitute the raw material for a versatile drama. Nevertheless, Bauck attaches a great deal of importance to Wagner:

> Although it is irrefutable that Wagner's production encompasses far too few elements to generate a more comprehensively based dramatic vitality,

it must nevertheless be recognized that within this more limited scope he has developed an unusual power, a living spirit, a design of massive, even at times imposing dimensions, and that this all springs from an imagination that surrounds all that enters its purview with burning colors.[41]

Because *Rienzi* was, according to Bauck, the composer's "first" work (which was untrue), he had not yet, in Bauck's view, learned to control his techniques: "This can be noted in the harmonies and modulations, curious and far-fetched at times, which sound strange, yet fail to surprise, and are unusual, without originality."[42] Bauck states that Wagner had been accused of poor insight in terms of the inventiveness of his melodies. Unlike the accusers, Bauck believes that although "we would not wish to call it unusually rich, yet this freshness cannot be overlooked, and is similarly in evidence in *Rienzi*."[43]

It is interesting that in his analysis, Bauck also refers to Wagner's future development. *Rienzi* was, without doubt, a promising work, but it also included elements that would later lead Wagner along the wrong paths. In *Rienzi*, Wagner was already willing to create unusual harmonies and modulations. According to Bauck, Wagner was not content to simply create something great; he strove for something unprecedented, and it was precisely this unprecedentedness that led to clashes of opinion. According to Bauck, this goal had blurred Wagner's capacity for self-criticism, and the succeeding works did not contain what *Rienzi* had promised.[44]

In *Tannhäuser* this baroque-grotesque mannerism reached a peak that—notwithstanding certain details of some beauty—can be said virtually to constitute the negation of musical civilization in the nineteenth century. At length, however, a kind of Nemesis brought *Tannhäuser* to the country that is the home of grace and refined taste, where it was the object of the most notable fiasco that has ever befallen any opera.[45]

Bauck refers to the Parisian *Tannhäuser* fiasco, in which "the home of grace and refined taste" rejected Wagner's projects out of hand. In *Rienzi*, Bauck had already discovered in embryonic form the richly baroque features of the grotesque that would later flourish in *Tannhäuser*. One might characterize Bauck as an anti-Wagnerian who was later hailed as a critic of Wagner. In all probability, Bauck's critical attitude hindered the reception of Wagner in Sweden. Bauck was an influential figure in the Swedish world of music: as a teacher he also influenced local students of music and their viewpoints on the new movements in music.

In the climate of the 1860s, Wagner did not attract many advocates in terms of Swedish publicity. The most ardent supporters of Wagner—Fritz Arlberg, August Söderman, and singer Fredrika Stenhammar—were for the most part influential on the performing side. The influence of the triumvirate was remarkable, for example, in the production of *Rienzi,* but their enthusiasm did not extend to the achievement of positive publicity during the 1860s. At the same time, Swedish critics, especially Wilhelm Bauck, took a rather reserved stand on Wagner. This probably slowed or minimized the success of Wagner's works on the Swedish stage. *Rienzi* was performed five times in summer 1865 and six times during the next season, 1865–66, but after that, the opera lost its audience.[46] The next Wagner premiere had to wait until 1872.

6

Institutionalizing a Composer

"The Emperor of New German Music"

After the scandal in Paris, the Wagner front was generally quiet for some time. There were performances but mainly in German theaters. In his letter to the publisher Franz Schott, Wagner listed all the towns that had sent him royalties by 20 November 1861, and the list of forty-six cities includes only a few from abroad. The composer, in fact, expresses his hope that the interest of outer-German, "ausser-deutsche," theaters, such as those in Stockholm, St. Petersburg, and Copenhagen, would increase in the future. Riga was, for Wagner, clearly a German center.[1]

In Sweden the only Wagner opera performed in the 1860s was *Rienzi*, and in Riga none of the composer's operas were premiered in that decade. At the beginning of the 1860s, the German Theater of Riga had drifted into a crisis on both the economic and the artistic levels, which brought all experimental efforts with new and unknown works to a halt. On 6 April 1861, the *Rigasche Stadtblätter* addressed this problem, noting that under the pressure of prevailing circumstances the orchestra had been reduced to twenty-four musicians. After the departure of Franz Thomé, the theater had rapidly fallen into decay.[2] The decline was, however, temporary, because the building of a new playhouse, to be opened in 1863, was to re-energize the theater.[3]

Tannhäuser, which had been the Livonians' perennial favorite, was occasionally staged: according to Carl Friedrich Glasenapp, the performance figures for *Tannhäuser* were as follows: it was performed twice in 1861, six times in 1864, twice in 1866, three times in 1867, and twice in 1869.[4] The statistics clearly do not indicate any signs of enthusiasm for Wagner. The repeat premiere of *Der fliegende Holländer* in November 1864 could be seen as a more vigorous attempt to revive interest in the composer. Apparently, interest in Wagner waned in the 1860s, for relatively small audiences attended the performances of *Der fliegende Holländer*. On 19 November, the *Rigasche Stadtblätter* reported that "Despite the good production of this opera in our theater, the first and second repeats of the work have been poorly attended, and the work is now in danger of being excluded from the repertoire."[5]

The Wagner front thus became quiet on both sides of the Baltic Sea. There are many reasons for this. The setback suffered by *Tannhäuser* in Paris had, doubtless, impeded the advance of Wagnerian innovation. More specifically, in French-oriented music centers such as Stockholm and St. Petersburg, the preconceptions of the public were apparently reinforced by the catastrophic Paris premiere. Another, far more significant, reason for this situation was the undeniable fact that Wagner's own productivity seemed to have slowed down. In the 1850s, *Der fliegende Holländer*, *Tannhäuser*, and *Lohengrin* quickly spread throughout Europe. At the same time, there had been an ongoing debate on the writings of Wagner's Zürich period and on the music of the future. In the 1860s the situation was entirely different: Wagner was still writing diligently, but he was not aiming for publicity in the same way as he had done previously. In his composing he concentrated on the completion of the *Ring* tetralogy, which did not take a definite shape until the 1870s. The planning of the tetralogy was part of the reason for the surprisingly long breaks between the premieres of Wagner's operas. *Lohengrin* had been premiered in 1850. The next work, *Tristan und Isolde*, was staged for the first time fifteen years later, in 1865. Besides this, only unfounded rumors about forthcoming innovatory work circulated; this did not inspire opera houses to call for new Wagner premieres. Wagner had published his poetic text *Der Ring des Nibelungen* in 1863, and this had a calming effect on the operatic world, which now settled down to wait for the new opera.

One must keep in mind that Wagner, in the 1850s, was still a touring conductor living on publicity. The situation changed when he was pardoned in 1861 and his return to German soil became possible. His adventures on the barricades were forgiven, and it appeared that the revolutionary had now quieted down. Simultaneously, the debate between the music journalists on the revolution in music and the music of the future came to an end. Wagner became increasingly interested in Germany and Germanness, although in a different sense than in the 1840s. When he was invited to the court of Ludwig II in 1864, he decided to concentrate on his great operatic project and endeavor to attain the position of a nationally accepted artist. Wagner wanted to acquire the blessing of the state and become an institution. Around the mid-1860s, Wagner was thus far less of a public figure, as he consciously directed himself toward the political powers, and this change is important to bear in mind from the perspective of the Wagnerian reception. Before this, he had dreamt of success in the main music centers of Europe. The setback in Paris, however, had meant an end to this hope, and once he was invited to Bavaria the offers of the aristocrats of St. Petersburg no longer seemed so tempting. The invitation to Munich was reported widely in the press. For instance, in May 1864, the *Rigasche Stadtblätter* reported that "the young King of Bavaria, Ludwig II, has sent Richard Wagner, the composer of *Tannhäuser*, an invitation as a result of which he will be endowed with a residence in Munich and an annual honorarium of 1200 gulden."[6]

The new situation encouraged Wagner to envisage a union of the German monarch and the artist. In consequence he produced a diary for Ludwig II, outlining a political program in which he tried to make the young king understand his role as a prince who might unite the divided German nation. The question of a united Germany was to trouble Wagner throughout the second half of the 1860s. The accelerating nationalism was heightened by military conflict. In the Austro-Prussian War (1866), Bavaria was allied with Austria, and thus came to be on the losing side. Following this, Wagner decided that it would be impossible for Bavaria and Ludwig to have any role in the unification of Germany. After 1866, Wagner began to orient himself more toward Prussia.[7] At the same time, he was again inspired to continue his literary work. The result was a series of articles, "Deutsche Kunst und deutsche Politik," which originally appeared in the *Süddeutsche Presse* in September to December 1867, and was reprinted in book form in 1868.[8] In his nationalistic writing, Wagner denigrated French civilization and described German culture as "the spring of the rebirth of the whole of mankind."[9] Besides these writings, Wagner finished *Die Meistersinger*, which, in terms of his German audience, produced a rebirth of interest in his work. The opera was premiered in Munich on 21 June 1868. *Tristan und Isolde*, premiered three years earlier, did not cause such a sensation: it was, after all, *Die Meistersinger* that, from the publicity viewpoint, seemed to continue the project that had originated in the 1850s. *Die Meistersinger* was a great success, particularly in German opera houses during the years 1869–70. In January 1869, it was performed in Dresden and Dessau, in February in Karlsruhe, and in March in Weimar and Mannheim. In 1870 the triumph continued; in February the work was performed in Vienna, and in March in Königsberg; in April it was Berlin's turn, and in December it was Leipzig's.[10]

Die Meistersinger aroused the attention of the international music world: it was, for instance, reported on both in Sweden and in Livonia. After a long silence, Wagner had created a popular piece that was comparable to *Tannhäuser*. Despite this, *Die Meistersinger* remained, for a long time and for a good reason, a wholly German phenomenon. The foreign opera houses decided to wait. In all probability, the news coverage concerning the national characteristics of *Die Meistersinger* caused the reservations. Could a comic opera created for Germans arouse the interest of foreign audiences who were accustomed to the serious features of *Tannhäuser*? One interesting matter is that, according to the Latvian musicologist Vita Lindenberg, surprising Baltic echoes can be found in *Die Meistersinger*: there is a direct reference to the so-called Lihgo-melody, which is known to be connected to the tradition of Livonian midsummer festivities, in the passage "Der Flieder war's: Johannisnacht!"[11] which occurs in Hans Sachs's Monologue in the third act. If this reference had been noticed, it would certainly have flat-tered the advocates of the rising Livonian nationalist movement, although its impact on the Baltic Germans who supported the German Theater of Riga might not have been so positive. Despite the reservations, the new opera by no means went unnoticed. *Die Meistersinger*'s Overture was per-formed on a festive occasion at the Riga Town Theater on 18 December 1869. The report in the *Rigasche Stadtblätter* was brief and negative: "The Introduction to *Die Meistersinger* is difficult, discursive, and boring; and also sounded totally cold."[12]

In Germany, the popularity of *Die Meistersinger* increased remarkably owing to the Franco-Prussian War in 1870: the market demanded a patriotic work.[13] The popularity of *Die Meistersinger* also convinced Wagner that it was now possible for him to become court musician to the united Germany.

Wagner was particularly pleased with the fact that Bavaria, after the outbreak of the war, decided to support Prussia. After all, there was no alternative. Following the Austro-Prussian War, Baden, Württemberg, and Bavaria retained their independence. They made a secret nonaggression pact with Prussia, agreeing that during a future war the Bavarian troops would operate under the king of Prussia.[14] Thus, in the Franco-Prussian War, the Bavarian army fought under the command of the Hohenzollern crown prince, the future Emperor Frederick III. Bavaria had, thus, publicly become subservient to Prussia's goals.[15]

Describing Wagner's relief on the day the war broke out, Cosima wrote: "The Bavarians, thank God, are going along with Prussia; the Austrians, dis-graceful as always, with France."[16] Wagner saw the war, above all, as a com-bined German struggle in which German culture was fighting a decisive battle against French degeneration. Shortly before the outbreak of the war, Wagner had begun to plan a manuscript on Beethoven. It was completed by the beginning of September.[17] In this text, Wagner dealt with the signif-icance of genius for the people. Without doubt, he wanted himself to be seen as a member of the line of German masters: Bach, Beethoven, Wagner . . .

Even though the antagonism between the Wagnerians and the anti-Wagnerians had been kindled in the 1850s, it was only in the early 1870s that the main battle lines were drawn up. In the ensuing conflict, high cal-iber weapons were increasingly used. In 1873, even the new edition of the *Brockhaus' Conversation-Lexikon* mentioned the process of institutionaliza-tion that was started around Wagner: "After the end of the Franco-Prussian War, certain influential friends at the Prussian Court undertook to have Wagner appointed to the post of director-general of music, unoccupied since the death of Meyerbeer."[18] Wagner wrote a hasty public protest, repu-diating the claim that his friends had attempted to acquire a position for him in Berlin.[19] Wagner's reply did not, however, reach the *Brockhaus* ency-clopedia, which was a standard-type reference work and was also widely used in the Baltic world. In Finland, for example, since no encyclopedia had yet been published locally, people wanted to acquire a *Brockhaus* or *Meyer* encyclopedia from Germany. Through channels such as this, information on the cultural debate spread rapidly.

Wagner even met Bismarck in Berlin on 3 May 1871, but the meeting proved to be a failure.[20] The composer realized that the only means left to him was to resort to "the people." Government funding for the Bayreuth operatic theater was beyond his reach, and the only solution was to appeal to public generosity. While governmental support was out of reach, Wagner had to acquire social acceptance by becoming a cultural institution not from the top down but from below. The strategy of institutionalization had to change. Following the example of the music publisher Emil Heckel of Mannheim, Wagner therefore became the first composer to found societies of enthusiasts who supported his position, that is, the Wagner societies that rapidly came into being throughout Germany. The societies undertook to raise funds for the Bayreuth Theater. This organization of Wagner enthusiasm in societies marks a significant turning point in the history of the Wagnerian reception (this point will be developed in the following chapters). Unlike other nineteenth-century composers, Wagner thus had his own network of societies who blew the trumpet on behalf of the master and maintained the mythology of his genius.

The Mastersingers of Riga

During the years 1868–71, then, the public image of Wagner changed abruptly. *Die Meistersinger* had elevated him into the limelight. The Overture to the opera had been performed, while it was still fresh, in Riga in December 1869, but the critics remained cool. Despite this, the theater's board of directors was interested in the work and decided to stage it. The Baltic-German minority in the Baltic provinces enthusiastically followed events in Germany, and, therefore, it is no wonder that the Riga theater was interested in performing the new, controversial work. A sign of the new importance of Wagner may also be traced in the fact that *Lohengrin* was apparently revived for the 1870–71 repertoire. The work was, however, limited to three performances in January 1871.[21]

Die Meistersinger was premiered, according to the Julian calendar, on 11 December 1871. For the first performance the theater printed an exceptionally large poster, which, along traditional lines, stated that the work would draw on "additional forces in the orchestra," and "new stage decor." The conductor was Julius Ruthardt, who later became an active member of the Riga Wagner Society; the stage direction was by Conrad Butterweck. The role of Hans Sachs was sung by Mr. Zöller, Pogner by Mr. Thümmel, Beckmesser by Mr. Bagos, Walther by Mr. Bary, and Eva by Ms. Radecke.[22] It is difficult to find out how far the orchestra was augmented. The *Rigaer*

Theater-Almanach (*Riga Theater Calendar*) for the year 1872 indicates that the orchestra normally contained thirty-five musicians.[23] Apparently, in *Die Meistersinger* there were about forty to fifty players. As for the singers, the most interesting artist in the cast was Luise Radecke, who had recently arrived in Riga from Weimar and quickly became the audience's favorite. In 1873, she was invited to Munich where, thanks to the Wagnerism of King Ludwig II, she had the opportunity to develop a deep understanding of the most central Wagner roles.[24]

Despite the unusually high price of the tickets, the attendance for the premiere was good, even though not all the seats in the auditorium were sold.[25] The work was of greater interest to the audience than *Lohengrin*, which had been performed in the previous year. Performances of *Die Meistersinger* continued to be popular in spring 1872.[26] In December 1871 and January 1872, the work was performed on seven occasions.[27] In addition to this, the opera returned to the stage twice during the spring of 1872, on 16 April and 19 May.[28] During that same spring, interest in Wagner in general was rising. *Lohengrin* was performed on 4 and 29 April as well as on 9 May. *Tannhäuser* was also performed twice during the fall of 1872.[29]

It is apparent that *Die Meistersinger* excited nationalist emotions among the Baltic Germans, which may help explain why the work was so quickly imported for staging in Riga. In other parts of the Baltic provinces, *Die Meistersinger* was not brought forward for stage production as quickly. The newspaper critics, however, followed the same lines as in the critique of *Lohengrin* sixteen years earlier, when Wagner's Germanness had been emphasized only in readers' columns, not in critics' reviews. The critic for the *Zeitung für Stadt und Land*, using the initial R., that is, Moritz Rudolph,[30] stated that it was too early to decide on the position the work would eventually hold in Wagner's overall oeuvre, or in the operatic literature in general. Despite this, Rudolph enthusiastically awaited the premiere: "The event that for so long has vividly occupied the attention of all those with a serious interest in our theater—and for the realization of which, on the day appointed, so many were recently so concerned—has now been brought to fruition."[31] Rudolph wrote in laudatory terms about the conductor who had succeeded in guiding the orchestra through such a demanding task. The singers were also commended, but the work itself apparently aroused mixed feelings. According to Rudolph, no applause was heard in the auditorium after the first act, but the audience joined in furious applause after the final act. It is possible that this was inspired by the exhortation to "respect the German masters," which was proclaimed in the finale of the work. This is, of course, mere speculation, since the critic does not offer any reason for the audience's reaction, which may have been inspired by motives other than nationalist sentiments. Thomas S. Grey has remarked that *Die Meistersinger* is open to various interpretations and carries no fixed meaning. Wagner added a few chauvinistic lines to the end of the opera to stress its contemporary relevance, but it is not certain that the audience agreed with these sentiments.[32] On the other hand, the spectators were undoubtedly aware of the nationalistic upheaval the opera had aroused in Germany and may have been receptive to such sentiments.

Moritz Rudolph, however, had no hesitations in concluding that "The first impression upon me of *Die Meistersinger* was magnificent, overwhelming."[33] According to Rudolph, the silence after Act I did not mean that the audience regarded the work as strange: perhaps the opera simply exceeded the limits of everyday experience. The sublimity of the experience is revealed in the critic's description: "Many a listener must have felt, as I did, like one who has experienced a great *natural phenomenon,* which persists indelibly in the memory long afterward—or one who has undertaken a sea voyage in a storm, and continues to feel the ground sway under his feet, long after he has regained *terra firma.*"[34] The *Rigasche Zeitung* also discussed *Die Meistersinger* in its three-part review written by "Fr. P." (Friedrich Pilzer). Pilzer, who was born in Nordhausen in the Harz Mountains region in 1837, had studied the theory of music and history in Berlin and achieved success as a poet and writer before his arrival in Livonia. In the summer of 1863, he moved to Riga and worked as a dramatist and secretary of the theater. From 1866, he also worked as a reporter for the *Rigasche Zeitung.*[35] At the beginning of his review, Pilzer referred to the heated debate in the German music world that had sprung up again in 1871: "The whole struggle that concerns Richard Wagner has gained more and more personal features."[36] In Pilzer's opinion, the people of Riga could accept a more dispassionate view of the matter.[37] This was true in the sense that no strong attacks on Wagner appeared in the public arena. The cultural forum of Riga was apparently lacking purists such as Wilhelm Bauck; at least, this basically negative attitude toward Wagner's music is not discernible in the newspapers of Riga. The specific position of the Baltic Germans may help to explain their willingness to accept Wagner's art.

In the second part of his review, Pilzer was mainly content to describe the plot of *Die Meistersinger.* On the whole, the most striking element of the opera was its polemic message, which the public was certainly able to interpret as a criticism of artistic life. Wagner himself parodied the critics in the figure of Beckmesser, but even so, the critics in Riga did not seem to be offended.[38] In the third part of his review, Pilzer summarized his views: even though there was little action in the work, the richness of detail and the beauty of the opera made *Die Meistersinger* a work that could be included with pride in the corpus of German opera.[39]

In general, *Die Meistersinger* was well received by the Riga public, but no signs of the institutionalization typical of the German discourse is distinguishable in the press reports. Nevertheless, the work was a success in Riga. When the spring season was over, the German Theater, following its usual traditions, also gave a few performances in Jelgava.[40] The choice of

Die Meistersinger for performance was, to a certain degree, due to Friedrich von Parrot, who was director of the theater in 1869–74. When, in 1890, Moritz Rudolph gathered together the biographies of the artists who were influential in Riga for the *Rigaer Theater- und Tonkünstler-Lexikon*, he described the Parrot era one of the best periods in the history of the theater.[41]

Despite the fact that no institutionalization can be perceived in Riga's reception of *Die Meistersinger*, the turbulent events in Germany were also felt in Livonia. After the unification of Germany, particularly after the negative reception of Wagner by the state, the Wagnerians organized themselves. Wagner gained appreciative supporters who accepted the role of missionary workers. One such was Munich Professor Ludwig Nohl (1831–85), who gladly used his works—on the history of music—as a means of strengthening Wagner's position. In January 1872, Nohl, almost by commission, lectured in close proximity to the Riga Theater in which the premiere of *Die Meistersinger* took place. Nohl gave lectures both in Riga and in Jelgava. According to Moritz Rudolph, Nohl was in on his way to St. Petersburg where he would seek sources for his Beethoven investigations.[42] On 16 January, he lectured on Ludwig van Beethoven in the museum's auditorium in Jelgava and on 19 January he lectured on "Richard Wagner and German Art."[43] On 18 January, Nohl talked about Wagner—and on 24 January he gave a lecture on Beethoven—in the hall of the Gewerbeverein in Riga. The Wagner lecture was a ticket-only occasion: the seats in the first row cost fifty kopecks, and all other seats cost thirty kopecks.[44] The content of Nohl's lectures can only be guessed at. Nohl belonged to the inner circle of Wagnerians who had great influence in increasing the support for their idol: other members of the circle included Peter Cornelius, Emil Heckel, Richard Pohl, Heinrich Porges, Hans Richter, Ludwig Schemann, Karl Tausig, and Hans von Wolzogen.[45] This group self-sacrificingly supported Wagner's Bayreuth project, and continued to spread the message of Wagnerism after the death of the maestro. Nohl had already met Wagner in Munich in 1864.[46] Nohl was particularly known as a Beethoven scholar, but at the beginning of the 1870s, he began to support Wagner's operatic project very strongly and to emphasize Wagner's closeness to German identity. It is probable that his lectures in Riga and Jelgava reflected the ideas in his book, *Gluck und Wagner*, published in 1870. In this work, Nohl analyzed the significance of three composers, Gluck, Beethoven, and Wagner, with respect to the development of German music drama. According to Nohl, Wagner had created for the German people their own, sorely needed, national drama. Wagner was, after all, the first composer who had specifically brought out the essence of Germanness.[47] In this interpretation, *Die Meistersinger* was a crucial work, and it was this message that Nohl must have wanted to bring to his Baltic public.

These years, then, generated an enthusiasm for Wagner in Riga, which, in the course of time, rooted itself in the Riga Wagner Society. The key role in channeling this enthusiasm was Carl Friedrich Glasenapp (who was born in Riga in 1847). He had studied philosophy and comparative philology at the University of Tartu and had worked as a home teacher in Pärnu. From 1875 onward, he worked as an *Oberlehrer* (senior teacher) in Riga. In the present study, the role of Glasenapp and the activity of the Riga Wagner Society will be examined in detail in the following chapters. For the moment, it is sufficient to state that the change in Wagner's position in Germany was reflected in Riga far more clearly than in the other Baltic regions. The existence of an active society in Riga reveals the truth of this. Wagner acquired a local pressure group of his own that attended to his interests and took care that the composer's name was publicized in musical circles in Riga.

During the 1870s, Wagner's music was heard in Riga with considerable frequency: *Tannhäuser* and *Lohengrin*, especially, could hardly be avoided by the audience. For instance, during February and March 1876 the top-class tenor Alexander Hesselbach visited the town, performing the title roles in both *Tannhäuser* and *Lohengrin*.[48] Besides *Die Meistersinger*, the only new Wagner opera performed in Riga during this decade was *Rienzi*, which was premiered on 28 January 1878. The performance was conducted by Julius Ruthard, and the stage direction was by Conrad Butterweck.[49] The demanding title role was interpreted by Rudolf Engelhardt, who sang in Riga in 1877–80 and was characterized by Moritz Rudolph as "a brave Wagner singer" and "the first and the only Rienzi of Riga."[50] Ida Beber, who later achieved great success as a Wagner soprano in Leipzig, sang the role of Irene.[51] The role of Colonna was sung by Eduard Thümmel, Adriano by Antonie Theissing, and Orsini by Wilhelm Zöller.[52]

Rienzi, in a way, represented the closing of a circle, as the critic for the *Zeitung für Stadt und Land*, apparently Moritz Rudolph, stressed: this was a work that Wagner had started to compose in Riga four decades earlier.[53] The town thus had its own influence on the history of the birth of the work. Of interest, however, in this respect, is Wagner's earlier statement that *Rienzi* could never be performed in Riga!

The basically positive outlook of the Riga public toward Wagner is seen in the fact that considerably less attention was paid to the faults in *Rienzi* in Riga than elsewhere (we need only remind ourselves of the critique of the Stockholm production in 1865). In 1878, Wagner had already secured his position. It was thus possible to interpret *Rienzi* as a work created during his younger days, when the composer's will to express himself was stronger than his ability to carry out his wishes. By the late 1870s, Wagner had already established his position as a great artist and, therefore, *Rienzi* could be seen as "a notable work of the genius, the poet-composer Richard Wagner." The *Zeitung für Stadt und Land*, for its part, declared that the finales of Acts I and II already contained, in a very early form, the stylistic features characteristic of the composer of *Der fliegende Holländer, Tannhäuser,* and

Lohengrin.[54] Friedrich Pilzer in the *Rigasche Zeitung* remarked that in *Rienzi*, Wagner was clearly directed toward French opera—that is, toward the style of Halévy and Meyerbeer—but in fact the composer was still clearly looking for his own personal means of expression.[55] Despite its pompous details, the music contained "features of grandeur."[56]

All this reflected the idea that Wagner belonged to the Pantheon of Music, making it justifiable to perform this work. This position came to be widely appreciated and accepted in Riga during the 1870s, and it was certainly influenced by the vigorous Wagnerian activities in the town. At the same time, Wagner productions emerged on to the stage in Sweden. *Rienzi* had been incorrectly interpreted as the music of the future, or in Bauck's case, as the very last sign of life before the final negation of Western music culture. While Riga, by 1872, already had a thirty-eight year tradition of performance of Wagner's music, Sweden was still taking its first steps toward it.

"Shrieks and Signals"

The history of Swedish Wagner performances continued in 1872, when the Royal Opera House decided to include *Der fliegende Holländer* in its repertoire. Seven years had elapsed since the last Wagner performance, which suggests that Wagnerians like Arlberg or Söderman were not, after all, very successful in spreading interest in their idol. The situation would not, in fact, have been any different if *Tannhäuser*, which was also Tichatschek's specialty, had been selected instead of *Rienzi* for performance in 1865. In the climate of 1872, the selection of *Der fliegende Holländer* can also be regarded as being rather odd. During the years 1868–71, interest in Wagner had been at a high point, mainly thanks to *Die Meistersinger*, and, simultaneously, there had been much commotion over the *Ring* tetralogy, which, over these years, was in the process of creation. It seems that owing to the cool reception of *Rienzi* there was a desire to produce a work of Wagner's from as early a period as possible; this, it was hoped, would guarantee a greater success than the selection of a more recent Wagner opera.

Der fliegende Holländer was performed on 24 January 1872. The role of Daland was sung by Anders Willman, Senta by Fredrika Stenhammar (see figure 6.1), and the Dutchman by Fritz Arlberg. In comparison with the posters in Riga, the advertisements for the Stockholm premiere did not emphasize spectacle. This was apparently because visual grandeur was simply expected from all new works produced by a house directed toward *grand opéra*. The scenery is not described in the poster, but it is noteworthy that the conductor's name is also missing: the names of the composer; Fritz Arlberg, who had translated the libretto into Swedish;, Fritz Ahlgrensson, who was in charge of the stage decor; and Peter Fredrik Lindström, who was responsible for the stage effects, are, however, mentioned.[57]

Figure 6.1. Fredrika Stenhammar (1836–80) as Senta in 1872. Archives of the Royal Theaters, Sweden.

What was expected from a new work in Stockholm was unquestionably spectacle, not genuine, fresh music. Göran Gademan has examined the publicity preceding *Der fliegende Holländer,* which seems to reflect such expectations. The basics of its story must have been familiar to the audience, who already expected mighty views of white-capped stormy waves and a gloomy ghost-ship.[58] A clear parallel to *Der fliegende Holländer* is seen in Giacomo Meyerbeer's *L'Africaine,* in which Vasco da Gama's sailing ship was

tossed about in the waters off Madagascar. This work gained extensive
advance publicity in Sweden in the 1860s. When it was performed in Berlin
in 1865, the *Dagens Nyheter* reported on the stormy applause given to the
five-hour spectacle.[59] In Stockholm the work had already been performed
during the 1866–67 season, an amazing twenty-one times. During the following season it was performed twenty-six times.[60] The chronicler in the
Stockholm Dagblad stated that, with regard to visual splendor, the audience
expected *Der fliegende Holländer* to outdo *L'Africaine*. But, according to the
chronicler, after the curtain rose, many members of the audience were
faced with the question: "But where are the *four* ships?"[61] If the expectations of the audience were so great, a disappointment was unavoidable.
Wilhelm Bauck, who had now moved to the service of the *Dagens Nyheter*,
confirmed these expectations in the first lines of his article:

> *Der fliegende Holländer* has often been spoken of; one expected to be per-
> mitted to see not merely *one* ship, but two; the African lady should have her
> skin darkened, Mr. Lindström should be raised to knighthood in the
> Order of Wasa, and Mr. Ahlgrensson appointed to an associate professor-
> ship at the Academy of Arts.[62]

It was, for the most part, sheer curiosity that attracted the public to the performances, and during the premiere season the work was performed on
about ten occasions: during the following season it was less successful and
was performed only three times before it disappeared from the eyes of
the citizens of Stockholm.[63] According to Gösta Percy's interpretation, the
ten performances in spring 1872 show that the public was interested
in the work, and its exclusion from the repertoire is hard to explain.[64] But
it is difficult to estimate the enthusiasm of the public merely on the basis of
the number of performances: frequency of performance does not reveal
the size of the audiences. It is also difficult to imagine that the Royal Opera
House would have excluded from its repertoire a work that attracted full
houses. It is thus probable that the attitude of audiences was mixed, and
the attempt to convert them ended in failure.

The attitude of the press toward the work was also mixed. In Gösta
Percy's view, the lines drawn up on the battlefield were illogical, with the
liberal newspapers sharing an uneasy relationship to the opera, while the
conservative press was far more positive.[65] The negative views were, on
this occasion, much stronger than in the case of *Rienzi*, understandably,
because this was, after all, the first time that the public had encountered
Wagnerian music drama. The *Post-och inrikes tidningar* paid particular attention to the noisy nature of the music, which was "for the most part hector-
ing, on occasion demonic, yet spiritual; and to be truly understood, needs
to be heard several times. The accompaniment to the song is at times quite
gentle, but at times so powerful that Mrs. Stenhammar and Mr. Arlberg

Figure 6.2. Royal Opera of Stockholm. Postcard by Förlag Herman Pettersson, Stockholm. Author's postcard collection.

sometimes appeared rather weak."[66] During the 1850s, in Finland and the Baltic provinces, Wagner's music was not accused of being noisy, and this was apparently due to the relatively small size of the orchestras: an orchestra certainly could not be noisy if it contained only twenty musicians. In the 1870s, at the Royal Opera House in Stockholm (see figure 6.2) as in Riga, in which the size of the orchestra had been continually increasing, the situation was different. The remark on the volume of the music is confusing, considering that *Der fliegende Holländer*, after all, represented only the very beginning of the development that finally led to the use of a massive orchestra. The later *Ring* tetralogy was deliberately planned so that the orchestra could be placed under the stage, and this was realized at the Bayreuth Theater in such a way that the volume of sound would not overwhelm the singers. When the same works were performed in ordinary theaters the singers were compelled to make extreme efforts to be heard above the orchestra, and thus Wagnerian singing was apt, in more difficult environments, to degenerate into shouting. It appears that *Der fliegende Holländer* had already aroused in the Stockholm audience an impression that the singers were shouting. Hence *Aftonbladet* claimed that the music was "ett kaos af skrik och signaler," a chaos of shrieks and signals.[67] This state of affairs was not, however, blamed on the singers: on the contrary, the singers were praised in all the reviews. *Aftonbladet* noted that "Mrs. Stenhammar and Messrs. Arlberg and Willman performed their congenial tasks with talent and were rewarded by two curtain calls after the curtain had fallen."[68] In addition, the orchestra conducted by Ludvig Norman, who had been confronted with a difficult task, excited a great deal of sympathy. The *Nya Dagligt Allehanda* also mentioned the merits of the singers. Negative criticism was focused only on Fritz Arlberg, whose voice was too low for the part of the Dutchman. Yet Arlberg could not be blamed for this: "It must, however, be admitted that the composer himself seems to have described the Dutchman by emphasizing the dark sides of the character."[69]

The use of the words "shrieks and signals" by *Aftonbladet* is an interesting attempt to describe Wagner's music. It is apparent that Wagner was experienced as being an exponent of a totally new kind of music. The word "shriek" could, of course, refer to the new fashion of Wagnerian singing in contrast to Italian *bel canto*,[70] or possibly to the desperate attempts of the singers to rise above the "rumbling" music produced by the orchestra. The words "shrieks and signals" might also have been intended to convey the idea of a certain incoherence through which the composer, according to the critic, strove to surprise the listener by interrupting his narrative with shouting and abrupt noises. The critic for *Aftonbladet* certainly meant to imply incoherence when he used the word "chaotic."

The "shrieks and signals" were sometimes followed by sensitive moments or even by jocular scenes.[71] This deviates from Bauck's review in the *Dagens Nyheter*, for Bauck saw no signs of sensitivity or humor in *Der fliegende Holländer*: "The plot, although exceedingly simple, is truly beautiful. If only it were not so serious, so tragic! The music clings closely to the text; that is precisely Wagner's strength. But that also makes it very serious. One longs for something that would thrill one to the power of melody, but this longing is never satisfied."[72] Probably the "signals" could be interpreted as signs of monotony and uneventfulness, that is, in contrast to melodies. According to Bauck, amidst the monotonous recitatives, there was clearly a need for more melodies, but Wagner did not offer these. It is possible that Bauck somewhat overinterpreted the work, being aware of Wagner's operatic theories, according to which the composer strove to get rid of an opera of set pieces and to place increasing stress on drama (that is, classical tragedy reborn). But, in fact, both in *Tannhäuser* and in *Lohengrin* there are clear signs of separate numbers. Such scenes in *Der fliegende Holländer* include, for example, the Chorus of the Norwegian Sailors and the Spinning Song; these pieces, in particular, were successful on their own as arrangements in the 1850s and spread rapidly. Wagner himself declared later that in *Der fliegende Holländer* he had been too much of a prisoner of old, traditional opera. The *Dagens Nyheter* accordingly stated that Wagner was well aware of the problems in his early works: "the fulfillment did not yet match the goal."[73]

The reference to "signals" in *Aftonbladet* could also be associated with Wagner's method of using musical motifs. Use of the word "signal" could in this interpretation imply that Wagner did not fully develop his melodies, but allowed only brief motifs, a few bars in length. It is possible that the critic was here referring specifically to a theme in the overture that resembled a fanfare or a signal.

It is evident that audiences or at least critics saw Wagner as a representative of a totally new music. In this project, *Der fliegende Holländer* signified a starting point: in its essence, the new style would be established in the succeeding works, and the new music was certainly experienced as difficult to comprehend. This is suggested with regard to *Der fliegende Holländer* by a remark in *Aftonbladet* stressing that "one should hear this opera several times."[74] Compared to Meyerbeer's works, *Der fliegende Holländer* seemed difficult to comprehend. On the other hand, the difficulty of Wagner's music may also have been the secret of his popularity. His works were not fixed in the listener's mind after one performance; on the contrary, one had to listen to the work once more. Could such a feature, after all, have been the seed of the addiction to Wagner?

On the whole, compared to the publicity aroused by *Rienzi*, the reception of *Der fliegende Holländer* seems to suggest a number of important changes in the awareness of Wagner. Particularly striking in the *Dagens Nyheter* and *Aftonbladet* was the large amount of background information given about the work, which shows clearly that the columnists had followed Wagner's accomplishments carefully, and that they also had read Wagner's writings. Wilhelm Bauck even described the origin of the opera: "In the summer of 1839, the twenty-six-year-old Wagner journeyed from Riga to London by sailing vessel in order to continue his voyage to Paris."[75] The idea of composing *Der fliegende Holländer* stemmed from this voyage. In the passage below, Bauck cites Wagner's own text, without mentioning the source of the quotation:

> "This sea voyage," he says, "I shall never forget; it lasted three and a half weeks, and was full of mishaps. Three times we encountered powerful storms, and once the captain found it necessary to run for a Norwegian port. This voyage through the Norwegian archipelago had a powerful impact on my imagination; the tale of the Flying Dutchman, reinforced by the stories told by the sailors, took on a very distinctive coloring, which could only be provided by the adventures which I lived through at sea."[76]

Even though Bauck does not give information about the source, it is obvious. Although, in the 1860s, Wagner had already started to dictate his autobiography to Cosima, the only relevant text that was available to the public was the *Autobiographische Skizze*, published by the *Zeitung für die elegante Welt* in 1843. Bauck had translated the description of the voyage word by word from this text.[77]

After the unification of Germany, Wagner had deliberately started to establish his position as an institution. This project involved the republishing of his previous literary works. In 1868, inspired by the popularity of *Die Meistersinger,* Wagner had produced a new edition of *Oper und Drama.* During the same year, he molded *Das Judentum in der Musik* into book form; this later became one of the key works of Wagner's anti-Semitism. It had originally appeared in the *Neue Zeitschrift für Musik* newspaper on 3 and 6 September 1850, but, at that time, Wagner had been hiding under the pseudonym K. Freigedank.[78] It was apparently easy to guess who was behind this pseudonym, but in any case, by 1869, Wagner was prepared to take personal responsibility for denigrating Jews. These republications were only an overture to a larger project, the fulfillment of which began immediately after the *Reichsgründung.* Wagner strove to immortalize his thoughts for posterity and to present the German people with his complete literary works. The *Gesammelte Schriften und Dichtungen* appeared in nine volumes during 1871–73. The tenth volume was published posthumously in 1883.[79] This series of works was available in Sweden, for Bauck had discovered the text of *Autobiographische Skizze* in the first volume of the series published in 1871.[80] The series does not seem to have come into Bauck's hands alone, for the *Nya Dagligt Allehanda* critic also refers to the first volume. In the preface to the series, Wagner described the basics of his art-theory and expressed his attitude toward his own early works such as *Rienzi* and *Der fliegende Holländer.*[81]

It seems that *Gesammelte Schriften und Dichtungen* was highly influential in inspiring the Swedish Wagner discourse in the 1870s. Wagner's Zürich period writings, of which there had been no new editions, were now available in full. The pattern that had been followed in Germany and in Livonia in the 1850s was also followed in Sweden in the 1870s. Wagner first became known through his theories, and only after this through his operas. In Sweden, Wagner's writings were brought to the public's attention through his complete works of 1871–73, at a time when only *Rienzi* and *Der fliegende Holländer* were familiar to the public. The other operas were only on the horizon.

One question that needs to be asked is why the Swedes followed chronological order in their schedule and, hence, performed *Der fliegende Holländer* after *Rienzi.* According to Göran Gademan, performing the works in a systematic and chronological order was a conscious decision. After resigning from the director's post, Ludvig Josephson had—in his book *Våra teaterförhållanden* (*The Conditions in Our Theaters,* 1870)—proposed to the board of directors that, after *Rienzi,* they should select *Lohengrin,* which had recently (in 1870) achieved success in Copenhagen. Contrary to this, the board decided to follow chronological order, probably thinking that the audience, having followed Wagner's development, could thus more easily comprehend his art.[82] It is, of course, possible that *Der fliegende Holländer* aroused interest owing to its Scandinavian connections. The events portrayed in the opera, which took place off the coast of Norway, may themselves have been engaging enough. Another reason could be the possibilities for spectacle offered by *Der fliegende Holländer* through its stormy sea and ghost-ship. The board of the theater possibly saw a connection with Meyerbeer's *L'Africaine*, which had gained a reputation due to its impressive scenery. At least, the public and the critics voiced such views.

Der fliegende Holländer did not, however, turn out to be a success comparable to that of *L'Africaine*; Edholm, the director of the theater, probably realized that *Lohengrin* would have been a better choice. According to Josephson's proposal, the following Wagner production was to be *Lohengrin* and not *Tannhäuser*, which would have continued the chronological line.

It is the performance of *Lohengrin* that is customarily regarded as a turning point in the Swedish reception of Wagner. It must, however, be remembered in this context that Stockholm is not the whole of Sweden, even though the Royal Opera had a significant influence as, from Stockholm, innovatory productions tended to spread to the rest of Sweden. *Lohengrin* was premiered in Stockholm on 22 January 1874. Statistics indicate that it was an indisputable success. Twenty-one performances were recorded in the files for the season of 1873–74.[83] Considering that the premiere was held in January, this means that the opera was performed almost weekly during the spring. After the 1859–60 season, the only opera that had surpassed twenty performances in its premiere season was Meyerbeer's *L'Africaine* (which, over the course of the 1866–67 season, was staged twenty-one times). In the 1870s, only Andreas Randel's lyric play *Värmlänningarna* in the 1878–79 season (twenty-six performances) and Giuseppe Verdi's *Aida* in the 1879–80 season (twenty-five performances) enjoyed greater success than *Lohengrin*.[84] One could conclude that, by the 1870s, Wagner had become one of the most popular of the composers whose works were presented by the Royal Opera House.

At the premiere of *Lohengrin*, on 22 January 1874, the singers of the old guard found themselves in the limelight. Hjalmar Håkansson performed the part of Heinrich the Fowler, Oscar Arnoldson was Lohengrin (see figure 6.3), Fredrika Stenhammar was Elsa, and Fritz Arlberg was Telramund.[85] One of the nobles of Brabant was Carl Fredrik Lundqvist, who later, in his memoirs, described the premiere as "magic."[86] The scenery was again designed by Fritz Ahlgrensson, and Peter Fredrik Lindström was again responsible for the stage effects. Arlberg, who had translated both *Rienzi* and *Der fliegende Holländer* into Swedish, had, however, retired as translator: the libretto was translated into Swedish by Frans Hedberg, who was also responsible for the stage direction.[87]

The critics gave mainly positive reviews. The *Stockholms Dagblad* declared that the music was too loud in certain passages, for, among others, Fritz Arlberg's baritone was drowned by the volume of sound.[88] *Aftonbladet* stressed

Figure 6.3. Oscar Arnoldson (1830–81) as Lohengrin in 1874. Archives of the Royal Theaters, Sweden.

that the audience was far more interested in the noisy highlights than in the ethereal Overture of the opera:

> The superb introduction, which describes the bliss of those dedicated to the service of the Grail, left the audience relatively unmoved, but the other brilliant numbers of the opera lacked nothing in depth and vital impression. The great duet between Lohengrin and Elsa, of the highest interest

from a psychological perspective as well as in purely musical terms, yielded Mrs. Stenhammar and Mr. Arnoldson a storm of applause, while Lohengrin's departure, the incomparably pure mood of which was fully matched by Mr. Arnoldson, led after the end of the opera to a double curtain call.[89]

The critic for *Aftonbladet* acknowledged Wagner as a great composer who had been faithful to his convictions, but also emphasized that parts of the work were overwhelmingly difficult. The role of Ortrud was "unrewarding," the part played by the orchestra massive, and the staging requirements abnormal. The visual element was connected with the swan of Lohengrin, which was to be seen in both the first and third acts. At the beginning of the opera, Lohengrin appears on the folded wings of the swan. In the Stockholm performance, two swans were used, in order to create an impression of depth. At the beginning, a small swan and Lohengrin in puppet form were seen moving behind the stage; after a while, a larger swan carrying Oscar Arnoldson emerged on to the stage.[90] According to *Aftonbladet*, the effect was impressive: "The swan, which easily can become dangerous as a total effect, left very little to be desired." In contrast to this, the scene with the dove was problematic. The ropes that supported the dove were too clearly distinguishable.[91] Wilhelm Bauck in the *Dagens Nyheter* commented on the special effects: "The appearance of the knight, with swan and shell, in the spotlights—the magnificent wedding procession, with all its intrigues, etc.—will be all the more successful if the costumes, decor and stage machinery of the production are designed with as much taste as magnificence, and especially if the swan is given enough furore."[92]

Bauck wrote a lengthy review in the *Dagens Nyheter* on 30 January 1874, beginning with a description of the content of the libretto, which in its religiosity presented "a kind of freemasonry." He compared Wagner to two other composers, Carl Maria von Weber and Giacomo Meyerbeer. In his evaluation of the libretto he took Weber as an object of comparison: "Wherefore does the libretto of the *Freischütz*, in which strange events also occur, stand so high above that of *Lohengrin*? It is because the *Freischütz* derives from the solid popular imagination, in the depths of the forest, whereas the adventures of *Lohengrin* are based upon a clerical fraud woven by cunning monks."[93] The result was that the text of the *Freischütz* sounded poetic and romantic, whereas the verses of *Lohengrin* were cold and prosaic. In Bauck's view, this was also the reason why Weber's work was musically far more rewarding and that Wagner had been compelled to resort "in abundance to pomp and celebrations to noise and spectacles in order to mask his inability." Finally, Bauck stated: "That is how the great opera reform is presented. What it requires is only the operation, with a sublime Mormon myth, of the Zürich spectacles that fell from the Heavens."[94] Bauck wondered what made Wagner so popular. Had the pair of spectacles that fell from the Heavens (that is, Wagner's theory) caused the audience to see something that did not exist in his works? One of the reasons for Wagner's popularity was, according to Bauck, the composer's striving for spectacle. In order to gain popularity, Wagner had resorted to the old prescription: "trombones and trumpet, glittering knights, gilded soldier-puppets, ostentatiously decorated bishops, warlike duels, festival processions, shells, swans, and doves, magic miracles, shrieks, and turmoil on the stage, thunder, and rattling in the orchestra: where is the audience who could resist such wonderful things?"[95]

Bauck was, after all, so interested in Wagner that he made himself acquainted with Wagner's thoughts through *Gesammelte Schriften und Dichtungen.* In his review of *Lohengrin,* he focused on Wagner's *Das Judentum in der Musik,* not to emphasize the contrast between the Christianity of *Lohengrin* and the anti-Semitism of Wagner, but in order to show how strongly Wagner had attacked Giacomo Meyerbeer. In fact, Wagner, in his text, had used the term "a well-known Jewish composer," but everyone knew to whom the taunt referred. When Wagner originally wrote the text, his relationship with Meyerbeer was extremely hostile; this was due to his own failure in Paris. Shortly before Wagner wrote the text, extreme attacks on Meyerbeer had been made in the *Neue Zeitschrift für Musik.* Theodor Uhlig, one of Wagner's closest friends, had employed the expression "hebraic art-taste" in regard to Meyerbeer and his new work, *Le prophète.*[96] The fact that *Le prophète* has many features in common with *Rienzi*—and that even *Lohengrin* is not lacking in effects that are typical of *grand opéra*—is something of a paradox, and this discrepancy was also noticed by Bauck: "Wagner had tried in his *Das Judentum in der Musik* to disparage Meyerbeer, but the truth is that both of these composers are striving for grandiose stage effects." Bauck then began to compare Wagner to Meyerbeer: "M. has *style*, W. only *mannerism.* M. understood how to proportion a colossal subject into a suitable form, W. did *not* comprehend this. M. created vast views and genuine colorful combinations of instruments, W. moves masses, M. impresses, W. makes noise."[97] The worst aspect of Wagner, according to Bauck, was "wild instrumental noise." It must be admitted that there were beautiful passages in the work, for instance, "a remarkably beautiful Bridal Song," but "the endless recitatives" made the work chaotic. In criticizing Wagner, Bauck was extremely severe, but similar comments also appeared in the writings of other reviewers. The critic for *Aftonbladet* stated: "If some of the longueurs were to be abridged, and certain loud but empty passages were excluded, the totality would be thereby considerably improved."[98] In short, Wagner's music seemed in certain passages to be disproportionally extended, becoming too long and monotonous in its character, besides which, most of its noisy effects could not be regarded as well grounded at all.

The *Nya Dagligt Allehanda,* for its part, also dealt with *Lohengrin.* Instead of striving, in the fashion of Bauck, to show how Wagner differed from other composers, the writer attempted to reduce this impression. Even though Wagner himself had tended to distance himself from the past and had emphasized the future, he had ardently admired not only Mozart, Gluck, and Beethoven but also Meyerbeer.

Overall, *Lohengrin* clearly divided the press into two camps. The attitude of the *Dagens Nyheter, Aftonbladet*, and the *Stockholms Dagblad* was, if not hostile, at least reserved, whereas the *Nya Dagligt Allehanda* and the *Post-och inrikes tidningar* took a positive stand.[99] The audience's attitude was positive, from the evidence of the performance figures. It seems the audience was also divided into antagonistic groups, although audience reactions are not generally speaking as easy to assess as those of the critics. On this occasion, however, Wagner became a subject of sharp debate in the readers' columns. Two pseudonyms, the "Spectator" and the "Auditor" regularly appeared in the columns of *Aftonbladet* and the *Dagens Nyheter*: the writers behind these pseudonyms started a debate on Wagnerian sensibility. The discourse was opened by the Spectator's three-part article on *Lohengrin*, which appeared in *Aftonbladet* on 21, 23, and 24 December 1874.[100] One of the ideas put forward in the article was that many cases parallel to that of Wagner could be found in the history of opera, and more generally, in the history of music. According to the Spectator, Wagner in fact, continued Weber's style, in which the borderlines between the aria and the recitative gradually became blurred. Accordingly, leitmotifs could already be found in Cherubini's and Weber's works. The significance of Wagner was not an essential question in the debate, for neither the Spectator nor the Auditor regarded Wagner as an epoch-making composer. The question was rather how the significance of Wagner should be comprehended, and in which historical trend Wagner should be placed. The Auditor responded to the Spectator by emphasizing that, instead of Weber, many other central figures of the history of music can be distinguished in Wagner's background, including, among others, Mozart, Beethoven, and Spohr.[101]

An interesting feature is that the debate was conducted in *Aftonbladet* and the *Dagens Nyheter*, whose critics shared a negative attitude toward Wagner. Negative views were reiterated in this debate. Commenting on the Auditor's first contribution, the editor of the *Dagens Nyheter* remarked that the Auditor's opinions followed those of the eminent critic for the newspaper, Wilhelm Bauck.[102] The identities of the Spectator and the Auditor have not yet been discovered, but the collection of newspaper cuttings in the Archives of the Royal Theaters in Stockholm indicates that three people, Stig Björkman, Jacob Bonggren, and T. Husén, used Spectator as their pseudonym.[103] It is hardly likely that Bauck was behind the debate, although the discourse reflected his ideas. Another critic who comes to mind is Adolf Lindgren, who began his career in 1874 in *Aftonbladet* and whose writings on Wagner resemble the theorizing of the Spectator. Lindgren's contribution to Wagnerian awareness among Swedes during the 1870s is so important that it cannot be ignored here. Lindgren approached the main problems concerning Wagner in his long article, "Richard Wagners sträfvanden, i kritisk belysning" ("The Goals of Richard Wagner, in a Critical Perspective"), published in the journal *Svensk tidskrift för politik, ekonomi och literatur* in 1875. Even though Lindgren does not seem to have been one of the participants in the debate, he had probably been influenced by the debate when he wrote his own analysis. Early in the article, Lindgren reveals that he is well aware of the German discourse and has become acquainted, for instance, with Ludwig Nohl's works. Lindgren states that his goal is to make clear to Swedish intellectuals that Wagner is not only an influential figure in the sphere of music but that he is, above all, a figure of intellectual history. The literary output of the composer totals 3,502 which, according to Lindgren, is an enormous output, so much so that it certainly requires a more detailed analysis.[104] Lindgren exhibits an almost perfect knowledge of *Das Kunstwerk der Zukunft* and *Oper und Drama*, which contain the kernels of Wagner's art-theory. As in the debate between the Spectator and the Auditor, Lindgren highlights the connections with the history of music in Wagner's theory. He concludes that the idea of a fusion of different forms of art is not new. In particular, Lindgren mentions Carl Maria von Weber, but he also emphasizes that Herder and Goethe had already presented the idea of a universal work of art (*Universalverk*).[105] Furthermore, he sees Meyerbeer as diametrically opposed to Wagner:

> Weber wished to have a drama in which every scenic nuance could rise to the level of his noble, soulful melody; Meyerbeer, on the other hand, wanted an unprecedentedly noisy, historical-romantic, diabolical-religious, bigoted-sensual, frivolous-pious, mystical-audacious, sentimental-bourgeois dramatic miscellany, in order to be able to discover there the material for atrociously bizarre music. The secret of Meyerbeeresque opera is in its effects.[106]

Lindgren, at first, seems to subscribe to Wagner's idea that music has unfortunately become an end in itself, and not the means it should be: "We have thus become convinced of what was said in the beginning, that the means of expression was made a goal, and the goal a means."[107] At the end of the article, however, he concludes that there is every reason to question what Wagner, in fact, meant by the concept of drama, and how dramatization really comes into being.[108]

An interesting feature in Lindgren's analysis is that, despite his references to Wagner's Schopenhauerian writing (*Beethoven*, 1870), he emphasizes the texts of the Zürich period. At that time, at the end of the 1850s and the beginning of the 1860s, Wagner was still ensnared by anarchist ideas. This is reflected in Lindgren's interpretation of Wagner's thought:

> Now we cannot deny our historical conditions, nor the political period in which we live. But the task of the future must be—to annihilate the state.

> For the essence of the political state is arbitrariness, whereas the essence of free individuality is necessity. Granted, the individual is inconceivable without other individuals, in other words, a society. But this society must not be the state, where the individual is isolated, egoistical, loveless. The fall of the state, therefore, means nothing other than the self-realization of society's religious consciousness in the face of its own human essence.[109]

Lindgren, however, sees Wagner's anti-statism as connected with socialism: "State to Wagner is nothing else but a mechanism of social control by the police, and in his tendency to demolish the state, he can be compared to the worst members of the First International."[110] It is clear that Lindgren was not aware of Wagner's strong desire to connect himself to the political development of Germany, particularly in the post-1871 period. Wagner's revived statism was evidently better known on the other side of the Baltic Sea, because news of Germany rapidly reached local newspapers, but Lindgren's main sources consisted of Wagner's collected writings, in which the anti-statist angle is striking.

In general, the newspapers did not comment on Wagner's political aspect, despite the fact that the composer was frequently mentioned as an exponent of the German national spirit. Nevertheless, Wagner was not often explicitly associated with current policy. Is it possible, however, that Lindgren's text reveals that Wagner as late as the mid-1870s was still viewed as an anti-statist radical whose writings might be politically questionable?

At the end of his article Lindgren admits that owing to his theories, Wagner is "a real epoch-making personality who has a significant influence on contemporary music."[111] In Lindgren's view, it is impossible to deny Wagner's influence: in this respect, particularly in the field of opera, Wagner could be compared with Gounod and Verdi. As for the composers of the past, Wagner could be likened to Gluck who had vied with Piccini and with the representatives of traditional Italian coloratura opera. In similar fashion, Wagner began to oppose Meyerbeer and the New Italian Rossinian style. Wagner had a coherent, recognizable style, which, according to Lindgren, was perfectly clear in *Tristan und Isolde*, a work that would not be performed in Sweden until the following century. "It might be possible that this style is false," concludes Lindgren, "but it is, however, a style."[112]

The debate between the Spectator and the Auditor, like Lindgren's article, revealed that Wagner was publicly discussed during the 1874–75 season. The professionals and devotees of Swedish opera also made personal contact with Wagner. In June 1874, Wagner received an honorary award of one 1,000 francs from the Stockholm Royal Opera, which led him to write a letter (see figure 6.4) to the director of the theater, Erik af

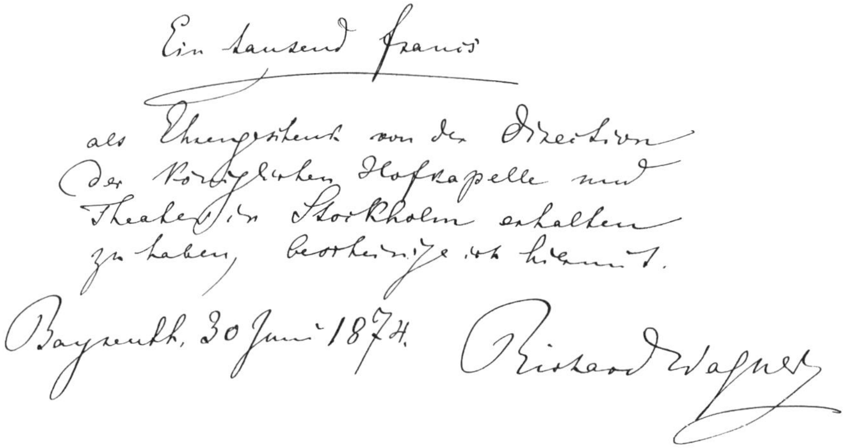

Ein tausend francs
als Ehrengeschenk von der Direktion
der Königlichen Hofkapelle und
Theater in Stockholm erhalten
zu haben, bescheinige ich hiermit.

Bayreuth, 30 Juni 1874. Richard Wagner

Figure 6.4. Richard Wagner's letter to Erik af Edholm, 30 June 1874. Stockholm City Archive, Stockholm.

Edholm.[113] In July of that same year, Wagner made contact with Ludvig Josephson and told him that he was planning the Bayreuth performances of the *Ring* for the summer of 1876. Among other items, Wagner was looking for theater costumes.[114]

The cycle of Wagner performances did not end with *Lohengrin*. The next work to come before the Stockholm opera public would be *Tannhäuser*, which had been pushed aside by *Lohengrin* as a deviation from chronological order. On 16 August 1876, Richard Henneberg's German Opera Company performed the work at the Mindre Teatern in an abridged version with limited forces. The title role was performed by Franz Ferenczy.[115] In the review in the *Dagens Nyheter*, Bauck's criticism was harsher than ever. He described the plot of the opera as stupid, and most of the music as "psalm-like declamation without form in slow motion, and worst of all was the opera's merciless length."[116] Bauck treated the Overture to the opera with extreme severity:

> The Overture (Allegro) is one of the strangest curiosities in the opera. Where has the composer found these harmonies, often enough with little regard for consistency or harmony, patched together with flint-hard melodies, and the rest of the score of the movement filled up with a motif whose unending shapelessness torments the ears as much as does the noise produced by the abuse of instrumental registers. Berlioz, who has taken the trouble to count, has identified this motif twenty four times in the Andante, and 118 times in the Coda to the Allegro; consequently, in the course of this Overture one is subjected 142 times to this motif, which most

of all resembles the toothless mumblings of an old woman lapsing into second childhood. If this is to continue, we shall soon put to shame the Chinese, who have up to now been considered unbeatable in the art of combining, in their music, noise with monotony.[117]

Monotony was again one of the most frequent epithets applied to Wagner's music. Bauck, when associating Wagner with Chinese music, admitted that Wagner represented otherness, while revealing his total inability to understand the language of an alien, different music. Finally, Bauck revealed a total indifference toward Wagner's entire operatic reform:

> Wagner's so-called reform consisted of the inspiration to approximate song, by means of shapeless declamation, to speech; but he failed to see what every beginner knows, that (with the exception of recitativo) this conflicts with the nature of music; it becomes no more than *half* music. Is dramatic character absent from the regular tonalities of Mozart, Weber, Boieldieu? Wagner's reform is nothing other than a colossal misconception.[118]

Aftonbladet commented on *Tannhäuser* only in a short news item stating that the opera deserved to have been performed under better conditions: as a total work and on a larger stage.[119] Nor was the public particularly interested in the performance, even though, thanks to the first Bayreuth Festival, Wagner's name had continually been in the public eye. For instance, *Aftonbladet* had recently quoted the descriptions of the Bayreuth Festival published in the Berlin *National-Zeitung*. There was, however, enough interest to make the Royal Opera embrace *Tannhäuser*. Despite this, the production was completed only two years later, and the work was premiered on 4 December 1878. The title role was sung by Oscar Arnoldson, the part of Hermann, Landgrave of Thuringia, by Anders Willman, Elizabeth by Fredrika Stenhammar, and Wolfram by Carl Fredrik Lundqvist. The libretto was translated into Swedish by Frans Hedberg.[120] The cast was thus the same as in *Lohengrin* except that the long-term Wagner enthusiast, Fritz Arlberg, was missing.

Adolf Lindgren reviewed the opera in a three-part article.[121] In his view, the Royal Opera had corrected its error: *Tannhäuser* was a central work in Wagner's production and should, accordingly, have been performed much earlier.[122] On the whole, Lindgren praised the performance, but it was played only nine times during the 1878–79 season.[123]

History Writing and Legitimation

It is interesting to scrutinize the establishment of Wagner's position in the Baltic world through music history writing, not only through opera performances and the discourse surrounding them. The first comprehensive works of music history were written at the end of the nineteenth century; around the Baltic Sea, this development took place during a period when it was necessary to take a stand on Wagner's works and their significance from the point of view of music history. In this connection, it is essential to keep in mind that German music literature was well known in the whole Baltic world, in Sweden, Finland, and the Baltic provinces. In Baltic-German intellectual circles, but also in Sweden and Finland, it was customary to read German literature. In the German language sphere, the most influential writers of comprehensive music histories were included Raphael Georg Kiesewetter, August Wilhelm Ambros, Hugo Riemann, and Guido Adler. For example, Kiesewetter's *Geschichte der europäisch-abendländischen oder unserer heutigen Musik* (1834) and Ambros's *Geschichte der Musik* (1862–78) were highly influential works and were read by both devotees of music and professional musicians.[124]

The debate on Wagner quickly found its way into the histories of music. Wagner also had enthusiasts among music scholars, who were certainly not afraid of canonizing their idol. The music historians Franz Brendel, Ludwig Nohl, and Richard Pohl were supporters of Wagner, and even members of his inner circle. Thus, the views of Nohl and Pohl could be seen as largely reflecting Wagner's own opinions. During the period from the late 1840s to the early 1850s, Wagner already had a clear idea of his own position in the history of music. This was obvious in his own texts, *Das Kunstwerk der Zukunft* and *Oper und Drama*. Wagner believed that his own texts functioned as a watershed in the entire history of music. Throughout his theoretical writings, he was careful to define his own place and, hence, to justify his existence. First, he described music as it had been in the past, and then he described what it could be in the future. After this, he made it clear that he himself represented the new trend. In other words, Wagner first created a theory of music drama and through this made the reception of his own works possible. It is therefore no wonder that it became easy to identify the epoch-making qualities of Wagner by acknowledging, in Ludwig Köhler's fashion, that there was music "before and after Wagner."[125]

One of the earliest music scholars to campaign for Wagner was Franz Brendel, who, from 1844, had been responsible for the *Neue Zeitschrift für Musik*, which had been founded by Robert Schumann.[126] By 1859, Brendel was already classifying Wagner as one of the leading figures in the New German School of Music (*neudeutsche Schule*). The term New German School was created by Brendel, and he categorized Franz Liszt and Hector Berlioz as exponents of the same movement, even though the former was Hungarian and the latter French. According to Carl Dahlhaus, this could be interpreted to signify that the concept "German," in Brendel's view, was an ideal not an ethnic category.[127]

In Brendel's comprehensive history of music, *Grundzüge der Geschichte der Musik,* published in 1861,[128] Wagner was endowed with a key position, even though his most significant works had not yet been composed.[129] Brendel mentioned that Wagner's next project was the fulfillment of his dream, *Der Ring des Nibelungen,* which would become one of the greatest achievements of German art.[130] Brendel thus appreciated Wagner through his theories, because he placed a work that did not even exist at that time in a significant position in the history of music.

Ludwig Nohl, who was known as a Beethoven scholar and whose lectures in Riga and Jelgava have already been mentioned in this study, was also one of Wagner's acquaintances. In *Gluck und Wagner* (1870), Nohl illustrated the significance of three composers, Gluck, Beethoven, and Wagner, for the development of German music drama. In *Allgemeine Musikgeschichte* (1880), Nohl continued his interpretation. Following Brendel's patterns, Nohl directed his attention toward the future in focusing attention on Wagner's opera *Parsifal,* which was to be premiered at Bayreuth two years later, in 1882.[131]

Brendel's and Nohl's historical descriptions end with an emphasis on the future. The same outline is followed by Richard Pohl.[132] As Brendel placed stress on the forthcoming *Ring* tetralogy and Nohl on *Parsifal,* so Pohl, at the end of his description, purposefully concentrated on the Bayreuth Festival, which he saw as a goal of Wagner's entire artistic activity. Without Bayreuth, Wagner's art would remain a broken-winged bird that would never be able to rise into the sky. The German people should comprehend the great mission of Wagner's art and thus guarantee an ideal environment for Wagner's works.[133]

It is interesting that the music *historians* Brendel, Nohl, and Pohl laid strong emphasis on the *future* and argued that Wagner represented something that had not yet been realized. To them, Wagner was a herald of a new age who could open a way to an entirely new world. Brendel's, Pohl's, and Nohl's efforts were exactly suited to Wagner's own goals (that is, to his attempts to create a community that would favor art).

The music historians who belonged to Wagner's inner circle blew the trumpet on behalf of their idol; but there were also antagonistic views. One of the most controversial questions in the German world of music was the question of the heritage of Beethoven. Some thought that Brahms was the best successor of Beethoven, who had continued Beethoven's work with his symphonies; others thought that Wagner, whose roots were in Beethoven's last symphony, the finale of which was based on the human voice, was the best successor of Beethoven.[134] The historical paradox of the Wagnerians is seen in this struggle. They ardently defended the idea that Wagner really continued Beethoven's work, but they also strongly emphasized that Wagner represented the artwork of the future. The anti-Wagnerians gladly addressed this paradox. Wilhelm Mohr sharply observed that the

Wagnerians had forgotten to differentiate between what Wagner would really have liked to create (art-theory); what he had been able to create (the cultural-political situation, the prevailing conditions); and what he had accomplished (the actual works of art).[135] Along these lines, Emil Naumann stressed the distinction between Wagner's thoughts and his accomplishments. In *Zukunftsmusik und die Musik der Zukunft* (1877), Naumann strove to show that Wagner's *Zukuftsmusik* was nothing radically new and different. Wagner had taken his idea of a total work of art directly from the heritage of Romanticism.[136] As a composer, Wagner could be grafted on to the same tree trunk as Bach, Gluck, Haydn, Mozart, or Beethoven.[137] On the whole, however, Naumann is ready to compromise. Unnecessary debate is in his view pointless: Bayreuth could remain as a Wagner center, but one should not neglect the works of Bach, Mozart, or Beethoven.[138]

Wagner critics could be found among the music historians, even though Wagner had tried to guarantee himself a place in history through the creation of an entire art-theory for the reception of his works. Emil Naumann did not, however, deny Wagner's skills or even his genius as a composer: he merely stated that Wagner's modernism was only seemingly radical.

In Sweden, in the writing of music history, Wagner was coolly avoided for a long period of time. German books were, of course, read and interpreted, but the attitude of the Swedish literature toward Wagner was one of indifference. The most eminent and prolific Swedish music historian was Wilhelm Bauck, who tended in his works to see beyond Germany and thus interpreted French music as a significant factor in the future. In 1862, Bauck published his *Handbok i musikens historia från fornverlden intill nutiden*, which was directed to students of music and in general to those with an interest in music. In this work, Bauck provides little information on Wagner, even though the question of Wagner had been one of the hottest disputes of the decade. Instead, Bauck describes Meyerbeer in depth and in laudatory terms.[139] In contrast to Brendel and Nohl, Bauck held that historical writing could describe only processes that have ended. This was, in fact, a widely shared view among historians. There was an effort to keep history apart from the present and from the future. In the preface to his book, Bauck explains that he has consciously avoided "describing many of the recent phenomena that had appeared in Germany, particularly R. Wagner and his methods of comprehending dramatic compositions." Bauck states that "the question has not yet completely come to an end, as is required for a historical description."[140] At the end of Bauck's work is a survey of the history of musicology and the historiography of music. Bauck's description of François-Joseph Fétis's *Biographie universelle des musiciens* reveals that it is one of Bauck's sources of inspiration.[141] In contrast to this, Bauck's evaluation of Brendel's *Geschichte der Musik* is controversial. In Bauck's view, Brendel's work is excellent as far as early music is concerned, but the closer the narrative comes to the present time, the more it reminds one of a polemic text: "The tone of the book sinks into fanaticism and sounds non-sensical."[142] In this comment, Bauck, of course, is referring to Brendel's Wagnerism, but he avoids dealing directly with Wagner in his text. He mentions Wagner once in reference to the work *Beethoven, ses critiques et ses glossateurs* by Alexander Ulibischeff, who died in 1859 but believed that Wagner was one of the recent plagiarists of Beethoven.[143]

Apparently, Bauck subscribed to the idea that, in 1871, the debate on Wagner was still so fierce that he could not accept Wagner's theories of music for inclusion in his reference book, *Musikaliskt real-lexikon. Handbok i musikvetenskap för musikstuderande såväl som för tonkonstens vänner i allmänhet.*[144] It is probable that Bauck followed the same principles in his lectures at the Royal Academy of Music. Bauck's notes for his lectures on the history of music have survived and are to be found in the Music Library of Sweden. The records clearly reveal that the book Bauck published in 1862 was very closely based on his lectures. A few dates, on the basis of which it is possible to conclude which details from the notes have been included in the book, can be found in the material. The earliest date is 1843. In the passage titled "Encomion Musices," there is a note, "Obs. tryckes i helhet!" (N.B., to be printed in total), which reveals that the notes were, without alteration, used as a starting point in the composition of the book. Later, printed pages from the finished book were added to the pile of notes. Many of the dates were from the 1870s. The role of Charles Gounod seems to be emphasized on the last pages of the notes. Bauck appears to regard Gounod as one of the most talented contemporary composers.[145]

In 1888, Bauck published a revised edition of his history of music. The title of the book was *Handbok i musikens historia från äldsta tider intill våra dagar:* on its back cover, H. Köstlin's *Geschichte der Musik* is mentioned as having been used as a source for the description of the most recent period in the text. Unlike Bauck's previous work, the revised edition clearly lays stress on the recent history of Italian, French, and German music, and also gives a brief account of the music of England, Russia, Belgium, and the Nordic countries. By the year 1888, even Bauck had been forced to accept the significance of Wagner, and he could no longer ignore him. Wagner had died five years earlier and had already passed into history, becoming, in earthly terms, a completed process that could and should be taken as a subject in the study of history. Bauck devotes as much as eight passages to Wagner, and unexpectedly criticizes the Meyerbeerian concept of opera because "Meyerbeer too often resorts to the mind of the large audience, which is receptive only to external effects, and thus, through this, often misuses both the text and the musical content of the opera; for instance, his way of using the coloratura aria as an operatic bravura often creates a painful impression." It was precisely this Meyerbeerian "misuse" that the

"highly gifted creator of the contemporary opera" Richard Wagner strove
to combat.[146] The largest amount of space in Bauck's text concerning Wagner is taken up with a description of the various phases of the composer's
life, but the evaluation of Wagner's significance still remains brief. Bauck
also refers to the debates on Wagner in this statement: "There has hardly
been any other composer who has found such faithful and enthusiastic
friends and admirers as Richard Wagner, but hardly anyone that, at the
same time, has had as strong and unbending adversaries as he has had."[147]
In his summary, Bauck states that, despite the fact that the field was divided
into Wagnerians and anti-Wagnerians, after the completion of *Parsifal*
(1882), both parties had to admit that "Wagner must be categorized as one
of the most significant personalities in the history of music."[148]

Bauck was an influential music historian in Sweden, and the change in
his attitude could certainly reflect a broader gradual erosion of opposition
to Wagner. Even though no other books that could compete with Bauck's
were obtainable in Swedish, Wagner's position was analyzed in a number
of specialist works. The most important of them was Adolf Lindgren's
sixty-seven-page book, *Om Wagnerismen* (*On Wagnerism*, 1881), which was
published by the author in the series *I tidens frågor*. The book was based on
Lindgren's article, "Richard Wagner's sträfvanden, i kritisk belysning"
(1875). Having in his previous articles noted the necessity for a more thorough analysis of Wagner, Lindgren now wished to scrutinize his subject in
greater depth. The amount of material on which his knowledge was based
was still limited, but, by the year 1881, he had had time to become more
closely familiar with Wagner's literary *Nachlass*. In 1875, Lindgren, in light
of the texts of the Zürich period, had regarded Wagner as a socialist, but
now he claimed that Wagner, as a political thinker, had changed, particularly in the 1860s. The work *Über Staat und Religion* was far from being
anarchist nihilism: "The same man that in his previous writings took the
role of an anti-statist who was as irreconcilable as the worst kind of socialist
and a member of the First International Workingmen's Association" now
wrote with sympathy about the state and even about the monarchy.[149]

The emphasis of Lindgren's book is, however, not on politics but on
aesthetics. He highlights the central principles of Wagner's art-theory, that
is, the idea of a total work of art and the leitmotif technique, the relationship of drama to music, the meaning of myth, and so on. Lindgren's goal
was to place Wagner in the framework of intellectual history and music,
thereby making it easier to analyze Wagner's role and significance. At the
end of his book, Lindgren evaluates the popularity of Wagner's operas
and their possibility of international success. The key, according to Lindgren,
underlay the works themselves, the operas, which "he had already
distanced from the aria and the ballet and simultaneously changed to
an altogether more lively 'flow' without breaking the musical forms."[150]
This formulated by Lindgren as an axiom, that "the popularity of the

Wagnerian operas is inversely related to their underlying Wagnerism." What is most important in the evaluation of Wagner's career is the relationship of practical composing to theorizing. In Lindgren's view, Wagner became more and more theoretical in his later works, and thus, more and more unsuitable for reception by audiences. The best of Wagner, according to Lindgren, was *Lohengrin*, which had been completed "before the emergence of the essential theoretical Wagnerism," and which (at the beginning of the 1880s), was still unquestionably the most popular of Wagner's works: it was known "from Stockholm to Naples, from New York to St. Petersburg."[151] In Stockholm, *Lohengrin* had been nicknamed "Lundgren" and "Långrin."[152]

One should remember that Lindgren used the term "Wagnerism" in a very limited sense: referring to Wagner's theory of opera, and thus to "an artistic movement" like the other "-isms" of art. Lindgren, in other words, did not employ the term Wagnerism to mean a collective movement or an activity of Wagner enthusiasts. The title of Lindgren's study, *Om Wagnerismen*, therefore, implies a scrutiny of Wagner's theory of opera. Lindgren does refer to the antagonism that existed between the Wagnerians and the anti-Wagnerians, but he does not directly classify the ideological world of the Wagnerians as being Wagnerism. Overall, he condemns all conflict and antagonism between musical trends, because such confrontation focuses too much attention on nonessential matters, while failing to discover the essential in Wagner. As an example of this, Lindgren mentions the opera *Harald der Wiking* (*Harold the Viking*) by the young Swedish composer Andreas Hallén. The work, which was influenced by Wagner, had recently been performed in Leipzig, and was reviewed both in the Wagnerian journals (*Musikalisches Wochenblatt, Neue Zeitschrift für Musik, Allgemeine deutsche Musikzeitung*) and in the anti-Wagnerian press (*Musikwelt, Musikalisches Centralblatt, Signale*). The press views of the work varied so much that one could not help concluding that the debate itself may have prevented the critics from hearing what kind of music Hallén, as a matter of fact, had composed.[153]

In terms of the Baltic world, Lindgren's *Om Wagnerismen* was an exceptionally long and detailed analysis of Wagner's aesthetics. Wagner was later analyzed in many treatises and articles in Sweden, at the end of the nineteenth century. Andreas Hallén wrote many essays on Wagner and even made a compilation of them to be published in book form as *Musikaliska kåserier* (1894).[154] In 1891, Oscar Bensow published a four-part study, *Richard Wagner som skapare af musikdramat* (*Richard Wagner as a Creator of Music Drama*).[155]

The Swedish music writers were also well known in Finland where the public was kept abreast of Swedish accomplishments. Some indigenous music literature was published in Finland, but no comprehensive history of music was published in Finnish during the nineteenth century, not to mention any investigations of Wagner. The most influential Swedish-language writer in Finland was the composer and ardent Wagnerian, Martin Wegelius (1846–1906). Wegelius was indisputably a leading personality in Finnish musical life during the last decades of the nineteenth century and influenced succeeding generations not only as a man of letters but also as a critic and teacher. Jean Sibelius was one of his students.

Wegelius had acquired his knowledge abroad. He had studied in Vienna in 1870–71, at the Leipzig Conservatory in 1871–73, and in Munich in 1877–78.[156] During these sojourns abroad, he soon became acquainted with Wagner's music, which was frequently performed in Germany during the 1870s. As late as the 1860s, Schubert and Schumann had been his idols as composers, but now his admiration for them was to fade.[157]

Wegelius endeavored to complete a book on Wagner, but the work remained unfinished. The last page of the manuscript, which is kept in the library of the Sibelius Academy in Helsinki, is numbered 323, but pages 207–8, 212–67, and 272–84 are missing from the text.[158] According to an estimate made by Finnish musicologist Veikko Helasvuo in 1946, the manuscript dates to the period from the late 1880s to the early 1890s.[159] The handwriting alters on page 313, indicating that the text before that change had been written during the same period (the 1880s), probably after Wagner's death in 1883. A little later, probably in the early 1890s, Wegelius again started to work on the text and strove to finish his project. The work, however, was still to remain incomplete. The unfinished manuscript is lacking an overall evaluation and summary.

The work as planned was based on Wagner's biography. Wegelius inserted into the biographical skeleton several analyzes of Wagner's works and theories. He pays a surprising amount of attention to Wagner's hostility against the Jews. The Swedish music writers dealt with Wagner's politics only briefly and almost totally ignored the racist element in his work, but Wegelius proceeds differently. He analyzes the two-part article *Das Judentum in der Musik* (1850), in detail[160] and seems to agree with many of the ideas Wagner presents there. As in Germany, anti-Semitic thinking in Finland strengthened its hold in the 1880s.[161] Wegelius states: "In Germany it is an open secret that there is not a single liberal, political newspaper that would not, more or less, be dependent on the Jews: whether they are owners, or, at least, shareholders, codirectors, or writers for the paper."[162] Wegelius's motive is, however, revealed on page 134 of the manuscript. He was striving to show that, in his thoughts, Wagner was far from agreeing with "the anti-Semitic agitation of our days," for Wagner suggested "a complete assimilation of the Jews," rather than a separation of the Jews from society (which was the declared goal of political anti-Semitism in the 1880s). The actual commentary seems to show that Wegelius's text originated in the 1880s, around the middle of that decade.

Despite recent criticism by such scholars as Paul Lawrence Rose, Marc A. Weiner, and Joachim Köhler, who see Wagner's anti-Semitism as all-encompassing and far-reaching,[163] Wagner in fact maintained an ambivalent attitude toward the anti-Semitic movement. He was willing to see himself as a representative of Jew-hatred, but he strove to distance himself from the anti-Semitic parties organized in the 1880s. When arrangements for an anti-Semitic petition were being made, Wagner refused to sign it.[164] The petition stated that the worst enemy of the German people was the Jewish element of society, which dominated the entire empire. The largest proportion of capital had, according to the petition, accumulated in Jewish hands. Furthermore, the petition suggested that strong measures needed to be taken for the liberation of the German people. These included restrictions on the immigration of Jews; the dismissal of Jews from important posts; an increased emphasis on Christian education in the schools, and an acceptance of Jewish teachers only in exceptional cases. Among those who signed the petition were the pianist-conductor Hans von Bülow (Cosima Wagner's first husband) and Hans von Wolzogen, the editor in chief of the *Bayreuther Blätter,* the Wagnerians' most important news-organ.[165] Despite Wagner's indifferent attitude toward this petition, the adherents of anti-Semitism came to dominate the Bayreuth Circle, and after the death of Wagner, a large number of racial questions were addressed in the *Bayreuther Blätter.* Wagner had also grown interested in racial doctrines, especially after becoming acquainted with Count Gobineau, the author of the *Essai sur l'iné-galité des races humaines* (1853–55), in December 1876.[166] Wegelius mentions the friendship between Wagner and Gobineau at the end of his manuscript. Wegelius makes use of context to describe Gobineau's views on Aryanism and the superiority of the white race.[167] It seems that Wegelius is continuing the project launched by the *Bayreuther Blätter* in which Wagner was molded into a Gobineauan figure, a genius of the Aryan race. In fact, Wegelius's text reflects Wagner's own ambivalence: Wegelius repudiates Wagner's anti-Semitism but, on the other hand, legitimates its existence. It is more than likely that Wegelius also propagated Wagner's racial ideas in his teaching at the Helsinki Conservatory.

The largest part of Wegelius's Wagner manuscript is, however, devoted to a description of Wagner's life history, his works, and his aestheic views. Compared to other works from the Baltic world, Wegelius's text comes closer to the worldview of the German Wagnerians. If the work had been published, it would certainly have aroused attention both in Sweden and in Germany. Apparently Wegelius decided to concentrate instead on a much larger project. He devoted himself to writing a comprehensive history of music. Wilhelm Bauck's books were well-known in Finland, but Wegelius probably thought there would be a demand for a different, Wagner-style interpretation of history. This comprehensive history, *Hufvuddragen af den västerländska musikens historia från den kristna tidens början till våra dagar,* appeared in three volumes during the years 1891–93. It was also published in Finnish, having been translated into that language in 1904 by Axel Törnudd under the title *Länsimaisen musiikin historia pääpiirteissään kristinuskon alkuajoista meidän päiviimme.*

Wegelius's history of music ends with Wagner, in a fashion similar to Brendel's history, which dates from the previous decade. Wegelius's sources were Ambros's unfinished work, *Geschichte der Musik,* and the supplementary volume, *Geschichte der Musik des 17., 18., and 19. Jahrhunderts* (1882–87), written by Wilhelm Langhans. Wegelius's basic view on history, however, comes from Wagner. This conclusion has also been reached by the Finnish music historian Matti Huttunen, who has studied Wegelius's idea of history. Wegelius's standpoint is in one way dominated by the Wagnerian idea of the history of the development of opera and in another way by the Gobineauan racial interpretation. In Wegelius's history, opera is endowed with a specific position, which culminates in the last section dealing with Wagner. Wagner "shared a kinship of spirit with Bach and Beethoven and was comparable to them."[168] Wagner's creation, the total work of art, was equal to the art of ancient Greece in its universal significance:

> It is true that Wagner achieved this ideal, and thus fused within the limits of a *single* work of art everything that music had previously obtained from each separate genre in isolation, which makes his life's achievement one of the most brilliant in the history of music. The fact that at the same time, bard and musician in one person, he succeeded in bringing the two sister arts— poetry and music—to permeate each other in a manner achieved by no one previously, and moreover, to perfect their effect by indissolubly melding them in union with the plastic vitality of the dramatic action, endows his life's achievement with an even greater scope in cultural history; for here, we see the classical "triad" realized in a manner that has been unknown in the annals of art since the demise of Greek tragedy; here, manifestly, is more than the Florentines in their boldest dreams dared to imagine.[169]

In its Gobineauan features, Wegelius's view of history was more akin to that of the Wagnerians than to that of Wagner. As Huttunen notes, Wegelius follows racial interpretations throughout his work.[170] In fact, he presents his Gobineauism in the first few pages of the book. He states that "since the earliest times, music has been practiced as art among the Aryan peoples," and that "with these peoples, the creators and transmitters of human culture, music became spread around the world, and has been maintained— like other forms of culture—for so long, and in such measure, as the Aryan element has exercised its influence." Gobineau had already written texts opposing the mixing of races. Wegelius applies this idea in this statement: "where this was neutralized by the effect of racial mixing, and disappeared, or was only weakly maintained, amid the surrounding masses, here there began a period of decadence for music."[171]

Following Wagner's ideas, Wegelius emphasized the significance of national thinking. He roundly condemned composers who had relinquished their national identity. His targets were mainly Jews, and frequently the same composers that Wagner denigrated. Wegelius argues that Felix Mendelsohn has as much originality "as he has German nature," and further opines that "An impartial examination of the Jewish musicians of our century cannot well yield any other result than this, that the Semitic soul is characterized by a great receptivity, but that in terms of musical creativity, it is totally impotent."[172]

It is interesting to note that the Swedish music literature never went this far in the application of the Wagnerians' ideas. In Sweden, critical voices such as those of Bauck and Lindgren were clearly dominant, whereas one of the leading figures of the Finnish world of music, Martin Wegelius, was an ardent Wagner enthusiast. Nevertheless, Wegelius's work appeared in Swedish, and it could thus be read in all the Nordic countries.

It is impossible, in the end, to estimate how widely Wegelius's history was read, but was reviewed recently after its publication by Adolf Lindgren in *Aftonbladet*. Lindgren admitted that the work was well written, although he could not abide Wegelius's admiration of Wagner.[173] But even in Sweden, Richard Wagner's position had become established; at the beginning of the 1880s, even Wilhelm Bauck attempted to end the controversy, although he remained critical of Wagner, at least, in public. Wagner had in the 1870s and 1880s gradually become an institution, but clearly this process took different forms on the eastern and western sides of the Baltic Sea.

Pilgrimage to Wagner

The Founding of the Bayreuth Festival

Throughout the nineteenth century, the history of the Wagnerian reception and Wagnerism was closely related both to local music culture and to German developments, which were vigilantly followed in newspapers and by means of tourist and study trips to Germany. In the 1850s, Wagner's plan to perform the *Ring* tetralogy in an operatic theater specifically built for it had been reported in the newspapers. This project became a central issue for the devotees of Wagner. When money in aid of the Bayreuth Festival House began to be collected through the Wagner societies in 1871, campaigners for the composer throughout Europe knew that the pilgrimage to Wagner would soon become a reality. Then the devotees of music from the Baltic world could also gather in close proximity to their master's art.

The idea of pilgrimage was certainly present in Wagner's mind; the principles of *Kunstreligion* (art-religion) included the idea that art should not be spread among the public; instead, members of the public should direct themselves toward art. This idea was reinforced by Wagner's efforts to make his art unsuitable for performance in local, hence often modest, conditions. The idea of pilgrimage had already been put forward by Wagner in his novella *Eine Pilgerfahrt zu Beethoven* (1840), completed during his Paris period: in Beethoven's place, as a great German genius, there would now be Wagner.

Originally, Wagner planned that Munich would be a great center of his music. Having been expelled from the court of Ludwig II at the end of 1865, he came to the conclusion that Munich should be replaced by Nuremberg, which he thought suitable for the performance of *Die Meistersinger* and, consequently, also for his other forthcoming operas. Nuremberg, however, was to be dismissed in 1869 when Wagner heard from Hans Richter that there was an excellent operatic theater in the town of Bayreuth.[1] Margrave Frederick (1735–63), who was married to Friederike Wilhelmine Sophie, "the favorite sister of Frederick the Great," had maintained his court at Bayreuth. The young margravine was interested in the arts, and like her brother, she was interested in composing (among other works, the opera Argenore). To be able to enjoy opera, the margrave

Figure 7.1. City of Bayreuth. Postcard by Verlag Paul Himml, Bayreuth. Author's postcard collection.

built the Operatic theater of Bayreuth. The opera house was completed in 1747, and, in its time, was one of the largest playhouses in the world. Its acoustics were exceptionally fine.[2]

Wagner visited Bayreuth (see figure 7.1) on his way to Berlin on 17–20 April 1871 and discovered that the town was perfectly suited to his purposes. Unfortunately, the stage facilities of the famous baroque theater proved to be out of date. The theater would not be suitable for Wagner's works, which required complex scenic designs. Therefore, an entirely new operatic theater needed to be built in the town. The town fathers were, of course, interested in the project, for it could raise Bayreuth again to its former fame.[3] Inspired by his experience, on 20 April, Wagner wrote to Lorenz von Düfflipp, the secretary of Ludwig II, with the information that he had decided to choose Bayreuth as the location of the forthcoming music festival.[4]

Bayreuth, which prior to Wagner was mainly known as the home town of the writer Jean Paul, was well suited to Wagner's purposes. The town was situated close to the northern frontier of Bavaria and was almost at the center of Germany. Its location was more advantageous than Munich, which lay too far to the south, roughly in the middle of Bavaria. Bayreuth was preferable to Nuremberg, because with the exception of Jean Paul and baroque architecture, it had nothing that could compete with Wagner performances.

In 1868, in *Deutsche Kunst und deutsche Politik*, Wagner had argued that theater should be the kernel of national education.[5] If the Wagner theater
arose in Bayreuth, it would stand, at least geographically, at the heart of
Germany. Thus, people all over Germany could easily make pilgrimages to
the fount of spiritual rebirth.

Wagner's plan now moved forward quickly. On 11 May 1871, he wrote
to Dr. Carl Landgraf that he was planning to arrange a great music festival
in Bayreuth within two years, in 1873. Wagner also informed Landgraf that
he was going to return to German soil, to his new home town, in order to
better arrange the forthcoming cultural event.[6]

Wagner tried continually to get support and patronage from the state for
his art. But he also began to plan an alternative solution based on direct support from the people. Having met Bismarck on 3 May 1871, only to leave
Berlin empty-handed, he immediately began to solicit financial support from
the people. By 12 May, he had already written an open letter, "Ankündigung
der Festspiele," in which he publicly presented his Bayreuth plan. The intention was to build a large Festspielhaus in Bayreuth before summer 1873.[7]

Wagner began to bring his proposal to fruition as a private project, but
his mind was still occupied with the idea of social acceptance. The most
important thing was to start the project and then hope that the German
nation would, at last, understand what kind of gift it had received. Wagner
explained this clearly to his economic adviser, the banker Friedrich Feustel:
"With this building we are offering only the outline of our idea, and hand-
ing it over to the *nation for completion* as a monumental edifice."[8] The theater was to be a simple wooden house. The money saved during its building
was to be used for the special equipment and decor needed to make the
experience complete. The total costs of the project were 300,000 taler, of
which 100,000 taler were reserved for the construction of the theater,
50,000 taler for the performance equipment, and 150,000 taler for the performance costs of the first festival.[9]

In spring 1871, Wagner had already started to raise money. Before
returning to Triebschen in May 1871, he visited Leipzig, Frankfurt, Darmstadt, and Heidelberg to inspire his supporters.[10]

At the beginning, the work was met with enthusiasm among Wagner's
Berlin friends. One of the most active was the Polish-born pianist Karl
Tausig, whose energy seemed to be inexhaustible. He made speeches on
behalf of Wagnerism in the capital city of the new Germany, where the message of Wagnerism had not in its entirety reached the populace. Tausig's
sudden death of typhus at the age of twenty-nine was a serious loss to
Wagner.[11] After Tausig's death, enthusiasm in Berlin weakened considerably. This was partly because it had become clear that Wagner intended to
base his festival in the distant town of Bayreuth.[12]

By the end of 1871, it was evident that waiting for money to come in
was not enough: Wagner's account had not increased by much: something

had to be done quickly, if the first festival was to be arranged in 1873. To speed up the collection of money, Wagner decided to issue 1,000 patronage certificates (*Patronatschein*), each priced at 300 taler. The purpose of the certificates was to create a firm financial base for the festival.[13] The high price of the certificates, however, caused problems. A means needed to be created by which low-income Wagnerians could support the project. A useful proposal was put forward by a Mannheim music publisher, Emil Heckel, who, by June 1871, had already established a Wagner society (Richard Wagner Verein) in his native town. Following Heckel's idea, Wagner decided, without delay, to found Wagner societies throughout Germany. The purpose of the societies was to arrange events and occasions for collecting money.[14] The societies could purchase patronage certificates on behalf of those members who could not invest 300 taler.[15] The proposal seemed to be a good one. The foundation of these patrons' associations was intended to guarantee that all enthusiasts had a chance to support the project.

Societies soon began to be founded. In 1871, the Mannheim Society already had sister groups in Leipzig, Vienna, and Berlin.[16] Wagner wrote out details of his projects in order to provide information for the societies.[17] In addition, he convinced them that he had always striven to contribute to the essence of the German spirit.[18]

During 1872, the societies' activities spread rapidly throughout Germany. Organizations of enthusiasts came into being almost in every town. When enough money had been collected, the essential work could begin. With solemn ceremony, the foundation stone of the opera house was laid on the hill close to Bayreuth on 22 May 1872.[19]

As the foundation stone was being laid, Wagner realized that the music festival could not be arranged for the following year. A great deal of money still had to be raised. The design of the structure had to be corrected, and the last part of the tetralogy, *Götterdämmerung*, had not yet been orchestrated. The festival would probably need to be postponed, at least until 1874.[20]

Wagner's plans were still too optimistic. At the end of 1872, Wagner and his financial supporter Feustel could see that the Wagner societies, despite all their efforts, had failed to collect enough money. The problem continued after the turn of the year, and no change was in sight. By August 1873, only a third of the patronage certificates had been purchased.[21] The situation seemed hopeless. Wagner could do nothing but seek state support again. Already on 24 June 1873, he had written a humble letter to Bismarck, asking directly for financial support, but Bismarck was unbending; no money was given.[22]

From the very beginning, Ludwig II had regarded the Bayreuth project as absurd and unrealistic.[23] Wagner knew this, and it was for this reason, in the first place, that he decided to accomplish his project without a patron.

Figure 7.2. Festspielhaus of Bayreuth. Photo: Hannu Salmi.

Now, however, he found it necessary, once again, to request Ludwig's assistance. At the end of January 1874, Ludwig made a donation of 100,000 talers.[24]

Ludwig's support was decisive. In a letter to Lorenz von Düfflipp, Wagner gave his opinion that the theater would be completed by the summer 1875.[25] This schedule was also extended. Not until 1876 did the theater (see figure 7.2) stand ready to receive the first festival audience.[26] "Wagner's iron will made it possible to realize the idea," wrote Marie zu Hohelohe later in her memoirs.[27] This was undoubtedly true. Without Wagner's vision and persistence the Bayreuth project would never have come to fruition. At the opening ceremony on 13 August 1876, Wagner could state that utopia had, at least for the time being, become reality. Germany now had its national theater.

The Bayreuth Festival was a unique cultural event at the time, and even Emperor Wilhelm I of Germany honored it with his presence.[28] A surprise guest at the festival was Emperor Dom Pedro II of Brazil, who was touring Europe at that time.[29] Only Bismarck refused to attend.[30] Naturally, Wagner's most enthusiastic supporters came to the festival, including Friedrich Nietzsche, Wilhelm Tappert, Ludwig Nohl, Richard Pohl, Gottfried Semper, and Karl Klindworth.[31] Professional musicians came from all over the world. The most famous were the Norwegian Edvard Grieg and the Russian Peter Tchaikovsky. Grieg wrote a series of articles for the Norwegian paper *Bergenposten* and attended not only the performances but also the rehearsals.[32]

Figure 7.3. Auditorium of the Festspielhaus, Bayreuth. Postcard by Verlag v. Chr. Senfft, Bayreuth, 1906. Author's postcard collection.

The festival started with the performance of *Das Rheingold*, for which the auditorium (see figure 7.3) was filled to capacity. The experience, for many Wagner enthusiasts, was unforgettable. The Festspielhaus had on its completion, and still has, one of the largest opera stages in the world. Wagner had designed the theater to resemble a classical amphitheater. The auditorium was designed in the form of a geometrical sector, which permitted equal visibility from every seat. No boxes had been built. The orchestra was separated from the audience by a large parapet: one could not therefore see the source of the music. In addition, the auditorium was constructed entirely of wood (which had been proven by Gottfried Semper to be the best material from an acoustical perspective). The first audience could thus experience something that could not be experienced in any other opera house. The uniqueness of the theater was evidently associated with Wagner's idea of making his festival into something resembling a religious rite. Art could therefore be followed in Bayreuth with a devotion like that in Ancient Greece.

When the last performance of the festival on 18 August was over, Wagner made a short speech, whose motives were clear to the audience. Wagner's last, emphatic words were: "Wollen Sie, so haben wir eine Kunst" (If you want, you will have real art).[33] The audience, the "German people," were now responsible for whether art had come for good or not. Responsibility for its

continuance was transferred to the people. The 1876 festival resulted from
many years' work, during which Wagner had come to realize that arranging
the next festival would be very demanding. In Wagner's inner circle the continuance of the festival was a constant subject of discussion. Wagner himself
believed that the next festival could be fixed for the following year, if only
permanent support from the state or, at least from the societies, could be
organized. Wagner's closest friends, Liszt and Bösendorfer, believed that permanent support could be arranged. The impresario Angelo Neumann was
much more pessimistic, considering the schedule too tight.[34] Eventually,
Neumann was proved right. No permanent support for the festival was
found. Wagner had to struggle until the year 1882 before the Wagnerians
could again gather in the Festspielhaus.

The 1876 Bayreuth Festival was covered in newspapers throughout
Europe. The atmosphere of the festival was thus conveyed to those who
could not make the pilgrimage to Germany. Almost all the major newspapers from the shores of the Baltic Sea sent special reporters to Bayreuth,
used their correspondents already in Germany, or cited German newspapers. Of the Riga newspapers, both the *Rigasche Zeitung* and the *Zeitung
für Stadt und Land* received dispatches directly from their own reporters.
The conductor Julius Ruthardt was writing for the *Rigasche Zeitung*,[35] and
Georg von Petersen for the *Zeitung für Stadt und Land*.[36] The latter series of
articles was also reprinted by the *Mitausche Zeitung*[37] in Jelgava and the
Libausche Zeitung[38] in Liepaja. Ruthardt's writing was full of praise, and in
many passages it clearly countercriticized the arguments of Heinrich Dorn
in the *Spenersche Zeitung*. According to Dorn, the theme of the *Ring*, even at
its best, was suitable only for an Icelandic national drama.[39] Dorn had himself
previously composed an opera based on *Das Nibelungenlied*, and perhaps for
this reason, he disliked Wagner's competing interpretation. In the original
Nibelungenlied, Brynhild is an Icelandic princess, and, therefore, there is an
Icelandic connection. The Scandinavian orientation was, however, reinforced in Wagner's interpretation, for he included material from *Edda* and
the *Völsunga-Saga*. In fact, only the last part of the *Ring* is, in part, based on
Das Nibelungenlied; the rest of the material is conspicuously Nordic. This
interpretation apparently irritated Dorn, who saw the work more as a
national drama of Iceland than of Germany. In Ruthardt's view, this critique was unnecessarily harsh: even though Wagner was not, perhaps, infal-
lible, he had left his mark on all of contemporary music. It is, therefore, no
wonder that after the performance of *Götterdämmerung* a female member of
the audience exclaimed: "Bravo, Wagner! Bravo, Maestro! Musica bella!
Musica bellissima!"[40]

Most of the reporters at Bayreuth filled their columns with descriptions
of the unique operatic theater, the drama itself, and the technical innovations that were necessary. Georg von Petersen's style is typical: Wagner's
work was already "a remarkable work of cultural history."[41] Of the Riga

newspapers, the *Neue Zeitung für Stadt und Land* also published an account of the Bayreuth events in an article that appeared in sections. The anonymous author says he is "coolly considering" and concludes: "I have dipped my pen neither in venom nor in honey."[42]

In Estonia, the *Revalsche Zeitung* dealt with the Bayreuth Festival largely in articles composed by many writers. To begin with, the paper published a three-part report by its correspondent, exclusively for Tallinn readers. The anonymous writer describes his journey by special train from Leipzig to the small northern Bavarian town. His attention is focused on the sparkling eyes of the Wagner enthusiasts and on the religious tone of the assembly: "Bayreuth! Anyone who happens to mention this word in Germany today can be certain that he arouses the attention of believers in the music of the future in the same way as a Muslim who speaks disparagingly of Mecca."[43] The writer continues by describing the unique stage of the Festspielhaus, and the giant orchestra located deep in the pit. Wagner had created music for "an imaginary theater," but he was "a man of victorious self-awareness and imposing genius," and he had succeeded in building at least one theater suitable for his works.[44] After this report, the *Revalsche Zeitung* published descriptions of the music presented at the festival. Some of them, as stated by the paper, had been collected from letters sent to the editor by the music critic for the paper; others were quotations from writings in the German newspapers.[45]

The press in Finland and in Sweden also paid a great deal of attention to the events in Bayreuth. The newspapers did not, in the main, send their own reporters to Germany, but they received articles from participants in the festival. The *Helsingfors Dagblad* published a series of articles penned by the young Finnish critic and composer Martin Wegelius, whose series of reports became the most thorough analysis of Wagner that had yet been published in Finland.[46] In his six-part series, Wegelius approached the music he had heard in a coolly analytical fashion, although he later became one of the most ardent advocates of Finnish Wagnerism and Wagner activity. Wegelius's writings were later published in a collection of letters, *Konstnärsbrev*.[47] Not all newspapers succeeded in acquiring original material for publication, but they endeavored to report on what was seen as a significant musical event. The *Helsingfors Dagblad* also published articles from the Central European papers, among others, Eduard Hanslick's review of the *Ring* on 1 September 1876.[48]

Bayreuth aroused similar interest in Sweden. On 24 August 1876, the *Nya Dagligt Allehanda* published, with a new introduction, a translation of a feuilleton by Karl Frenzel, which had originally appeared in the Berlin *National-Zeitung*. The *Nya Dagligt Allehanda* had for a long time been publishing adverse criticism of Wagner, as Wilhelm Bauck had worked as a reporter on the paper until 1871. Frenzel's article presented an ironic picture of Wagner, in which the Bayreuth Festival was seen as an event principally for high society. According to this article, the festival was a significant

Figure 7.4. Rhinemaidens, Minna Lammert and Marie and Lilli Lehmann, in the first production of *Das Rheingold* in 1876. National Archive of the Richard Wagner Foundation, Bayreuth.

cultural event on which the attention of the whole civilized world was focused, but many celebrities were seen at the event, including artists, writers, musicians, singers, scientists, and politicians. Following the example of society diarists, Frenzel also noted those who were not present. "Where were Verdi, Gounod, Brahms, and Joachim?" Instead, the festival was attended by "the well-known aristocratic society ladies of Berlin, Vienna, and St. Petersburg who constitute the essential moving force in Wagnerism." Frenzel also demonstrated the contradictions between fiction and reality. How modest, after all, was Siegfried's struggle against the dragon compared to the efforts required by the members of the audience in the acquisition of any form of refreshment.[49]

Wagner was also topical in Sweden because Henneberg's German opera company performed *Tannhäuser* in Stockholm at the beginning of August 1876. The performance was originally planned for 6 August but was delayed until 16 August.[50] The *Dagens Nyheter* stated: "This was one of the first fruits of the struggle for reform that will be crowned by Wagner through the performance of his drama cycle *Der Ring des Nibelungen* at Bayreuth, on one of these days."[51] Counter-publicity was created by Wilhelm Bauck's thoroughly critical review of *Tannhäuser* on 23 August.[52] The critical attitude of the Swedish press toward Wagner was intensified by *Aftonbladet*, which used a sizable amount of space to give examples of the negative reception of the work. For instance, it published several articles, mainly put together from German and Austrian newspapers. The central source was again the Berlin *National-Zeitung*. The author of the first article, in which several sources are used, states that, however cool and reserved a visitor happens to be toward the worship of Wagner, he cannot but admire the fact that Wagner had been able to finish his project. It was not a work for the whole nation: Wagner had created his art for a small circle, even though he claimed to speak in the name of the German people.[53] In the second installment of the series, *Aftonbladet* directly quotes Karl Frenzel's writing on the high society life and the general atmosphere of Bayreuth. The beginning of the article is typical: Frenzel describes Bayreuth as grotesque; the rococo splendor is in perfect harmony with a petit-bourgeois idyll.[54] The third installment of the series is calmer and apparently consists of a synopsis of the *Ring* culled from several newspapers.[55] Ample space was given to the reviews by the *Daily News* and the *Neue Freie Presse*,[56] but *Aftonbladet* continued its negative line in other parts of the article. Surprisingly, however, the paper quoted the correspondent who wrote in the *Helsingfors Dagblad* as M. W. (that is, Martin Wegelius), who was classified by the *Aftonbladet* critic as an admirer and friend of the composer.[57]

On the whole, the descriptions of Bayreuth published in the Finnish and in German newspapers of the Baltic provinces are positive and calmly analytical, but the Swedish papers, particularly the *Nya Dagligt Allehanda* and *Aftonbladet*, filled their columns with harsh criticism. The Finnish and the rest of the Baltic press focused on the music and the drama, but in Sweden, the emphasis was placed on the social dimension and the high-society aspect of Wagnerian activity; on the eastern side of the Baltic Sea, these aspects were excluded from the local newspapers.

Tourists on the Green Hill

At the time of the first Bayreuth Festival, Wagner was known throughout Europe: his projects had been discussed by the newspapers, and in music circles there was no uncertainty over the objectives of his projects. Even before the festival, Bayreuth aroused so much interest that, when news reports on the forthcoming festival spread, the most ardent Wagnerians began to prepare themselves without delay for their journey to Germany.

Interest in Wagner, even in the Baltic world, was so strong that a trip to the northern Bavarian town was seen by many as an obvious necessity. As has already been stated, religiosity was always associated with Wagner. The mystical and transcendental tone in which people tended to speak of him was influenced by the prevailing situation in music, politics, and intellectual life.

Wagner emphasized that he was the advocate of the future, the exponent of the artwork of the future, and, in that sense, a seer. The correspondent for the *Revalsche Zeitung*, accordingly, called Wagner "a prophet of the music of the future" (Profet der Zukunfsmusik).[58] The future spoke through him. Wagner aimed for fame, but, at the same time, he composed music and poetry for works that required exceptional resources and were extremely difficult to perform. In Central European opera houses, his works could become part of the basic repertoire, but in the Baltic world, his works could not be heard very often. This inaccessibility heightened the religious element in Wagnerism. Attending a Wagner opera was a unique occasion, and the Bayreuth Festival theater became the shrine of this uniqueness. Wagnerians in the Baltic world, as well as Wagnerians worldwide, thus assembled at Bayreuth. Pilgrimage was also one of Wagner's own goals. When the German-born Finnish musician Richard Faltin met Wagner at Bayreuth in 1876, and mentioned that some poor attempts to perform the master's works had taken place in Finland, Wagner laconically answered: "Oh, you should rather come to Bayreuth!"[59]

This suggestion of Wagner's was followed not only by the Finns but by Wagnerians in other countries. During the nineteenth century, the Bayreuth Festival was held thirteen times. The repertoire was as follows:

1876 *Der Ring des Nibelungen* (3 performances)
1882 *Parsifal* (16)
1883 *Parsifal* (12)
1884 *Parsifal* (10)
1886 *Parsifal* (9), *Tristan und Isolde* (8)
1888 *Parsifal* (9), *Die Meistersinger von Nürnberg* (8)
1889 *Parsifal* (9), *Tristan und Isolde* (3), *Die Meistersinger von Nürnberg* (5)
1891 *Parsifal* (10), *Tristan und Isolde* (4), *Die Meistersinger von Nürnberg* (4), *Tannhäuser* (4)
1892 *Parsifal* (8), *Tristan und Isolde* (4), *Die Meistersinger von Nürnberg* (4), *Tannhäuser* (4)
1894 *Parsifal* (9), *Lohengrin* (6), *Tannhäuser* (5)
1896 *Der Ring des Nibelungen* (5)
1897 *Parsifal* (8), *Der Ring des Nibelungen* (3)
1899 *Parsifal* (7), *Die Meistersinger von Nürnberg* (5), *Der Ring des Nibelungen* (2)[60]

A more detailed examination of journeys to Bayreuth and the numbers of people who performed the pilgrimage is necessary here. Information on these journeys to Bayreuth is available in various sources. Newspapers, memoirs, and private correspondence contain stories and recollections of experiences at Bayreuth. The most significant archival material for the investigation of Wagneristic tourism is provided by the lists of visitors (*Fremdenlisten*) published by the festival organizers. The organizers collected

Table 7.1. Swedish, Finnish, Baltic, and Russian visitors to Bayreuth in 1876, 1882, 1888, 1891, 1896, and 1899.

Year	1876	1882	1888	1891	1896	1899	Average	Total
Sweden	4	11	5	12	22	36	15	90
Finland	3	8	3	1	5	22	7	42
The Baltic provinces	11	19*	21	33	9	22	19	115
Russia	41	78	71	44	76	85*	66	395
Total	59	116	100	90	112	165	107	642

*Whenever an asterisk appears in the table, the note "mit Famille" (with the family) has occurred in the lists. In both cases, however, only one guest was accompanied by his family.

information on visitors' accommodation and recorded their name, place of residence, address while attending the festival, and also, in many cases, occupation. The lists of visitors were published in booklet form and sold at a relatively low price, but, unfortunately, they have not survived in their entirety. The finest collection of lists is to be found in the Wagner Archives in Bayreuth. Lists of visitors from the 1890s can also be found in Fredrik Vult von Steijern's Wagner Collection in the Royal Library of Sweden.

The use of the visitor lists is, to a certain extent, problematic. The surviving lists are discontinuous. For the nineteenth century festivals, lists are to be found only for the years 1876, 1882, 1888, 1891, 1896, and 1899. The information on 1884, 1886, 1889 and 1897 is incomplete, and the lists for the years 1883, 1892, and 1894 have probably not survived at all, at least not in Bayreuth or Stockholm.[61] The Finnish composer Jean Sibelius visited the 1894 Bayreuth Festival, but his name is not recorded in the extant lists.[62] Even if a complete collection had survived, nothing could guarantee that the compilers had managed to record every single visitor. One problem is that visiting musicians and artists would have been constantly on the move. They might have been living temporarily in Germany and recorded the town in which they were studying or working as their place of origin. In such a case, an investigator might be able to identify the permanent inhabitants of a given region among the visitors, but, unfortunately, it is not always possible to do this. Besides this, the compilers of the lists may have misinterpreted the handwritten hotel register records and therefore recorded the visitors' names and place of residence in such a way that identification of the registrant is far from easy. An example of this is Martin Wegelius, whose surname, according to some recordings, is Wegelind,[63] according to others Wegelink.[64]

Despite these problems, the lists of visitors do provide a general idea of the number of visitors from Sweden, Finland, and the Baltic provinces to the Bayreuth Festival. In table 7.1 the analysis is limited to those festivals for which complete lists have survived, but it shows the visitors' various places of residence. Russian Wagner tourists are also counted, for purposes of comparison. It must be noted, however, that many of the visitors were accompanied by servants, and the lists never identified maids or servants, not to mention information on the total numbers of hired people who accompanied visitors. Therefore, this group has been completely omitted from the lists.

As is revealed in table 7.1, which indicates the number of visitors from the area around the Baltic Sea, most came from Russia. The Baltic provinces were also well represented, comprising the second largest group. The third largest group is Swedish, and the fourth largest is Finnish. The geographical distribution broadened noticeably in all areas toward the end of the century. In 1876, St. Petersburg, Riga, Helsinki, and Stockholm were most frequently given as places of residence, but toward the end of the century, as the number of visitors increased, their geographical spread also expanded. For instance, in the first festival, 63 percent of Russians were from St. Petersburg, but in 1896 the percentage was only 35.5.

The evidence for this trend is not entirely reliable, because toward the end of the century many Russians marked their home place merely as "Russland." According to the 1896 statistics, of the 76 visiting Russians, 27 registered as coming from St. Petersburg, and 33 as simply from Russia. However, the frequency of different places of origin increased considerably. Thus, at the 1896 festival, among the Russian visitors some were from as far away as Sverdlovsk (Jekaterinenburg), beyond the Ural Mountains.[65] There were also visitors from the present-day Ukraine (Kiev, Odessa, Kharkov, Jampol, Smela). The question of Russian origin is, of course, a difficult one, for, besides Finland and the Baltic provinces, the largest part of present-day Poland belonged to the Russian Empire. It is quite possible that the "Russia" category included visitors who came from these areas but recorded their place of origin as Russia. For example, the railroad official Friedrich Adelung, who participated in the 1888 and 1891 festivals, registered as being from "Radom, Russland," even though Radom is located south of Warsaw, in present-day Poland.[66] In the nineteenth-century Russian Empire, even naming one's place of residence was a political matter. It is thus possible that among those who recorded their place of origin as Russia, in the late 1880s and in the 1890s, there were also Russians who lived in the Baltic provinces, but wished to stress their Russianness. In contrast, the Baltic Germans, without exception, recorded that they were from Estonia, Livonia, or Courland.

Unfortunately, it is impossible even to guess how many Russians who lived in the Baltic provinces have been excluded from this cataloguing. At any rate, the lists of visitors clearly indicate a large number of visitors whose place of residence is specifically recorded as Estonia, Livonia, and Courland. Table 7.2 indicates the geographical distribution of Baltic visitors during the entire period.

Table 7.2. Geographical distribution of Baltic visitors to Bayreuth in 1876, 1882, 1888, 1891, 1896, and 1899.

Year	1876	1882	1888	1891	1896	1899	Total
Riga	6	15	12	25	5	16	79
Valmiera/Wolmar	1	–	–	–	–	–	1
Tartu/Dorpat	1	1	–	–	–	–	2
The rest of Livonia	1	2	3	8	4	–	18
Pärnu/Pernau	2	–	–	–	–	–	2
The rest of Estonia	–	–	–	–	–	1	1
Liepaja/Libau	–	1	2	–	–	5	8
The rest of Courland	–	–	4	–	–	–	4
Total	11	19	21	33	9	22	115

The indisputable center of Baltic Wagner enthusiasm was Riga, whose long tradition of Wagner cultivation is reflected in the large numbers of Riga residents who attended the Bayreuth Festival. A highly active Wagner society, whose history will be dealt with in chapter 8, functioned in Riga. The climax of this enthusiasm in Riga was reached during the 1880s and at the beginning of the 1890s. On the other hand, during the last decades of the nineteenth century, the position of the German minority in Riga began to weaken decisively, when the policy of Russification tightened, and the number of Baltic Germans decreased. Perhaps this political situation influenced the amount of Wagner enthusiasm, and Wagner became a symbol of Germanness for the diminishing minority.

In any case it appears that, according to the visitors' lists, enthusiasm for Wagner in the Baltic provinces was far more centralized than in Russia where, besides St. Petersburg and Moscow, there were two smaller centers, namely, Kiev and Odessa. It is, however, surprising that only a few Estonians are to be found in the lists of Bayreuth visitors. Tartu is represented by Emil Musso and Heinrich Zöllner,[67] but the city belonged to Livonia, not Estonia, at the time. The only Estonian visitors seem to have been Mr. and Mrs. Friedrich Specht from Pärnu in 1876 and W. Kentmann in 1899.[68] The last-named recorded his place of residence only as Estonia. The pilgrimage from Courland to Bayreuth was also modest in size. Courland occurs in the statistics only in 1882 and 1888. The records for the year 1882 include just one registered visitor from Courland, who was from Liepaja. In 1888, there were six Courlandian visitors, including Prince Biron with a retinue, Count Freytag von Löringhoff, and Mrs. Dr. Waldhauer.[69]

It appears that no geographical and regional expansion of the pilgrimage comparable to that of Russia took place in the Baltic provinces. The interest in Wagner remained largely Livonia-centered throughout the late nineteenth century. This was at least partly due to the fact that the position

Table 7.3. Geographical distribution of Swedish visitors to Bayreuth in 1876, 1882, 1888, 1891, and 1899.

Year	1876	1882	1888	1891	1896	1899	Total
Stockholm	2	10	4	3	18	26	63
Gothenburg	–	–	–	4	–	8	12
Malmö	–	–	–	1	–	–	1
Lund	–	–	–	2	–	–	2
Borås	–	–	–	1	–	–	1
Uppsala	–	–	–	–	1	–	1
Helsingborg	–	–	–	–	–	1	1
Skottorp	–	–	–	–	–	1	1
The rest of Sweden	–	1	1	–	3	–	5
Swedes living abroad	2	–	–	1	–	–	3
Total	4	11	5	12	22	36	90

of the German minority was weakening year by year, simultaneously with a decrease in the proportion of Germans in the total population. In contrast to this, a Russian-type regional expansion seems to have taken place in Sweden during the 1880s and the 1890s, as table 7.3 reveals. The most widely distributed selection of Swedish visitors to Bayreuth was recorded in 1891, when the visitors recorded came not only from Stockholm but also from Gothenburg, Malmö, Lund, and Borås. The largest number of participants are recorded in the year 1899, when 36 Swedes visited the Bayreuth Festival. Apparently, the enthusiasm of the Swedes continued through the turn of the century, for the 1901 list includes 26 Swedes.

Even though the regional distribution of the Swedish travelers appears to broaden toward the turn of the century, one should keep in mind that the total numbers are not high, since Wagner tourism was an exclusive hobby. A large majority of Swedish visitors still came from Stockholm. In total, at least 90 Swedish persons had visited Bayreuth by the end of the century (in actual fact, many more, for not all of them were registered in the lists of visitors, and only six festivals out of thirteen can be counted). Of the number actually counted, 63 persons, that is, 70 percent, were from Stockholm. The geographic distribution of visitors to Bayreuth was not as broad in Sweden as in Russia, where there were more centers of interest in Wagner, and where a wealthy aristocracy could afford to travel to Germany. The Swedish world of music, especially opera, was concentrated in Stockholm, the home of the Royal Opera House, where the possibility of becoming acquainted with Wagner's works was far better than in the rest of Sweden. There was also an active musical life in Gothenburg, which was reflected in high frequencies of Bayreuth trips at the end of the century.

Table 7.4. Geographical distribution of Finnish visitors to Bayreuth in 1876, 1882, 1888, 1891, 1896, and 1899.

Year	1876	1882	1888	1891	1896	1899	Total
Helsinki	3	7	1	–	4	20	35
Viborg	–	–	–	–	1	–	1
The rest of Finland	–	1	2	–	–	2	5
Finns living abroad	–	–	–	1	–	–	1
Total	3	8	3	1	5	22	42

The central position of cities is also noticeable in the Finnish statistics (table 7.4). The total number of Finnish visitors to Bayreuth during these years, according to the surviving lists, was 42, of which 35 (83 percent) were from Helsinki. Finnish Wagnerism, in fact, was extremely Helsinki-centered. This emphasis on the capital was reinforced even more by the music institutions founded in the 1880s—the Helsinki Philharmonia and the Helsinki Conservatory—which began to function in 1882. Turku, which had been an unquestionable cultural center in Finland, is notable for its lack of inclusion in the sources on the Finnish reception of Wagner. Besides Helsinki, only Viborg, close to St. Petersburg and a place where musical life was really active, is included in the statistics. Far-reaching conclusions cannot, however, be reached because the numbers are so small, and lists for only six festivals have survived. The results may be regarded as indicating a likely trend. I have not made a global analysis, but it seems that interest in the Bayreuth Festivals in the Baltic world was great, even from an international perspective.

In total, the 1876, 1882, 1888, 1891, 1896, and 1899 festivals were visited by 90 Swedish, 42 Finnish, 115 Baltic, and 395 Russian travelers. The Grand Duchy of Finland and the Baltic provinces were part of the Russian Empire, but the information on the places of residence of visitors is reasonably reliable. Some of the visitors from the Baltic provinces may have been registered as Russians if, on coming to Bayreuth, they recorded their place of residence as Russia. In six festivals, the total number of music tourists from Sweden, Finland, Estonia, Livonia, and Courland, was 247 persons (that is, approximately 41 per festival). If we assume that attendance was much the same at the festivals for which no complete lists are available, the number of visitors in the nineteenth century could have totaled 535 people. This is high, considering that the Bayreuth Festival was within the reach only of a very exclusive social class. On the whole, the visitors came from the largest cities, such as Stockholm, Helsinki, and Riga. Of the 247 persons listed, 72 percent came from these centers. These, then, were the most central bases for the reception of Wagner during the nineteenth century.

The Cultural and Social Boundaries of Wagnerism

In the study of Wagnerism and interest in Wagner, it is important to focus attention not only on geographical but also on social features. The spread of Wagner's music and enthusiasm for Wagner were not only horizontal processes in which they spread from one place to another. The reception of Wagner was also a vertical social phenomenon. There is every reason to claim that the real boundaries of Wagnerism were social.

In his writings, Wagner defined his field as German national art, and he characterized himself as a genius through whom the nation spoke. This was, of course, a matter of rhetoric, typical of a Romantic composer, through which the artist was looking to justify his goals. On the other hand, Wagner's utopia genuinely included the idea of an approach to a larger public. Without this, he would not have intended his *Kaisermarsch* to be a national piece of music or to continuously aim for national status. The Bayreuth Festival also, at least in theory, offered everyone the possibility of attending. The members of the Wagner societies had the right to obtain tickets for the festival at a relatively low price. The purpose of the Bayreuth Bursary was to pay for those who could not otherwise afford to journey to the shrine of Wagner's art.

These estimable principles, however, remained mere principles for a long time. The Swedish *Aftonbladet*, quoting a German paper, stated that Wagner's art was not a coherent expression of the national spirit as the art of classical antiquity had been. Bayreuth was not a new Hellas despite the claims of the most enthusiastic Wagnerians:

> This festival has frequently been compared with the great national festivals in Hellas. Nothing could be more false. Major national customs and traditions can no more be suddenly called forth from the soil than can great national art. They are created by the people themselves gradually over many decades, nay, over many centuries. On Greek as on German soil, for the national epic to reach full flower in *one* form of art (rather than *two* as is the case with Wagner's musical dramas) needed a full century, in order to grow to that superb fruition of beauty which will achieve the world's enrapturement for all eternity. Only then will Richard Wagner have created a national musical drama, when the German people have adopted his melodies and style and reproduce them by instinct. At present, however, Wagner's melodies are less than popular; they are for the most part accessible only to an insignificant circle of musicians and musically educated music lovers. For the public, his music remains a book sealed with seven seals, and one would do the members of the public an injustice to reproach them for this. The *Nibelungenlied* has gone from strength to strength, but Wagner's creations are foreign to the people, who can find no entry into them. We should look upon the theater in Bayreuth with a clearer vision than that of those enthusiasts who through their fanaticism have become known as Wagner's friends.[70]

During the first Bayreuth Festival, the most sarcastic journalist in attendance had already drawn attention to the festival's audience. Karl Frenzel had written in the *National-Zeitung* that ordinary people had nothing to do "on the Green Hills": "Wagner has composed his favorite work for his patrons and friends, singers, stage directors, and conductors: with the exception of a very small group of people, mainly wealth and civilization are represented; the large masses of the people have been totally prevented from taking part in this activity."[71] Frenzel's interpretation is overcritical and polemic, for Wagner's purpose was not to perform his works only for his patrons and friends: he aimed at a wider audience. The method of organizing the festival was the main reason for the fact that it was attended very largely by patrons (that is, those who were ready to invest their share in Wagner's art either through patronage certificates or as members of a Wagner society). The societies had recruited wealthy people who were willing to support the modern artistic goals; but they also attracted musicians, composers, and artists who were interested in Wagner's art. Wagner's specific objective of merging music and drama into a functional whole (a new type of music drama) meant that the profile of those who were interested in his art was not as narrow as that of those attending traditional musical events. Writers also felt an interest in the venture, and Wagner also roused a certain amount of interest among academics. He had achieved a reputation as an art-theorist, which explains the fact that scholars of music and literature also showed interest and curiosity.

Frenzel listed the names of celebrities, artists, writers, poets, composers, scholars, and politicians he had seen in the festival audience. A similar picture was painted by Martin Wegelius in his article for the *Helsingfors Dagblad*:

> In 1848, the young refugee revolutionary could hardly have guessed that he would one day welcome the German emperor and numerous other princely guests in a theater of his own design, constructed for one of his own works. There is perhaps no artist in the world who has had a public of such renown, in all respects, as that which today filled the Wagner Theater. Wherever I turned my gaze, I beheld celebrities representing every branch of art and literature. Yet one had little time to gaze around. As soon as Kaiser Wilhelm had taken his place, at a signal, all the gas lamps in the theater were turned low; it became so dark that one could barely make out those sitting in one's immediate vicinity.[72]

Frenzel and Wegelius were not the only ones to take note of the celebrities attending the festival. It was seen as such an important event that people interested in fashionable high society occasions also attended. Wagner's festival aroused pan-European or even global interest, which made the composer a topic of conversation.

In this atmosphere the nobility was at ease. According to Frenzel, the hereditary nobility was particularly well represented; among the nobility the most ardent patrons were to be found:

> Alongside, or to be more precise, in front of these "knights of the spirit," the foreground was taken by the hereditary nobility. With their Valkyrian girdles, their looks and smiles, famous aristocratic ladies from Berlin, Vienna, and St. Petersburg, who comprise the real moving force in Wagnerism, played the part that fell to them. Behind them could be seen their cavaliers, willing or reluctant followers of the prophet; and bringing up the rear, the vengeful chorus of Enthusiasts. Everyone is familiar with the story of the Patriarch Cyrilius, who entered the gates of Alexandria accompanied by a bodyguard of monks armed with cudgels. The message of this arrière-garde was the same: Strike! hew!—the appeal to brute strength. Indeed, the comment by one staunch Wagnerian after the last day's performance was apposite: "May God be praised and thanked," he effused to one of the ladies, "that no one has been struck down or battered to death!"—This may serve as an indication of the mood that prevailed at Bayreuth, notwithstanding the presence of all those noble and beautiful ladies.[73]

Frenzel focused attention on the aristocratic ladies who came from Berlin, Vienna, and St. Petersburg. The role of the aristocracy should not be overemphasized, but the fact is that Wagner did have wealthy aristocratic patrons. In Berlin, one of his most important patrons was Marie von Schleinitz. Wagner had achieved success in St. Petersburg during his visit to Russia. Grand Duchess Elena was particularly willing to support him financially, to such an extent, in fact, that Wagner even considered moving to Russia. Despite Wagner's former activities as an anarchist and revolutionary, he had enjoyed a close relationship with King Ludwig II of Bavaria from as far back as 1864. Wagner's royalism was probably apt to kindle enthusiasm in aristocratic circles.

Besides nobility, Frenzel also emphasizes femininity in his comments. The ladies were escorted by their companions, who were not as interested in the festival as their partners. The Russian composer Peter Tchaikovsky, who participated in the 1876 festival, also referred to femininity in his letter to the *Russky Viedomosty* newspaper. He describes the women attending the festival as "false" or "dishonest admirers" of Wagner. Tchaikovsky had been conversing about Wagner with a Russian businessman who had no knowledge at all of music. In his letter he also mentions the female members of the audience:

> I made acquaintance of a Russian business man who assured me that he acknowledges Wagner alone in the field of music. "But are you familiar with all the others?" I asked him. It turned out that my dear fellow-countryman had no idea about music but had the fortune to be personally acquainted with the Master and had been invited to his receptions. He was very flattered by this and felt it his duty to deny

everything which Wagner himself did not recognize. Wagner has, of course, a great many sincere and enthusiastic devotees among professional musicians. These, however, came to a conscious enthusiasm by means of study and if Wagner is to get any moral support in seeking out his Ideal it will be through the warm-hearted devotion of these people. It would be interesting to discover if Wagner is able to differentiate them from the horde of false admirers—the women in particular—who from their standpoint of ignorance are impatiently against all those who do not share their opinions.[74]

Gender among Wagnerian enthusiasts is in itself an important question, and is particularly worthy of analysis as Wagner is frequently associated with masculinity. Tchaikovsky's comment does not offer any jumping-off point from which to come to deeper conclusions. He regarded the women as "false admirers," being not only ignorant but also impatient, with a willingness to express ungrounded opinions. It might be suggested that Tchaikovsky's homosexuality was connected with his negative attitude toward femininity but, in this case, his personal motivations are not particularly important. Tchaikovsky's words can be judged as comments on the early Wagner audience. Was the women's role emphasized among Wagner's enthusiasts? The field of musical literature was overwhelmingly masculine in the German musical world during the nineteenth century.[75] Critics, writers of music, and scholars of music were, almost without exception, male. The same can be said of the newspaper debates on Wagner, which were conducted in the readers' columns by males. In this respect, the Wagnerian reception was no different from the reception of other composers. But why did Frenzel and Tchaikovsky focus attention on women? Or were the female members of the audience simply more willing to express their opinions?

These questions are difficult to answer, for there is no information with which to construct a gender profile of those listening to Wagner's music. Yet, after all, it would not be strange if females were attracted by Wagner's music. In many of his operas, Wagner dealt with themes that were connected with womanhood. In *Tannhäuser*, he had presented a twofold image of a woman in a way typical of Western culture: the sensual Venus and the chaste Elizabeth were opposing polarities. In his later works, however, Wagner strove to rid himself of these stereotypical images of femininity and to see the physical and the spiritual as an inseparable whole. This striving was perhaps most perfectly crystallized in *Tristan und Isolde*. Wagner had also dealt with the emancipation of women, in the second part of the *Ring*, *Die Walküre*. Here, Brünnhilde revolts against her father and will finally be condemned by him. In *Siegfried*, Wotan, the father (see figure 7.5), is forced to accept the futility of his attempts at manipulation, and he completely withdraws from the stage. The question of femininity puzzled Wagner, even on his deathbed. His last writing was a fragment of the text *Über das*

Figure 7.5. Franz Betz as Wotan in the first Bayreuth production of *Der Ring des Nibelungen* in 1876. National Archive of the Richard Wagner Foundation, Bayreuth.

Weibliche im Menschlichen (*The Human Womanly*) in which he opposes the arranged marriages of a class-based society:

> Whereas the fall of human races lies before us plain as day, we see the other animal species preserved in greatest purity, except where man has meddled in their cross-ing: manifestly, because they know no "marriage of convenience" with a view to goods and property. In fact they know no marriage at all; and if it is Marriage that

Table 7.5. Numbers of female Swedish, Finnish, and Baltic visitors to Bayreuth in 1876, 1882, 1888, 1891, 1896, and 1899.

Year	1876	1882	1888	1891	1896	1899	Total
Sweden	–	6	1	6	7	14	34
Finland	–	2	–	–	2	12	16
The Baltic provinces	3	10	9	18	6	10	56
Total	3	18	10	24	15	36	106

Table 7.6. Percentages of women among Swedish, Finnish, and Baltic visitors to Bayreuth in 1876, 1882, 1888, 1891, 1896, and 1899.

Year	1876	1882	1888	1891	1896	1899	Average
Sweden	–	54%	20%	50%	32%	39%	38%
Finland	–	25%	–	–	40%	54%	38%
The Baltic provinces	27%	53%	43%	54%	67%	45%	49%
Average	17%	47%	34%	52%	42%	45%	43%

> raises man so far above the animal world, to highest evolution of his moral faculties, it is the abuse of marriage, for quite other ends, that is the ground of our decline below the beasts.[76]

It would be interesting to discover how the upper-class ladies of the nineteenth century reacted to Brünnhilde who had clearly rejected class-based distinctions in society, but the surviving material from the Baltic world does not include any references to females' reactions to the composer. It is, however, possible to approach the subject on a more concrete level and to estimate the number of female visitors in the festival audience; although these figures, in themselves, do not reveal much of the visitors' actual experience.

Some of the records in the visitor lists, concerning female guests from Sweden, Finland, Estonia, Livonia, and Courland, are difficult to interpret. A couple of times the expression "mit Familie" (with the family) occurs in the lists, making it impossible to define precisely the size or the gender profile of the visiting family. In these cases my statistical tabulation is based on the probability of one daughter per family. It is, however, difficult to estimate the extent to which the members of a visiting family actually participated in the performances. The occurrence of female visitors in the lists is seen in table 7.5. The results are tabulated as percentages in table 7.6, but one should bear in mind that, for example, in the years 1876 and 1888 the numbers of visitors are so small that any conclusions based on these numbers are merely speculative. As the statistics indicate, the proportion of female

members among the visitors to six festivals is as high as to 43 percent; which
is relatively large. Almost half of the visitors from the Baltic provinces were
women. The proportion of Swedish and Finnish female visitors to the festivals is somewhat lower, at 38 percent. The statistics for Finland reveal that
in 1899, the majority of the Finnish visitors were female.

Traveling in Europe increased significantly during the nineteenth
century. Movement around the continent turned into tourism. Through
Thomas Cook's initiatives, conducted tours became familiar throughout
the Western world.[77] The spread of the railroad network also made traveling quicker and more convenient. Toward the end of the century, the
number of female passengers, traveling alone or in company, increased
considerably. Quite a large proportion of women came to Bayreuth without
traveling in the company of a male. On the basis of the *Fremdenlisten* it is difficult to reach any firm conclusions about the company in which people
arrived, but it is possible to calculate the number of wives, widows, and self-
employed women who traveled independently. Women accompanied by
their husbands were, without exception, registered with their husbands in
this fashion: "Siegert Emil, mit Gattin, Musikdirektor" (Siegert, Emil, with
wife, Music Director).[78] The 1882 festival was visited by Lilly Bäckström with
her lady companion, Miss Rosa Durrwang, and maid, and Baroness von
Hartmann with her daughters from Sweden. From Riga came Miss Emma
Sprost, the ladies Emilie Barth and Marie von Berens, and Therese Müller
with her daughters. Baroness Maydell was also among the Livonian visitors.[79] According to Frenzel, there were female aristocrats in abundance at
Bayreuth. The aristocracy was indeed well represented in the audience, but
the women who came alone or in female company do not appear to have
belonged to the nobility; they were rather members of the middle class or
classifiable as intellectuals. For example, the wives and daughters of Senators Mechelin and Munck from Finland participated in the 1899 festival.
The same festival was also visited by Amalie Ingman, wife of a procurator,
Marie Luise Wasenius, and Thérèse Hahl, who had already visited Bayreuth
in 1882, and who was reputed to have heard *Parsifal* on the Green Hill
thirteen times.[80]

In the study of the social boundaries of Wagnerism, gender is a significant factor, but at the same time, it is possible to scrutinize the Wagner
devotees' social background in general. Obviously, sources of information
on the relationship of a particular set of social affiliations with an interest
in music are scarce, especially if the investigation is limited to a single composer. How can we know who listened to Schubert or Chopin? The lists of
visitors to Bayreuth are, in this respect also, unique source material. In
addition to the visitor's name and place of residence, occupation, academic
degree, title, or some other indicator of social status were also included
in the lists, although not in all cases. In my analysis, I have divided the
Swedish, Finnish, and Baltic visitors roughly into groups. I have placed

those whose status is not mentioned in the sources in a group titled "others."

My classification requires some additional explanation. Occupational distinctions are not easy to draw. In my classification, the group titled "music" includes professional musicians, singers, teachers of singing, ballet dancers, opera and theater directors, and composers. The music business was also represented in the festival audience: for instance, R. E. Westerlund from Helsinki and Paul Nelder from Riga visited Bayreuth in 1899, but I have placed them in the group called "entrepreneurs." Among those titled "journalists" there are many who earned their living at least to some extent by writing reviews of music. These included, among others, the Swede Fredrik Vult von Steijern (1891, 1899) and the Livonian Carl Waack (1891). I have classified these as journalists, because on registering at Bayreuth, they specified their journalistic status. Many of those I have categorized as "academics" may have earned their living in the field of music. For example, the music writer Carl Friedrich Glasenapp worked for a long time at the Riga Polytechnicum.

Categorization of the aristocracy also constitutes a problem. Members of the nobility could function under other headings, for instance, in administration. In the group titled "nobility" I have included only those visitors who stated no other affiliation or occupation.

Table 7.7 appears to imply that the social spread of Wagner travelers was broader in the Baltic provinces than in Sweden and in Finland. On the other hand, with respect to Finland, the total actual count of visitors is so small that the occupational breakdown should not be overinterpreted. Perhaps table 7.8, in which the status categories have been represented as percentages, might be of help. A social breakdown for each region has been presented in this table, as has the percentage of the total number of Swedish, Finnish, and Baltic visitors in each social group.

Table 7.8 seems to indicate that in relation to social status there were significant differences between the Swedish, Finnish, and Baltic visitors to Bayreuth. For Finland, the groups representing music (38 percent) and administration (33 percent) stand out at the top of the scale. However, almost no journalists came from Finland. Although Martin Wegelius was prepared to publicize his experiences, the small number of journalists reflects the low status of music within the Finnish public sphere in general. The representation of the Finnish nobility and the bourgeois merchant class was also small. A typical Finnish visitor to Bayreuth was not a professional in music like Richard Faltin (1876, 1882, 1888), Edvard Fazer (1891), or Karl Flodin (1896); most often, he or, in the case of a woman, her husband was a government or municipal official. Many Finnish visitors also worked at the country's only university, in Helsinki. The first festival was visited by, among others, Fredrik Saltzmann (1839–1914), who at the time worked as docent of surgery at the University of Helsinki.[81] Professors

Table 7.7. Social status of Swedish, Finnish, and Baltic visitors to Bayreuth in 1876, 1882, 1888, 1891, and 1899.

	Music	Nobility	Entrepreneurs	Administration	Academics	Journalists	Others
Sweden							
1876	3					1	
1882	2	3		2		5	
1888	1			1		3	
1891	3	1		1	2	2	3
1896	5	1	1	2	4	2	7
1899	3	9		10		3	9
Total	17	14	1	16	6	7	28
Finland							
1876	2				1		
1882	3			2	3		
1888	2			1			
1891	1						
1896	4				1		
1899	4	2	2	11			3
Total	16	2	2	14	5		3
The Baltic provinces							
1876	2	2	1	2	1	1	2
1882	4	5	4	3		1	2
1888	1	6		8	4		2
1891	4	11	4	2	4	1	7
1896	1	2			1		5
1899		2	1	7	6		6
Total	12	28	10	22	16	3	24
Overall totals							
	45	44	13	52	27	10	55

Hans Seiling and August Fredrik Sundell attended the 1882 festival.[82] Sundell visited Bayreuth for a second time in 1884.[83]

   Among the Swedish visitors, the number of professionals in music was relatively low compared to the Finns, but the most widely known names in the field are, of course, to be found in the lists. The opera singer Fritz Arlberg, the number one Swedish campaigner for Wagner, participated in

Table 7.8. Social status of Swedish, Finnish, and Baltic visitors to Bayreuth (given as percentages) in 1876, 1882, 1888, 1891, 1896, and 1899.

	Music	Nobility	Entrepreneurs	Administration	Academics	Journalists	Others	Total
Sweden	19%	16%	1%	18%	7%	8%	31%	100%
Finland	38%	5%	5%	33%	12%	–	7%	100%
Baltic provinces	10%	24%	9%	19%	14%	3%	21%	100%
Baltic Sea Area	18%	19%	5%	21%	11%	4%	22%	100%

the 1876 and 1882 festivals. The 1876 festival was visited by Ludvig Josephson, later the director of the Royal Opera House in Stockholm. The 1891 festival was visited by conductor and composer Karl Valentin with his family, and the 1899 festival by music critic and composer Wilhelm Peterson-Berger. The opera director Axel Burén was at Bayreuth in 1896.[84] Swedish singers such as Johannes Elmblad, Olive Fremstad, and Erik Smedes were often in the cast of Bayreuth performances; singers were not always included in the lists of visitors.[85]

In the Swedish group, the proportion of government and municipal officials, and academics, is clearly lower than in the Finnish group. However, 16 percent of the Swedes came from the nobility. It is possible, even probable, that visitors who were members of the nobility worked in administration but registered their noble status rather than their middle-class occupation. On the other hand, Fredrik Vult von Steijern, a Swedish supporter of the Bayreuth Circle, whose enthusiasm for Wagner will be described in chapter 8, had an aristocratic background but always recorded his journalistic connections.[86]

Among the Baltic visitors, the occupational profile is broad and probably more evenly distributed than in the Finnish and Swedish group. An interesting feature is the clearly smaller representation of music professionals. It appears that devotion to Wagner was not just a matter for professionals. The largest number of representatives of the field of music came from Riga. These included the conductor Julius Ruthardt (1876), the pianist Heinrich Höhne (1882), the conductors Emil Siegert (1882) and Otto Lohse (1888), and the singing teacher Monica Hunnius (1896).[87] These visitors had an advanced and varied musical education, and their activity was reflected in the musical life of Riga. Ruthardt, for example, had born in Stuttgart in 1841 and had worked in Riga since 1871 as a conductor and composer. His output includes music for the Norwegian playwright Bjørnson's tragedy, *Hulda*.[88] Otto Lohse, born in Dresden in 1858, was also a versatile musician and composer. He was known first as a cellist and was already playing in the Bayreuth Festival orchestra in 1886.[89] From 1889, he worked as a conductor of the Riga

Town theater. Besides this, Lohse taught, wrote reviews for the *Zeitung für Stadt und Land*, acted as a musical leader in the Riga Wagner Society, and composed actively whenever time allowed. His output consisted mainly of choral and orchestral works. In addition, he composed a three act opera, *Der Prinz wider Willen* (*A Prince against His Will*). During the winter 1888–89 season, Lohse particularly influenced the Wagnerian reception in Riga by conducting a series of five historical concerts, the income from which was donated, without deductions, to the Bayreuth Patronage Society.[90]

Even though the majority of Baltic musicians and composers seem to have come from Riga, there were exceptions, such as Heinrich Zöllner, the music director of the University of Tartu and an eminent figure in his town. He was one of those at the 1882 festival who witnessed the premiere of *Parsifal*.[91] According to documents in the Estonian Historical Archives, Zöllner was a frequent visitor to Germany in the 1880s.[92] Zöllner also represented academics; these, at 14 percent of the Baltic group, comprised a larger percentage than in the Finnish or Swedish groups. Most of the Baltic academics were, however, from Riga. The only visitor from Tartu besides Zöllner was Emil Musso, a student who participated in the first festival in 1876.[93] The academics of Riga are well represented in the lists. Prof. Carl Bischoff participated in the festivals at least in 1888, 1896, and 1899. The 1888 festival was attended by Prof. Theodor Groenberg and the last festival of the century by the well-known mathematician Piers Bohl.[94]

The representation of nobility and merchants among the Baltic guests was notably large. Old German nobility still existed in the Baltic provinces, and many of its members visited Bayreuth, including Baron von Wöhrmann (1876) and Baroness Maydell (1882) from Livonia and Prince Biron (1888), Baron Freytag von Löringhoff (1888, 1891), Baron Konrad von Vietinghoff (1891), and Baron Arthur von Vietinghoff (1896) from Courland.[95] On the other hand, there was a large German merchant class in the Baltic provinces, and in Riga at least, these burghers were generous patrons of music. This merchant class offered ample support for Wagner.

If visits to Bayreuth are regarded as indicators of Wagnerism, the social boundaries of this phenomenon seem to change, to a degree, according to geographical region in the Baltic world. An interesting question is whether any changes, which are recognizable through records of visits to Bayreuth, took place in the social groups with an interest in Wagner during the years 1876–99. Table 7.7, in my opinion, implies that the social spread of Wagnerism in the Baltic provinces was already broad at the first 1876 festival, whereas in Finland and in Sweden it broadened later, as late as the 1890s. It must be remembered that Wagner's works had been heard continuously in Riga since the composer's period of residence in the town. The Baltic-German minority was also extremely interested in German cultural novelties, which offered a solid footing for Wagner. This appears to explain the fact that not only music professionals were enthusiastic about Wagner.

In the nineteenth century, Finnish interest in Wagner was probably the most limited, in terms of the different groups involved; apart from music professionals, generally speaking only academics and administrative officials were involved in the Wagnerian cult. Apparently, this situation continued until the 1899 festival. In Sweden, people interested in Wagner had begun to come from a broader social spectrum in the 1890s, rather earlier than in Finland. This difference between the two countries could, at least in part, be explained by economic conditions in Finland, which was one of the poorest countries in Europe. Only a small number of people could afford to attend operatic performances or make the trip to Bayreuth. On the other hand, opera, as part of the culture of the nobility and the bourgeoisie, had a long tradition in Sweden. Furthermore, in Sweden, Wagner's works had been performed in the Royal Opera House since the 1860s; therefore some indigenous Wagner enthusiasm had already been kindled. In Stockholm, opera was a form of art favored by the upper class and, hence, not only professionals within the field of music but also others were attracted to the south. Although Wagner's *Tannhäuser* had been performed in Finland in 1857, no other Wagner operas were performed there before the twentieth century. This situation made Finnish musicians, musicologists, and composers eager to travel to Germany, because they could not otherwise hear Wagner's works, and it explains why the proportion of music professionals in the Finnish group of visitors is larger than in the Swedish or the Baltic groups.

The Bayreuth lists of visitors, however, represent only a very narrow view of Wagnerism. In chapter 8, I will deal with the activity that was channeled into the functioning of the Wagner societies. A further scrutiny of the social spread of Wagnerism is thus made possible, by focusing attention on the question of which circles of devotees and professionals in the Baltic world regarded the provision of financial support of Wagner's projects as being truly important.

The Campaigners for Bayreuth

Patrons, Agents, Societies

The Wagner societies played an essential role in the fulfillment of the Bayreuth project from 1871 onward. As no support from the state was available, this network of societies seemed to be the only means by which the future of the festival could be guaranteed. In this situation, organizing a collection was a pioneering activity, but it was also apt to rouse suspicion among contemporaries, which explains the fact that enthusiasm was not as great as it might have been.[1] The first Bayreuth Festival led to organizational reforms, and, in 1877, a general Patronat-Verein was established as the parent organization of the societies. According to Paragraph I of the parent society's laws, the central activity of the societies was to work for the arrangement and fulfillment of the festival along Richard Wagner's lines. Paragraph II states that the societies should operate in two directions: they had to manage the financing so as to ensure the possibility of an annual festival; and they were to endeavor to spread the knowledge of Wagner's art. The third paragraph set out the membership fees and ticket prices. It was decided that the annual membership fee should be 100 German marks and the price of a ticket 100 marks. According to an additional clause, the societies were allowed to sell tickets to their members at a lower price than to nonmembers.[2]

After the first festival, Wagner concluded that, financially speaking, the project had been a complete failure. It had been a large-scale operation: the operatic theater had been built, the orchestra and soloists had been hired, and the costumes, stage decorations, and facilities had been acquired. The total cost was 1,281,000 German marks, and in addition, Wagner still owed 216,000 marks out of a loan he had received in 1873 from the Bavarian State Treasury. It was obvious that the next festival could not take place in the following year. Wagner considered withdrawing from the whole venture and selling his theater to the state of Bavaria or possibly to private entrepreneurs in the field.[3] He even planned to emigrate to the United States.

The debt to the Bavarian state was paid off in March 1878, after which the financial situation was eased. In the same year, Wagner decided that the

Ring would not be performed at Bayreuth until conditions were favorable. The opera cycle was licensed to be performed by other opera houses, and the first to seize this opportunity was Angelo Neumann, under whose leadership the *Ring* was staged in Leipzig as early as 1878.[4] Wagner could now concentrate all his efforts on the arrangement of the next festival around the aura created by his new work, *Parsifal.* The role of the Patronat-Verein was still important, as new patrons had to be recruited quickly in order to keep up financial support. The society also began to publish a journal to publicize Wagnerism, the *Bayreuther Blätter,* and strove to spread it beyond the borders of Germany as a connecting link to all Wagner enthusiasts. By subscribing, enthusiasts could support the Wagner project.

Interest in Wagner spread with rapidity through the activities of the Patronat-Verein, an internationally organized society. The organization also reached the Baltic world, above all Finland and the Baltic provinces, but it failed to find an agent in Sweden. However, Fredrik Vult von Steijern, an active supporter of the Bayreuth Circle who devoted himself to spreading the message of Wagnerism, was active in Sweden and also supported Wagnerian activities through his personal donations. The role of advocates and agents was accentuated in the late 1870s and 1880s. Every district had a leader or leaders representing the Bayreuth project: Vult von Steijern in Sweden, Faltin and Wegelius in Finland, and Glasenapp in Livonia. They embodied Wagnerism in the Baltic world. It is therefore essential to examine their personal Wagner histories and their energetic efforts to arouse a Wagner cult in their home countries.

Almost a Relative: Fredrik Vult von Steijern

Despite the success achieved by the Wagner operas of the 1870s, organized Wagnerism did not arise at an international level in the way that Wagner himself had wished. The sources do not mention any functioning Wagner society in Sweden during the nineteenth century. From the 1850s onward, Wagnerians such as August Söderman existed in Sweden, but devotees of Wagner's art did not function as members of a society. Adolf Lindgren in *Om Wagnerismen* understood Wagnerism as an aesthetic movement, not as a civic activity. Wilhelm Peterson-Berger, in his scrutiny of the Swedish reception of Wagner, does not refer to any society.[5]

If a Swedish society had existed in the nineteenth century, it would certainly have left traces in the Wagner Archives in Bayreuth. When the *Bayreuther Blätter* published a catalog indicating the donations received from different countries, money appeared to come from both Helsinki and Riga, but not from Stockholm.[6] The membership lists of the Patronat-Verein from 1885, 1891, 1892, 1894, and 1896 do not include a single Swedish name.[7]

Despite the lack of an agent of the Patronat-Verein in Sweden, the increase in interest in Wagner is surely indicated by the circulation of the *Bayreuther Blätter*. Subscriptions to the journal after the first Bayreuth festival were relatively modest. At the end of 1878, the *Bayreuther Blätter* published a catalog of the localities in which subscribers lived. The total circulation of the *Bayreuther Blätter*, at that time, was 1,232 copies, and subscribers lived in 188 locations including Stockholm with one copy and Gothenburg with as many as seven copies.[8] A catalog of subscribers to the *Bayreuther Blätter*, a memorandum of addresses, a book of accounts, and receipts have survived in the Hans von Wolzogen collection in the Wagner Archives. Through these sources it might be possible to identify the Swedish subscribers, but the material is far from perfect and does not reveal any overall picture of the history of the journal. The 1883 catalog of subscribers comprises 159 names, and the 1884 catalog 288 names, but not a single Swedish name is included.[9] The name of the Swedish opera singer J. Salomon is, however, found in the book of addresses.[10] Another Swedish name, Fredrik Vult von Steijern, is to be found in the pile of subscription receipts.

Vult von Steijern (see figure 8.1) was probably a regular subscriber to the journal, but the surviving receipts cover only two years (from 1917 and 1918). This Stockholm Wagnerian had a villa in Saltsjöbaden, and his subscription fees were paid from there.[11] Vult von Steijern was a contributor to the *Bayreuther Blätter*, and his name occurs in the membership list of the Patronat-Verein in the section titled "Ortsvertretung der Redaktion der Bayreuther Blätter" (Local Representatives of the Editors of the *Bayreuther Blätter*).[12] Vult von Steijern had a good relationship with the Bayreuth Circle, but the relationship was personal and did not have a wider impact on the Swedish reception of Wagner. The *Bayreuther Blätter* published writings by Vult von Steijern, including an article, "Aus dem Briefe eines Schweden über Bayreuth," in which he stresses the significance of Wagner in his own development: "It is only here at Bayreuth that all the regenerative significance of this art became perfectly clear to me."[13]

Fredrik Vult von Steijern was a reporter for the *Dagens Nyheter* and a writer of broad experience. His interest in music began in his youth, and he got to know Wagner's work at the Royal Opera performances in Stockholm. A good picture of Vult von Steijern's musical development is to be found in his diary, which he started in 1874. The diary is made up of several dozen volumes and is now in the collections of the Royal Library of Sweden.

Vult von Steijern was a regular concertgoer, but his comments prior to his trip to Germany in 1877 do not show him to be a great believer in Wagner. If his diary entries can be trusted, he had attended the Swedish *Lohengrin* premiere on 22 January 1874 but not the *Tannhäuser* performance by the German Henneberg Opera Company at Stockholm's Mindre Teatern on 16 August 1876. In 1876, he heard Wagner's music mainly as concert

Figure 8.1. Fredrik Vult von Steijern (1851–1919). Reproduced by Marie Persson, the Royal Library, National Library of Sweden.

numbers. On 19 November the pianist Richard Anderson played the Funeral March from *Götterdämmerung* at a matinee.[14]

Wagner appeared in Vult von Steijern's diaries, in the first place, during his 1877 journey to Germany and his visits to Leipzig and Nuremberg. On 29 April 1877, he heard *Tristan und Isolde*. He was, however, far more influenced by *Der fliegende Holländer* and *Tannhäuser*. According to his diary entry for 23 August, he describes the stirring impression *Der fliegende Hol-länder* had made upon him. At the same time, he reveals that he has seen the work on two previous occasions. In general, the diary entries are brief, and he is not inclined to provide detailed descriptions of his experiences. Therefore, the lines devoted to *Der fliegende Holländer* reveal a great deal. His Wagner fever continued in September, when, after a long interval, he saw *Tannhäuser*. He saw it again in November.[15] Vult von Steijern's enthusiasm for Wagner thus originated in these experiences. His descriptions of Swedish concerts changed abruptly in the following year: in December 1878, he saw *Tannhäuser* at the Royal Opera House four times in succession.[16] In 1884, he also saw Labatt's guest performance of *Tannhäuser* and praised it as the best performance, apparently, ever seen in Sweden.[17] In 1887, he saw *Die Meistersinger*, but no comments on this are to be found in his diary.[18]

Vult von Steijern's first visit to Bayreuth took place in 1891. He arrived on 15 August and attended the *Tristan* performance on the very same day. The following day was devoted to *Parsifal*. The lack of a performance on 17th August enabled Vult von Steijern to visit Wagner's grave in the yard of the Villa Wahnfried and the Hermitage outside Bayreuth. He met the Norwegian soprano Ellen Gulbranson and Cosima Wagner herself. The diary does not reveal how he became acquainted with Cosima, but it was probably arranged through Gulbranson. The appearance of Vult von Steijern's name as one of the reporters for the *Bayreuther Blätter* in 1891 is no coincidence. He apparently also became acquainted with many other members of the Wagner inner circle. This time, his visit to Bayreuth was brief. On 18 August, he attended a performance of *Tannhäuser* and on 19 August he saw *Parsifal* again. On the following day, he left for Würzburg.[19]

Vult von Steijern returned to Bayreuth in 1892. The first performance given in rain-drenched Bayreuth was *Parsifal*, of which Vult von Steijern recorded in his diary: "*Parsifal*. Wonderful—everything outside it was forgotten, only mere pleasure and, despite this, not the same renunciation as last year; how is it that do I not know when the performance will completely seize me?"[20] The next performance was *Tristan*: "Wonderful, wonderful—this performance is more rewarding than ever."[21] On 24 July, Vult von Steijern attempted to pay a visit to Cosima Wagner, but was not given an audience. A meeting was finally arranged on 30 July at a soirée held by Frau Wagner at the Villa Wahnfried. Vult von Steijern had the chance only to exchange a few words with Cosima, but Hans von Wolzogen introduced him to Felix Mottl, Albert Fuchs, and Wagner's English son-in-law Houston Stewart Chamberlain. On 2 August, Vult von Steijern met Wolzogen, with whom he took a long walk. On the following day, with his wife Gerda, he visited the Wolzogens. His relationship with Hans von Wolzogen, editor in chief of the *Bayreuther Blätter*, was extremely close. On 5 August, Vult von Steijern had a long discussion on Wagner with Wolzogen during a walking tour. On 7 and 8 August, Baroness von Wolzogen visited Fredrik and his wife Gerda.[22]

This time, Vult von Steijern's stay was long, and he attended almost all the performances that were given. Toward the end of the festival, his friendship with Chamberlain became much closer. After the performance of *Tristan und Isolde* on 20 August, Vult von Steijerns dined with the Wolzogens and the Chamberlains. On the eve of the festival's last performance, *Parsifal,* Vult von Steijern writes: "Farewell to all the acquaintances; the Wolzogens, von Groß, Kniese, Glasenapp, Ellis, and many others, last but not least Chamberlain; all of you with whom we have made friends."[23] In his writings, Chamberlain frequently stressed the racial side of his father-in-law: he saw the regenerative influence of Wagner's art as a racial question, and doubtlessly this political element was discussed during his encounters with Vult von Steijern. Unfortunately, the latter's diary entries are so brief that the content of his discussions in Bayreuth remains unclear. Writing in the *Bayreuther Blätter* in 1891, however, he referred to Chamberlain's and Wolzogen's views on Wagner as a manifestation of Aryan culture.

In 1894, after a year's absence, Vult von Steijern again visited Bayreuth. Although the visit was very brief, it included meetings with Cosima Wagner, Wolzogen, Chamberlain, and William Ashton Ellis.[24] The 1895 Bayreuth Festival was also excluded from his program, but he and his wife did spend October and November in Germany. The couple happened to be in Berlin during the premiere of *Die Walküre*, about which Fredrik wrote in his diary: "An unusually carefully constructed production."[25] On 8 October, he saw *Rienzi* for the first time in Dresden, which made "a particular impression" on him.[26] Together with the complete *Ring*, the Dresden repertoire included *Lohengrin, Die Meistersinger,* and *Tannhäuser.*[27] The Wagner repertoire in Dresden was probably more tempting than that of the Bayreuth Festival and, therefore, Vult von Steijern decided to put off visiting the festival until the next time. During his travels in Germany, he also obtained a copy of Chamberlain's biography of Wagner, which had recently been published.[28]

In 1896, Vult von Steijern again made a pilgrimage to Bayreuth, and, on 17 July, Chamberlain and Ellen Gulbranson were looking forward to meeting him at the railroad station on the arrival of his train from Dresden. On the very same evening, the group assembled at the Villa Wahnfried in the company of the opera singer Johannes Elmblad and the father of Wagnerian activities, Emil Heckel.[29] This visit was really long, and Vult von Steijern did not leave the festival town until 20 August. In a period of just over a month, he heard the *Ring* five times and attended the Wahnfried parties on three occasions. From this one could conclude that his relationship with Cosima had become closer.[30] During the following summer, Vult von Steijern again visited the festival, and he mentions in his diary that he was even allowed to sit beside Frau Cosima during the banquet, which doubtlessly reflects his popularity. The same table also included the leading figure in the Riga Wagner Society, Carl Friedrich Glasenapp.[31] It appears that Glasenapp was not one of Vult von Steijern's closest contacts, for there are few references to Glasenapp in the diary. On the other hand, the Vult von Steijern collection in the Royal Library of Sweden includes Glasenapp's *Richard Wagner als Mensch* (1890) with the author's dedication to his "friend."[32]

Vult von Steijern's contacts with Bayreuth were reinforced throughout the 1890s, and they continued into the second decade of the twentieth century. They were his personal contacts, however, and had no long-term impact on the Swedish reception of Wagner. As a reporter, Vult von Steijern's position was certainly influential. On the other hand, his name does not occur very often in the history of Swedish music and opera. Vult von Steijern's unique Wagner collection must, however, have had a significance of its own. He was an avid collector of anything connected with Wagner; amassing the composer's own texts and also biographies and treatises on the composer. The collection even includes lists of visitors to the Bayreuth Festival, lists that are not available as a complete series even at the Wagner Archives in Bayreuth. The availability of this extensive Wagner library made a remarkable contribution to Swedish knowledge of the composer.

It is very likely that Vult von Steijern exercised an influence on the operatic life of Stockholm despite his repeated disappearances into the background. For example, Vult von Steijern's name appears briefly in the source material on the Wagner performances planned in 1894–95. In fall 1893, Harald Molander had contacted Henrik Hennings in order to arrange a Wagner performance featuring Angelo Neumann's opera company in Stockholm and, possibly, in Copenhagen.[33] The plan fell through, but in May 1894, Hennings returned to the matter. Neumann's famous and highly appreciated tour did not reach Sweden, but the director of the Breslau (Wroclaw) theater, Dr. Loewe, decided to arrange performances in Copenhagen, and it was Hennings who took responsibility for the arrangements. Before the performances, Hennings proposed to Molander that, during the same tour, the show could be brought as far as Stockholm.[34] The correspondence was extended to Johannes Elmblad, and the price of the tickets and the tight schedule appeared to become a sticking-point. The Swedish side was also probably suspicious about the artistic standard of the performances, for Hennings can be seen trying to convince Molander and Elmblad of "the artistically high standard and solidity of the production."[35] Molander replied that the schedule, in the end, was too tight, and it would be impossible to make arrangements with the Royal Opera House in a tactful manner.[36] Molander also wrote to Elmblad and to Chamberlain Burén at the Royal Opera House. To Burén, Molander explained that there were too many go-betweens in the affair. Apparently, Vult von Steijern had also participated in the planning of the project, as Hennings had mentioned his name in a letter to Elmblad on 5 May 1894.[37] Molander also wrote to Loewe in Breslau (Wroclaw), stressing that financial conditions were a constraint. The lack of a guaranteed audience, which would have eliminated the risks, was also a problem: "One is apt to forget that there is no Wagner audience here; this audience will not become available as a gift, but, on the contrary, must be conquered using all possible means."[38] Attempts to change the schedule at the last moment would deal the whole affair "der Mord des ganzen Geschäft," a fatal blow.[39]

Vult von Steijern's role in this episode, or in Molander's words, "in this Wagner farce," is unclear, but it is clear that he participated in the preparations and preliminary negotiations. Vult von Steijern was without doubt ready to campaign for a Wagner repertoire in Stockholm by all possible means. It was accordingly no wonder that, when a staging of *Die Walküre* was finally announced at the Royal Opera House, and when the ticket booking list was made public, Vult von Steijern, Regeringsgatan 28, is in twenty-fifth position on the list. The name of bank director Ernest Thiel (1859–1947), who was Vult von Steijern's close friend, an ardent Wagnerian and a well-known collector of art, is also found on the list.[40] It seems that the Swedish campaigners for Wagner were either professionals in the field of music or representatives of the upper classes like Thiel or Vult von Steijern. The campaigners, however, did not come together to pursue their interests, and therefore no Wagner society came into being in Sweden during the nineteenth century.

The Representatives of Finland:
Richard Faltin and Martin Wegelius

Even though Swedish musical life was of higher caliber and its traditions were older than those in Finland, activities connected with Wagner met with greater appreciation in Finland. Overall, German music culture was dominant in Finland, whereas strong connections to France existed in Sweden. Contrary to conditions on the western side of the Baltic Sea, many Wagner operas could not for practical reasons be performed in Finland. Paradoxically Wagnerism was more active in Finland and was also channeled into societal activities.

One of the most important advocates of Wagnerism in Finland was Richard Faltin (1835–1918), whose background guaranteed him good contacts with Germany. Faltin was born into the bourgeois merchant family of Edward Faltin in Danzig (Gdansk) in 1835. He obtained his musical education in Dessau and Leipzig in the early 1850s.[41]

During 1854–55, Faltin studied at the Leipzig Conservatory. The most famous musicians there were Franz Brendel, Ferdinand David, Julius Rietz, Ignaz Mocheles, Louis Plaidy, and Moritz Hauptmann.[42] Although supporters of Mendelssohn were in the majority at the conservatory, genuine

Wagner enthusiasts could be found among the teachers there. One of the most significant of these was Franz Brendel (1811–68), who had been involved with Wagner as early as the late 1840s and early 1850s.[43] In 1859, Brendel claimed that Wagner was one of the leading figures in the New German School.[44] Similarly, in his comprehensive *Grundzüge der Geschichte der Musik,* he endowed Wagner with a key position as a pioneer of New German Music, even though Wagner's most significant works had not yet even been composed.[45]

Faltin had probably come to know Wagner's music during his student years. Faltin completed his studies at the conservatory in 1855, but remained in Leipzig until Easter the following year. Leipzig was the indisputable center of musical life in Germany, and it offered both employment and opportunities to attend interesting concerts.[46] At Easter 1856, the director of the Conservatory, Schleinitz, unexpectedly presented Faltin with three employment possibilities. The conservatory had received offers of employment from Jerusalem, Coburg, and Viborg. Finland, in the distant north, interested Faltin so much that he decided to accept the offer from Viborg and leave for Finland to teach piano, violin, choral and solo singing, and music theory at a Finnish music school. His decision was influenced by the fact that, during his studies in Leipzig, he had become acquainted with a Finnish student, Karl Johan Moring. Faltin had taught German to Moring, and Moring had taught Swedish to Faltin.[47] It should also be remembered that the Baltic provinces and the St. Petersburg region were traditional areas of employment for German musicians.

Faltin journeyed via Stockholm and Helsinki to Viborg to take up a position that would be significant in Viborg's musical life.[48] Faltin spent the rest of his life in Finland, and from 1869 onwards, he resided in Helsinki.[49] Frequently, however, he visited Germany, in order to keep up with new musical movements in his native country. During 1861–62, he continued his studies in Leipzig. During this period, he met Hans von Bronsart, who in 1860 had founded an association by the name of Euterpe. The society's purpose was to cultivate the music of composers characterized as exponents of the New German School (that is, the music of such composers as Berlioz, Liszt, and Wagner).[50] Through Bronsart and Euterpe, Faltin had close contact with the Wagnerians.

In Leipzig, Faltin was enthused by Wagner's music and did not hesitate to return to Germany when information on the Bayreuth Festival reached Finland. During the first festival, in 1876, *Der Ring des Nibelungen* was performed three times. Faltin wished to obtain tickets for all three cycles and was compelled to apply for a scholarship from the University of Helsinki, where he was employed as a music teacher from 1871 to 1896.[51]

Faltin traveled by boat from Helsinki to Travemünde, then continued his journey overland, via Danzig and Berlin, to Bayreuth. For part of the time, he journeyed in the company of the young Finn Martin Wegelius, who was on his way to hear Wagner.[52] Faltin was originally going to pay his traveling expenses by writing reports for the Helsinki *Morgonbladet*, but when he learned that Wegelius was intending to write similar articles for the *Dagblad*, he changed his mind and wrote home: "A comparison to Wegelius's report in the *Dagblad* will naturally turn into my own defeat."[53]

Faltin was greatly influenced by the Wagnerian ecstasy at Bayreuth. On the opening day, he wrote to his wife Olga:

> It was striking . . . how in the railway carriage from Berlin, the passengers were so different from normal travelers: Wagner, nothing else but Wagner; nothing else was spoken about except the Nibelungenring; the entire world appeared suddenly overtaken by myths and heroic sagas!—And all the life and bustle here in the streets of the town; the innumerable important and interesting faces one meets; not to mention the ceremonially bedecked town itself, the gates of honor and other festive decorations;—to cut it short, had I not been in festive mood already, I must perforce, nolens volens, have become so now.[54]

Besides Wegelius, Faltin also met many of his old friends, including the cellist Börngen who had earlier introduced Faltin to the director of the Würzburg Music School, Dr. Kliebert, who had then introduced Faltin to Richard Wagner's niece Franciska Ritter.[55]

Of greater importance to Faltin than society circles was the Festival House itself, which was built on the Green Hill and where the listeners were soon to assemble: "A bold, beautiful building, so simple, but, despite this, however, so ingeniously designed, without [even the] minimum [of] luxury; the auditorium being a work of art in itself."[56] After four days, when he had heard the *Ring* in its entirety, Faltin wrote:

> Oh, where can one find words to describe everything that Wagner, that divine artist, has donated to his contemporaries and to posterity in this work, written with his heart's blood! . . . I am inclined to believe that a work that seizes its hearers with such inescapable force must certainly belong among the most distinguished ever created. If formerly I doubted whether certain passages were musically practicable, such doubts are now entirely removed; it is all not merely practicable, but relatively easy to perform. The singers merely need, obviously, to be trained for this *German style* created by Wagner, just as they previously needed to be trained in the French or the Italian.[57]

A few days before the end of the festival, on 24 August, Faltin received an invitation from Franciska Ritter to visit the Wagners at the Villa Wahnfried. Naturally, he seized the opportunity to see the composer he so much admired. When he found that Mrs. Ritter had not yet arrived, Faltin decided to take the bull by the horns:

> When I learnt from the servants that Mrs. Ritter had not yet arrived, I plucked up my courage and made my way through the guests, both ladies and gentlemen, all the way to Wagner. I introduced myself; told him whence I came; and added that I could never have forgiven myself if, during a three weeks' sojourn in Bayreuth, I had not made at least one attempt to meet him in person. Now I was doubly happy to have achieved this aim.[58]

More than a hundred guests from different corners of the world had crowded into Wagner's home. The host mingled with the guests, addressing them, when required, in German, in French, or in English. After exchanging a few words, Wagner opened his Steinway and played the first four bars of the first movement of Beethoven's Eighth Symphony; then Camille Saint-Saëns seated himself at the grand piano and gradually moved from Beethoven to his own *Danse Macabre*. The climax of the evening came, however, when Franz Liszt, who, throughout the evening had been surrounded by his admirers, went to the keyboard and performed his *Soirées de Vienne*. "Liszt's technique is faultless!" wrote Faltin in his letter. "Even today, the maestro is able to put all his apprentices into his pocket."[59]

To Faltin the Bayreuth Festival was a significant turning point, as he now had the chance to hear Wagner's music in the form the composer himself wanted. At the same time, he became acquainted both with Wagner himself and with many Wagnerians. From the perspective of Finnish knowledge of Wagner, all of this was of great importance: in his position as a teacher of music at the University of Helsinki, he could now spread an interest in Wagner among his students. Having returned to Finland, Faltin began to act in support of Wagnerian ideas. He had been recruited as an agent for the Patronat-Verein, as a representative of the society in Finland. It is difficult to tell whether he was recruited at the 1876 festival or later through correspondence, for no signs of Faltin's activity appear in the archival material of the Patronat-Verein until the accounting period 1877–78. At this point, no Wagner society had been founded in Finland, but Faltin was offered direct membership of the Patronat-Verein for the sum of 15 German marks. For those who were willing to invest a larger amount, there was the possibility of contributing 50 German marks toward the foundation of the Richard Wagner School at Bayreuth.[60]

In January 1878, when the *Bayreuther Blätter* published the membership fees and donations received during the period from 16 September 1877 to 1 January 1878, under the category "Über 200 Mark" (More than 200 marks) the city of Helsinki and the name of Director of Music Faltin were listed, and a total of 292 reichsmarks. The payment from Finland was divided into subtotals: 150 marks came from membership fees and 142 marks as donations to the Patronat-Verein.[61] Since annual membership cost 15 marks, it is easy to deduce that there were ten Finnish members. Each member of the Patronat-Verein received the *Bayreuther Blätter*. According to the journal's own statistics, exactly ten copies were sent to Helsinki in 1878.[62] It is difficult to come to any conclusion on the origin of the 142-mark donation. In all probability, someone had made a contribution to the foundation of the Richard Wagner School, but the sum probably also included donations not subject to specific conditions.

It is notable that in the January 1878 statistics, the donations from Helsinki were rated as being the ninth largest. The largest sum of money, 1,600 marks, had come from Riga in Livonia; the second largest was from Viersen, and Worms was in third position. After that came Berlin, Göttingen, Heidelberg, Mainz, Cologne, and then Helsinki. The capital of Finland was ranked seventh in the membership figures.[63] In the following months, the amount of money sent from Finland did not, however, increase. Faltin either became tired of membership recruitment or failed to find new candidates. According to the new statistics published by the *Bayreuther Blätter* in March 1878, no payments appear to have been received from Helsinki since those recorded in the January statistics. In the list of donations, Helsinki had fallen to fourteenth position, and Munich had risen to first, Riga having fallen to second.[64]

Further statistics were published in October 1878. The Helsinki contribution remained the same. Its position was now thirtieth. The Finnish membership figures had not increased. By contrast, the membership figures for Riga were rising despite a slight slowing down toward the end of the year 1878. The number of members was 60 in January, 77 in March, and 80 in October.[65] In Finland the number of members remained at 10, all of them having been recruited in fall 1877.

The Patronat-Verein also sold patronage certificates at the price of 300 taler. The holder of the certificate was automatically given a seat for three *Ring* cycles (that is, for twelve operatic performances).[66] Apparently, the only Finnish holder of a patronage certificate was Faltin, whose name is to be found in the list of certificates in the society's archive. Faltin was the holder of patronage certificate number 478. In total, the list included 594 certificates. The list, however, is undated.[67]

Archival material indicating the changes in Finnish membership, and thus suggesting the level of Faltin's activity, can also be found in the files on the distribution of the *Bayreuther Blätter*. Information on circulation was given in July 1881. The paper was, at that time, sent to 8 members of the Patronat-Verein in Helsinki. Since all members received a copy, it is clear that the number of members had decreased after 1877–78. For the sake of comparison, one may look at the circulation figures for the year 1881, which are as follows: 9 in Moscow, 7 in St. Petersburg, 60 in Riga, 84 in Bayreuth, 92 in Munich, 99 in Berlin, and 126 in Vienna.[68]

A year later, in May–June 1882, there were 9 members in Helsinki, 8 in Moscow, 5 in St. Petersburg, and 40 in Riga.[69] A slight increase in the Helsinki membership occurs after that. At the end of 1883, 13 people from Helsinki were registered in the lists despite a radical decrease in overall Baltic and Russian membership. In St. Petersburg there were only 3 members, in Moscow only 2, and in Riga only 16, which, considering the number of members in 1881 (60), was a considerable change.[70] Wagner had died at the beginning of 1883, but it is difficult to discover whether this affected the activities of the society. In Finland, the figures appear to have risen slightly, but in Russia and in the Baltic provinces the statistics clearly reveal a decline.

Despite the relatively modest increase in the Helsinki membership figures, Faltin functioned loyally as a representative of the Patronat-Verein throughout the 1880s and 1890s. Information on his activity during this period is, once again, obtainable from the annual income and expenditure accounts of the *Bayreuther Blätter*. According to the August–September issue of 1884, the payments remitted through Faltin totaled 48 marks in membership fees and 80 marks in subscriptions. Nine Finns had also supported the Patronat-Verein through an additional donation of 10 marks. Here the donors are enumerated: they were Richard Faltin, Mrs. Frenckell, the conductor Bohuslav Hrimaly, Baron and Baroness Lamezan, the pianist H. von Mickwitz, Mrs. Adele Osberg, the engineer Max Seiling, and Martin Wegelius.[71]

The membership lists of the Allgemeine Richard Wagner-Verein for the period 1885–96 found in the Vult von Steijern Collection of the Royal Library of Sweden also give information on active Finnish society members. The information recorded in these files will be examined in the following paragraphs. This task is made easier by the fact that the names and occupations registered in the lists reveal the social characteristics of the members. In addition, the small number of active Finnish members makes it possible to catalog the persons concerned in detail. The 1885 membership included, besides *Orts-Vertreter* (local representative) Faltin, nine people: the pianist L. Dingeldey, the notary Viktor Ekroos, Mrs. Frenckell, Ms. Mickwitz, Mrs. Adele Osberg, the engineer Max Seiling, Prof. Sundell, Martin Wegelius, and the pianist Heinrich Wesing. The list does not mention anyone from Stockholm, St. Petersburg, or Tallinn; but the names of 67 members from Riga and 9 from Christiania (now Oslo) are included.[72]

Owing to the small number of members listed, far-reaching conclusions concerning the social aspect of Wagnerism cannot be reached. Of the 9 members, 3 were females whose social background was not specified. Among the male members, the field of music is well represented (Dingeldey, Faltin, Wegelius, Wesing), but the membership also includes a notary, an engineer, and a professor. The social breakdown is more clearly revealed in the membership lists for the following years.

In 1891, there were 11 Finnish members. The new members included the composer and writer Karl Flodin, the conductor Robert Kajanus, the merchant Woldemar Klärich, the opera singer Abraham Ojanperä, the *Konzertmeister* Anton Sitt, and Prof. F. J. Wiik; the continuing were Faltin, Wegelius, Ekroos, Sundell, and Wesing. The group was significantly more male than the group of 1885. The female members Mrs. Frenckell, Ms. Mickwitz, and Mrs. Osberg are missing. The twelfth member was the *lektor* (high school teacher) Anton Perret from Viborg. Apart from Perret, Finnish interest in Wagner was concentrated in the country's capital city., The number of Finnish members had remained almost static since 1877, despite the fact that individual members had come and gone. In Riga, by contrast, there was a decrease in membership around 1883, but later the figures started to rise. In 1885 the number of members was 67, whereas in 1891 the total number of members was three times larger, at 187.[73] The social profile of the Finnish membership appears largely similar to the profile revealed by the Bayreuth lists of visitors. Music professionals played a visible role in Wagnerian activities. This was, of course, to a large extent, due to the fact that Faltin and Wegelius were influential leaders of opinion in the Finnish music world. In this respect, they differ from the Swedish Wagnerian Vult von Steijern, who was a journalist, and also from the Livonian Glasenapp, who was a teacher, music scholar, and writer. Among the new Finnish members the field of professional music was represented by Flodin, Kajanus, Ojanperä, and Sitt, which means that all the leading figures of Finnish musical life were members of the Patronat-Verein. Even though the Patronat-Verein did not, essentially, organize any activity in Finland, the membership information reveals that the most central and influential professionals in Finland had a connection to Bayreuth.

In the 1890s, the size of the Finnish membership remained stable. In 1892 it was 10, during the years 1893 and 1894 it was 9, and by 1896 it had risen to 13.[74] The new members registered were, in 1892, the schoolmistress Olga Tavaststjerna;[75] and, in 1896, the conductor A. Leander; assistant to a senator O. Hj. Pesonius; R. E. Westerlund, Master of Arts; and Baron R. F. von Willebrand. Ekroos, Faltin, Flodin, Kajanus, Ojanperä, Sitt, Sundell, Tavaststjerna, and Wegelius were registered as continuing members.[76]

The mainstays of Finnish membership of the Patronat-Verein over the period from the late 1870s to the 1890s were, then, the same group of influential people. In addition to Faltin, the society's nucleus included Viktor Ekroos, A. F. Sundell, and Martin Wegelius. Of these, Faltin and Wegelius had attended the 1876 Bayreuth festival and retained the energy to struggle for the Wagnerian cause until the end of the nineteenth century.

In addition to Faltin, there is ample reason to treat Martin Wegelius (see figure 8.2) in more detail in the present chapter, as his activities as a Wagnerian were far more widely spread than those of Ekroos or Sundell. The Patronat-Verein did not create any bridges between devotees of Wagnerism,

Figure 8.2. Martin Wegelius (1846–1906). Library of the Sibelius Academy.

for the members were directly linked with the main office of Wagnerism. Through the *Bayreuther Blätter*, however, they received up to date information on "the holy of holies" and information on local societies in other countries. Martin Wegelius (1846–1906) deserves detailed examination in this study, for he attempted to broaden the activities of the society in Finland (even though he achieved only temporary success). Wegelius was one of the most important figures in Finnish music life, owing to the fact that, in 1882, he founded the Helsinki Conservatory (the later Sibelius Academy, whose significance, from the point of view of the education of musicians and composers, has been great). Wegelius also functioned as a music critic and lecturer. Besides this, as we have seen, he also wrote the first comprehensive history of music in Finland. Like the Swedish opinion leader Wilhelm Bauck, Wegelius was, at the same time, a critic, historian, and a teacher, and it is apparent that as a teacher he grafted his aesthetic and sometimes political views onto his students and thus exercised an influence on Finnish attitudes toward Wagner.

Like many of his contemporaries, Wegelius acquired his knowledge abroad. He studied in Vienna in 1870–71, at the Leipzig Conservatory in 1871–73, and in Munich in 1877–78.[77] As late as the 1860s, his ideal composers had been Schubert and Schumann.[78] Now, during his sojourns in Central Europe, he abandoned his old idols. He soon came to know Wagner's operas thoroughly. In this respect, his Leipzig years were of particular importance, for there Wegelius familiarized himself with *Die Meistersinger* (which had been premiered a few years earlier).[79]

At the beginning of 1876, Wegelius resigned from his post as leader of the Akademiska Sångföreningen (the Academic Singing Society). He departed for Bayreuth on 2 August. He had no intention of missing an opportunity to see Wagner's works performed at the playhouse designed by Wagner himself. It is little wonder that in one of his later articles on Bayreuth, he quoted Goethe's words: "Who would the poet understand, must go into the poet's land."[80]

Wegelius first sailed on the steamship *Alexander* to Lübeck in the company of Viktor and Ilta Ekroos who were, coincidentally, also traveling to Germany. From Lübeck he continued his journey to Leipzig where he met the Norwegian composer Selmer.[81] With Selmer and Faltin (who had recently joined the company), Wegelius arrived at Bayreuth on 12 August.[82] The reports composed by Wegelius for the *Helsingfors Dagblad* reveal his extremely analytical attitude toward the music he had heard. He was far less interested in highbrow society than was Faltin. After the performance of the second part of the *Ring, Die Walküre*, he wrote:

> Where *Das Rheingold* has something of an epic character, *Die Walküre* offers a series of scenes of the most passionate quality. This applies especially to the first and third acts, which incidentally are in a musical sense among the most popular, and direct in their impact, that Wagner has ever composed.[83]

Wegelius's reports were more descriptive and analytical than value oriented, and only later did he express his own subjective views in a more detailed way. The controlled and academically cool tone of his writings could also result from the fact that the Finnish readership was not yet able to comprehend the significance of Wagner. Wegelius's analyzes were apparently the first Wagner texts published in Finland; and in these, Wegelius was content to represent Wagner, rather than proclaiming him a classic among composers.

The emotions he experienced in the auditorium of the Festival theater were revealed much later in his comprehensive history of music, *Hufvud-dragen af den västerländska musikens historia från den kristna tidens början till våra dagar* (1891–93). The work was originally written in Swedish, but a Finnish translation by Alex Törnudd appeared in 1904. In the substantial section relating to Wagner, Wegelius describes his experiences:

> In the year 1876, when, for the first time, I heard the series *Der Ring des Nibelungen* at Bayreuth, during the first lengthy scene, I could only see through my receptive mind's *eye*, and for half an hour I was not conscious that simultaneously I was also hearing music. Not until my ability to judge (for some unknown reason) reawakened, did I start to wonder at this strange form of seeing—real "Hellsehen" [clairvoyance], which was totally beyond the limits of my experience, and which gave me a clear concept of the internal, spiritual life of the dramatis personae and of their external action. Not until then did my *ear* awake from sleep, and, to my great aston-ishment, I noticed that through that very organ, as in a dream, I had received the most logical and exact impressions concerning the internal purpose of the dramatic action, and soon I noticed that the motifs that the orchestra was developing were already familiar to me. I have never (one should also mention this) experienced anything like this anywhere else than at the Bayreuth theater, not even in hearing the work at an ordinary opera house.[84]

Wegelius had already been seized by very unusual feelings, when, in the course of boarding the Leipzig train on 20 August 1876, he offered his vale-dictions to Bayreuth.

The real canonization of Wagner was accomplished by Wegelius much later, in his book on the history of Western music. Wagner's striving for a fusion of arts (*Gesamtkunstwerk*) caused Wegelius to conclude that Wagner's life's work had great significance "in the perspective of universal intellec-tual history."[85] In the fusion of arts, no one else had succeeded as Wagner had: "the fact that Wagner had accomplished this, and had been able to compress into the frame of one artwork all that music hitherto had achieved in isolated territories, makes his life's work one of the most unique achievements in the history of music."[86] In confirmation of his appreciation of Wagner, Wegelius ends the chapter with words he appar-ently repeated in his lectures at the Helsinki Conservatory in the 1880s: Wagner was "heir apparent to the legacy of Bach and Beethoven, the only master comparable to them."[87]

Wegelius not only exercised an influence on the history of Wagnerism as a critic, writer, and lecturer: he was also an important participant in society activities. As previously stated, he was a long-term member of the Patronat-Verein. The activity of this group was, however, relatively modest; the members of the Patronat-Verein did not arrange any important society events in Finland. In order to share his enthusiasm for Wagner, Martin Wegelius founded a society called the Wagnerföreningen, whose members assembled during the winter of 1898–99. According to Karl Flodin's descriptions, a group of devotees of music participated in this activity, mainly to study the Wagner operas to be performed at the next Bayreuth festival. Wegelius lectured to two groups, mainly on *Die Meistersinger, Parsifal,* and the *Ring* tetralogy.[88] Wegelius's informal lectures were illustrated on the piano by Karl Ekman, who was sometimes assisted by R. E. Westerlund, if the piano arrangement required four hands. According to Flodin, most of the society members were Wegelius's friends or students of music, but a few other devotees of music from Helsinki participated.[89]

The Wagnerföreningen was not an official society, and, therefore, no reference to it is found in the register of associations. Nor were minutes of the meetings kept. The society's organization was probably similar to that of other groups previously founded by Wegelius for the performance of classical music. It was mainly a club of devotees in which the participants could perform or discuss music. Because of its unofficial status, there are, of course, no surviving membership lists. It is very likely that some members of the Patronat-Verein were also members of the Wagnerföreningen, but it is hardly probable that professionals such as the opera singer Abraham Ojanperä or the conductor Robert Kajanus participated in this activity. There is, however, one clue to the membership. The principal goal of the Wagnerföreningen was to study the works that would be performed in the 1899 festival. It is thus likely that, at least some of the society members were among the twenty-two visitors to Bayreuth in 1899. The Finns who visited the 1899 festival were Louise von Bonsdorff; Richard Faltin with his wife and daughter; Thérèse Hahl; Amalie Ingman, wife of the procurator; Ms. Aina Korhonen; the bank clerk Elis Lagus; the wife of Senator Mechelin with her daughter; Louise and Anna Munck; Dr. Pentzin; the bank clerk John Silén; Dr. Alvar Törnudd; the lawyer John Uggla; the state official Björn Wasastjerna; Ms. Marie Luise Wasenius; the music entrepreneur R. E. Westerlund with his wife; and Baron von Willebrand.[90] Further conclusions cannot be drawn. Some of these twenty-two visitors would seem to have also been members of Wegelius's society, but Wegelius himself, Karl Ekman, and R. E. Westerlund are not mentioned in the Bayreuth lists. Wegelius, it seems, was too busy to make the trip to the festival. Working day and night, however, was too much for Wegelius; his strength gave out, and with this, the activity of the Wagnerföreningen ceased.[91]

The modest success of the Wagner society piloted by Wegelius and Faltin's connection with the Patronat-Verein reveal that in Finland there was a genuine willingness to participate in social activities in the spirit that

Wagner himself intended. The goals involved the collection of funds for Wagner's artistic endeavors, the study of Wagner's works, and the publicization of Wagner's ideas. Wegelius for decades led various music associations and discussion clubs and invested their social activities with intellectual significance. Since such activities are largely of German origin, it is no wonder that they appeared in Finland where the influence of German culture had always been strong. The German tradition was even stronger in the Baltic provinces where the societies were more structured and active than in Finland.

Carl Friedrich Glasenapp and the Riga Wagner Society

The activities of the Wagnerföreningen can be characterized as modest and they soon came to an end. By contrast, the Wagner Society in Riga was extremely active. Not only due to the opera performances but also in light of this activity, Riga was the most active Wagner center in Baltic Sea area. The key person in all this was indisputably Carl Friedrich Glasenapp. Like Vult von Steijern, he belonged to the inner circle of Bayreuth, but he also tended, like Faltin and Wegelius, to direct his literary and social activity outward from Bayreuth. Any comparison between him and other Finnish and Swedish society members is, however, unfair, as Glasenapp, due to the influence he exercised, was unquestionably the most significant Wagner expert in the entire Baltic world and, besides that, an internationally known figure. After his death on 3 April 1915, the *Rigasche Rundschau* newspaper called him "a man who was a celebrity: not only of Baltic but also of European fame."[92]

Carl Friedrich Glasenapp, 1847–1915 (see figure 8.3), was the son of an elementary school teacher, Friedrich Glasenapp, and his wife Emilie (née Kuhlmann). Carl Friedrich completed his studies in Riga, and on doing so moved to Pärnu in Estonia to be employed as a gymnasium teacher. There he married Henriette Rambach in 1874.[93] In 1875, he moved with his family to Riga and at first worked as an *Oberlehrer* of German language and literature at the Riga Town School for Girls.[94] In the course of time, he moved to the Riga Technical High School or Polytechnikum (see figure 8.4), where he was employed as docent of the general history of literature.[95] In 1911, the title of *Wirklicher Staatsrat* (Councillor of State) was conferred on him for his achievements as a biographer of Wagner.[96] Four years later, on 1 April 1915, Glasenapp died of an apoplectic stroke at the age of 67.[97]

At a very early stage Glasenapp was already interested in Wagner's works. In the early 1860s, he had become acquainted with Wagner's texts and begun to compile a Wagner library for himself.[98] He probably also attended the Wagner performances at the Riga German theater, where his enthusiasm became even greater. He later became especially interested

Figure 8.3. Carl Friedrich Glasenapp (1847–1915). National Archive of the Richard Wagner Foundation, Bayreuth.

in the Wagnerian tradition associated with his native town. The literary *Nachlass* of Glasenapp in the Bayreuth Wagner Archives includes a catalog in which he had painstakingly recorded, on the basis of newspaper advertisements, all the *Tannhäuser* performances in Riga during the 1853–75 period.[99] In the 1860s, there was no real Wagner premiere in Riga. *Lohengrin* had been performed in 1855, and *Die Meistersinger* would be premiered only in 1871. However, *Tannhäuser* was performed several times.

Figure 8.4. Glasenapp's workplace, the Polytechnikum of Riga. Postcard by Verlag Lenz & Rudolff, Riga. Author's postcard collection.

In the 1876–77 period, Glasenapp published his first biography of Wagner, titled *Richard Wagners Leben und Wirken*, which culminates in the accomplishment of the Bayreuth project. Glasenapp became a regular visitor to Bayreuth, met Cosima and Richard, and enjoyed the friendship of both of them. In fact, he soon became court historian to the Bayreuth Circle and was allowed access to sources that were considered secret and sensitive, and were thus not for the eyes of others. Glasenapp was also allowed to read Richard's original autobiography, which was completed in 1880 (a revised edition was released much later, in 1911). He was also allowed to read Cosima Wagner's diaries (which were not published until 1976–77).[100] The long-term result of Glasenapp's work was a six-part biography, *Das Leben Richard Wagners* (see figure 8.5), printed in Leipzig during the years 1894–1911. This work was regarded as authoritative for decades to come. Glasenapp was lucky to be able to use unique source material. Therefore his book became a standard reference work, to which other scholars were almost forced to refer, because the original sources were not available to them. At the time of its publication, Glasenapp's book was one of the most comprehensive composer biographies ever published. It is still worth consulting because of its unique material. The problem is, however, that Glasenapp was a worshiper of Wagner. He continued the process of myth-making that Wagner himself had started in *Mein Leben*. Despite its painstaking attention

Das Leben

Richard Wagners

in sechs Büchern

dargestellt

von

Carl Fr. Glasenapp.

Vierte, neu bearbeitete Ausgabe.

Erster Band.

(1813—1843.)

Leipzig

Druck und Verlag von Breitkopf und Härtel

1905.

Figure 8.5. Title page of the first volume of Glasenapp's Wagner biography. Carl Fr. Glasenapp, *Das Leben Richard Wagners*. Vol 1: 1813–43. 4th edition (Leipzig: Breitkopf & Härtel, 1905).

to minute detail, the book has serious lacunae, and Glasenapp tends to underestimate Wagner's political activities, for example.

Glasenapp's Wagner publications made him world famous, but he remained loyal to Riga, maintaining a widespread network of contacts in Germany and in the Baltic world. He traveled regularly in Central Europe, not only to hear Wagner's music but also to keep abreast of current continental streams in art. He also knew personally many of the Wagnerians in the Baltic world. At Bayreuth, he became acquainted with Vult von Steijern, with whom he maintained close contact. After the turn of the century, Glasenapp also had links with Finland, mainly through the agency of Richard Faltin. He had heard that Faltin had published a memoir in an article titled "En soiré hos Wagner" in the journal *Finsk musikrevy* 7 (1905), and Glasenapp wished to publish the text in German in *Die Musik*. Faltin, flattered by the request, sent Glasenapp his next article, "Erinringar från Bayreuth" ("Reminiscences of Bayreuth"), which had been published in *Finsk musikrevy* 13 (1906).[101]

Like Faltin, Glasenapp was extremely energetic in his activities on behalf of the Patronat-Verein. He became a representative of the society at the same time as Faltin did; hence, Wagnerians of Riga also participated in the collaborative Wagner activity. Unlike the Helsinki members of the Patronat-Verein, the members of Riga did not directly join the parent society but founded a local organization. This organization was active from the start. In January 1878, the *Bayreuther Blätter* reported that Riga had sent more money than any other town, 1,600 German marks, of which 900 marks were membership fees. This means that 60 members had been recruited in 1877, a figure that clearly reveals the Riga enthusiasts' readiness for Wagnerian activities. There were more supporters of the Patronat-Verein in Riga than in any town in Germany. An interesting feature is that all the membership fees were remitted to the Patronat-Verein through representatives. In other words, private individuals did not directly approach Bayreuth; everything was channeled through representatives. The *Vertretung* (representation) of Riga was the largest. Four names are mentioned in connection with Rigan representation in the Patronat-Verein: C. F. Glasenapp, J. Ruthardt, M. Rudolph, and G. Engelmann.[102] Owing to the varied social backgrounds of this quartet, the society spread its tendrils widely. Glasenapp was an academically educated teacher, Ruthardt a conductor, Rudolph a music critic, and Engelmann a bookshop proprietor. Glasenapp, Ruthardt, and Engelmann had already attended the 1876 Bayreuth Festival.[103]

The Riga Wagner Society was already very active in the autumn of 1877. This is revealed in the correspondence between Gustav Engelmann and Carl Friedrich Glasenapp. The society arranged soirées in which fragments from Wagner's works were performed and discussed with enthusiasm.[104] The activity thus considerably deviated from that of the Finnish membership of the Patronat-Verein and more closely resembled that of Martin Wegelius' Wagnerföreningen. An exceptional feature was the society's activity as a pressure group whose purpose was to encourage the performance of Wagner operas in Riga. There is evidence of this kind of "militant mission" when Wagner licensed the *Ring* for performance in opera houses other than Bayreuth—the idea of having *Das Rheingold* performed in the local theater was in society members' minds. The idea was proposed in

March 1878[105] but the project did not come to fruition. *Das Rheingold* was not premiered until 1890.[106]

The society remained lively until the 1890s. In the beginning, during the fall of 1877, the enthusiasm was great, but after that, the increase in membership slowed down. In March 1878, the total number of members was 77; in October 80.[107] A slight change is seen in the October statistics of the *Bayreuther Blätter*, which reveal that among those representing Riga, Moritz Rudolph had been replaced by Otfried Rötscher. The pianist Rötscher, born in 1840, had been Hans von Bülow's student; he lived in Tartu for a long period and gave concerts throughout Livonia, Courland, and Germany. In the middle of the 1860s, however, he suffered an attack of muscular paralysis and was forced to give up his career as a pianist for seven years. During this time, he concentrated on teaching, conducting, and piano. When he recovered, he returned to the concert halls. From 1875 onward he lived in Riga and gave concerts both in the Baltic provinces and in Germany.[108]

Many of the leading figures in the music life of Riga were active in the society, a fact that guaranteed a large membership. The membership lists of the society, in which the names and frequently also occupations and even addresses of members have been recorded, have survived from the 1880s and 1890s. According to the 1885 list, there were 67 Riga members. The society still had four notable members; in addition to Glasenapp, Alexander von Döllen, the conductor Otto Lohse, and *Oberlehrer* Hermann Westermann were especially active.[109] Alexander von Döllen had acted as the society librarian during the three previous years and he was still in charge of the library in 1885. The library was located on Nicolaistrasse.[110] In 1885, the membership included the merchant J. Bach; the director Heinrich Back; the town librarian Georg Berkholz; Baroness Louise von Brümmer; Professor Theodor Groenberg; the inspector Karl Haller; Consul Alexander von Heymann; the secretary Oskar Mertens; Lieutenant General von Mirkowitz; the music entrepreneur Paul Nelder; Baron von Vegesack; Baroness von Wöhrmann; and the merchant Louis Zietemann. There were 26 women and 41 men.[111] The gender and occupational breakdown is fairly similar to that in the Bayreuth lists of visitors. Undoubtedly, the members of the society were among the most influential figures in local cultural life and probably had connections with other parts of Livonia as well as the other Baltic provinces. The librarian Georg Berkholz, for example, had extensive working experience in the Baltic provinces and in Russia. Like Theodor Groenberg, he had studied at the University of Tartu. As a Livonian, it was natural for him to receive his education in Tartu, where he studied philosophy in 1836–37. After that, he worked as a home teacher in Livonia and Russia and as a librarian in St. Petersburg, ultimately in the library of Princess Elena Pavlovna. It is quite possible that Berkholz had already become acquainted with Wagner's works, at least his literary works, at that time, as the princess was one of the most ardent Wagnerians in St. Petersburg. During the 1860s, Berkholz moved to Riga, where he spent the rest of his life as a town librarian.[112]

In 1891, the society's membership was at a record size; almost three times higher than earlier and later figures). A total of 187 people, 54 women and 133 men, were registered as members. The large number of members from outside Riga is striking. In the 1880s, the society's activity was widely spread in the Baltic provinces and reached even further afield: included in the list, for example, were Wilfried and Fanny Anders from St. Petersburg, the bookshop proprietor O. Nähring from Pärnu, and Prof. Alexander Rizzoni, whose place of residence was registered as Rome.[113] Alexander von Döllen, who had been among the leading figures in the society, resided in Griva near Daugavpils (Dünaburg). Thus, Riga offered a connecting link to those interested in Wagner, for no other Wagner society existed in its vicinity.

The society's membership included members of the nobility, government and municipal officials, magistrates, councillors of state, and privy councillors. The society had attracted the highest and most distinguished members of the Baltic aristocracy, including Barons Karl and Alexander Freytag von Loringhoven.[114]

The reason for the rapid growth of membership in the Riga Wagner Society is difficult to determine. In any case, during subsequent years the size of the membership stabilized at the level of the year 1885. According to the 1892 list, there were 60 members, and in 1893 and 1894 the number remained the same.[115] In 1896 the number of members showed a decrease of 10.[116] The number of women in 1892 was 15, in 1893 17, in 1894 18, and in 1896 16. A core group, which guided the society's activity, regularly reappears. Besides Carl Friedrich Glasenapp, among the leading loyal figures were his wife Henriette, their daughters Eva and Senta, and their son Kosmos Glasenapp. Prof. Max Glasenapp, the music entrepreneur Nelder, Prof. C. A. Bischoff, Marie von Schilling (wife of a councillor of state), Ms. Emma Sprost, Prof. Theodor Groenberg, the conductor Carl Waack, Baron Adalbert von Krüdener, and the lawyer Harald von Wahl, were all regular members.

But what was the reason for the sudden growth in the 1891 membership figures? Probably the society arranged a campaign to recruit new members. It was far from easy to acquire tickets for the Bayreuth Festival, and in those days, as at present, a good way to obtain tickets was to join a Wagner society. Perhaps the knowledge of this possibility spread more widely than before and made those interested in Wagner participate in the society. The increase in membership is also reflected in the lists of visitors to Bayreuth. In 1891, the number of Baltic visitors was exceptionally large. The average number of Baltic participants in the festivals during the years 1876, 1882, 1888, 1891, 1896, and 1899 was 19, but the 1891 festival was visited by 33 people. In fact, if the year 1891 is excluded from the count, the average would be only 16. There were 25 Riga visitors out of the 33 Baltic participants in 1891.

As mentioned before, the 1891 Wagner society list includes members who lived outside Riga, and these also raised the membership figures. Another reason for the rapid growth in the society's activity was social change in Riga. The population of Riga had increased rapidly, particularly in the 1880s. In 1836, the population had been 67,378, but by 1881 it was 179,111. After this, growth clearly accelerated, and, in 1897, the population stood at 255,973. The industrialization of the town had taken place with surprising speed, which shook the social power structures. In particular, the balance between ethnic groups changed due to the rapid population growth. In 1897, out of the Riga population, 41.64 % were Letts, 25.53 % Germans, 16.94 % Russians, 6.45 % Jews, 5.03 % Poles, and 2.29 % Lithuanians.[117] Even though the Germans still made up a quarter of the population, the percentage of Germans in the total population had decreased. The German minority, without doubt, felt its position threatened, and this fear was reinforced by the tsarist policy of Russification. Was the Wagner society, after all, a fortress of German culture in which Germans assembled to be guided by the interests they shared? The membership lists do not include any names of the rising Lettish intelligentsia, not to mention Russians, Jews, Poles, or Lithuanians. Another factor could be internal developments within the German minority. One quarter of the population was German speaking, but a remarkably high proportion had recently arrived from Germany (*Reichsdeutsche*). Bernhard Hollander stated in his *Riga im 19. Jahrhundert* (1926) that it was difficult for the new German arrivals to integrate into municipal and social life during the social turmoil and economic boom.[118] The Wagner society, apparently, in this respect, offered a splendid possibility for socializing, considering that the society members were keen observers of cultural events in Germany and also arranged events at which German art was celebrated.

The Riga Wagner Society's activity was lively throughout the nineteenth century. At first, collective studies of Wagner's works played a central role, as they did in the Finnish Wagnerföreningen. During the winter of 1878–79, the society arranged five study evenings (*Studienabend*) under the guidance of the conductor Julius Ruthardt: the subtle nuances of *Die Walküre* were analyzed with precision during these sessions. The *Bayreuther Blätter* noted this activity and mentioned that the tenor Rudolf Engelhardt had performed at these soirées.[119] Engelhardt's career as a heroic tenor lasted from 1877 to 1880, when he had influence in Riga and performed the role of Rienzi, for example. After his Riga period, he retired from the stage and worked as a land surveyor in Sachsen-Meiningen until his death in 1886.[120]

The arrangement of study evenings remained the central activity of the society throughout the century. In the autumn of 1884, there were four study evenings, again on the subject of *Die Walküre*. The conductor Otto Lohse accompanied the singers of the Riga theater on the piano, and participants in the study evening listened to a lecture on the structure of the work. At the evening's end, chairman Hermann Westermann thanked all the participants in a concluding speech.[121] In the spring of 1886, the subject of analysis was *Tristan und Isolde*. On 16 February, Westermann lectured on the plot of *Tristan*, and two days later, the first act of the opera was performed as part of a study evening. The role of Isolde was performed by Mrs. Aman, and Mr. Lorenz was Tristan. The soloists were assisted by a chorus of singers including members of the local male chorus and technical school students under the leadership of Otto Lohse. On 24 February, Glasenapp lectured on the themes of the first act with music samples performed by Lohse.[122] In autumn 1886, the operas studied were *Der fliegende Holländer*[123] and *Parsifal*,[124] in spring 1887 *Tristan und Isolde*,[125] and in fall 1887 *Die Walküre* again.[126]

The personality cult surrounding Wagner was also important to the society's activities. This can be seen after Wagner's death in 1883. On 13 February, a year after the tragic loss of the master, the Riga Wagner Society under the guidance of Hermann Westermann assembled to honor the memory of the composer.[127] The death of Wagner had a deep and ongoing effect on the society's activities, making the personality cult even more important. Assemblies were arranged on the anniversaries of Wagner's death and birth. On 22 May 1886, the society arranged a birthday celebration (*Geburtsfeier*) in the Schwarzhäuptersaal, at which Westermann gave a speech, and the Overture to *Die Meistersinger* was performed as a piano transcription for four hands by court pianist Carl Pohlig and Otto Lohse. In addition to this, the audience heard "Wach' auf!" and "Ehrt eure deutschen Meister" from *Die Meistersinger* performed by a chorus of a hundred singers. The next number was a performance of the entire first act of *Tristan,* and the occasion ended with the Overture and the Final Chorus from *Parsifal.*[128]

In the encouragement of the cult of personality, not only Westermann but also Glasenapp performed an important role, for Glasenapp was a diligent performer at the society's functions. For example, a thirty-two-page book, *Richard Wagner als Mensch*, was based on a lecture Glasenapp gave to the society. Considerable demand for the work existed, as is seen in the fact that a third printing of it appeared in 1890. In his lecture, Glasenapp depicted Wagner as a "patient," "tender," and "caring" genius who had been fascinated by the pleasures of life. Glasenapp particularly stresses Wagner's excellent memory: the master had memorized the story of his younger days as a conductor in detailed perfection.[129]

As well as the glorification and mythologizing of Wagner, a general interest in German culture was also to be seen in the society's program:

attention was focused not only on Wagner's works but also on German art: the society especially promoted Bach, Mozart, and Beethoven. On the 200th anniversary of Bach's birth, on 21 March 1885, the Riga society arranged a concert to honor the composer; on this occasion, a pamphlet, *Von Bach zu Wagner, ein Gedenkblatt,* which contained Wagner's thoughts on Bach, was sold to benefit the scholarship fund.[130] In fall 1885, the society organized a Beethoven soirée during which the audience could hear piano sonatas, songs, and the Sonata for cello in A Major. A message concerning Wagner had, however, been introduced into the concert: the concluding number was Isolde's "Love-Death," performed in a piano transcription made by Franz Liszt.[131] Apparently, the society's goal was to raise the German masters on to a pedestal and at the same time to remind the public of Wagner's connections with his models. In spring 1886, it was Mozart's turn. An outstanding Mozart program was performed at the concert of 30 April, and again Wagner's comments, this time on Mozart, were sold as a complementary text. The Beethoven theme continued in November 1886, when Carl Pohlig started a series of eight concerts in which he performed Beethoven's piano sonatas. The series ended in March of the following year. In October 1886, Pohlig had performed a piano version of Liszt's Dante Symphony.[132] In fall 1887, using words and melodies, Pohlig told of the history of music in a series of *Historische Konzerte.*[133]

Unlike the Finnish society, the Riga Wagner Society was, in general, directed toward publicity. Wagner was publicly associated with the tradition of German music, which as a project can be paralleled with tendencies in the writing of music history. Images associated with the past were evoked through historical concerts as they were through literature. This was accentuated by the fact that Wagner was presented as belonging to the same tradition as Bach, Mozart, and Beethoven. This process clearly began after Wagner's death: it was a process not only of the institutionalization of Wagner but also of his elevation on to a pedestal, his inclusion in the canon of art. The Riga Wagner Society participated energetically in this process.

In the 1880s, the Riga Wagner Society was extremely lively; several lectures, meetings, and concerts were arranged every month. New methods for addressing the public were constantly sought and apparently produced results, for, in 1891, the society's membership was larger than ever. The society also boasted its own library, from which material on Wagner could be borrowed for use at home. The impact of the Riga Wagner Society was not limited to Livonia, or even to the Baltic provinces in general. The society's publications spread not only to Germany but all over Europe. The concerts arranged by the society enlivened musical life throughout Livonia and offered models for the activities of other Wagner devotees. It is even possible that Martin Wegelius received an impetus to start his own study evenings through the *Bayreuther Blätter,* for there is a strong resemblance between Wegelius's study evenings and the practical pursuits of the Riga Wagner Society. The members in Riga drew their own map with regard to the possibilities offered by an interest in Wagner, and this had a broader European significance. Thus, the *Bayreuther Blätter* wrote in its January 1887 issue that the Riga Wagner Society was "ein Vorbild für alle Vereine," a paragon for all the other societies.[134] In the history of Wagner enthusiasm and the Wagner cult, the Baltic Sea was thus not "a chilly, peripheral backwater" but an active cultural area whose ideas were echoed everywhere in Europe.

Conclusion

The Final Chord

When Richard Faltin met Wagner in Bayreuth in 1876 and told him about the sporadic attempts to perform the master's music in Finland, Wagner answered politely: "Oh, you should rather come to Bayreuth! I am happy, however, that there are people up there who like my music."[1] Finland, like the whole Baltic world, was "up there," far away from the Europe in which Wagner particularly wanted to succeed. In 1876, the center of everything was Bayreuth: Wagner undoubtedly wished to promote this centralized worldview of Wagnerism and hoped that his disciples and followers would support his venture both intellectually and financially. Early in his career Wagner had already realized that the performance of his works required sizable investments, such that only large and established opera houses could fulfill the demanding prerequisites. Thus, when he was leaving Livonia in 1839, Wagner had surmised that the remote city of Riga could never be an arena for his works. As an opera composer, Wagner accordingly did not work to ease the spread of his works by giving consideration to the conditions prevailing in the opera world: he forged his works for the future. Perhaps Wagner's somewhat cynical comment to Faltin refers simply to the fact that in 1876 Bayreuth was the only place in which performances satisfying Wagner's requirements could be produced.

Wagner was by no means unconcerned about the Baltic world. When making preparations for the Bayreuth festival in 1874, he had even turned to the Royal Opera in Stockholm to ask for help. Contrary to his assumption in the 1830s, Riga became an especially important Wagner center, even from a Europe-wide perspective. Riga was also the residence of Carl Friedrich Glasenapp, whose work in transmitting the Wagner image and recording Wagner knowledge was crucial.

Reactions to Richard Wagner's ideas and output in the Baltic world have been the main topic of this study. It seems clear that the Baltic Sea region and German culture were in close interaction throughout the period investigated. The participants in this negotiation were not at all mutually unreachable, despite the geographical distances between them. Information moved quickly and, typically for the period, newspapers copied items from other newspapers. The press frequently dealt with Wagner's artistic plans as well as his biographical vicissitudes. Interaction was also seen in the form of movements of musicians and compositions. Through bookstores and libraries, sheet music was widely distributed. German music journals that were followed on both sides of the Baltic Sea relayed the debate that was going on in Central Europe. This interaction accelerated gradually in the course of the nineteenth century: developments in the means of transport, especially through the extension of the rail network, made quicker and more regular transportation possible.

The interaction between German music culture and the Baltic world was closely connected with Wagner's personal activities. When he met Faltin in 1876, Wagner was already an established artist who felt no need to leave his bastion: the rest of the world had to come to him. But in his early career, Wagner, like many other musicians before him, went to seek new experiences in the Baltic world. However, he longed for a breakthrough in the music centers of Europe and traveled directly from Riga to the heart of the contemporary musical world, Paris, with great expectations. After his Dresden period (1842–49), Wagner once again had to return to his migratory life and worked as a conductor all over Europe. He got his best offer from Russia, and arrived there in spring 1863. Indisputably, this concert tour strongly encouraged enthusiasm for Wagner in St. Petersburg, an enthusiasm that lasted even after he had found his royal benefactor in Munich. Later it was Russian aristocrats, in particular, who traveled to the Bayreuth festival and gave their financial support to Wagner's ambitious venture.

Wagner began to systematically plan the accomplishment of his project. This was largely carried out after the political unification of Germany in 1871, when Wagner personally began to influence the instutionalization of his own position, especially when it had become obvious that the new *Reich* took a rather reserved stand on his ideas. Wagner edited a collection of his writings under the title *Gesammelte Schriften und Dichtungen* (1871–73), offering a wider audience the opportunity to acquaint themselves with his thinking. At the same time, he urged his supporters to found Wagner societies that could subsidize the Bayreuth project.

Although, in making these plans, Wagner primarily thought of German audiences, at the same time he made a wider influence possible and fostered interaction between the distant north and his own cultural sphere. German cultural phenomena were watched carefully in the Baltic world, where inspiration in educational, scientific, and artistic matters often came from Germany. *Gesammelte Schriften und Dichtungen* made Wagner's texts available also to the northern, as well as the German public. In Sweden, Wilhelm Bauck's opera reviews reveal that the publication of the first volume of the series in 1871 had not gone unnoticed beyond the borders of Germany. The Swedish, Finnish, and Baltic provinces Wagnerians subscribed to the *Bayreuther Blätter*, which became an important channel for information. The Wagner societies, too, offered a possibility of engaging with Wagner's project. Wagner himself had given a crucial impetus to this arrangement, conscious of the fact that he had followers all around Europe who needed societies to which they could attach themselves.

Thus, Wagner's personal contribution was of great importance to his reception in the Baltic world: the activities of the societies, trips to

Bayreuth, and literary publicity were to encourage Wagner enthusiasts who, by these means, could reinforce their interest. Now they had a direct connection to Bayreuth, and Wagner did almost nothing to further the presentation of his works in the Baltic Sea region, despite the fact that arrangements of his works satisfying the smaller-scale demands of the area were easily made. Arrangements, however, proved to be crucial in the spreading of Wagner's music, irrespective of what he himself thought about them. By the second half of the 1850s, the music of *Tannhäuser* and *Lohengrin*, in particular, was already well known throughout the Baltic world. Two-and four-hand piano transcriptions based on Wagner's operas were available from the 1850s onward and gradually the array of instruments for which arrangements were made expanded. Nevertheless, at the end of the 1860s, the arrangements were mostly from *Tannhäuser, Lohengrin*, and *Der fliegende Holländer*. The range of Wagner arrangements started to grow at the beginning of the 1870s when *Tristan und Isolde, Die Meistersinger von Nürnberg, Das Rheingold,* and *Die Walküre* also appeared in the music catalogs. Although home and salon music constituted an international sector of music culture, there were some regional differences. Sometimes home music resonated with concerts and opera performances, which raised certain works to greater popularity. For example, Filip von Schantz's concert activity increased the sale of the *Tannhäuser* March. During the 1860s, Schantz conducted the piece successfully in his concerts—and this was consciously exploited in the marketing of arrangements.

In addition to homes and salons, Wagner's music could be heard in concert halls from the 1850s onward. In fact, the first performances of the *Tannhäuser* Overture in Stockholm and St. Petersburg were given at almost the same time in spring 1856. Wagner pieces were quite popular in the repertoire of military bands: in Sweden the oldest arrangements that have been dated go back to the year 1860. Wagner's music probably attracted military musicians all over Europe; *Blackwood's Edinburgh Magazine* wrote in November 1861 that "Wagner's stormy marches are magnificent when played by a military band in the open air."[2]

No complete Wagner opera was staged in Sweden until 1865 (and, in Russia, none until 1868). However, both in Sweden and in Russia, real enthusiasm started to grow during the subsequent decade. The Wagner premieres of the 1870s, *Der fliegende Holländer* in 1872, *Lohengrin* in 1874, and *Tannhäuser* in 1878, influenced the establishment of Wagner's position in Sweden. The performance of *Lohengrin* in 1874 was particularly groundbreaking.

In Livonia, the situation was entirely different from that in Sweden. Wagner's works had already been performed in Riga in the 1840s and 1850s: *Der fliegende Holländer* was produced in 1843, *Tannhäuser* in 1853, and *Lohengrin* in 1855. *Tannhäuser*, in particular, appealed to the Livonian public and was presented several times during the following decades. The next

Wagner premiere had to wait, however, until the 1870s; by then, through the *Reichsgründung*, Wagner had acquired a new political significance that influenced his reception in general: *Die Meistersinger* was premiered in 1872 and *Rienzi* in 1878. Furthermore, the end of the century was more lively in Riga than in Stockholm. While the Swedish public had the opportunity to experience *Die Meistersinger* in 1887 and *Die Walküre* in 1895, the audience in Riga was already familiar with *Die Walküre* by 1889, *Das Rheingold* by 1890, and *Siegfried* by 1898. The excitement in Riga concerning Wagner was mirrored in the local area. The *Tannhäuser* of Riga inspired the premiere of the opera in Tallinn in December 1853. The Riga German Opera also presented the work in Helsinki as a guest performance in summer 1857.

Comparing the Swedish performances to those in Livonia, one has to remember that the resources of the Stockholm Royal Opera were different from those of the operatic theater in Riga, not to mention the modest theaters of Tallinn and Helsinki. In Stockholm, as in St. Petersburg, the opera flourished under the patronage of the hereditary ruler; in displaying the power of the monarch, it was probably fulfilling functions very similar to those it had fulfilled in earlier centuries. During the 1850s, Wagner was known as a radical revolutionary who seemed to support the bourgeoisie rather than the aristocracy or the monarch. Undoubtedly, the inclusion of a Wagner opera in the Stockholm repertoire, or in St. Petersburg, would have been politically risky in those circumstances. When the year 1864 arrived, everything changed: Wagner obtained the patronage of King Ludwig II of Bavaria. Now, it was surely much more appropriate than previously to stage his operas in Stockholm or St. Petersburg. Wagner's relatively slow reception in Sweden was also influenced by the fact that local operatic life had long been more oriented toward France than toward Germany. This probably led to the decision to initiate Wagnerian performances with *Rienzi*, Wagner's most Gallic opera.

The Riga German Opera, which had performed Wagner since 1843, was an entirely different matter. As an institution supported by German merchants and other members of the bourgeoisie, it was willing to give space to innovative German music. The fashionable works of the period, such as the operas by Meyerbeer, Auber, and Halévy, were not neglected, but the relationship to German culture was basically closer in Riga than it was in Sweden. Interestingly enough, the Baltic-German cultural impact reached the north, Estonia and even Finland; that is, the area between the Swedish and Russian cultures. Because German culture traditionally had a strong foothold in Finland, it is no wonder that the Finns had contacts with the Baltic Germans. In fact, before the visit of the Riga opera company led by Franz Thomé in summer 1857, Helsinki had already been visited by many other ensembles that originated in Estonia and Livonia. The interaction between Finland and the Baltic provinces was indisputably fostered by the fact that these regions were in a somewhat similar political position.

They all belonged to the Russian Empire, although Finland was clearly more independent than Estonia and Livonia.

The reception of Wagner's operas in the Baltic world was by no means a coherent, monolithic phenomenon; there seem to have been interesting dissimilarities and disparities that cannot be explained simply by different schedules in the performance of his works but need to be understood in the context of larger cultural traditions. In Sweden, the general attitude toward Wagner's works was clearly more critical than it was in Finland or in the Baltic provinces. At least in terms of Swedish literary publicity, negative and reserved attitudes came to the foreground. Because the Swedish operatic tradition was more French oriented, the adoption of Wagner's ideas became a more difficult matter, as these ideas conflicted with the dominant ideology. On the other hand, Wagner was never attacked with the harsh criticism peculiar to the most ardent anti-Wagnerians in Germany. However, in Sweden, for example, discussion of the "noisiness" of Wagner's music was given more space in the publicity than on the other side of the Baltic Sea. During the 1860s and 1870s, many European newspapers and journals had transmitted views in which Wagner's orchestration was associated with excessive noise-making. In 1872, the music of *Der fliegende Holländer* was described as a "chaos of shrieks and signals." In March 1875, the Austrian satirical magazine, *Kikeriki!*, described a Wagner concert in which musicians plucked the harp with a rake, played a horrified cat with a bow, rubbed basins with a knife, and finally threw pieces of glass into a kettle.[3] In Germany, the March 1871 issue of the *Allgemeine Musikalische Zeitung* described how a Wagnerian musician, Karl Ludwig Eberle, had sustained permanent mental damage from listening to Wagner's music.[4] In England, the words of a German critic were quoted, arguing that Wagner's music "would make a deaf man hear, and a hearing man deaf."[5] The Swedish critics, too, with Wilhelm Bauck at their head, emphasized Wagner's supposedly unhealthy, noisy aspects. By contrast, on the eastern side of the Baltic Sea this kind of criticism played hardly any role. In this connection, however, one has to remember that the orchestra of the Riga theater was not as large as the ensemble in the Royal Opera in Stockholm. When *Tannhäuser* was played by twenty or thirty musicians, there was not much room for the creation of "noisy effects."

Despite the considerable differences in the reception of Wagner's operas, there were similarities as well. An intriguing fact is that *Tannhäuser* played a central role in the expansion of Wagner's reputation. In Sweden, general Wagner fervor did not arise until the premiere of *Lohengrin* in 1874, but music from *Tannhäuser* had been heard there in different forms since the 1850s. As has been stated earlier in this study, according to the calculations of Gösta Percy, out of all the music performed in Swedish orchestral concerts over the years 1857–84, as much as 60 percent came from *Tannhäuser*. In the Baltic provinces as well as in Finland, the position of this

opera was at least as solid. *Tannhäuser* had been a tremendous success in the
Riga Opera in 1853, and it was continuously performed in the following
decades. Its strong position in terms of the Wagnerian reception was due to
many factors. First, it was Wagner's first popular work, and it had already
gained wide international attention as early as the beginning of the 1850s,
so it was quite natural that it also aroused curiosity in the Baltic world. Second, in company with *Der fliegende Holländer* and *Lohengrin, Tannhäuser*
belonged to Wagner's Romantic operas, in which traditional roots were dis-
tinctly present. It was easy to extract numbers from it and arrange them
either for piano or for various ensembles. Also Franz Liszt and Hans von
Bülow had produced their own *Tannhäuser* transcriptions and thus promoted the success of the opera. Thanks, perhaps, to this popular publicity,
especially within the area of home and salon music, *Tannhäuser* strengthened its place in the opera world. The third factor was most probably the
fact that, in Central Europe, the work came powerfully into the limelight in
the 1850s and provided the first encounter with the composer for many
later Wagnerians. In the case of foreign musicians and composers who studied in Germany during the 1850s, it was most probably *Tannhäuser* that they
first had a chance to become acquainted with, and later they often recalled
their first experiences. Besides its traditionality, the opera, of course, also
included much that was new—it had the "modern" aspects that one would
expect to find if one had followed the furious debate aroused by Wagner's
theoretical writing. The composer August Söderman had seen *Tannhäuser*
in March 1857 and was enthralled by it. So was the singer Fredrika Stenhammar, who later got the chance to interpret many Wagner characters on
the stage in Stockholm. Stenhammar heard *Tannhäuser* in Leipzig in May
1853, four years earlier than Söderman. In her letter to a Mrs. Schäfer, she
reports that this opera, in particular, was exceptionally popular at the time.
She believes its music is more magnificent than any other she has ever
heard. Her short account ends with the remark that it would be impossible
for Mrs. Schäfer to understand Wagner's music without listening to it herself:
"You can have no conception of this."[6]

The critic and composer Wilhelm Peterson-Berger also examined the
position of *Tannhäuser* in his *Richard Wagner som kulturföreteelse* (1913). This
book was based on the lectures Peterson-Berger had given in Stockholm
during the winter of 1912–13. For example, he described, in the third person, the birth of his own enthusiasm for the composer, and ended by arguing that his passion started with *Tannhäuser*. This opera, he argues, is the
most accessible in Wagner's oeuvre: it reveals itself most easily to a Wagner
novice. Owing to his strongly religious background, Peterson-Berger was
attracted by the work's similarity to divine ritual. It was like a public spiritual ceremony with a powerful erotic undertone. *Tannhäuser* included religious motifs, such as sin, regret, prayer, forgiveness, damnation,
pilgrimage, and the theme of the madonna.[7] Peterson-Berger observed the

overall Catholic tenor of the work; perhaps it was this religious message, intermingled with erotic sensualism and love, that made it so popular. It has to be remembered that religion and spiritual life were still significant in the worldview of the nineteenth-century bourgeoisie. Wagner had combined elements of the sacred and the profane, through Tannhäuser's wandering between Venus and Elizabeth. In *Der fliegende Holländer* and *Lohengrin*, religion was also important. In the former case it was associated with the qualities of Gothic romance, in the second with demonic, heretical features. Although the first Swedish Wagner production had been *Rienzi*, the works specifically listed by Peterson-Berger, *Tannhäuser, Lohengrin*, and *Der fliegende Holländer*, aroused tremendous local enthusiasm during the 1870s.

An interesting issue in the history of Wagner's reception is the question of who the followers of Wagner's ideas and art actually were. And further: who were those militant Wagnerians who tried to advance the enterprise of their idol? In Sweden, there were devoted Wagnerians as early as the 1850s. August Söderman, Fritz Arlberg, and Fredrika Stenhammar were anxious to advocate for Wagner, but their position in local musical life was probably not strong enough to raise the popularity of his operas, at least during the 1850s. In Riga, on the other hand, Wagner aroused serious discussion among the critics and among the directors of the theater, a discussion that soon led to a more favorable atmosphere. People had been writing about Wagner throughout the Baltic world from the beginning of the 1850s, but it seems that there was no actual Wagner debate in Sweden and Finland before the 1870s. The Finnish author and journalist Zacharias Topelius and the Swedish composer J. A. Josephson argued about the ideas in Wagner's *Oper und Drama* in their correspondence, but this never became a public debate. In the press of the Baltic provinces, Wagner's name occurred more frequently: Oscar von Riesemann's essays and reviews in 1860, in particular, offered a distillation of Wagner's basic art-theoretical concepts for public judgment. Furthermore, the press in Riga had already dealt conspicuously with Wagner in the 1850s. Wagner was, however, most noticeably brought into the public eye in 1876, when newspapers all around the Baltic world reported over a period of several weeks on what had happened and what had been seen and heard in the first Bayreuth Festival. Even such small papers as the *Libausche Zeitung* and the *Mitausche Zeitung* discussed the ideas and art of Richard Wagner. The largest newspapers, such as *Aftonbladet* in Stockholm, the *Helsingfors Dagblad* in Finland, the *Revalsche Zeitung* in Tallinn, and the *Rigasche Zeitung* in Riga, published long accounts of the events in Bayreuth.

When the first Bayreuth Festival began, Wagner's position was stable and well established all around the Baltic world. If there had been some delay in the Swedish reception of Wagner compared with the Livonian one, they were now on the same level. This change was influenced by Wagner's own activity. Bayreuth became more important to Wagnerians than local performances. This centralization even makes it possible to study the Wagnerians of the Baltic world at a concrete level, because Wagnerian tourism has left traces in the archives. Even though the lists of visitors to the festival have not survived as a complete series, information on 247 Wagner tourists from Sweden, Finland, and the Baltic provinces can be found in these lists. In sum, at least ninety Swedish, forty two Finnish, and 115 Baltic guests participated in the festivals of 1876, 1882, 1888, 1891, 1896 and 1899. Wagnerian activity was clearly concentrated, as over 70 percent of all guests came from the major centers, Stockholm, Helsinki, and Riga. Tallinn, the present capital of Estonia, was not one of these centers, nor was Tartu, which had traditionally been a cultural center; at that time located on the Livonian side of the border. It seems that Wagnerian tourists came from the cities where musical life was lively and where it had already been possible to gain exposure to Wagner's works. The stimulus for the journeys to Bayreuth was not a desire to compensate for a lack of opera at home: the voyage did not counterbalance any inability to experience opera in local theaters. Here, we might refer to a general principle in the relationship between communication and physical mobility. During the last few centuries, the continuously increasing exchange of information has not lessened the need for mobility; indeed, the trend seems to be in the opposite direction. While information and cultural products have moved across borders, tourism has also increased. Perhaps this was the case in the reception of Wagner as well: local performances, fragments heard in concerts, and news spread through the press generated an increased interest in traveling abroad in order to listen to Wagner.

The borders of Wagnerian activity were not only geographical but also social. Joseph Horowitz has remarked that, in the United States of the 1890s, women in particular showed great interest in Wagner's art.[8] During his attendance at the Bayreuth Festival in 1876, Peter Tchaikovsky had already noted the significant role of women in the audience. I have not had any general statistics on gender roles in Bayreuth at my disposal, but among the guests coming from the Baltic world, 43 percent were women. The proportion of female visitors was at its highest in 1891, when they made up 52 percent of the Wagner tourists from Sweden, Finland, and the Baltic provinces. The proportion of women attending was close to that of men, but from the cultural perspective of the late nineteenth century, female participation must be considered quite high. The opportunities for women to travel had, however, improved in the course of the century, as may be reflected in these figures. In the Baltic world, the number of female visitors was highest in Livonia, especially in Riga. Remarkably, in 1896, 67 percent of all the Baltic visitors were women. It would be interesting to make larger-scale comparisons, at the European level, but this would be a topic for another investigation.

The Bayreuth lists of visitors have also made it possible to scrutinize the social profile of the guests. It seems that in the Baltic provinces the social map was far more complex than in Sweden and Finland, where Wagnerian activity rested on quite a narrow base. In the case of Finland, professionals in the field of music and government and municipal officials formed the largest segment. Among Swedish visitors, however, the role of musicians, critics, and other professional musicians, like that of officials, was weaker, while the occupational variety was clearly broader than in Finland. Furthermore, among visitors from the Baltic provinces, the number of professional musicians was fairly modest, but overall the social distribution was broad. This tells us that in Riga, from which most of the Baltic guests came, enthusiasm for Wagner was not solely a professional matter; it had a broader social relevance connected to the position of the Baltic-German population. In Livonia, Wagnerism thus crossed social borders, giving an opportunity to librarians and merchants as well as aristocrats and academics to assemble around Wagner's art.

It was characteristic of Baltic enthusiasm for Wagner that those who traveled to Bayreuth and those who participated in society activities first and foremost represented the diminishing Baltic-German population: there are no Estonian or Latvian names to be found on the visitor lists. It is quite probable that symbolic references to German culture were associated with Wagner's image during the 1870s and 1880s, when the composer himself was so immersed in his Teutonic devotions that the Estonian and Livonian majority were unwilling to identify with him. In fact, the situation in the Baltic provinces comes near to the Finnish situation. The first Finnish name to be found in the visitor lists is that of Ms. Aina Korhonen, who traveled to Bayreuth in 1899, at the very turn of the century. The rest of the Finnish guests belonged to the Swedish-speaking Finnish population (with the exception of Faltin, whose native language was German). In Finland, concert and operatic life was primarily promoted by the Swedish-speaking middle and upper classes, and it took time for the Finnish-speaking population to become acquainted with it. Because the Swedish-speaking minority had enjoyed close relations with both Sweden and Germany for a long time, it was natural that the encounter with Wagner and Wagnerism occurred among them. In Finland and in the Baltic provinces, there was unavoidably a cultural political dimension to Wagner that was missing in Sweden. In addition, German cultural influence had traditionally been stronger on the eastern side of the Baltic Sea; and it is conceivably for this reason that the Swedish reception of Wagner was quite different from the reception in Finland and the Baltic provinces. Taking a stand in favor of Wagner was not necessarily a political issue as it may have been among the Swedish-speaking population in Finland and among the Baltic Germans in Livonia. This difference may well be reflected in the fact that the Swedish Wagnerians never formed any Wagner society of their own.

At this point, it is crucial to note that, even if Wagner's name had been bound up with politics since the 1840s, he cannot simply be interpreted as the epitome of Germanness. Wagner presented a political issue in many different ways. As a modernist, he evoked mixed feelings and voiced a critique of dominant cultural policy. Furthermore, he was an ex-revolutionary whose activities could still arouse suspicion in the 1860s, as the secret files of the Russian police reveal. This changed in the 1870s, when Wagner's name was often associated with the rising German state, despite the fact that he never received any official support from the new *Reich*. But the Wagnerians trumpeted so loudly for their master that many contemporaries saw Wagner as a German *par excellence*. To be sure, Wagner gave rise to national sentiments in Livonia, where there was an active German minority. His operas could be celebrated as a counterbalance to the fact that the political role of the minority was gradually diminishing. Still, it is difficult to figure out how spectators really perceived Wagner on the basis of performances. Wagner was himself ambivalent in his attitude toward the nation-state. His operas became platforms for various, even opposing, interpretations. Even if he became a canonized composer by the 1880s, he remained a cultural threshold that divided, and still divides, opinions.

In conclusion, attention should also be paid to the temporal nature of Wagner's project. It was not planned just for the present day but broadened into the future. In his theoretical texts, written at the end of the 1840s and the beginning of the 1850s, Wagner had already propagated his ideas on the "artwork of the future." He wanted to construct his works more for the future than for the present. For precisely this reason he planned his music dramas as large-scale enterprises, with the result that most opera houses of the time could not produce them, even if they had the desire to do so. This orientation toward the future was also understood by contemporaries. Wagner's writings had been read throughout the Baltic world since the 1850s, but, instead of the "artwork of the future," journalists and critics referred to the "music of the future" (*Zukunftsmusik, framtidsmusik*), thus following the same incorrect pattern that was so often put forward in the Central European musical press. Wagner wanted to publicly disengage himself from this concept in "*Zukunftsmusik*" (1860), but his voice was drowned out by the media. Contrary to Wagner's opinions, attention, in terms of public discourse, was more often focused on music than on drama.

The fact that Wagner in his writings was oriented toward the future and seriously pondered things to come was by no means unconventional in the cultural context of the nineteenth century. Interest in speculation about the future had increased enormously and, in the second half of the century, led to the expansion of science fiction and utopian literature. Wagner, however, was exceptional in trying to grasp the future development of *art*, an area that has seldom interested visionaries of the future. To Wagner, this was also a personal decision: he saw himself as a neglected artist and explained that he represented a future world that had not yet been realized. Wagner also provided information on his plans to the public, in the form of scenarios that would come into existence sooner or later.[9] Perhaps this particular strategy explains why the Bayreuth Festival commanded such enormous attention in the press: Wagner had talked openly about his ambitions for decades before the final realization of the project.

It is hardly a coincidence that a Swedish journalist, Claës Lundin, kept Wagner in mind while writing his utopian novel *Oxygen och Aromasia* (1878). This work is a biting satire on the age of extreme capitalism in the remote future of the year 2378.[10] Because of Wagner's noisy music, the art world has started to employ odors and aromatic sensations, instead of sounds, in the creation of artworks:

> The Music of the Future, which had first made its breakthrough early in the nineteenth century, during the succeeding two centuries underwent such development, and achieved such a perfection, not least due to the phonograph, that it became more than the ear could bear. The famous Richard Wagner, inventor of the Music of the Future, had dealt the human eardrum such a blow that in the end people could no longer hear anything at all; and by means of the phonograph, his disciples had sent their trombone blasts around the entire World. Mankind had long been deaf, stone deaf, until in the end the ear became regarded as a useless appendage of the body.
>
> It was at this time that friends of the arts and chemists began to devote their attention to the long-disregarded nose. In preceding centuries the sensitivity of the olfactory organ had not improved; on the contrary, it had deteriorated, on account of nicotine. Yet could not this state of affairs be amended? None of the human senses affects the feelings so powerfully as that of scent. It was therefore obvious that the means of art should be deployed to make use of this sense. Thorough investigations were initiated into the distinctive character and effects of scent; the laws of olfactory harmony and disharmony were formulated, first empirically, but then in theoretical terms. Chemistry was able to supply, at a steadily falling cost, the necessary scents, and once the Ododion had been publicly displayed as an astounding piece of equipment, it soon began to be deployed by artists and so, in the course of time, within the home as well. This was the end of music, and the Music of the Future had a future no more.[11]

Lundin plays with the thought of Wagner's music as unhealthy or even damaging noise: the whole of mankind has been deafened by the Wagnerian resonance. These kinds of mental images of the "music of the future" were being constructed as early as the 1860s and 1870s, especially by the Central European press. Lundin wrote his novel at a time when Wagner had frequently been in the news columns in Stockholm. The premieres at the Royal Opera had evoked strong reactions that reached the readers' columns. Soon, in the late summer of 1876, the publicity culminated in the reports on the Bayreuth Festival. There seemed to be no limit to Wagner's success.

An arresting feature in Lundin's narrative is the combination of modern technology and the "Music of the Future." Wagner, as far as is known, never showed any interest in mechanical music. There were, however, mechanical instruments and music boxes before Thomas A. Edison presented his phonograph to the public in 1877, but Wagner seems to have paid no attention to these. Nonetheless, Lundin's point is not to focus on Wagner's preferences. The phonograph could, in any case, be a vehicle for the promotion of Wagner. In the nineteenth century, mechanical music had no practical meaning for the diffusion of Wagner's art, but in the twentieth century Lundin's vision has in part been realized: records—and later films and videos, CDs and DVDs—have changed the distributional possibilities and the reception of music. Through the radio, music has stretched "around the entire World," but the "Music of the Future" has not vanished. Perhaps Lundin was correct, in the sense that, in the history of nineteenth-century music, Wagner more than anybody else has had a profound impact on future development. The result may not have been the "death of the ear" but an indisputable transformation of music, which could hardly be understood without considering Richard Wagner's ideas and works.

Notes

Prelude

1. *Aftonbladet* (25 January 1872).

2. In the case of Estonia, Livonia, and Courland, the cities also have German names. Tallinn was Reval, Pärnu was Pernau, Tartu Dorpat, Liepaja Libau, Jelgava Mitau, and Daugavpils Dünaburg.

3. John Louis DiGaetani, "Wagnerian Patterns in the Fiction of Joseph Conrad, D. H. Lawrence, Virginia Woolf, and James Joyce" (Ph.D. diss., University of Wisconsin, 1973); also John Louis DiGaetani, *Richard Wagner and the Modern British Novel* (Rutherford, NJ: Fairleigh Dickinson University Press, 1978).

4. Elwood Hartman, *French Literary Wagnerism* (New York: Garland, 1988).

5. Erwin Koppen, *Dekadenter Wagnerismus: Studien zur europäischen Literatur des Fin de siècle* (Berlin and New York: de Gruyter, 1973).

6. Raymond Furness, *Wagner and Literature* (Manchester: Manchester University Press, 1982).

7. William J. McGrath, "Wagnerianism in Austria: The Regeneration of Culture through the Spirit of Music" (Ph.D. diss., Univ. of California, Berkeley, 1965); Edgard de Brito Chaves Júnior, *Wagner e o Brasil* (Rio de Janeiro: Emebê, 1976); *Wagner i Catalunya: Antologia de textos i gràfics sobre la influència wagneriana a la nostra cultura* (Barcelona: Edicions del Cotal, 1983); Anne Dzamba Sessa, *Richard Wagner and the English* (Rutherford, NJ: Fairleigh Dickinson University Press, 1979); Stoddard Martin, *Wagner to 'The Waste Land': A Study of the Relationship of Wagner to English Literature* (Totowa, NJ: Barnes & Noble Books, 1982); Gerald Dale Turbow, "Wagnerism in France 1839–1870: A Measure of a Social and Political Trend" (Ph.D. diss., University of California, Los Angeles, 1965); *Von Wagner zum Wagnerisme: Musik, Litteratur, Kunst, Politik*, ed. Annegret Fauser and Manuela Schwartz (Leipzig: Leipziger Universitätsverlag, 1999); Karel Wauters, *Wagner en Vlaanderen 1844–1914: Cultuurhistorische Studie* (Ghent: Secretariaat van de Koninklijke Academie voor Nederlandse Taal-en Letterkunde, 1983); Ute Jung-Kaiser, *Die Rezeption der Kunst Richard Wagners in Italien* (Regensburg: Bosse, 1974); Rosamund Bartlett, *Wagner and Russia* (Cambridge: Cambridge University Press, 1995); and Joseph Horowitz, *Wagner Nights: An American History* (Berkeley: University of California Press, 1994).

8. *Wagnerism in European Culture and Politics*, ed. David C. Large and William Weber, in collaboration with Anne Dzamba Sessa (Ithaca, NY: Cornell University Press, 1984).

9. Erwin Koppen, "Der Wagnerismus—Begriff und Phänomen," in *Richard-Wagner-Handbuch*, ed. Ulrich Müller and Peter Wapnewski (Stuttgart: Kröner, 1986), 609–10. In fact, Koppen argues that Wagnerism started during the 1860s, but I have proposed a slightly earlier date, as the debate on Wagner's theory of art had already started during the 1850s.

10. During the nineteenth century, present-day Estonia and Latvia were divided into three provinces, Estonia, Livonia, and Courland, which all belonged to the Russian Empire. The province of Estonia was not identical to present-day

Estonia: Dorpat/Tartu, for example, was at that date on the Livonian side of the border.

11 Fernand Braudel: *La Méditerranée et le monde méditerranéen à l'époque de Philippe II* (Paris: Colin, 1949).

12. David Kirby, *Northern Europe in the Early Modern Period: The Baltic World 1492–1772* (London: Longman, 1990); and David Kirby, *The Baltic World 1772–1993: Europe's Northern Periphery in an Age of Change* (London: Longman, 1995).

13. Kirby, *Northern Europe*, ix.

14. For further details, see Heinrich W. Schwab, "Der Ostseeraum. Beobachtungen aus seiner Musikgeschichte und Anregungen zu einem musikhistoriographischen Konzept," in *Nordisk musikkforskerkongress Oslo, 24.–27. juni 1992* (Oslo: Det historisk-filosofiske fakultet, Universitet i Oslo, 1992), 12.

15. Ibid., 15.

16. Ibid., 11–12.

17. See note 7 above.

18. For further details, see Emerich Kastner, *Die dramatischen Werke Richard Wagners: Chronologisches Verzeichnis der ersten Aufführungen*, 2nd ed. (Leipzig: Breitkopf und Härtel, 1899), 38–43.

19. On reception, see Tony Bennett and Janet Woollacott, *Bond and Beyond: The Political Career of a Popular Hero* (New York: Methuen, 1987), 59–65; Hans Robert Jauss, *Ästhetische Erfahrung und literarische Hermeneutik* (Frankfurt am Main: Suhrkamp, 1982), 665–66; Hannu Salmi, "Sociohistorical Context and the Change of Meanings in Cinema, Especially from the Perspective of Using Filmic Evidence in Historical Studies," in *On the Borderlines of Semiosis: Proceedings from the ISI conference in Imatra, July 1991*, ed. Eero Tarasti (Imatra: International Semiotics Institute at Imatra, 1993), 301–11.

20. Horowitz, *Wagner Nights*, 213–39.

Chapter 1

1. See Wilhelm Bauck, *Handbok i musikens historia från fornverlden intill nutiden: För tonkonstens idkare såväl som för dess vänner i allmänhet* (Stockholm: Hirsch, 1862), 294.

2. For further details, see Hannu Salmi, *Richard Wagner Suomessa: Suomalaisen Wagner-reseption mahdollisuudet 1800-luvulla* (Oulu: University of Oulu, 1991), 150–51.

3. *Rigasche Stadtblätter* (26 March 1853). In the course of his career, Thomé worked as far away as Laibach (Ljubljana), Trieste, Lemberg (Lvov), Graz, Riga, and finally Prague, where in 1862 he founded the first theater to perform in the Czech language; see Richard Wagner, *Sämtliche Briefe* (Leipzig: Deutscher Verlag für Musik, 1967–2000; Wiesbaden: Breitkopf & Härtel, 1999–), 5:566. (Hereafter referred to as Wagner, *Sämtliche Briefe*.)

4. *Eesti muusika biograafiline leksikon* (Tallinn: Valgus, 1990), 25; Juhan Aavik, *Eesti muusika ajalugu*, vol. 2: *Kunstmuusika* (Stockholm: Estniska Kultursamf., 1969), 139.

5. *Rigasche Stadtblätter* (11 April, 2 May, 23 May, 20 June, and 25 July 1857).

6. Ibid, (21 July 1855).

7. *Lithuania. An Encyclopedic Survey*, ed. Johan Zinkus (Vilnius: Encyclopedia publishers, 1986), 362.

8. Vida Bakutyte, "Musical Life in Vilnius at the Time of Ole Bull's Visit (1841)," in *Nordisk musikkforskerkongress Oslo, 24.–27. juni 1992* (Oslo: Det historisk-filosofiske fakultet, Universitet i Oslo, 1992), 450–52.

9. Fabian Dahlström and Erkki Salmenhaara, *Suomen musiikin historia 1: Ruotsin vallan ajasta romantiikkaan* (Porvoo: WSOY, 1995), 137–38.

10. Ibid., 1:136–38. In his analysis Dahlström refers to Carl-Allan Moberg's *Drag i Östersjöområdets musikliv på Buxtehudes tid* (1957). For a full account, see Greger Andersson, "Der Ostseeraum als Musiklandschaft. Musik—Musikinstitutionen—Repertoires im 17. und 18. Jahrhundert. Präsentation eines Forschungsprojekts," in *Balticum—A Coherent Musical Landscape in 16th and 18th Centuries*, ed. Irma Vierimaa, 9–17 (Helsinki: University of Helsinki, 1994). See also Heinrich W. Schwab, "Der Ostseeraum. Beobachtungen aus seiner Musikgeschichte und Anregungen zu einem musikhistoriographischen Konzept," in *Nordisk musikkforskerkongress Oslo, 24.–27. juni 1992*, 11–33 (Oslo: Det historisk-filosofiske fakultet, Universitet i Oslo, 1992).

11. Dahlström and Salmenhaara, *Suomen musiikin historia*, 1:187–88.

12. K. E. Eurén, *Höyrykoneet: Niiden keksintö ja käytäntö* (Hämeenlinna: Eurén, 1863), 86.

13. Harry Herbert Tobies. *Das Baltikum: Siebenhundert Jahre Geschehen an der Ostsee* (Berg: VGB, 1994), 462–64.

14. See Martin Gregor-Dellin, *Richard Wagner: Sein Leben, Sein Werk, Sein Jahrhundert* (Munich: Piper, 1980), 104–5; Wagner, *Sämtliche Briefe*, 1:51–52. See also Derek Watson, *Richard Wagner* (London: Dent, 1979).

15. See especially Wagner, *Sämtliche Briefe*, 1:44 and 323.

16. See Werner Breig, "Wagners kompositorisches Werk," in *Richard-Wagner-Handbuch*, ed. Ulrich Müller and Peter Wapnewski (Stuttgart: Kröner, 1986), 364–65; Breig incorrectly gives the date as March 1835. For full details of this and other works, see *Wagner Werk-Verzeichnis (WWV): Verzeichnis der musikalischen Werke Richard Wagners und ihrer Quellen*, ed. John Deathridge, Martin Geck, and Egon Voss (Mainz: Schott, 1986). The correct date is corroborated by Wagner himself in various biographical sources: see, for example, "Die rothe Brieftasche" in Wagner, *Sämtliche Briefe*, 1:82.

17. See Gregor-Dellin, *Richard Wagner*, 116–17.

18. Wagner arrived in Berlin on 18 May 1836, soon after the failure of the first performance of *Das Liebesverbot*; see Wagner, *Sämtliche Briefe*, 1:82–83.

19. These letters may be found in ibid., 1:263–314.

20. Wagner's letter to Minna, postmarked Berlin, 20 June 1837, in *Letters of Richard Wagner: The Burrell Collection* (New York: Macmillan, 1950), 43; for the original German, see Wagner, *Sämtliche Briefe*, 1:263.

21. Wagner's letter to Schumann, 3 December 1836, in Wagner, *Sämtliche Briefe*, 1:317.

22. Wagner, *Sämtliche Briefe*, 1:318.

23. Henry Bacon, *Oopperan historia* (Helsinki: Otava, 1995), 246; Oswald Georg Bauer, *Richard Wagner Goes to the Theatre*, trans. Stewart Spencer (Bayreuth: Leitung der Bayreuther Festspiele, 1996), 48. Spontini had written *Fernand Cortez* in 1809 but revised it on several subsequent occasions. It was probably the fourth version, dating from 1832, that Wagner saw in Berlin.

24. See Gregor-Dellin, *Richard Wagner*, 119.

25. This is stated by Wagner himself in *Mein Leben*, ed. Martin Gregor-Dellin (Munich: List, 1976), 133.

26. Wagner's letter to Minna, 21 May 1836, in Wagner, *Sämtliche Briefe*, 1:265.

27. Wagner's letter to Minna, 6 June 1836, in *Letters of Richard Wagner*, 63; Wagner, *Sämtliche Briefe*, 1:301. Wagner himself wrote this letter over a period of days, beginning on 6 June and ending on the 21st. The advice to Minna to use pressure in persuading Hübsch to agree to her request was offered on the 13th (mistakenly dated the 12th by Wagner).

28. *Letters of Richard Wagner*, 63; Wagner, *Sämtliche Briefe*, 1:302

29. Wagner, *Mein Leben*, 136; Richard Wagner, *My Life* (London: Constable, 1911), 157.

30. Wagner, *Mein Leben*, 136; Wagner, *My Life*, 157.

31. Wagner, *Mein Leben*, 134–35; see also Gregor-Dellin, *Richard Wagner*, 120.

32. Wagner mentions this plan in his letter to Robert Schumann of 3 December 1836; Wagner, *Sämtliche Briefe*, 1:318. Unfortunately, his letter to Scribe has not survived.

33. Wagner, *Mein Leben*, 136–37.

34. Gregor-Dellin, *Richard Wagner*, 120–21.

35. *WWV*, 152–54. According to the editors of the *WWV*, this overture was not premiered in Riga until 19 March 1838 (Julian calendar). Erwin Kroll had earlier argued that Wagner had conducted it in Königsberg, his evidence for this claim being Eduard Sobolewski's review of Wagner's Königsberg concerts in the *Neue Zeitschrift für Musik* 6 (1837): 120. But, as the editors of the *WWV* point out, the description in the *Neue Zeitschrift* does not necessarily refer to *Rule Britannia*. They remain convinced, therefore, that the first performance of *Rule Britannia* took place in Riga in March 1838. Cf. Erwin Kroll, *Musikstadt Königsberg: Geschichte und Erinnerung* (Freiburg i. Br.: Atlantis, 1966), 144.

36. Carl Friedrich Glasenapp, *Das Leben Richard Wagner*, 4th ed. (Leipzig: Breitkopf & Härtel, 1905), 1:275–76; Vita Lindenberg, "Richard Wagners Wirken in Riga," in *Opern und Musikdramen Verdis und Wagners in Dresden. 4. Wissenschaftlicher Konferenz zum Thema: 'Dresdner Operntraditionen,'* ed. Günther Stephan, Hans John, and Peter Kaiser (Dresden: Hochschule für Musik Carl Maria von Weber, 1988), 704. Both Glasenapp and Lindenberg refer to Wilhelm Tappert's article "Perkunos und Lohengrin," *Musikalisches Wochenblatt* 18 (1887): 413.

37. Lindenberg, "Richard Wagners Wirken in Riga," 705.

38. Bauer, *Richard Wagner Goes to the Theatre*, 44; Kroll, *Musikstadt Königsberg*, 143–45; *WWV*, 151.

39. *WWV*, 150.

40. Kroll, *Musikstadt Königsberg*, 117–18; Bauer, *Richard Wagner Goes to the Theatre*, 43.

41. Gregor-Dellin, *Richard Wagner*, 122–23.

42. Wagner, *Mein Leben*, 149–50.

43. Schindelmeisser was Heinrich Dorn's stepbrother. Dorn had conducted Wagner's Overture in B-Flat Major in Leipzig on 25 December 1830. He moved to Riga in 1833.

44. Wagner's letter to Louis Schindelmeisser, 7 June 1837, in Wagner, *Sämtliche Briefe*, 1:328.

45. Wagner's letter to Minna, postmarked Berlin, 20 June 1837, in Wagner, *Sämtliche Briefe*, 1:330–32.

46. Lindenberg, "Richard Wagners Wirken in Riga," 692.

47. Constantin Mettig, *Geschichte der Stadt Riga* (Riga: Jonck & Poliewsky, 1897), 392.
48. Heinrich Bosse, "The Establishment of the German theater in 18th Century Riga," *Journal of Baltic Studies* 3 (1989): 210–11. The Vietinghoff family could trace its origins back to Westphalia, but they had lived in Livonia since the fourteenth century; see *Deutschbaltisches biographisches Lexikon 1710–1960*, ed. Wilhelm Lenz (Cologne: Böhlau, 1970), 834.
49. Ilona Breģe, "Rīgas Pilsētas teātris 1782–1863. Das Rigaer Stadt-Theater 1782–1863," in *No Fītinghofa tēatra līdz Vāgnerzālei. Vom Vietinghoff-Theater bis zum Wagner-Saal* (Riga: Das Deutsche Kulturinstitut Lettlands, 1992), [9] (Breģe's article is unpaginated). First staged in 1773, Monsigny's opera was performed in Riga in German as *Die schöne Arsena*.
50. Ibid.," [9–11]. *Zémire et Azor* by André Grétry (1741–1813) dates from 1771, *Die Jagd* by Johann Adam Hiller (1728–1804) from 1770. Georg Benda (1722–95) was born Jiří Antonín Benda. He was a Czech composer who moved to Prussia in 1742 and made a name for himself with his comic operas, melodramas, and operettas, though the lack of any clear-cut divisions between the various musical genres at this time means that they could all equally well be described as operas. Both *Der Dorfjahrmarkt* and *Ariadne auf Naxos* were first staged in 1775.
51. For further details, see Henrik Knif, "Opera seria—välttämätön ylellisyys. Barokkioopperan suojelijat ja yleisö," *Tiede ja edistys* 1 (1992): 17–26; and Henrik Knif, *Gentlemen and Spectators: Studies in Journals, Opera and the Social Scene in Late Stuart London* (Helsinki: Finnish Historical Society, 1995), 209–25.
52. The Birons were a Courland family who had been raised to the nobility in Poland in 1638. From 1737 the title of Duke of Courland was conferred on the head of the family; see *Deutschbaltisches biographisches Lexikon*, 67.
53. Breģe, "Rīgas Pilsētas teātris 1782–1863. Das Rigaer Stadt-Theater 1782–1863," [13].
54. Lindenberg, "Richard Wagners Wirken in Riga," 693.
55. Breģe, "Rīgas Pilsētas teātris 1782–1863. Das Rigaer Stadt-theater 1782–1863," [15].
56. These vocal societies may be seen as the male-voice equivalent of the fashionable salon societies favored by women. Originally, they were convivial occasions at which members sat round a table (hence their name) singing hunting and drinking songs. From these activities the male-voice choirs emerged.
57. Lindenberg, "Richard Wagners Wirken in Riga," 694–96; Breģe, [15].
58. Quoted by Lindenberg, "Richard Wagners Wirken in Riga," 702. Dorn's memoirs were first published in the *Rigasche Stadtblätter* 21 (1870).
59. Rechnung für Musikdirektor Wagner von S. Sternberg 6.3.1838 (1378 f., 1 apr., 9666 l., 1–3 lp.), The Latvian State Historical Archives, Riga.
60. Wagner's *Autobiographical Sketch* is reproduced in Wagner, *Sämtliche Briefe*, 1:95–114, esp. 104.
61. Wagner, *Mein Leben*, 152–55.
62. Wagner, *Mein Leben*, 152–53; Wagner, *My Life*, 177; Gregor-Dellin, *Richard Wagner*, 124–25.
63. Wagner, *Sämtliche Briefe*, 1:104; Engl. trans. from *Wagner: A Documentary Study*, ed. Herbert Barth, Dietrich Mack, and Egon Voss (London: Thames & Hudson, 1975), 14. The *Autobiographical Sketch* first appeared in Laube's radical *Zeitung für die elegante Welt* on 1 and 8 February 1843.

64. This is the date given by Raimond Skrābāns in *Izcilie pasaules mūziķi Rīgā: Apceres par mūzikas sakariem XIX gadsimtā* (Riga: Zinātne, 1993), but Wagner himself in his letter to Schindelmeisser of 17 Sept. states that it took place on the 16th; Wagner, *Sämtliche Briefe*, 1:335.

65. Skrābāns, *Izcilie pasaules mūziķi Rīgā*, 84.

66. Wagner, *Mein Leben*, 155; Wagner, *My Life*, 180–81.

67. This is Wagner's own comment; see Wagner, *Mein Leben*, 156.

68. Wagner, *Mein Leben*, 156; Wagner, *My Life*, 181.

69. Wagner, *Mein Leben*, 156–57; Wagner, *My Life*, 182.

70. Skrābāns, *Izcilie pasaules mūziķi Rīgā*, 84–85.

71. Wagner, *Mein Leben*, 154; Wagner, *My Life*, 179.

72. Wagner, *Mein Leben*, 154; Wagner, *My Life*, 179.

73. See the concert advertisement in Skrābāns, *Izcilie pasaules mūziķi Rīgā*, 89.

74. Breģe, "Rīgas Pilsētas teātris 1782–1863. Das Rigaers Stadt-theater 1782–1863," [16].

75. Gregor-Dellin, 126; see also Wagner, *Mein Leben*, 158.

76. Lindenberg, "Richard Wagners Wirken in Riga," 699–700. Lindenberg quotes the *Zuschauer* 4770 (1838). See also Wagner's own description of the Jelgava performances in Wagner, *Mein Leben*, 159.

77. For more information about this program, see Skrābāns, *Izcilie pasaules mūziķi Rīgā*, 89.

78. Quoted by Gregor-Dellin, *Richard Wagner*, 127; Engl. trans. from *Wagner: A Documentary Study*, 160. See also Skrābāns, *Izcilie pasaules mūziķi Rīgā*, 85 and 89.

79. See Tobies, *Das Baltikum*, 557.

80. Eugène Scribe and G. Delavigne, *Robert af Normandie. Opera i fem akter*, 7th ed. (Stockholm: Albert Bonniers förlag, 1873), 54–55.

81. Booklet accompanying the CBS recording of *Le prophète* (M3K 79400), 310–11. The libretto was again by Scribe.

82. Eugène Scribe, *Hugenotit. Opera viidessä näytöksessä*. (Helsinki: Suomalainen teatteri 1876), 84–85.

83. The letter to Schumann is dated 3 Dec. 1836. The one to Lewald is undated, but according to Glasenapp (*Die Leben Richard Wagners*, 1:272), it was written on 12 Nov. 1838. See Wagner, *Sämtliche Briefe*, 1:318 and 350n1.

84. Wagner, *Sämtliche Briefe*, 1:323–27. According to the first published edition of this letter, it was written on 4 February 1837.

85. Tobies, *Das Baltikum*, 557.

86. Vilho Niitemaa and Kalervo Hovi, *Baltian historia*, 2nd ed. (Helsinki: Tammi, 1991), 89–90.

87. Lindenberg, "Richard Wagners Wirken in Riga," 704. Lindenberg mentions Werner's play (erroneously calling it *Das Kreuz am Baltischen Meer*), but fails to prove that Wagner knew it. Friedrich Ludwig Zacharias Werner (1768–1823) was one of the most popular playwrights of the Romantic period in Germany. He devoted himself to religious themes while cultivating a sensationalist element in the form of scenes of torture and carnality. Among his plays were dramatic adaptations of the lives of Luther and Attila. See *Kansojen kirjallisuus*, vol. 7 (Porvoo: WSOY, 1976), 123–24.

88. Lindenberg, "Richard Wagners Wirken in Riga," 705.

89. See Bauer, *Richard Wagner Goes to the Theatre*, 44.

90. *WWV*, 164–92.

91. Wagner, *Sämtliche Briefe*, 1:104–5; Engl. trans. from *Wagner: A Documentary Study*, 14.

92. Wagner, *Sämtliche Briefe*, 1:105. (The full score of act 2 was not completed until September 1839.)

93. Wagner, *Sämtliche Briefe*, 1:105.

94. Wagner, *Mein Leben*, 167.

95. See Wagner, *Sämtliche Briefe*, 1:364–65 for the composer's undated letter to Henriot of [June 1839].

96. Gregor-Dellin, *Richard Wagner*, 132–33.

97. Wagner, *Mein Leben*, 168.

98. Wagner, *Mein Leben*, 168–69.

99. Wagner, *Mein Leben*, 169; Wagner, *My Life*, 196.

100. Wagner, *Mein Leben*, 169; Wagner, *My Life*, 196–97.

101. Wagner, *Mein Leben*, 170–71; Wagner, *My Life*, 197–98.

102. Wagner, *Mein Leben*, 171; Wagner, *My Life*, 199.

103. Wagner, *Mein Leben*, 174; Wagner, *My Life*, 202–3.

104. Martin Wegelius, *Länsimaisen musiikin historia pääpiirteissään kristinuskon alkuajoista meidän päiviimme*, trans. Axel Törnudd (Helsinki: Holm, 1904), 571.

Chapter 2

1. Salmi, *Richard Wagner Suomessa*, 155–56.

2. Tallinna Kõrgem Muusikakool was founded in 1919. As of 1923, its name was Tallinna Konservatoorium. A High School of Music was also founded in Tartu in the same year (from 1925 onwards Tartu Konservatoorium). On this point, see *Eesti muusika biograafiline leksikon* ed. Ela Eelhein et al, (Tallinn: Valgus, 1990), 302.

3. Of the Swedes who studied in Leipzig, one could mention August Söderman (1832–76) and Ludvig Norman (1831–85); of the Finns Carl Gustaf Wasenius (1821–99), Filip von Schantz (1835–65), Richard Faltin (1835–1918), Martin Wegelius (1846–1906), and Robert Kajanus (1856–1933); and of the Estonians Rudolph Griwing (1853–1922), Ernst Reinecke (1856–1911), and Adalbert Wirkhaus 1880–1961). See Wilhelm Bauck, *Handbok i musikens historia från äldsta tider intill våra dagar* (Stockholm: Hirsch, 1888), 259–61; Dahlström and Salmenhaara, *Suomen musiikin historia*, 1: 424, 449, 454, 495, 508–9; and *Eesti muusika biograafiline leksikon*, 99, 204, 292.

4. For example, Martin Wegelius, a Finn, made friends with the Norwegian composers Edvard Grieg, Johan Svendsen, and Christian Sinding. See Dahlström and Salmenhaara, *Suomen musiikin historia*, 1:496.

5. See especially Dorothee Eberlein, "Zwischen Petersburg und Leipzig. Zur Ausbildung musikalischer Formen in den baltischen Ländern um 1900," in *National Movements in the Baltic Countries during the 19th Century*, ed. Aleksander Loit (Stockholm: University of Stockholm, 1985), 455–56. Among the Estonians who studied in St. Petersburg, Adelheid Hippius (1853–1942), Johannes Kappel (1855–1907), Friedrich August Saebelmann (1851–1911), and Rudolf Tobias (1873–1918) are

particularly worthy of mention. See, for example, *Eesti muusika biograafiline leksikon*, 48–49, 76, 219; Eberlein, "Zwischen Petersburg und Leipzig." 459. Later visitors to St. Petersburg were, among others, Mart Saar (1882–1963), Artur Lemba (1885–1963), Juhan Aavik (1884–1982), and Peeter Süda (1883–1920). At the turn of the twentieth century in particular, St. Petersburg also attracted visitors from Latvia and Lithuania. Latvia provided, among others, Jāzeps Vītols (1863–1948), Emīls Melngailis (1874–1954), Emīls Dārziņš (1875–1910), and Alfrēds Kalniņš (1879–1951). Lithuanian visitors included Konstantin Galkauskas (1875–1963), Česlovas Sasnauskas (1867–1916), Nikas Petrauskas (1873–1937), and Jurgis Karnavičius (1884–1941). An interesting exception among the Lithuanians was the famous composer Mikalojus Čiurlionis (1875–1911), who studied both in Warsaw and in Leipzig.

6. *Eesti muusika biograafiline leksikon*, 132–33.

7. *Post-och inrikes tidningar* (2 May 1865). Door had already given concerts in the Nordic countries in 1857 when Pacius heard him in Stockholm in the spring of 1857. Pacius wrote with enthusiasm to his friend Zacharias Topelius: "Apropos, hier ist ein ausgezeichneter Klavierspieler, Herr Door aus Wien, der mit erster Gelegenheit nach Finnland zu reisen gedenkt, um dort Konzerte zu geben. Sey gut und bereite seine Ankunft bestens vor. Ihr werdet Freude an ihm haben, es ist ohnedies ein eben so anspruchsloser als ausgezeichneter Künstler." Pacius' letter to Topelius 26 March 1857, in Zacharias Topelius, *Konstnärsbrev. Z. Topelius' brevväxling med författare, konstnärer, skådespelare och musiker*, ed. Paul Nyberg, vol. 1 (Helsinki: The Society of Swedish Literature in Finland, 1956), 208. The letter was dated in March, but it also includes passages written during the months of June and July.

8. *St. Petersburger Zeitung* (27 February/11 March 1853).

9. *Rigasche Stadtblätter* (11 October, 13 October 1856).

10. *Helsingfors Tidningar* (1 July, 9 July 1857).

11. *Svenska tidningen* (7 November 1857).

12. *Åbo Tidningar* (6 October, 17 October, 22 October 1821).

13. Marko Lehti, "Suomalaisten Tallinnan-matkailun alkuvaiheet. Tallinna fennomaanien silmin 1800-luvun jälkimmäisellä puoliskolla," in *Matkakuumetta: Matkailun ja turismin historiaa*. With English summaries, ed. Taina Syrjämaa. (Turku: University of Turku, 1994), 94–95. See also *Åbo Tidningar* (22 June 1842). The route of the Furst Menschikof was soon extended to St. Petersburg. See also the advertisement in the paper *Svenska tidningen* (9 May 1857).

14. *St. Petersburger Zeitung* (18 February/2 March 1853, 22 February/6 March 1853).

15. The vessel was used by Franz Thomé with his family when he came to Riga in order to work as the director of the Riga German theater in July 1853: "Das Dampfschiff Düna, welches am 22. Juni von Stettin hieselbst anlagte, brachte uns auch den neuerwählten Theaterdirector Herrn F. Thomé nebst 2 Kindern und einige der neu engagirten Glieder unserer Bühne." *Rigasche Stadtblätter* (30 July 1853).

16. David Kirby, *The Baltic World, 1772–1993: Europe's Northern Periphery in an Age of Change* (London: Longman, 1995), 165.

17. *Reval/Tallinn. Porträt einer Ostseestadt*, ed. Erik Thomson (Cologne-Rodenkirchen: Liebig Druck & Verlag, 1979), 103.

18. *Suomen taloushistoria*, 1: *Agraarinen Suomi*, ed. Eino Jutikkala, Yrjö Kaukiainen, and Sven-Erik Åström (Helsinki: Tammi, 1980), 483.

19. It is probable that many of Wagner's works and themes were arranged for mechanical instruments in the nineteenth century, but the scrutiny of this popularization has been excluded from the present study. Rolls manufactured for player pianos, for example, on the basis of Franz Liszt's and Frédéric Chopin's compositions have survived, and it is therefore highly possible that Wagner's most famous melodies have also been transferred through perforation on the surface of rolls to be performed on the pianola.

20. Andreas Ballstaedt and Tobias Widmaier, *Salonmusik: Zur Geschichte und Funktion einer bürgerlichen Musikpraxis* (Stuttgart: Steiner, 1989), 34–38.

21. Ibid., 60–78.

22. Ibid., 79.

23. Admittedly, mechanical recording had a drastic effect on the publishing of sheet music, which was driven to a crisis at the beginning of the twentieth century.

24. Wagner's letter to Breitkopf & Härtel, 6 June 1855, in Richard Wagner, *Sämtliche Briefe*, 7:202–3.

25. Ibid., 203.

26. See, for example, Wagner's letter to Breitkopf & Härtel, 20 June 1853 and 9 January 1854, in Wagner, *Sämtliche Briefe*, 5:333, 490–91.

27. Dahlström and Salmenhaara, *Suomen musiikin historia*, 1:482–83.

28. *Förteckning öfver nya sång-och pianokompositioner. Att tillgå hos Musik-och Bokhandlare i Sverige, Norge, Danmark och Finland samt direckt från Abr. Hirschs Förlag* (Stockholm: Hirsch, s.a.), Music Catalogs, the Music Library of Sweden, Stockholm. The year of printing is missing in Hirsch's catalog, but apparently it was published after 1885.

29. This information is based on the lists of publishers at the Music Library of Sweden. I should like to express my particular thanks to Veslemöy Heintz, who gave me fullest access to the archival materials and kindly guided me in the use of these files.

30. The information concerned is based on my observations of the Ephemera Collection at the Library of the Latvian Academy of Sciences and notation advertisements published in the newspapers.

31. The advertisement of J. Deubner, *Rigasche Zeitung* (8 June 1857), Extrablatt. The advertisement emphasizes the large network of the company: "J. Deubner, Buch-und Musikalienhändler in Riga, und in den Buchhandlungen Dorpats, Revals und Mitaus."

32. *Rigasche Stadtblätter* (23 December 1871).

33. Gumpert had a library of sheet music as early as the 1840s. See, for example, *Förteckning öfver N.J. Gumperts musikaliska lån-bibliothek N:o 1 till 3*. Jemte första och andra supplementet (Gothenburg: Gumpert, 1846), The Music Library of Sweden, Stockholm.

34. *Katalog öfver J. E. Sundbergs Musikhandel och Musik-Lånbibliotek i Göteborg* (Gothemburg: Sundberg, 1875), The Music Library of Sweden, Stockholm.

35. *Katalog öfver Musikalier, som äro att tillgå uti Clara Öhrströms Musikhandel och Musik-Lånebibliothek i Malmö* (Malmö: Öhrström, 1871), The Music Library of Sweden, Stockholm.

36. See, for example, *Förteckning över musikalier i Abr. Hirschs musikhandel och musikaliska låne-institut i Stockholm* (Stockholm: Hirsch, 1852); *Förteckning N:o 2 öfver de musikalier som äro att tillgå i Eduard Josephsons musikhandel och musik-lånebibliothek i Stockholm* (Stockholm: Josephson, 1853); *Katalog öfver Musikalier som äro att tillgå uti Abr. Lundquists Musikhandel och Musiklånbibliothek* (Stockholm: Lundquist, 1858);

Katalog öfver Musikalier som äro att tillgå uti Rylander & Komp. Musik-lånbibliothek i Stockholm (Stockholm: Rylander, 1851), The Music Library of Sweden, Stockholm.

37. *Fjerde Supplementet till förteckning öfver N.J. Gumperts Musikaliska Lånbibliothek* (Gothenburg: Gumpert, 1850), 9. The Music Library of Sweden, Stockholm.

38. *Katalog öfver Musikalier som äro att tillgå uti Rylander & Komp. Musikhandel och Musiklånbibliothek i Stockholm* (Stockholm: Rylander, 1851), 71–72. The Music Library of Sweden, Stockholm.

39. Ibid., 87.

40. *Musikaliskt Lån-Bibliothek i Lund* (Lund: A. B. Heinzelmann, 1853), The Music Library of Sweden, Stockholm.

41. *Abr. Hirschs Musik-Katalog. Förteckning öfver musikalier i Abr. Hirschs musikhandel och musikaliska låne-institut i Stockholm* (Stockholm: Hirsch, 1852), 116. The Music Library of Sweden, Stockholm. The copies were sold with the numbers 9224 and 9225. *Les deux Grénadiers* cost one crown and the Carnival Song 24 pence (öres).

42. *Nya Musikalier från Utlandet inkomna i December månad hos Abr. Hirsch* (Stockholm: Hirsch, 1855), The Music Library of Sweden, Stockholm. Apparently, the question was of the same lyric pieces on which Wagner, Breitkopf & Härtel, Franz Liszt, and Hans von Bülow were in correspondence in December 1853 and in January 1854. Wagner himself had arranged five pieces from *Lohengrin* for solo voice and piano: "Elsa's Traum," "Schluss des ersten Aktes," "Morgenlied und Männerscene," "Hochzeitmusik und Brautlied," and "Einzug des Heeres." See Wagner's letter to Hans von Bülow 25 November 1853, in Wagner, *Sämtliche Briefe,* 5:475–76. Wagner asked Hans von Bülow to make arrangements from the pieces only for piano. Later, he asked Liszt to revise Bülow's accomplishment. See Wagner's letter to Franz Liszt, 17 December 1853, in Wagner, *Sämtliche Briefe,* 5:484–86.

43. *Sjette Supplementet till förteckning öfver N.J. Gumperts Musikaliska Lånbibliothek* (Gothenburg: Gumpert, 1855), The Music Library of Sweden, Stockholm.

44. *Fjerde Supplementet till förteckning öfver N.J. Gumperts Musikaliska Lånbibliothek* (Gothenburg: Gumpert, 1857), The Music Library of Sweden, Stockholm.

45. Cf. Wagner's letter to Breitkopf & Härtel, 9 January 1854, in Wagner, *Sämtliche Briefe.* 5:491.

46. Franz Liszt, *Zwei Stücke aus Wagners Tannhäuser und Lohengrin, Femte Supplementet till förteckning öfver N.J. Gumperts Musikaliska Lånbibliothek* (Gothenburg: Gumpert, 1857), The Music Library of Sweden, Stockholm. The same music publication can be found in other catalogs as well, e.g., in the Beyer catalog of 1865. Cf. G. P: son Beyer, *Förteckning öfver en i priset betydligt nedsatt samling musikalier hvilka tillhört ett genom branden i Carlstad skingradt musikaliskt lånebibliothek. G P: son Beyers Bokhandel* (Carlstad: Beyer, 1865), The Music Library of Sweden, Stockholm.

47. Franz Liszt, *Zwei Stücke aus R. Wagner's Tannhäuser und Lohengrin: für das Pianoforte von Franz Liszt* (Leipzig: Breitkopf & Härtel, 1853).

48. *Förteckning N:o 2 öfver Musikalier i Abr. Hirschs musikhandel och musikaliska låne-institut i Stockholm* (Stockholm: Hirsch, 1859), The Music Library of Sweden, Stockholm.

49. The history of the interpretation of opera will be treated in detail in the following chapters.

50. For the performance history of *Tannhäuser* in the Baltic Sea area, see, in particular, Hannu Salmi, "Thüringenistä koilliseen. Richard Wagnerin Tannhäuserin esityshistoriaa Itämeren alueella," *Suomen Wagner-Seuran julkaisu* 6 (1995): 4–9.

51. *Rigasche Zeitung* (7 February 1855). The same advertisement appeared repeatedly in *Rigasche Zeitung* on 8 February, 18 February, and 14 March 1855.

52. Ibid. (14 March 1855, 16 April 1855).

53. Ibid. (16 April 1855).

54. Cf. Hannu Salmi, *"Die Herrlichkeit des deutschen Namens . . ."*: *Die schriftstellerische und politische Tätigkeit Richard Wagners als Gestalter nationaler Identität während der staatlichen Vereinigung Deutschlands* (Turku: University of Turku, 1993), 65–66, 108–11; Hannu Salmi, *Imagined Germany: Richard Wagner's National Utopia.* (New York: Peter Lang, 1999), 11–12, 50–51, 131–33.

55. *Rigaer Theater- und Tonkünstler-Lexikon nebst Geschichte des Rigaer Theaters und der Musikalischen Gesellschaft,* ed. Moritz Rudolph (Riga: R. Kymmel, 1890), 88.

56. *Beilage zur Rigaschen Zeitung* (11./23. December 1871).

57. *Nya Musikalier utkomna hos Elkan & Schildknecht i Stockholm samt tillgängliga hos alla Herrar Bok- och Musikhandlare i Sverige* (Stockholm: Elkan & Schildknecht, 1864), The Music Library of Sweden, Stockholm.

58. Dahlström and Salmenhaara, *Suomen musiikin historia,* 355–56.

59. Wegelius, *Hufvuddragen af den västerländska musikens historia,* 3 vols. (Helsinki: Holm, 1891–93), 3:571.

60. Martin Wegelius, "Wagner-Biography," 52–53. An unpublished manuscript in the Library of the Sibelius Academy, Helsinki. According to the estimations made by Veikko Helasvuo, the text was written in the late 1880s and early 1890s. Cf. Veikko Helasvuo, "Martin Wegeliuksen Wagner-elämäkerta," *Musiikkitieto* 11 (1946): 70–71.

61. *Revue européenne* (1 April 1861).

62. Cf., for example, *Abr. Hirschs Musik-Katalog. Förteckning öfver musikalier i Abr. Hirschs musikhandel och musikaliska låne-institut i Stockholm* (Stockholm: Hirsch, 1852), The Music Library of Sweden, Stockholm.

63. *Förteckning öfver musikalier i Elkan & Schildknechts musikhandel och musiklånebibliothek i Stockholm* (Stockholm: Elkan & Schildknecht, 1859), 20, 30–31. The Music Library of Sweden, Stockholm.

64. *Förteckning öfver musikalier i Elkan & Schildknechts musikhandel och musiklånebibliothek i Stockholm* (Stockholm: Elkan & Schildknecht, 1859), 34, 42, 44–46, 56, 63, 66, 74–76. The Music Library of Sweden, Stockholm. Similar arrangements of Wagner are also found in the other sales catalogs of 1859. Hirsch, for example, marketed Beyer's cycle, *Révue mélodique,* in which the arrangement Opus 112 contained melodies from Rossini's *Guillaume Tell,* Weber's *Oberon,* Donizetti's *Lucrezia Borgia,* and other popular operas as well: among others, *Der fliegende Holländer.* Adaptions of *Tannhäuser* could be found alongside Cramer's *Les Fleurs des opéras* in, e.g., G. W. Marks's *Potpourris sur les Motifs des Opéras,* H. Albert's *Bluettes des meilleurs Opéras* (Op. 8, no. 15), Beyer's *Repertoire des jeunes pianistes* (Op. 36, no. 52), and Cramer's *Le jeune Pianiste* (Op. 84, no. 22). For a full account, see *Förteckning N:o 2 öfver Musikalier i Abr. Hirschs Musikhandel och Musikaliska Låne-Institut i Stockholm* (Stockholm: Hirsch, 1859), The Music Library of Sweden, Stockholm.

65. Ibid., 89–91. *Das Liebesmahl der Apostel* is composed for male chorus and orchestra. In the arrangement rendered by Elkan and Schildknecht, the piano substitutes for the orchestra.

66. *Förteckning öfver Musikalier i Elkan & Schildknechts Musikhandel och Musik-Lånebibliothek i Stockholm* (Stockholm: Elkan & Schildknecht, 1870), The Music Library of Sweden, Stockholm.

67. Ibid., 42–43, 84.

68. Ibid., 13.

69. Ibid., 26–27.

70. *Katalog öfver Musikalier som äro att tillgå i Abr. Lundquists Musikhandel och Musik-Lånbibliothek i Stockholm* (Stockholm: Lundquist, 1876), The Music Library of Sweden, Stockholm.

71. Ibid., 10–11, 32.

72. *Annals of Opera 1597–1940*, Compiled from the Original Sources by Alfred Loewenberg, with an Introduction by Edward J. Dent (Cambridge: W. Heffer & Sons, 1943), 417.

73. The Bridal Chorus from *Lohengrin* and the Pilgrims' Chorus from *Tannhäuser* were also arranged for cornet solo and duo. See *Carl Blosfeld, Musikalienhandlung, Riga, Alexander-Boulevard No 1, Riga*, Music Catalogs, The Library of the Latvian Academy of Sciences, Dept. of Rarities, Riga. The year is not recorded in Blosfeld's catalog, but it was apparently printed at the very end of the nineteenth century.

74. *Carl Blosfeld, Riga. Billige Bandausgaben*, The Library of the Latvian Academy of Sciences, Dept. of Rarities, Riga. In this case, the year is also missing.

75. Gösta Percy, "Något om Wagner-traditionen i Sverige," in *Operan 200 år: Jubelboken*, ed. Klas Ralf (Stockholm: Prisma, 1973), 95. About Foroni, see Angelo Tajani, *Jacopo Foroni: Från barrikaderna till Kungliga Operan*, trans. Vibeke Emond (Höör: Två kronors förlag, 2002).

76. P. Vretblad, "Arlberg, Georg Efraim Fritz," in *Svenskt biografiskt lexikon* (Stockholm: Albert Bonniers förlag, 1920), 2:185–86. Arlberg also composed songs for solo voice in the style of Wagner, among others, *Två visor om döden*, Op. 2 (1869), in which he makes use of the infinite melody in the song "Der Tod, das ist die kühle Nacht." Cf. *Musiken i Sverige: Den nationella identiteten 1810–1920*, ed. Leif Jonsson and Martin Tegen (Stockholm: Fischer, 1992), 375–76. Cf. Axel Helmer, *Svensk solosång 1850–1890. 1: En genrehistorisk studie* (Stockholm: Svenskt musikhistoriskt arkiv, 1972), 269–74.

77. Hallén was an ardent Wagnerian who also applied the style of his paragon to his composition. The influence of both Wagner and Liszt are already recognizable in his early composition, the symphonic poem *Frithjof och Ingeborg* (1872). Hallén also experimented with mythological-historical opera in his work *Harald der Wiking* (Harald the Viking)—with a libretto by Hans Herring—which was premiered in the German language in Leipzig in 1881 and in Swedish in Stockholm in 1884. Stylistically, the work can be likened to *Die Walküre* and *Tristan*. On this subject, see Martin Tegen, "Tre svenska vikingaoperor," *Svensk tidskrift för musikforskning* 42 (1960): 12–14. See also *Musiken i Sverige*, 405–6, 434.

78. Percy, "Något om Wagner-traditionen i Sverige," 95.

79. Edbergska programsamlingen, The Music Library of Sweden, Stockholm.

80. Maria Collan-Beaurain, *Fredrik Pacius: Lefnadsteckning*. Helsingfors: Söderström & Co., 1921, 196. Collan-Beaurain cites Pacius' diary entry on 22 August 1857.

81. Dahlström and Salmenhaara, *Suomen musiikin historia*, 1:340.

82. Ibid., 1:355–56, 489.

83. Collan-Beaurain, *Fredrik Pacius*, 272. Collan-Beaurain cites Pacius's diary entry on 18 December 1867.

84. Fredrik Pacius's letter to Karl Collan, 26 April 1870, in Collan-Beaurain, *Fredrik Pacius*, 274.

85. Fredrik Pacius, *Die Loreley* (master tape from 1959), The Sound Archive of the Finnish Broadcasting Company, Helsinki. Cf. Dahlström and Salmenhaara, *Suomen musiikin historia*, 1:369.

86. August Meissner was born in Grabow in 1833 and died in Stockholm in 1903. He acted as a conductor and violinist from 1855 in Gothenburg and as of 1860 in Helsinki, assuming the same tasks in 1868 in Stockholm. For further details, see Gustaf Hilleström, *Kungl. Musikaliska Akademien. Matrikel 1771–1971* (Strängnäs: Nordiska Musikförlaget, 1971), 186.

87. *Hufvudstadsbladet* (1 June 1865). The review is signed only with the initials H. P., but they clearly refer to Hermann Paul. Paul was born in Schwedt an der Oder in Prussia in 1827 and died in Helsinki in 1885. He acted as a permanent critic on the staff of *Hufvudstadtsbladet* from 1865 to 1878. He toured widely as a violinist in the Baltic Sea area from 1858 to 1862. On this subject, see Jukka Sarjala, *Musiikkimaun normitus ja yleinen mielipide: Musiikkikritiikki Helsingin sanomalehdistössä 1860–1888*. (Turku: University of Turku, 1994), 263.

88. Ibid., 490–91.

89. Olavi Kasemaa, "Neue Gesellschaft—Neue Musik," in *National Movements in the Baltic Countries during the 19th Century*, ed. Aleksander Loit (Stockholm: University of Stockholm, 1985), 436–37. The Tartu Brass Band was founded in 1820 and the Väägvere Band in 1839.

90. Ibid., 438.

91. *Eesti muusika* (Tallinn: Eesti raamat, 1968), 1:31; Kasemaa, "Neue Gesellschaft—Neue Musik," 438–39.

92. By 1901 the situation had basically changed. According to the estimate of Olavi Kasemaa, there were possibly 64 orchestras during that time in Estonian towns. Of these, 17 were in Tallinn, with an equal number in Tartu. Narva (10), Pärnu (5) and Viljandi (5) were also active in this respect. See especially Kasemaa, "Neue Gesellschaft—Neue Musik," 443. During the 1870s, the largest towns in Estonia were indisputably Tallinn and Tartu, which also had the largest population in musical education. In 1881, the number of inhabitants in Tallinn was 50,342, in Tartu 29,974, in Pärnu 12,966 and in Viljandi 5,325. No tabulated statistical figures indicating the population of Narva have survived from that year. At any rate, the other Estonian towns were communities of fewer than 5,000 people. For further information, see *Statistiline album: Album statistique* (Tallinn: Riigi statistika keskbüroo, 1925), 1:3–5.

93. Kasemaa, "Neue Gesellschaft—Neue Musik," 446.

94. *Eesti muusika*, 1:97–99.

95. "Beschreibung der Festlichkeiten bei den Jubelfeier der Kaiserlichen Universität Dorpat am 12. und 13. December 1852," *St. Petersburger Zeitung* (8/20 January 1853).

96. O. R., "Musikleben in Reval während der Winter-Saison 1859/1860," *Revalsche Zeitung* (5 July 1860).

97. Ibid.

98. "Symphonie-Concert," *Extrablatt zur Revalschen Zeitung* Nr. 96 (22 October 1860). The review is not signed, but in all probability it is the work of Oscar von Riesemann.

99. "Musikalische Abendunterhaltung," *Pernausche Zeitung* (30 January, 31 January 1881).

100. *Pernausche Zeitung* (13 February 1881). The original name of the song was *Suomis Sång* (1854).

101. *Pernausche Zeitung* (8 May 1881).

102. Helmer, 212; Gunnar Jeanson, *August Söderman: En svensk tondiktares liv och verk* (Stockholm: Bonnier, 1926), 22–41; *Musiken i Sverige*, 262.

103. "Großes Orchester-Concert von der Hapsalschen Bade-Capelle," *Pernausche Zeitung* (15 May 1881).

104. "Concerte des Cornett-Quartetts und Quintetts vom Rigaschen Stadt-Theater-Orchester," *Pernausche Zeitung* (30 June 1881).

105. This is reported by *Pernausche Zeitung* (9 June 1881).

106. Livregementets dragoner, Regementsmusikens notarkiv 162b; Livregementets dragoner, Regementsmusikens notarkiv, Vol. 1694, The Military Archives of Sweden, Stockholm.

107. Norrlands artilleriregemente, Musikkåren, Serie D2, Vol. 1, The Military Archives of Sweden, Stockholm.

108. Södra Skånska Regementet, Musikkåren, Serie D1, Vol. 3, The Military Archives of Sweden, Stockholm.

109. Livgrenadjärregementet, Musikkåren, Series DII, Vols. 1 & 2, The Military Archives of Sweden, Stockholm.

110. Jonköpings regemente, Musikkåren, Series D1, Vol. 1, The Military Archives of Sweden, Stockholm.

111. "Pilgrimskör ur Tannhäuser," Livregementets dragoner, Regementsmusikens notarkiv, Vol. 1694, The Military Archives of Sweden, Stockholm. The arrangement was written in a 14-page score, and the transcription required two cornets, a French horn, a trumpet, a tenor horn, a bass horn, and percussion.

112. "Ouverture till Flygande Holländaren," Södra Skånska Regementet, Musikkåren, Serie D1, Vol. 3, The Military Archives of Sweden, Stockholm.

113. Bartlett, 13. Conversely, Wagner could be heard surprisingly early in Norway, when the Villa-Colonna-Capellet, the Christiania Orchestra, and a chorus of one hundred singers performed the march from the opera *Tannhäuser* under the baton of F. Beyer in September 1852. For further details, see Harald Herresthal, "Det borgerlige musikkonsum i Christiania på 1850-talet," in *Nordisk musikkforskerkongress Oslo, 24.–27. juni 1992. Innlegg og referater* (Oslo: Det historisk-filosofiske fakultet, Universitet i Oslo, 1992), 169.

114. Wilhelm Bauck, *Musik och theater. Samlade kritiska uppsatser dels ur journaler och tidskrifter, dels ur konsthistoriska föreläsningar, hållna i K. Musikaliska Akademien* (Stockholm: Norstedt & S, 1868), 65–67. Wilhelm Bauck wrote his review on the concert given by Mr. Richard in Stockholm on 16 March 1861 in the *Nya Dagligt Allehanda*. The review was re-published in Bauck's book *Musik och teater*.

Chapter 3

1. *Annals of Opera 1597–1940*, Compiled from the Original Sources by Alfred Loewenberg, with an Introduction by Edward J. Dent (Cambridge: W. Heffer & Sons, 1943), 431–32.

2. Later, from 1855, Hoffmann acted as the director of the Josefstädter theater in Vienna. In his memoirs Richard Wagner has had difficulties with his reminiscences of Johann Hoffmann and calls him incorrectly Joseph. On this point, see especially Wagner, *Mein Leben*, 799.

3. *Rigasche Stadtblätter* (14 April 1843).

4. *Rigasche Zeitung* (19 January 1843).

5. Epp Lauk et al., "A Retrospective Look at the Development of the Media in the Baltics," in *Toward a Civic Society. The Baltic Media's Long Road to Freedom. Perspectives on History, Ethnicity and Journalism*, edited by Svennik Høyer, Epp Lauk, and Peeter Vihalemm (Tartu: Baltic Association for Media Research, 1993), 52.

6. *Theater-Anzeige: Der fliegende Holländer*, Theaterzettel 1843, Nr. 171, The Library of the Latvian Academy of Sciences, Dept. of Rarities, Riga.

7. *"Abonnement suspendu": Der fliegende Holländer*, Theaterzettel 1843, Nr. 172, The Library of the Latvian Academy of Sciences, Dept. of Rarities, Riga.

8. Ibid. In the advertisement, the role of the Helmsman is mentioned to be performed by Mr. Sammt. The singer's falling ill is mentioned in the review of *Der Zuschauer*, which also indicates that the stand-in for the role was Johann Hoffmann. See also *Der Zuschauer* (25 May/6 June 1843), 400.

9. "Bosco in Riga," *Rigasche Zeitung* (27 March 1843); "Aus Mitau," *Rigasche Zeitung* (18 March 1843); *Rigasche Zeitung* (16 September 1843); *Rigasche Zeitung* (27 November 1843).

10. *Rigasche Zeitung* (17 June and 15 July 1843).

11. "Eingesandt," *Der Zuschauer* (25 May/6 June 1843), 400.

12. Wagner's letter to Robert Schumann, 16 June 1843, in Wagner, *Sämtliche Briefe*, 2:282.

13. Wagner's letter to Minna, 18 June 1843, in ibid., 2:283.

14. Wagner's letter to Franz Löbmann, 9 December 1843, in ibid., 2:343.

15. Wagner's letter to Samuel Lehrs, 7 April 1843, in ibid., 2:234.

16. See ibid., 2:250. Wagner began composing after 19 July.

17. The premiere of *Der fliegende Holländer* in Kassel was on 5 June 1843, only a short time after the Riga performance, which was, according to the Julian calendar, on 22 May (Gregorian calendar, 3 June). See ibid., 2:250.

18. Wagner's letter to Ferdinand Heine, in ibid., 2:314–15. The date is not recorded, but it is possible to ascertain that the letter has been written at the beginning of August 1843. See also *Illustrierte Zeitung* (7 October 1843).

19. Wagner's letter to Franz Löbmann, 9 December 1843, in Wagner, *Sämtliche Briefe*, 2:343.

20. Hans-Joachim Bauer, *Richard Wagner-Lexikon* (Bergisch Gladbach: Lübbe, 1988), 502. See also Wagner's letter to Liszt, 16 June 1852, in Richard Wagner, *Sämtliche Briefe*, 4:392.

21. Wagner's letter to Theodor Uhlig 27 September 1852, in ibid., 5:55.

22. Wagner's letter to Theodor Uhlig, 1 November 1852, in ibid., 5:91.

23. *Rigaer Theater-Almanach für das Jahr 1853* (Riga, 1852).

24. According to the Gregorian calendar, on 18 January 1853. See also the advertisements for the premiere of the work in the *Rigasche Zeitung* on 30 December 1852, 2 January, 3 January, and 9 January 1853.

25. *Tannhäuser*, Theaterzettel 1853, The Library of the Latvian Academy of Sciences, Dept. of Rarities, Riga.

26. The statement made above refers to the Pacius quotation from the year 1857 presented in the previous chapter: "Icke som det nyare spektakelgörandet af Wagner et consortes där ingenting finnes bakom. . . ." Maria Collan-Beaurain, *Fredrik Pacius: Lefnadsteckning* (Helsinki: Söderström & Co., 1921), 272.

27. *Tannhäuser*, Theaterzettel 1853, The Library of the Latvian Academy of Sciences, Dept. of Rarities, Riga.

28. Wagner's letter to Franz Liszt, 19 February 1853, in Wagner, *Sämtliche Briefe*, 5:197. In German: "In Russland (Riga) hat die Aufführung stattfinden dürfen!!"

29. See the table in ibid., 5:473.

30. Wagner's letter to Franz Löbmann, 1 June 1853, in ibid., 5:309.

31. *Rigasche Stadtblätter* (26 February 1853).

32. "Tannhäuser in Riga," Aufzeichnungen von Carl Friedrich Glasenapp, Glasenapp-Nachlaß (Hs 218), National Archive of the Richard Wagner Foundation, Wahnfried House, Bayreuth.

33. *Rigaer Theater- und Tonkünstler Lexikon nebst Geschichte des Rigaer Theaters und der Musikalischen Gesellschaft*, ed. Moritz Rudolph (Riga: R. Kymmel, 1890), 4.

34. *Extrablatt zur Rigaschen Zeitung* (10 January 1853).

35. Ibid.

36. Wagner's letter to Ferdinand Heinelle, in Wagner, *Sämtliche Briefe*, 2:314–15. The letter was apparently written in August 1843.

37. *Extrablatt zur Rigaschen Zeitung* (14 January 1853).

38. Ibid.

39. On the concept of *Gefühlsverständnis*, see Hannu Salmi, *"Die Herrlichkeit des deutschen Namens. . .": Die schriftstellerische und politische Tätigkeit Richard Wagners als Gestalter nationaler Identität während der staatlichen Vereinigung Deutschlands* (Turku: University of Turku, 1993), 141–42.

40. See Jukka Sarjala, *Musiikkimaun normitus ja yleinen mielipide: Musiikkikritiikki Helsingin sanomalehdistössä 1860–1888* (Turku: University of Turku, 1994), 150.

41. Cf. Wagner's own words in a letter to Ludwig II, 10 October 1864, in *König Ludwig II. und Richard Wagner. Briefwechsel*, ed. Otto Strobel (Karlsruhe: Braun, 1936–39), 1:28–29. Wagner equated himself with Columbus, who, with the economic assistance of Queen Isabella, had discovered America. Wagner needed similar support from his own patron Ludwig!

42. *Extrablatt zur Rigaschen Zeitung* (10 January 1853); *Extrablatt zur Rigaschen Zeitung* (14 January 1853).

43. *Extrablatt zur Rigaschen Zeitung* (17 January 1853).

44. Joachim Raff, *Die Wagnerfrage. Erster Theil: Wagner's letzte künstlerische Kundgebung im "Lohengrin"* (Braunschweig: Vielveg, 1854), 4.

45. Ibid., 4–5.

46. Wagner's letter to Franz Brendel, 2 February 1853, in Wagner, *Sämtliche Briefe*, 5:174–75.

47. *Rigasche Stadtblätter* (7 January 1855).

48. The full title of the book is Friedrich Hinrich: *Richard Wagner und die neuere Musik: Eine kritische Skizze aus der musikalischen Gegenwart* (Halle: Schrödel und Simon, 1854).

49. *Rigasche Stadtblätter* (20 January 1855).

50. Wagner, *Sämtliche Briefe*, 5:472–73. See also Bauer, *Richard Wagner-Lexikon*, 255. *Lohengrin* was also performed in the East-Prussian Stettin (now Szczecin in

Poland) in November 1854, but I have not succeeded in dating the performance exactly.

51. *Rigasche Stadtblätter* (26 February, 26 March 1853).

52. *Rigasche Stadtblätter* (30 July 1853).

53. Wagner's letter to Franz Löbmann, 1 June 1853, in Wagner, *Sämtliche Briefe*, 5:309–10.

54. Wagner's letter to Breitkopf & Härtel, 15 June 1854, Wagner, *Sämtliche Briefe*, 6:152.

55. *Lohengrin*, Theaterzettel 1855, The Library of the Latvian Academy of Sciences, Dept. of Rarities, Riga.

56. "Die Aufführung von R. Wagner's Lohengrin," *Extrablatt zur Rigaschen Zeitung* (29 January 1855). In German: "Endlich haben wir am 24. Januar R. Wagner's "Lohengrin" auf Riga's Bühne zum ersten Male gehört."

57. "Die Aufführung von R. Wagner's Lohengrin," *Extrablatt zur Rigaschen Zeitung* (29 January 1855). In German: "fast den ganzen Weg durch labyrinthische musikalische Felsenriffe in dunklester Nacht, nur selten von eigenen Consonanzen-Blitzen erleuchtet."

58. Ibid.

59. Ibid.

60. See closer Kurt Overhoff, *Die Musikdramen Richard Wagners: Eine thematisch-musikalische Interpretation*, 2nd ed. (Salzburg: A. Pustet, 1984), 391, 395.

61. *Rigaer Theater-Almanach für das Jahr 1856*, 6. At that time, the orchestra consisted of six violins, two violas, two cellos, two double basses, two flutes, two oboes, two clarinets, two bassoons, four French horns, a trombone, two trumpets, a harp, and timpani.

62. "Die Aufführung von R. Wagner's Lohengrin," *Extrablatt zur Rigaschen Zeitung* (29 January 1855).

63. Ibid.

64. *Rigasche Stadtblätter* (27 January 1855).

65. *Lohengrin*, libretto, in Richard Wagner, *Dichtungen und Schriften*, ed. Dieter Borchmeyer (Frankfurt am Main: Insel Verlag, 1983), 2:192.

66. Ibid., 2:196.

67. *Rigaer Theater- und Tonkünstler Lexikon*, 197–98.

68. *Rigasche Zeitung* (18 February 1855).

69. "Tannhäuser in Riga," Aufzeichnungen von Carl Friedrich Glasenapp, Glasenapp-Nachlaß (Hs 218), National Archive of the Richard Wagner Foundation, Wahnfried House, Bayreuth.

70. "Richard Wagner's Plan zu einer komischen Oper," *Extrablatt zur Rigaschen Zeitung* (19 February 1855).

71. For more details, see Salmi, *"Die Herrlichkeit des deutschen Namens. . . ,"* 107, 212–13.

72. Ibid., 213.

73. *Rigasche Stadtblätter* (12 January 1856).

74. *Rigasche Zeitung* (20 February 1857).

75. Wagner's letter to Luise Meyer, 26 March 1857, in Wagner, *Sämtliche Briefe*, 8:293.

76. *Rigasche Zeitung* (2 July 1855).

77. Bauer, *Richard Wagner-Lexikon*, 502.

78. *Rigasche Stadtblätter* (3 February 1866).

79. Elmar Arro, *Geschichte der estnischen Musik* (Tartu: Akadeemiline kooperatiiv, 1933), 1:52–53.

80. *Reval/Tallinn: Porträt einer Ostseestadt*, ed. Erik Thomson (Cologne-Rodenkirchen: Liebig Druck & Verlag, 1979), 40–43.

81. *Revaler Theater-Almanach mit dem Repertoir der vom 1852 bis März 1853 gegebenen Vorstellungen für Freunde der Schauspielkunst*, ed. Alexander Borosska (Tallinn, 1853), 7–21.

82. Kristel Pappel, "Die ersten Aufführungen von Wagners Opern am Revaler Theater," in *Das deutschsprachige Theater im baltischen Raum, 1630–1918*, ed. Laurence P. A. Kitching, 139–44 (Frankfurt am Main: Peter Lang, 1997).

83. Wagner's letter to Wilhelm Fischer, 11 July 1853, in Wagner, *Sämtliche Briefe*, 5:354. Wagner mentions Tallinn in his letter to Minna on 28 July 1853, in ibid., 5:382.

84. Wagner's letter to Franz Liszt, 16 November 1853, in ibid., 5:470. This letter reveals that Wagner asked more money for *Lohengrin* than for *Tannhäuser*. He says to Liszt that he will have at least 25 louis d'or. See ibid., 5: 468.

85. Pappel, "Die ersten Aufführungen von Wagners Opern am Revaler Theater."

86. In the fifth volume of Wagner's *Sämtliche Briefe* there is a table concerning the performances of Wagner's operas during 1852–54, in which the premiere in Tallinn is assigned to the year 1854. This is because, according to the Gregorian calendar, the premiere was on 2 January 1854. See further Wagner, *Sämtliche Briefe*, 5:44.

87. *Revaler Theater-Almanach 1853*, 3–6; *Rigaer Theater-Almanach 1852*, 3–6.

88. Pappel, "Die ersten Aufführungen von Wagners Opern am Revaler Theater." The date of the Darmstadt premiere is based on the information given in the fifth volume of *Sämtliche Briefe*. See Wagner, *Sämtliche Briefe*, 5:472. The Darmstadt premiere was conducted by Wagner's friend Louis Schindelmeisser as his first assignment as the *Kapellmeister* of the local theater. The rehearsals of *Tannhäuser* probably began in mid-August 1853. See Wagner's letter to Louis Schindelmeisser, 13 August 1853, in ibid., 5:395.

89. Pappel, "Die ersten Aufführungen von Wagners Opern am Revaler Theater."

90. Lauk et al., "A Retrospective Look," 53, 73. There might, however, have been comments on opera performances in the newspapers of other towns. I have gone through also *Dörptsche Zeitung* from the years 1853–54, but the paper does not usually mention anything about the events in Tallinn. This is because, at that time, Tartu belonged to Livonia, not Estonia. *Dörptsche Zeitung* commented much more on the events of Riga than Tallinn.

91. O. R., "Richard Wagner und die Zukunftsmusik," *Extrablatt zur Revalschen Zeitung* (14 November 1860).

92. *Deutschbaltisches biographisches Lexikon*, 633–34.

93. Pappel, "Die ersten Aufführungen von Wagners Opern am Revaler Theater."

94. *Theatralisches Vergißmeinnicht, oder: Letztes Flüstern des Souffleurs*, ed. Christian Müller (Tallinn, 1861), 4–7.

95. *Extrablatt zur Revalschen Zeitung* (19 November 1860); *Theatralisches Vergißmeinnicht*, 3. Pappel writes the name incorrectly as Bratsch. Cf. Pappel, "Die ersten Aufführungen von Wagners Opern am Revaler Theater." Perhaps this was the same Bartsch who in 1857 had worked in Düsseldorf and planned to organize a performance of *Lohengrin*. See further Wagner's letter to Jakob Bartsch, 17 March 1857, in Wagner, *Sämtliche Briefe*, 8:289–90.

96. *Extrablatt zur Revalschen Zeitung* (19 November 1860).

97. Ibid.

98. *Theatralisches Vergißmeinnicht;* Pappel, "Die ersten Aufführungen von Wagners Opern am Revaler Theater."

99. *Extrablatt zur Revalschen Zeitung* (19 November 1860).

100. Ibid.

101. *Annals of Opera,* 450–51.

102. *Reval/Tallinn,* 43.

103. *Annals of Opera,* 418–19.

104. "Musikleben in Reval während der Winter-Saison 1859/1860," *Revalsche Zeitung* (5 July 1860).

105. O. R., "Richard Wagner und die Zukunftsmusik," *Extrablatt zur Revalschen Zeitung* (14 November 1860).

106. Ibid.

107. Ibid.,"

108. On Feuerbach's influence see Bryan Magee, *The Tristan Chord: Wagner and Philosophy* (New York: Henry Holt and Company, 2000), 51.

109. Voltaire: *Dictionnaire philosophique* (A Gotha: C. G. Ettinger, 1786), 2:445–48. Voltaire employs the word *événemen,* not *événement.*

110. O. R., "Richard Wagner und die Zukunftsmusik," *Extrablatt zur Revalschen Zeitung* (14 November 1860).

111. Cf. Wagner, *Opera and Drama,* Richard Wagner's Prose Works. Translated by William Ashton Ellis. Vol. 2, 1–376. London: Kegan Paul, Trench, Trubner & Co., 1893; (reprint, Lincoln: University of Nebraska Press, 1995), 17.

112. *Extrablatt zur Revalschen Zeitung* (19 November 1860).

113. Carl Dahlhaus, "Wagners Stellung in der Musikgeschichte," in *Richard-Wagner-Handbuch,* ed. Ulrich Müller and Peter Wapnewski (Stuttgart: Kröner, 1986), 61–62.

114. Raff, *Die Wagnerfrage,* 4–5.

115. Collan-Beaurain, *Fredrik Pacius,* 196. Collan-Beaurain quotes Pacius's diary entry on 22 August 1857.

116. Sarjala, *Musiikkimaun normitus ja yleinen mielipide,* 200.

117. Gregor-Dellin, *Richard Wagner,* 460, 873–74.

118. This has been remarked by Sarjala. See Sarjala, *Musiikkimaun normitus ja yleinen mielipide,* 201. See also Friedrich Wieck, *Clavier und Gesang: Didaktisches und Polemisches* (Leipzig: F. Whistling, 1853).

119. Gregor-Dellin, *Richard Wagner,* 874.

120. Jürgen Kühnel, "Wagners Schriften," in *Richard-Wagner-Handbuch,* ed. Ulrich Müller and Peter Wapnewski (Stuttgart: Kröner, 1986), 526. See also Richard Wagner, *Ausgewählte Schriften* (Leipzig: Verlag Philipp Reclam, 1982), 179–230. Wagner's writing has been dated as "Paris, im September 1860."

121. Wagner, *Ausgewählte Schriften,* 179–80.

122. Ibid., 193.

123. Ibid., 208.

124. Dahlström and Salmenhaara, *Suomen musiikin historia,* 1:344–45. See also Wäinö Sola, *Wäinö Sola kertoo* (Porvoo: WSOY, 1951), 72–73; Anders Ramsay, *Muistoja lapsen ja hopeahapsen,* trans. Antti Nuuttila (Porvoo, WSOY, 1987), 1:186.

125. Eino E. Suolahti, *Helsingin neljä vuosisataa* (Helsinki: Otava, 1972), 175. See also Ramsay, *Muistoja lapsen ja hopeahapsen*, 191–92.

126. Dahlström and Salmenhaara, *Suomen musiikin historia*, 1:345; Sven Hirn, *Alati kierueella: Teatterimme varhaisvaiheet vuoteen 1870* (Helsinki: Helsinki University Press, 1998), 149.

127. Hirn, *Alati kiertueella*, 149–50.

128. Hannu-Ilari Lampila, *Suomalainen ooppera* (Porvoo: WSOY, 1997), 33–34.

129. Cit. Collan-Beaurain, *Fredrik Pacius*, 151.

130. See Suolahti, *Helsingin neljä vuosisataa*, 176.

131. Topelius's letter to Pacius, 7 June 1851, in Zacharias Topelius, *Konstnärs-brev: Z. Topelius's brevväxling med författare, konstnärer, skådespelare och musiker*, ed. Paul Nyberg (Helsinki: The Society of Swedish Literature in Finland, 1956), 1:197.

132. This is how the scene was interpreted also in Sweden where Pacius's opera had been performed in autumn 1856 and in spring 1857. Pacius wrote to Topelius in March 1857: "Ein wahrer Scandal ist der Judenscene. Anstatt die zu mildern, ist sie hier auf eine widrige Weise hervorstehend. Sie wird durch ein paar ächt polnische Judenphysionomien dargestellt, mit langen schwarzen Caftans, und fällt, anstatt ins Komische, ins Tragische. Der grösste Theil der Musik ist gestrichen, und dagegen von Jolin ein platter, langweiliger Dialog hinzugesetzt, der kein Ende nimmt. Ich habe mich lebhaft dagegen aufgelehnt, allein vergebens, und ich begreife nicht die Direction, der grösste Theil des Publikums besteht aus Juden, die über diese fatale Scene sehr entrüstet sind." Pacius's letter to Topelius, 26 March 1857, in ibid., 204.

133. Suolahti, *Helsingin neljä vuosisataa*, 176.

134. Lampila, *Suomalainen ooppera*, 34.

135. *Rigasche Stadtblätter* (11 April 1857).

136. *Extrablatt zum Rigaschen Zeitung* (22 May 1857).

137. Heikki Waris, "Helsinkiläisyhteiskunta," in *Helsingin kaupungin historia* (Helsinki: Helsingin kaupunki, 1950), vol. 3, part 2, p. 11.

138. *Helsingfors Tidningar* (1 July 1857). On the repertoire, see also ibid., (11 July 1857, 12 August 1857, 19 August 1857).

139. *Rigasche Stadtblätter* (23 May 1857); *Finlands Allmänna Tidning* (9 July 1857).

140. *Helsingfors Tidningar* (1 July 1857).

141. *Rigaer Theater-Almanach für das Jahr 1856*, 6.

142. *Suometar* (31 July 1857).

143. *Helsingfors Tidningar* (12 August 1857).

144. Ibid.

145. Sarjala, *Musiikkimaun normitus ja yleinen mielipide*, 257.

146. *Finlands Allmänna Tidning* (12 August 1857).

147. See for example *Åbo Underrättelser* (21 August 1857).

148. *Helsingfors Tidningar* (19 August 1857).

149. *Finlands Allmänna Tidning* (12 August 1857).

150. *Helsingfors Tidningar* (26 August 1857).

151. *Rigasche Stadtblätter* (25 July 1857).

152. The author recalls the verses of Scribe incorrectly. In Meyerbeer's opera, the chorus scene of the first act begins thus: "A la Finlande buvons, buvons, buvons!

A notre prince trinquons!" "Söder om Östersjön," *Helsingfors Tidningar* (3 October 1857).

153. "Den moderna operan," *Svenska tidningen* (27 July 1857).

154. Greve was born in Holstein, Germany. In the beginning, his talents seemed to lead to a career as a violinist. In 1842, the director of the Turku orchestra and the music school F. W. Siber invited the 22-year-old Greve to Turku as a violinist in his orchestra, as his assistant conductor, and as a teacher at the music school. Finally, Greve worked as the conductor of the orchestra of the Turku Music Society, in which position he remained until 1846. In summer 1845 he studied in Leipzig under the guidance of Ferdinand David. In 1846–47, he continued his studies under the guidance of both David and Felix Mendelssohn, the founder of the Leipzig Conservatory. After his studies, Greve returned to Turku and continued his activities as a conductor and composer. Further details are found in Dahlström and Salmenhaara, *Suomen musiikin historia,* 1:421–24.

155. See Topelius's letter to Conrad Greve, 12 May 1850, in Topelius, *Konstnärsbrev,* 278–80.

156. Dahlström and Salmenhaara, *Suomen musiikin historia,* 1:345–46.

157. Topelius's letter to J. A. Josephson, 4 December 1853, in Topelius, *Konstnärsbrev,* 1:319.

158. Josephson's letter to Topelius, 8 April 1854, in ibid., 1:324–25.

159. Josephson's letter to Topelius, 7 January 1857, in ibid., 1:329–30.

160. Topelius's letter to Josephson, 5 April 1857, Zacharias Topelius's collection (Coll. 244), Helsinki University Library, manuscript collection. See also Topelius, *Konstnärsbrev,* 1:332.

161. *St. Petersburger Zeitung* (15/27 January 1853).

162. Topelius's letter to Josephson, 5 April 1857, Zacharias Topelius's collection (Coll. 244), Helsinki University Library, manuscript collection. See also Topelius, *Konstnärsbrev,* 1:332–34.

163. Pacius's letter to Topelius, 26 March 1857, in Topelius, *Konstnärsbrev,* 1:202–3. See also Dahlström and Salmenhaara, *Suomen musiikin historia,* 1:350–51.

164. Pacius's letter to Topelius, 26 March 1857, in Topelius, *Konstnärsbrev,* 1:202–3.

165. Fredrik Cygnaeus, *Samlade arbeten III. Literatur-historiska och blandade arbeten* (Helsinki: G. W. Edlund, 1883), 148.

166. Timo Tiusanen, *Teatterimme hahmottuu: Näyttämötaiteemme kehitystie kansanrunoudesta itsenäisyyden ajan alkuun* (Helsinki: Kirjayhtymä, 1969), 103–8.

167. Karl Flodin and Otto Ehrström, *Richard Faltin och hans samtid* (Helsinki: H. Schildt, 1934), 215.

168. Salmi, *Richard Wagner Suomessa,* 147–48.

Chapter 4

1. For a full account, see the catalog of works, *Richard-Wagner-Handbuch,* ed. Ulrich Müller and Peter Wapnewski (Stuttgart: Kröner, 1986), 831–32.

2. *Revue européenne* (1 April 1861).

3. Wegelius, *Hufvuddragen af den västenländska musikens historia,* 3:582.

4. The farce was composed by Karl Binder. See Hans-Joachim Bauer, *Richard Wagner-Lexikon* (Bergisch-Gladbach, 1988), 502. For more information with regard to the success of *Tannhäuser*, see Wagner's own description of the matter his letter to Franz Liszt of 16 November 1853 in Wagner, *Sämtliche Briefe*, 5:470–71.

5. Wagner, *Mein Leben*, 725.

6. Niitemaa and Hovi, *Baltian historia*, 310–13.

7. Ibid., 311.

8. Wagner, *My Life*, 854; Wagner, *Mein Leben*, 727–28.

9. Wagner, *Mein Leben*, 728.

10. The documents concerning Richard Wagner, Russian State Archive, Moscow (Gosudarstvennyi Arhiv RF, GARF), F. 109, Op. 3, D. 2266, L. 1–7. The surviving documents also include an advertisement of a concert arranged in St. Petersburg on 19 February 1863. The archive material of the secret police has been treated by Evgenii Braudo in his writing *Vagner v Rossii. Novye materialy k ego biografi* (Petrograd, 1923). The author also published his finds in Germany in the form of a brief article: see Eugen Braudo, "Richard Wagner unter russischer polizeilicher Aufsicht. Aus den Akten der russischen Geheimpolizei," *Die Musik* 10 (1923/24).

11. The entry in the memorandum of the Russian Secret Police concerning Richard Wagner on 11 February 1863, F. 109, Op. 3, D. 2266, L. 1–2, Russian State Archive, Moscow.

12. The recording concerning Richard Wagner in the memorandum of the Russian Secret Police, 12 February 1863, F. 109, Op. 3, D. 2266, L. 3, Russian State Archive, Moscow.

13. The recording concerning Richard Wagner in the memorandum of the Russian Secret Police, 15 February 1863, F. 109, Op. 3, D. 2266, L. 4, Russian State Archive, Moscow.

14. The recording concerning Richard Wagner in the memorandum of the Russian Secret Police, 20 February 1863, F. 109, Op. 3, D. 2266, L. 5, Russian State Archive, Moscow.

15. The recording concerning Richard Wagner in the memorandum of the Russian Secret Police, 15 April 1863, F. 109, Op. 3, D. 2266, L. 6, Russian State Archive, Moscow.

16. Rosamund A. Bartlett, *Wagner and Russia* (Cambridge: Cambridge University Press, 1995), 299. Cf. the concert poster in Russian and French, 19 February 1863, F. 109, Op. 3, D. 2266, L. 7, Russian State Archive, Moscow. Bartlett has, in the appendices of her treatise, scrutinized the programs of all the concerts given by Wagner. According to Bartlett, the program of the concert held on 19 February included the *Lohengrin* Overture and Senta's Ballad from *Der fliegende Holländer*. There is, however, no mention of these numbers in the printed concert poster; instead, it mentions The Pilgrims' Chorus from *Tannhäuser*. The poster was printed a week before the concert, on 12 February, i.e., on the day of Wagner's arrival in St. Petersburg. It is therefore probable that the program indicated by the poster was agreed upon through correspondence in advance but was changed after Wagner's arrival.

17. Bartlett, *Wagner and Russia*, 299–301. *Die Walküre* was premiered in Munich only in 1870, and *Siegfried* in Bayreuth in 1876.

18. Ibid., 299–301. *Tristan und Isolde* was premiered in Munich in 1865 and *Die Meistersinger von Nürnberg* also in Munich in 1868.

19. Ibid., 11.

20. William Weber, "Wagner, Wagnerism, and Musical Idealism," in *Wagnerism in European Culture and Politics*, ed. David C. Large and William Weber, in collaboration with Anne Dzamba Sessa (Ithaca, NY: Cornell University Press, 1984), 40.

21. Bartlett, *Wagner and Russia*, 13.

22. Ibid., 15–16; Ludmila Poljakowa, "Wagner und Russland," in *Richard Wagner—Leben, Werk und Interpretation: Internationales Kolloquium* (Leipzig: Karl-Marx-Universität, 1983), 307; Sergej Martynow, "Richard Wagner in Russland. Zum 100. Todestag des Musikdramatikers,"*Sowjetunion Heute* 2 (1983): 60.

23. Martynow, "Richard Wagner in Russland," 60.

24. Cit. Marina M. Godlewskaja, "Richard Wagner in St. Petersburg," in *Wagner in St. Petersburg* (Bayreuth: Bayerische Vereinsbank, 1993), 13.

25. Martynow, "Richard Wagner in Russland," 60–61.

26. Wagner, *My Life*, 711–12; Wagner, *Mein Leben*, 604.

27. Bartlett, "Wagner and Russia," 15.

28. Ibid., 16.

29. Ibid., 17.

30. Fremdenlisten 1876, A 2500 I, National Archive of the Richard Wagner Foundation, Wahnfried House, Bayreuth. See also *Bayreuth: The Early Years: An Account of the Early Decades of the Wagner Festival As Seen by the Celebrated Visitors & Participants*, Comp., ed., and with an introduction by Robert Hartford (London: Gollancz, 1980), 52.

31. For a full account of the criticism of the Russian press, see, in particular, Bartlett, "Wagner and Russia," 29–35.

32. Ibid., 34.

33. "Das erste Wagner-Concert," *St. Petersburger Zeitung* (21 February/5 March 1863).

34. Ibid.

35. *St. Petersburger Zeitung* (12/24 March 1863).

36. Wagner, *My Life*, 858; Wagner, *Mein Leben*, 731.

37. For more detail, see Bartlett, "Wagner and Russia," 28–29.

38. *Åbo Underrättelser* (14 August 1869). Cf. *Borgå Bladet* (3 December 1863). The original in French: "Je pars pour l'Allemagne. Adieu, charmant pays! Adieu Russes bien aimés, noble et intelligent nation! Vous seules avez su apprécier ma musique divine; vous seuls avez applaudi mes créations sublimes, pendant que Paris, ce centre de l'ignorance les sifflait! . . . Pour vous recompenser, chers Sarmathes mélomanes, je jure devant ce torrent, de composer un opéra, dont les héros principal sera l'Imatra; les autres rôles seront remplis par les rochers, les sapins, les poissons, etc. . . . Peut-être trouverai-je utile de mettre aussi en scène un homme— mais ce point n'est pas encore décidé. Richard Wagner."

39. For more details, see the *Åbo Underrättelser* (14 August 1869). Cf. Sven Hirn, *Imatra som natursevärdhet till och med 1870: En reselitterär undersökning med lokalhistorisk begränsning* (Helsinki: Finnish Academy of Science and Letters, 1958), 161.

40. Hirn, *Imatra som natursevärdhet*, 161–62. Apparently, the reporter of *Åbo Underrättelser*, who published the news item of the inscription on the wall of the pavilion at the edge of the Imatra rapids, had read the Swedish newspaper discovered by Hirn. *Åbo Underrättelser* begins its own piece of news by stating: "Apropos

musik, så läste vi nyligen en notis att Richard Wagner komponerat en opera vid namn 'Imatra.' " For further details, see *Åbo Underrättelser* (14 August 1869).

41. Hirn, *Imatra som natursevärdhet,* 282. See also Salmi, *Richard Wagner Suomessa,* 143–68.

42. For this discovery I am indebted particularly to musicologist Matti Huttunen, who found the envelope in question when skimming A. B. Marx's work. Faltin's library is now retained in the collections of the Helsinki University Library.

43. *Åbo Underrättselser* (14 August 1869).

44. Cf. Wegelius, *Länsimaisen musiikin historia pääpiirteissään kristinuskon alkuajoista meidän päiviimme,* trans. Axel Törnudd (Helsinki: Holm, 1904).

45. Cf. Bruno Nurmi, *Richard Wagner* (Porvoo: WSOY, 1923). See also Hannu Salmi, " 'Richard Wagner, suuri sävelseppo ja runoilija. . .' Bruno Nurmen Wagner-elämäkerta (1923)," *Synteesi* 1–2 (1991): 92–100.

46. Tauno Silvonen, "Onko Richard Wagner käynyt Suomessa," *Musiikkitieto* 9–10 (1936): 150–51.

47. Hirn, *Imatra som natursevärhet,* 161–62.

48. Seppo Heikinheimo, "Kävikö Wagner Imatralla?" *Helsingin Sanomat* (9 December, 1984).

49. Petri Sariola, "Kävikö Richard Wagner Suomessa?" *Kaleva* (13 December 1995).

50. Cosima Wagner's diary entry on 11 July 1869, in Cosima Wagner, *Die Tagebücher,* 2 vols., ed. and annotated Martin Gregor-Dellin und Dietrich Mack (Munich: Piper, 1976–77), 1:126.

51. Hirn, *Imatra som natursevärhet,* 161.

52. See, e.g., Wagner, *Mein Leben,* 730.

53. Richard Wagner, *Der Ring des Nibelungen: Ein Bühnenfestspiel für drei Tage und einen Vorabend* (Leipzig: Verlagsbuchhandlung von J. J. Weber, 1863).

54. For more information, see *Richard-Wagner-Handbuch,* ed. Ulrich Müller and Peter Wapnewski (Stuttgart: Kröner, 1986), 832.

55. *Der Große Brockhaus: Handbuch des Wissens in zwanzig Bänden.* 15th ed. (Leipzig: Brockhaus, 1933), 16:454.

56. W. J. Rose, "Social Life before the Partitions," in *The Cambridge History of Poland.* Vol. 2: *From Augustus II to Pilsudski (1697–1935).* Edited by W. F. Reddaway, J. H. Penson, O. Halecki, and R. Dyboski (Cambridge: Cambridge University Press, 1951), 80–87.

57. See, e.g. *König Ludwig II. und Richard Wagner: Briefwechsel.* 5 vols., ed. Otto Strobel (Karlsruhe: Braun, 1936), 4:19.

Chapter 5

1. For further details, see Helmer, *Svensk solosång 1850–1890,* 212.

2. August Söderman's letter to Fritz Arlberg, 15 February 1857, cited in Gunnar Jeanson, *August Söderman: En svensk tondiktares liv och verk* (Stockholm: Bonnier, 1926), 28–29.

3. Jeanson, *August Söderman,* 27–29.

4. Söderman's diary recording in 1857, cited in ibid., 29. The original notebook is found in the library of the Swedish Royal Academy of Music.

5. *Extrablatt zur Rigaschen Zeitung* (14 January 1853).

6. Söderman's diary recording 1857, cited in Jeanson, *August Söderman*, 29.

7. Helmer, *Svensk solosång 1850–1890*, 212.

8. Taneli Kuusisto, *Musiikkimme eilispäivää* (Porvoo: WSOY, 1965), 177. Kuusisto's work includes two interviews with Armas Järnefelt; the earlier interview is from 1933 (pp. 177–80), and the later one from 24 April 1943 (pp. 166–77).

9. Ibid., 169–70.

10. Helmer, *Svensk solosång 1850–1890*, 212.

11. *Musiken i Sverige: Den nationella identiteten 1810–1920*, ed. Leif Jonsson and Martin Tegen (Stockholm: Fischer, 1992), 262.

12. Göran Gademan, *Realismen på operan: Regi, spelstil och iscensättningsprinciper på Kungliga Teatern 1860–82* (Ph.D. diss., University of Stockholm; Stockholm: Stift. för utgivning av teatervetenskapliga studier, 1996), 53.

13. Marina M. Godlewskaja, "Richard Wagner in St. Petersburg," in *Wagner in St. Petersburg*, ed. Bärbel Hamacher (Bayreuth: Bayerische Vereinsbank, 1993), 17–18; Rosamund A. Bartlett, "Wagner and Russia: A Study of the Influence of the Music and Ideas of Richard Wagner on the Artistic and Cultural Life of Russia and the Soviet Union 1841–1941." (Ph.D. thesis, St. Anthony's College [Oxford], 1990), 311.

14. Gademan, *Realismen på operan*, 52–54.

15. Ibid., 44–45.

16. Ibid., 340.

17. Gösta Percy, "Något om Wagner-traditionen i Sverige," in *Operan 200 år: Jubelboken*, ed. Klas Ralf (Stockholm: Prisma, 1973), 99.

18. Gademan, *Realismen på operan*, 220; Percy, "Något om Wagner-traditionen i Sverige," 99.

19. *Aftonbladet* (4 March 1865).

20. *Neueste Nachrichten* (12 February 1865); *Allgemeine Zeitung* (14 February 1865). See also Hannu Salmi, *"Die Herrlichkeit des deutschen Namens . . .": Die schriftstellerische und politische Tätigkeit Richard Wagners als Gestalter nationaler Identität während der staatlichen Vereinigung Deutschlands* (Turku: University of Turku, 1993), 175–76.

21. *Allgemeine Zeitung* (15 February 1865).

22. Wagner had commissioned a portrait of himself from his friend Friedrich Pecht. The Cabinet Secretary Pfistermeister told Ludwig that Wagner intended to make a request for the payment of 1,000 florins for this work of art. On presenting the King with the portrait, Wagner had broken the etiquette of the Court by addressing Ludwig with the words "mein Junge." When this reached Ludwig's ears, he declined audience.

23. *Allgemeine Zeitung* (19 February 1865). The anonymous writer was poet Oskar von Redwitz. On this point, see Salmi, *"Die Herrlichkeit des deutschen Namens . . ."* 176.

24. *Aftonbladet* (9 May 1865).

25. *Post- och inrikes tidningar* (7 June 1865); *Aftonbladet* (7 June 1865); Gademan, *Realismen på operan*, 219–20. The libretto was also published. Cf. Richard Wagner, *Rienzi, den siste folktribunen. Tragisk opera i fem akter af Richard Wagner.* Stockholm,1865.

26. On these points, see the premiere poster of *Rienzi*, The Archives of the Royal Theaters, Stockholm.

27. *Dagens Nyheter* (7 June 1865).

28. *Post- och inrikes tidningar* (9 June 1865).

29. See e.g. *Aftonbladet* (9 June 1865).

30. *Dagens Nyheter* (9 June 1865).

31. *Aftonbladet* (9 June 1865).

32. *Dagens Nyheter* (9 June 1865).

33. *Dagens Nyheter* (9 June 1865).

34. C. V. A. Stranberg had functioned as the critic of *Stockholms Dagblad* from 1852 to 1864. He switched to *Post- och inrikes tidningar* in 1865. In regard to all these points in general, see Gademan, *Realismen på operan*, 63.

35. *Post- och inrikes tidningar* (15 June 1865).

36. C. F. Hennerberg, "Carl Wilhelm Bauck," in *Svenskt biografiskt lexikon*. (Stockholm, 1920), 2:772–73.

37. Wilhelm Bauck, *Musik och theater* (Stockholm: Norstedt & S, 1868), 65–68.

38. Ibid., 58–59.

39. Ibid., 62.

40. Ibid., 59.

41. Ibid., 59–60.

42. Ibid., 60. Bauck did not know that Wagner had, previous to *Rienzi*, already composed two operas: *Die Feen* and *Das Liebesverbot*.

43. Ibid., 60.

44. Ibid., 62.

45. Ibid., 63.

46. Joseph Tichatschek was interested in visiting Sweden again. During spring and summer 1866, he negotiated with both the stage director, Ludvig Josephson, and with the director of the theater, Erik af Edholm. In March 1866, Tichatschek proposed that the theater would take Halévy's *La Juive* instead of *Rienzi*. See Joseph Tichatschek's letter to L. O. Josephson, 12 March 1866, L. O. Josephson Collection (Ep.J. 5), The Royal Library of Sweden, Stockholm. However, in July 1866, Tichatschek proposed to Edholm that the Royal Opera House would arrange one more performance of *Rienzi*. See Tichatschek's letter to Erik af Edholm, 20 July 1866, Erik af Edholm Collection, The Stockholm City Archive, Stockholm. At that time, Tichatschek had some personal problems, but they were no obstacles to his willingness to perform in Stockholm. His son had participated in the Austro-Prussian War in 1866, and had already been pronounced dead, but by a miracle he was found alive in a prisoner-of-war camp. See Tichatschek's letter to Erik af Edholm, 22 July 1866, Erik af Edholm Collection, The Stockholm City Archive, Stockholm.

Chapter 6

1. Wagner's letter to Franz Schott, 20 November 1861, in Richard Wagner, *Sämtliche Briefe*, 13:292–99.

2. *Rigasche Stadtblätter* (6 April 1861).

3. Ilona Breģe, "Rīgas Pilsētas teātris 1782–1863: Das Rigaer Stadt-Theater 1782–1863." In *No Fītinghofa teātra līdz Vāgnerzālei: Vom Vietinghoff-Theater bis zum Wagner-Saal* (Riga: Das Deutsche Kulturinstitut Lettlands, 1992), [24].

4. "Tannhäuser in Riga," Aufzeichnungen von Carl Friedrich Glasenapp, Glasenapp-Nachlaß (Hs 218), National Archive of the Richard Wagner Foundation, Wahnfried House, Bayreuth.

5. "Der fliegende Holländer. Oper von Richard Wagner," *Rigasche Stadtblätter* (19 November 1864).

6. "Richard Wagner in München," *Rigasche Stadtblätter* (21 May 1864).

7. Hannu Salmi, *"Die Herrlichkeit des deutschen Namens . . .": Die schriftstellerische und politische Tätigkeit Richard Wagners als Gestalter nationaler Identität während der staatlichen Vereinigung Deutschlands* (Turku: University of Turku, 1993), 164–207.

8. Ibid., 207–8.

9. Richard Wagner, *Deutsche Kunst und deutsche Politik* (Leipzig, 1868), 53–54.

10. Salmi, *"Die Herrlichkeit des deutschen Namens . . .,"* 217–18.

11. Vita Lindenberg, "Richard Wagners Wirken in Riga," in *Opern und Musikdramen Verdis und Wagners in Dresden: 4. Wissenschaftlicher Konferenz zum Thema 'Dresdner Operntraditionen,'* ed. Günther Stephan et al., (Dresden: Hochschule für Musik Carl Maria von Weber, 1988), 705.

12. *Rigasche Stadtblätter* (31 December 1869).

13. On the early reception of *Die Meistersinger,* see Thomas S. Grey, "Wagner's *Die Meistersinger* as National Opera (1868–1945)," in *Music and German National Identity,* ed. Celia Applegate and Pamela Potter (Chicago: University of Chicago Press, 2002).

14. Diether Raff, *A History of Germany: From Medieval Empire to the Present,* trans. Bruce Little (Oxford: Berg, 1988), 134–35; Walter Bussmann, "Vom H. Römischen Reich deutscher Nation zur Gründung des Deutschen Reiches," in *Handbuch der europäischen Geschichte,* ed. Theodor Schieder (Stuttgart: Union Verl., 1981), 5:576.

15. Bussmann, "Vom H. Römischen Reich," 5:601–2; Robert W. Gutman, *Richard Wagner: The Man, His Mind, and His Music* (New York, NY: Harcourt, Brace & World, 1968), 308. Both Württemberg and Bavaria mobilized immediately on day following the declaration of the war. See, for example, Eduard Baltzer, *Unter dem Kreuz des Kriegs: Betrachtungen über die Ergebnisse von 1870–71 in gleichzeitigen Aufzeichnungen von Eduard Baltzer* (Nordhausen: F. Förstemann, 1871), 6.

16. Cosima's diary entry, 19 July 1870, in Cosima Wagner, *Diaries.* Vol. 1: 1869–1877, ed. and annotated Martin Gregor-Dellin and Dietrich Mack, trans. Geoffrey Skelton (London: Collins, 1978), 246. Cf. Cosima Wagner, *Die Tagebücher,* 2 vols. (Munich: Piper), 1:259.

17. The manuscript was completed on 7 September 1870; see *König Ludwig II. und Richard Wagner: Briefwechsel,* 5 vols., ed. Otto Strobel (Karlsruhe: Braun, 1936), 5:215. The copied version was not, however, finished until 28 September.

18. *Brockhaus' Conversations-Lexikon. Supplement zur elften Auflage. Encyklopädische Darstellung der neuesten Zeit nebst Ergänzungen früherer Artikel* (Leipzig: Brockhaus, 1873), 2:686.

19. Richard Wagner, "Protest," in *Sämtliche Schriften und Dichtungen,* Volks-Ausgabe. 6th ed. (Leipzig: Breitkopf & Härtel, 1911–16), 16:54.

20. Salmi, *"Die Herrlichkeit des deutschen Namens . . . ,"* 159–65.

21. "Theater. Rückblick auf den Januar 1871," *Rigasche Stadtblätter* (11 February 1871). See also *Rigaer Theater-Almanach für das Jahr 1872* (Riga, 1872), 8. *Lohengrin* was performed only on 2, 9, and 17 January 1871.

22. *Die Meistersinger von Nürnberg*, Theaterzettel 1871, The Library of the Latvian Academy of Sciences, Dept. of Rarities, Riga.

23. *Rigaer Theater-Almanach für das Jahr 1872*, 5–7.

24. *Rigaer Theater- und Tonkünstler-Lexikon nebst Geschichte des Rigaer Theaters und der Musikalischen Gesellschaft*, ed. Moritz Rudolph (Riga: R. Kymmel, 1890), 190–91.

25. *Zeitung für Stadt und Land* (14/26 December 1871).

26. *Rigaer Theater-Almanach für das Jahr 1873* (Riga, 1872), 8–10.

27. *Rigasche Zeitung* (8/20 January 1872). The advertisement states that the seventh performance of *Die Meistersinger* was given on 9 January. The *Rigaer Theater-Almanach* later indicated that after 9 January, the work was not performed until April.

28. *Rigaer Theater-Almanach für das Jahr 1873*, 8–12.

29. Ibid., 8–12. The performances were on 27 September and on 14 October 1872.

30. Moritz Rudolph was born in Leipzig in 1843, and he first studied cello, and later piano at the Leipzig Conservatory. In April 1865, he moved to Jakobstadt in Courland in order to work as a teacher of music in a girls' school, and in autumn 1867 he moved to Riga. From the summer of 1871, he wrote music reviews for the *Zeitung für Stadt und Land*, which later took the name *Rigaer Tageblatt*. For a full account of this, see *Rigaer Theater- und Tonkünstler-Lexikon*, 203–4.

31. *Zeitung für Stadt und Land* (14/26 December 1871).

32. Grey, "Wagner's *Die Meistersinger* as National Opera (1868–1945)," 83–84.

33. In German: "Der erste Eindruck, welcher ich von den Meistersingern erhielt, war ein großartiger, überwältigender."

34. *Zeitung für Stadt und Land* (14/26 December 1871).

35. *Rigaer Theater- und Tonkünstler-Lexikon*, 181–82.

36. In German: "Der ganze Kampf, der in der deutschen Musikwelt um Richard Wagner entbrannt ist, hat mehr und mehr ein persönliches Gepräge angenommen."

37. "Richard Wagner's Meistersinger," *Rigasche Zeitung* (22 December/3 January 1872).

38. *Rigasche Zeitung* (23 December/4 January 1872).

39. *Rigasche Zeitung* (24 December/5 January 1872).

40. "Theater in Mitau," *Rigasche Zeitung* (31 May/12 June 1872).

41. *Rigaer Theater- und Tonkünstler-Lexikon*, 178.

42. Ibid., 172.

43. *Rigasche Zeitung* (15/27 January 1872); *Rigasche Zeitung* (18/30 January 1872).

44. *Rigasche Zeitung* (15/27 January 1872); *Rigasche Zeitung* (20 January/3 February 1872).

45. Wagner's friends for a long time also included Franz Liszt, Anton Pusinelli, August Röckel, and Otto Wesendonck, but these men were supporters rather than disciples.

46. See Wagner, *Mein Leben*, 760.

47. Ludwig Nohl, *Gluck und Wagner: Über die Entwicklung des Musikdramas* (Munich: Finsterlin, 1870), 247. Apparently, the thought of Wagner's Germanness and the idea of seeing his art as a German national drama rapidly spread from the German histories of music abroad. For instance, the Italian Filippo Filippi in his

work *Musica e musicisti* (1876) regarded Wagner as the first genuinely German opera composer to emphasize Germanness and to direct his works clearly to his own nation. On this subject, see especially Filippo Filippi, *Musica e musicisti; Critiche, biografie ed escursioni* (Milan: Ricordi, 1876), 316–18.

48. *Rigaer Theater- und Tonkünstler-Lexikon*, 96.

49. *Rienzi,* Theaterzettel 1878, The Library of the Latvian Academy of Sciences, Dept. of Rarities, Riga.

50. *Rigaer Theater- und Tonkünstler-Lexikon,* 55.

51. Ibid., 14.

52. *Rienzi,* Theaterzettel 1878, The Library of the Latvian Academy of Sciences, Dept. of Rarities, Riga. See also *Rigaer Theater- und Tonkünstler-Lexikon,* 244–45, 274.

53. *Zeitung für Stadt und Land* (3/15 February 1878).

54. Ibid.

55. *Rigasche Zeitung* (31 January/12 February 1878).

56. *Rigasche Zeitung* (30 January/11 February 1878).

57. See especially the premiere poster of *Der fliegende Holländer,* The Archives of the Royal Theaters, Stockholm.

58. Göran Gademan, *Realismen på operan: Regi, spelstil och iscensättningsprinciper på Kungliga Teatern 1860–82* (Ph.D. diss., University of Stockholm; Stockholm: Stift. för utgivning av teatervetenskapliga studier, 1996), 228–29.

59. *Dagens Nyheter* (24 November 1865).

60. Gademan, *Realismen på operan,* 340.

61. *Stockholms Dagblad* (27 January 1872). See also Gademan, *Realismen på operan,* 228–29. In Swedish: "Men var äro de *fyra* skeppen?"

62. *Dagens Nyheter* (25 January 1872). Bauck had been moved from the *Nya Dagligt Allehanda* to the *Dagens Nyheter* in 1871. For more information, see C. F. Hennerberg, "Carl Wilhelm Bauck," in *Svenskt biografiskt lexikon* (Stockholm, 1920), 2:772–73.

63. Gademan, *Realismen på operan,* 343; Gösta Percy, "Något om Wagner-traditionen i Sverige," in *Operan 200 år: Jubelboken,* ed Klas Ralf (Stockholm: Prisma, 1973), 100. Thus, 10 performances were given in spring 1872 and the other three performances in the autumn of the same year.

64. Percy, "Något om Wagner-traditionen i Sverige," 100.

65. Ibid., 100.

66. *Post- och inrikes tigningar* (25 January 1872).

67. *Aftonbladet* (25 January 1872).

68. Ibid.

69. *Nya Dagligt Allehanda* (29 January 1872).

70. This difference should not be taken literally, for, in fact, it is possible to see many connections between Wagnerian singing and bel canto!

71. *Aftonbladet* (25 January 1872).

72. *Dagens Nyheter* (25 January 1872).

73. *Nya Dagligt Allehanda* (29 January 1872).

74. *Post- och inrikes tigningar* (25 January 1872).

75. *Dagens Nyheter* (25 January 1872).

76. Ibid.

77. Cf. "Autobiographische Skizze," in Wagner, *Ausgewählte Schriften* (Leipzig: Verlag Philipp Reclam, 1982), 88–89. The original text is as follows: "Diese Seefahrt

wird mir ewig unvergeßlich bleiben; sie dauerte drei und eine halbe Woche und war reich an Unfällen. Dreimal litten wir von heufigstem Sturme, und einmal sah sich der Kapitän genöthigt, in einem norwegischen Hafen einzulaufen. Die Durchfahrt durch die norwegischen Scheeren machte einen wunderbaren Eindruck auf meine Fantasie; die Sage vom fliegenden Holländer, wie ich sie aus dem Munde der Matrosen bestätigt erhielt, gewann in mir eine bestimmte, eigentümliche Farbe, die ihr nur die von mir erlebten Seeabenteuer verleihen konnten."

78. Jürgen Kühnel, "Wagners Schriften," in *Richard-Wagner-Handbuch,* ed. Ulrich Müller and Peter Wapnewski (Stuttgart: Kröner, 1986), 521.

79. Richard Wagner, *Gesammelte Schriften und Dichtungen,* 9 vols. (Leipzig: Siegel's Musikalienhandlung, 1871–73); Richard Wagner, *Gesammelte Schriften und Dichtungen,* vol. 10 (Leipzig: Siegel's Musikalienhandlung, 1883).

80. Wagner, *Gesammelte Schriften und Dichtungen,* vol. 1, (1871). "Autobiographische Skizze" is on pages 4–19.

81. *Nya Dagligt Allehanda* (29 January 1872).

82. Gademan, *Realismen på operan,* 220. See also Ludvig Josephson, *Våra teaterförhållanden. Betraktelser och uppsatser* (Stockholm: Samson & Wallin, 1870).

83. Gademan, *Realismen på operan,* 343.

84. Ibid., 338–43. In the early 1880s, among the popular operas the highest pinnacles were also reached by Meyerbeer's *L'Étoile du nord* during the period 1881–82 (22 performances), Arrigo Boito's *Mefistofele* during the period 1882–83 (22 performances), and Adolphe Adam's *Konung för en dag* (Si j'étais roi) 1881–82 (22 performances).

85. On this point, see especially the premiere poster of *Lohengrin,* The Archives of the Royal Theaters, Stockholm.

86. Percy, "Något om Wagner-traditionen i Sverige," 100. Further details may be found in Carl Fredrik Lundqvist, *Minnen och anteckningar,* 2 vols. (Stockholm: Hugo Gebers, 1908–9).

87. See the premiere poster of *Lohengrin,* The Archives of the Royal Theaters, Stockholm.

88. *Stockholms Dagblad* (25 January 1874).

89. *Aftonbladet* (23 January 1874).

90. Gademan, *Realismen på operan,* 232–34.

91. *Aftonbladet* (23 January 1874).

92. *Dagens Nyheter* (30 January 1874).

93. Ibid.

94. Ibid.

95. Ibid.

96. Paul Lawrence Rose, *Wagner: Race and Revolution* (New Haven, CT: Yale University Press, 1992), 76–77.

97. *Dagens Nyheter* (30 January 1874).

98. *Aftonbladet* (23 January 1874).

99. *Nya Dagligt Allehanda* (23 January 1874), *Post- och inrikes tidningar* (27 January 1874), *Dagens Nyheter* (30 January 1874), *Aftonbladet* (3 February 1874), *Stockholms Dagblad* (3 February 1874).

100. *Aftonbladet* (21, 23, 24 December 1874).

101. *Dagens Nyheter* (12, 23 January 1875).

102. *Dagens Nyheter* (12 January 1875).

103. *Lohengrin.* Polemik mellan Auditor och Spectator. Musikhistoria: Kompositörer 7991, The Archives of the Royal Theaters, Stockholm.

104. Adolf Lindgren, "Richard Wagners sträfvanden, i kritisk belysning." *Svensk tidskrift för politik, ekonomi och literatur* (1875): 244.

105. Ibid., 245–46.

106. Ibid., 252.

107. Ibid., 252.

108. Ibid., 268.

109. Ibid., 255.

110. Ibid., 262.

111. Ibid., 271.

112. Ibid., 272.

113. Richard Wagner's letter to Erik af Edholm, 30 June 1874, Erik af Edholm Collection, The Stockholm City Archive, Stockholm.

114. Richard Wagner's letter to Ludvig Josephson, 17 December 1874, Ep.J. 5:11, The Royal Library of Sweden, Stockholm.

115. Percy, "Något om Wagner-traditionen i Sverige," 100–101.

116. In Swedish: "mestdels af psalmodiserande deklamation utan form, i långsamt tidmått, ch det värsta är dess obarmertiga längder."

117. *Dagens Nyheter* (23 August 1876).

118. Ibid.

119. *Aftonbladet* (17 August 1876).

120. *Tannhäuser och Sångarstriden på Wartburg,* poster, The Archives of the Royal Theaters, Stockholm.

121. *Aftonbladet* (3, 4, and 7 December 1878).

122. *Aftonbladet* (7 December 1878).

123. Percy, "Något om Wagner-traditionen i Sverige," 101.

124. Matti Huttunen, *Modernin musiikinhistoriankirjoituksen synty Suomessa.* English summary: *The Beginnings of Modern Music History Writing in Finland* (Helsinki: Finnish Musicological Society, 1993), 30–33.

125. See Ludwig Köhler, "Jenseits und Diesseits Wagner," *Signale für die Musikalische Welt* (11 March 1869).

126. Franz Brendel (1811–68) was a critic and a music scholar with whom Wagner was involved already in the late 1840s and early 1850s. For further information, see Wagner, *Mein Leben,* 479, 480, 493, 518.

127. Carl Dahlhaus, *Richard Wagner's Music Dramas,* trans. Mary Whittall (Cambridge: Cambridge University Press, 1979), 82.

128. The book is based on the lectures given by Brendel at the conservatories of Leipzig and Prague. See Franz Brendel, *Grundzüge der Geschichte der Musik,* 5th ed. (Leipzig: Heinrich Matthes, 1861), title page.

129. Ibid., 59–62.

130. Ibid., 60.

131. Ludwig Nohl, *Allgemeine Musikgeschichte* (Leipzig: Reclam, 1880), 305.

132. Richard Pohl (1826–96) was a composer and a music scholar. He already knew Wagner in the 1850s (see Wagner, *Mein Leben,* 513). Since 1864, Pohl acted as a reporter of the *Neue Zeitschrift für Musik.* At the beginning of Wagner's Munich period, the paper was totally in the hands of the Wagnerians; the editor-in-chief was

still Franz Brendel and the reporters were Richard Pohl and Heinrich Porges, who had been employed in 1863.

133. Richard Pohl, *Richard Wagner* (Leipzig: Breitkopf & Härtel, 1884), 195–98.

134. See especially Dahlhaus, *Richard Wagner's Music Dramas*, 82–84. In Emil Naumann's view, the question was of a kind of "party-struggle." In the polemic writing, *Wagnerianismus* was known as being aggressively noisy, and *Brahmanenthum*, instead, as being more moderate. See Emil Naumann, *Zukunftsmusik und die Musik der Zukunft* (Berlin: C. Habel, 1877), 30.

135. Wilhelm Mohr, *Richard Wagner und das Kunstwerk der Zukunft im Lichte der Baireuther Aufführungen* (Cologne, 1876), 1–4.

136. Naumann, *Zukunftsmusik und die Musik der Zukunft*, 27.

137. Ibid., 31.

138. Ibid., 36. Naumann, as a matter of fact, states that the battle between the supporters of Wagner and those of Brahms is useless, because both of the composers have continued the surviving heritage in their own fashions. See ibid., 30. Naumann's attempt to draw the gap between the two sides together is interesting considering the bitterness peculiar to the clashes of the divergent opinions. Several odd interpretations of Wagner's music thus appeared in the press. For example, in spring 1871, the *Neue Freie Presse* published a piece of news of the death of the Berlin Court Theater musician Karl Ludwig Eberle. Eberle, who had died at the age of 45, was known as a Wagner enthusiast, and he had actively taken part in the campaign on behalf of Wagner. According to the newspaper, Eberle had died because Wagner's music had ruined his mental health ("allein das unablässige Studium der Wagner'schen Musik, zu deren enragirten Parteigängern er zählte, hat allmälig seine geistige Gesundheit vollständig zerrüttet"). On this subject, see especially the *Allgemeine Musikalische Zeitung* (8 March 1871). The paper quotes the news item of the *Neue Freie Presse* with the headline "Wirkung Wagner'schen Musik auf die 'geistige Gesundheit.'"

139. Bauck, *Handbok i musikens historia från fornverlden intill nutiden* (Stockholm: Hirsch, 1862), 254–59.

140. Ibid., vii–viii.

141. Ibid., 282–83. Despite this, in the preface, Bauck does not mention Fétis's book as his source, but, in this respect, rather refers to Kiesewetter or Forkel. See ibid., vii.

142. Ibid., 282.

143. Ibid., 283.

144. Wilhelm Bauck, *Musikaliskt real-lexikon: Handbok i musikvetenskap för musikstuderande såväl som för tonkonstens vänner i allmänhet* (Stockholm: Hirsch, 1871), passim.

145. Wilhelm Baucks musikhistoriska föreläsningar, The Music Library of Sweden, Stockholm.

146. Bauck, *Handbok i musikens historia från äldsta tider intill våra dagar* (Stockholm: Hirsch, 1888), 217–18.

147. Ibid., 222.

148. Ibid., 224.

149. Adolf Lindgren, *Om wagnerismen* (Stockholm: Z. Haeggströms förlagsexp., 1881), 30–32.

150. Ibid., 51.

151. Ibid., 52.

152. Ibid., 63.

153. Ibid., 59.

154. Andreas Hallén, *Musikaliska kåserier: Stockholmsminnen från åren 1884–1894* (Stockholm: G. Chelius, 1894).

155. Oscar Bensow, *Richard Wagner såsom skapare af musikdramat* (Stockholm: G. Chelius, 1891).

156. *Suomen säveltäjiä* (Porvoo: WSOY, 1965), 1:225.

157. See, e.g., Martin Wegelius, *Konstnärsbrev* (Helsinki: Söderström, 1918), 1:13.

158. The unpublished manuscript of Martin Wegelius' Wagner biography, the Library of the Sibelius Academy, Helsinki.

159. Veikko Helasvuo, "Martin Wegeliuksen Wagner-elämäkerta," *Musiikkitieto* 11 (1946): 71.

160. The unpublished manuscript of Martin Wegelius' Wagner-biography (pp. 124–36), the Library of the Sibelius Academy, Helsinki.

161. This is perceivable also in the thoughts of Zachris Topelius; see Nils Erik Forsgård, *I det femte inseglets tecken. En studie i den åldrande Zacharias Topelius livs- och historiefilosofi* (Helsinki: The Society of Swedish Literature in Finland, 1998).

162. The unpublished manuscript of Martin Wegelius' Wagner biography (p. 133), the Library of the Sibelius Academy, Helsinki. In Swedish: "Däremot är det i Tyskland en öppen hemlighet, att det knappast finnes en liberal politisk tidning, som icke är mer eller mindre beroende af judar, vare sig att de äro egare af tidningen, eller endast aktionärer, meddirektörer eller följetonister deri."

163. Rose, *Wagner: Race and Revolution*; Marc A. Weiner, *Richard Wagner and the Anti-Semitic Imagination* (Lincoln: University of Nebraska Press, 1995); Joachim Köhler, *Wagner's Hitler: The Prophet and His Disciple*, trans. and with an introduction by Ronald Taylor (Oxford: Polity Press, 2000).

164. Hannu Salmi, *Imagined Germany: Richard Wagner's National Utopia* (New York: Peter Lang, 1999), 199–200.

165. Petition in der Judenfrage an Fürst Bismarck, Hs 100a, National Archive of the Richard Wagner Foundation, Wahnfried House, Bayreuth.

166. Cosima Wagner describes Richard's encounter with Gobineau in her diary, see Cosima Wagner, *Die Tagebücher*, 1:1017.

167. The unpublished manuscript of Martin Wegelius' Wagner biography (pp. 285–86), the Library of the Sibelius Academy, Helsinki.

168. Martin Wegelius, *Hufvuddragen af den västerländska musikens historia från den kristna tidens början till våra dagar* (Helsinki: Holm, 1893), 3:576.

169. Ibid., 544.

170. Huttunen, *Modernin musiikinhistoriankirjoituksen synty Suomessa*, 40–44.

171. Martin Wegelius, *Hufvuddragen af den västerländska musikens*, 1:2.

172. Ibid., 3:455.

173. Karl Flodin, *Martin Wegelius: Levnadsteckning* (Helsinki: The Society of Swedish Literature in Finland, 1922), 440–41.

Chapter 7

1. Manfred Eger, "Die Bayreuther Festspiele und die Familie Wagner," in *Richard-Wagner-Handbuch*, ed. Ulrich Müller and Peter Wapnewski (Stuttgart: Kröner,

1986), 593. Richter apparently told of Bayreuth on his visit to Triebschen between 2 and 5 April 1869. On this subject, see Cosima Wagner, *Die Tagebücher*, 2 vols., ed. and annotated by Martin Gregor-Dellin and Dietrich Mack (Munich: Piper, 1976–77), 1:80–81.

 2. For further details, see Luisa Hager and Lorenz Seelig, *Markgräfliches Opernhaus Bayreuth. Amtlicher Führer* (Bayreuth: Bayer. Verwaltung der Staatl. Schlösser, Gärten und Seen, 1987).

 3. See Cosima's diary entries on 17–20 April 1871, in Cosima Wagner, *Die Tagebücher*, 1:378–79. See also Derek Watson, *Richard Wagner* (London: Dent, 1979), 246–47; Curt von Westernhagen, *Wagner*, 2nd ed. (Zürich: Atlantis Verlag, 1979), 408–9.

 4. Wagner's letter to Düfflipp, 20 April 1871, in Detta Petzet and Michael Petzet, *Die Richard Wagner-Bühne Ludwigs II* (Munich: Prestel, 1970), 808.

 5. Wagner, *Deutsche Kunst und deutsche Politik* (Leipzig, 1868), 42.

 6. Wagner's letter to Carl Landgraf, 11 May 1871, in Wagner, *Briefe 1830–1883* ed. Werner Otto (Berlin: Henschel, 1986), 342–43.

 7. Richard Wagner, "Ankündigung der Festspiele," in *Sämtliche Schriften und Dichtungen*, 6th ed., vol. 16 (Leipzig: Breitkopf & Härtel, 1911–16), 131–32.

 8. Wagner's letter to Friedrich Feustel, 12 April 1872, in Richard Wagner, *Selected Letters*, ed. and trans. Stewart Spencer and Barry Millington (London: Norton, 1987), 793.

 9. An exact copy of the statements of the budget is included in the appeal published in the paper *Musikalisches Wochenblatt*, through which the readers were encouraged to support the project. On this question, see "Deutsche Festspiele in Bayreuth: Aufruf des Academischen Wagner-Vereins zu Berlin," *Musikalisches Wochenblatt* (26 April 1872).

 10. Watson, *Richard Wagner*, 254–55. See also Cosima's diary entries on 12–16 May 1871, in Cosima Wagner, *Die Tagebücher*, 1:387–89. When writing the appeal to raise money for the foundation of the festival, Wagner was visiting Leipzig.

 11. See Cosima's diary entries on 18–20 July 1871, in Cosima Wagner, *Die Tagebücher*, 1:415–18.

 12. Watson, *Richard Wagner*, 254–55.

 13. Veit Veltzke, *Vom Patron zum Paladin: Wagnervereinigungen im Kaiserreich von der Reichsgründung bis zur Jahrhundertwende* (Ph.D. diss., University of Bochum (Bochum: Brockmeyer, 1987), 86–103 and passim; Frank B. Josserand, "A Study of Richard Wagner's Nationalism." (Ph.D. diss., University of Texas, Austin, 1957), 325–26. Later, the number of the patronage societies was raised to 1300. This was due to the fact that in the course of the work Wagner's budget proved to be too optimistic.

 14. Veltzke, *Vom Patron zum Paladin*, 15–23; Eger, "Die Bayreuther Festspiele und die Familie Wagner," 594–95. Wagner commented on the significance of Heckel to Richard Pohl on 7 November 1871: "Der 'Allgemeine deutsche Wagnerverein,' diese ganz ausgezeichnete Inspiration unseres Freundes Heckel möge nun über die germanische Welt und zunächst das Deutsche Reich dahinfluten!" Wagner, *Briefe 1830–1883*, 350–51.

 15. Watson, *Richard Wagner*, 254; Westernhagen, *Wagner*, 412.

 16. See, e.g., Wagner's letter to Richard Pohl, 7 November 1871, In Wagner, *Briefe 1830–1883*, 350–51. The Berlin-Wagner Society was founded by

Bernhard Löser, a tobacconist in Berlin whose admiration of Wagner was not diminished by the composer's anti-Jewishness. See, for example, Wagner, *Briefe 1830–1883*, 482.

17. This writing was: Richard Wagner, *Bericht an den Deutschen Wagner-Verein über die Umstände und Schicksale, welche die Ausführung des Bühnenfestspieles "Der Ring des Nibelungen" begleiteten* (Leipzig, 1872).

18. Ibid., 33.

19. See, e.g., Josserand, "A Study of Richard Wagner's Nationalism," 329.

20. See, e.g., Watson, *Richard Wagner*, 259.

21. Eger, "Die Bayreuther Festspiele und die Familie Wagner," 595.

22. Wagner's letter to Bismarck, 24 June 1873, in *Richard Wagner an Freunde und Zeitgenossen*, ed. Erich Kloss. (Leipzig, 1912), 560–61.

23. See, e.g., Robert W. Gutman, *Richard Wagner: The Man, His Mind, and His Music* (New York: Harcourt, Brace & World, 1968), 313.

24. Eger, "Die Bayreuther Festspiele und die Familie Wagner," 596.

25. See Wagner's letter to Düfflipp, 10 January 1874, in Petzet and Petzet, *Die Richard Wagner-Bühne Ludwigs II*, 822.

26. See e.g. Josserand, "A Study of Richard Wagner's Nationalism," 338–39.

27. Marie zu Hohenlohe, *Erinnerungen an Richard Wagner* (Weimar, 1938), 17. Marie zu Hohenlohe was the daughter of Princess Caroline von Sayn-Wittgenstein, the mistress of Franz Liszt. Marie, who was born in 1837, later married the Duke Hohenlohe-Schillingsfürst. Marie herself did not visit Bayreuth until the spring of 1889. See ibid., 24.

28. For a full account of the visit of Wilhelm I to Bayreuth, see, for example, Cosima Wagner's diary entry on 12 August 1876, in Cosima Wagner, *Die Tagebücher*, 1:998. Wilhelm I arrived at Bayreuth on 12 August, a day before the opening of the festival. Richard Wagner received the Emperor at the railway station, where the Emperor flattered the composer through calling the occasion 'a national celebration': "Richard empfängt auch den Kaiser, welcher sehr freundlich gestimmt vom Nationalfest spricht. Endlich!" See also Ludwig Schemann's description of the incident, Ludwig Schemann, *Meine Erinnerungen an Richard Wagner* (Stuttgart: F. Frommanns Verlag, 1902), 14–15.

29. See Cosima's diary entry on 13 August 1876, in Cosima Wagner, *Die Tagebücher*, 1:998. See also Eger, "Die Bayreuther Festspiele und die Familie Wagner," 596.

30. Robert von Keudell has described Bismarck's predilections for music in his memoirs *Fürst und die Fürstin Bismarck: Erinnerungen aus den Jahren 1846 bis 1872* (Berlin: Spemann, 1901). According to Keudell, Bismarck loved music, particularly Beethoven and Schubert, but Wagner was not his favorite. Keudell puts forward the fact that Bismarck, who hated opera, never visited the Berlin Opera House, nor did he later visit Bayreuth (61–68).

31. See Fremdenliste No. 1, 14 August 1876, Fremdenliste No. 3, 16 August 1876, Fremdenliste No. 4, 17 August 1876, Fremdenliste No. 6, 21 August 1876; National Archive of the Richard Wagner Foundation, Wahnfried House, Bayreuth.

32. See *Bayreuth: The Early Years: An Account of the Early Decades of the Wagner Festival As Seen by the Celebrated Visitors & Participants*, Comp., ed., and with an introduction by Robert Hartford (London: Gollancz, 1980), 61. See also Fremdenliste No. 4, 17 August 1876, Fremdenliste No. 5, 20 August 1876; National Archive of the Richard Wagner Foundation, Wahnfried House, Bayreuth.

33. Wagner's speech has been described by, among others, Ludwig Schemann and Martin Wegelius; see Schemann, *Meine Erinnerungen an Richard Wagner*, 15; Martin Wegelius, *Konstnärsbrev*, 2 vols., ed. Otto Andersson (Helsinki: Söderström, 1918–19), 2: 66–69. Schemann stresses the idea that it was only on this occasion that Wagner was able to speak directly to his *own* audience. Wegelius' description is mainly laconically illustrative.

34. On this point, see Angelo Neumann, *Erinnerungen an Richard Wagner*, 5th ed. (Leipzig: L. Staackmann, 1907), 21–22. The Viennese piano manufacturer Ludwig Bösendorfer proposed to Wagner that the festival be moved to Leipzig where it could be rearranged in the following year. This move was not, however, accepted by Wagner.

35. Julius Ruthardt, "Briefe aus Bayreuth," *Rigasche Zeitung* (20 July/1 August, 23 July/4 August, 26 July/7 August, 28 July/9 August, 29 July/10 August, 7/19 August, 10/22 August 1876).

36. Georg v. Petersen, "Die Bühnenfestspiele in Bayreuth," *Zeitung für Stadt und Land* (6/18 August, 7/19 August, 10/22 August, 11/23 August 1876).

37. *Mitausche Zeitung* (7 August 1876). A week later, the *Mitausche Zeitung* quoted Eduard Hanslick's writing in the Viennese paper *Neue Freie Presse*. See Eduard Hanslick, "R. Wagner's Bühnenfestspiele in Bayreuth," *Mitausche Zeitung* (14 August and 21 August 1876).

38. *Libausche Zeitung* (10 August, 12 August, 14 August, 17 August 1876).

39. Julius Ruthardt, "Briefe aus Bayreuth III," *Rigasche Zeitung* (26 July/7 August 1876).

40. Julius Ruthardt, "Briefe aus Bayreuth VII," *Rigasche Zeitung* (10/22 August 1876).

41. Georg v. Petersen, "Die Bühnenfestspiele in Bayreuth I," *Zeitung für Stadt und Land* (6/18 August 1876).

42. "Die Bayreuther Festspiele," *Neue Zeitung für Stadt und Land* (13/31 August 1876).

43. "Aus Baireuth," *Revalsche Zeitung* (12 July/2 August 1876).

44. *Revalsche Zeitung* (22 July/3 August and 23 July/4 August 1876).

45. See, e.g., *Revalsche Zeitung* (5/17 August 1876; 6/18 August 1876, 10/22 August 1876; 13/25 August 1876).

46. "Festtheatern i Bayreuth och Richard Wagners 'Ring des Nibelungen,'" *Helsingfors Dagblad* (12 August, 21 August, 26 August, 9 September, 24 September, 25 October, 26 October 1876).

47. Wegelius, *Konstnärsbrev*, 2: 45–109.

48. "Fest-skådespelet i Bayreuth (Kritikens dom öfver det wagnerska musikdramat)," *Helsingfors Dagblad* (1 September 1876).

49. "Festspelen i Baireuth," *Nya Dagligt Allehanda* (24 August 1876).

50. *Dagens Nyheter* (26 July 1876, 17 August 1876).

51. *Dagens Nyheter* (17 August 1876).

52. "Tyska operan, *Tannhäuser*, af R. Wagner," *Dagens Nyheter* (23 August 1876).

53. "Richard Wagners festföreställningar i Baireuth I: Wagner-teatern," *Aftonbladet* (16 August 1876).

54. "Richard Wagners festföreställningar i Baireuth II: Festspelens allmänna karakter (Ur National-Zeitung), af Karl Frenzel," *Aftonbladet* (16 August 1876).

55. "Richard Wagner festföreställningar i Baireuth III: Den dramatiska diktens innehåll," *Aftonbladet* (18 August 1876).

56. *Aftonbladet* (17 August 1876, 18 August 1876).
57. "Richard Wagners festföreställningar i Baireuth V: Medaljens frånsida," *Aftonbladet* (30 August 1876).
58. "Aus Baireuth," *Revalsche Zeitung* (12 July/2 August 1876).
59. Richard Faltin, "En soiré hos Richard Wagner," *Finsk musikrevy* 7 (1905): 123. In German: "Ach! kommen Sie lieber nach Bayreuth."
60. *Bayreuth: The Early Years*, 266. The festival did not take place in 1900. The first festival in the twentieth century took place in 1901, and its repertoire included *Der fliegende Holländer* (5 performances), *Parsifal* (7 performances), and *Der Ring* (2 cycles).
61. It is, of course, possible that the lists concerned could be found in the private archive of a visitor to Bayreuth, but I have not succeeded in finding such a collection.
62. On Sibelius' relationship to Wagner, see Erik Tawaststjerna, *Sibelius*, vol. 1: 1865–1905, trans. Robert Layton (London: Faber and Faber, 1976).
63. Fremdenlisten 1876, National Archive of the Richard Wagner Foundation, Wahnfried House, Bayreuth.
64. Fremdenlisten 1882, National Archive of the Richard Wagner Foundation, Wahnfried House, Bayreuth.
65. Fremdenlisten 1896, Fredrik Vult von Steijern Wagner Collection, The Royal Library of Sweden, Stockholm.
66. Fremdenlisten 1888–91, National Archive of the Richard Wagner Foundation, Wahnfried House, Bayreuth.
67. Fremdenlisten 1876, 1882, National Archive of the Richard Wagner Foundation, Wahnfried House, Bayreuth. The student Emil Musso from Tartu participated in the 1876 festival and Heinrich Zöllner, the composer and teacher of the University of Tartu, the 1882 festival.
68. Fremdenlisten 1876, National Archive of the Richard Wagner Foundation, Wahnfried House, Bayreuth; Fremdenlisten 1899, Fredrik Vult von Steijern Wagner Collection, The Royal Library of Sweden, Stockholm.
69. Fremdenlisten 1888, National Archive of the Richard Wagner Foundation, Wahnfried House, Bayreuth. The spelling of Prince Biron's name has presented difficulties; it occurs twice in the lists and has been recorded incorrectly (Biror and Bison!). For further information about Prince Biron's and Freytag von Löringhoff's ancestral background, see *Deutschbaltisches biographisches Lexikon*, 67, 227.
70. "Richard Wagners festföreställningar i Baireuth I: Wagner-teatern," *Aftonbladet* (16 August 1876).
71. "Richard Wagners festföreställningar i Baireuth II: Festspelens allmänna karakter (Ur National-Zeitung), af Karl Frenzel," *Aftonbladet* (16 August 1876).
72. M. W., "Festtheatern i Bayreuth och Richard Wagners 'Ring des Nibelungen' II," *Helsingfors Dagblad* (21 August 1876); Wegelius, *Konstnärsbrev*, 2:54–55.
73. "Festspelen i Baireuth," *Nya Dagligt Allehanda* (24 August 1876).
74. *Bayreuth: The Early Years*, 55–56.
75. On the gendered nature of the nineteenth-century music culture, see Marja Mustakallio, *"Teen nyt paljon musiikkia": Fanny Henselin (1805–1847) toiminta modernisoituvassa musiikkikulttuurissa* (Åbo: Åbo Akademi University Press, 2003), 58–64. See also Pirkko Moisala and Riitta Valkeila, *Musiikin toinen sukupuoli: Naissäveltäjiä keskiajalta nykyaikaan* (Helsinki: Kirjayhtymä, 1994).
76. Wagner, "The Human Womanly," in *Richard Wagner's Prose Works*, trans. William Ashton Ellis, (London: Kegan Paul, Trench, Trubner & Co., 1896), 6:335.

77. Janne Ahtola, "Thomas Cook & Son—perheyrityksenä maailmankartalle," in *Matkakuumetta: Matkailun ja turismin historiaa,* with English summaries, ed. Taina Syrjämaa (Turku: University of Turku, Department of History, 1994), 39.

78. Fremdenlisten 1882, National Archive of the Richard Wagner Foundation, Wahnfried House, Bayreuth.

79. Ibid.

80. Fremdenlisten 1899, National Archive of the Richard Wagner Foundation, Wahnfried House, Bayreuth. See also Karl Flodin and Otto Ehrström, *Richard Faltin och hans samtid* (Helsinki: H. Schildt, 1934), 214–15.

81. *Kuka kukin oli—Who Was Who in Finland: Henkilötietoja 1900-luvulla kuolleista julkisuuden suomalaisista* (Helsinki: Otava, 1961), 449. Saltzmann had become Doctor of Medicine and Surgery in 1867, and worked as a Docent of Surgery between 1871 and 1879, as well as Professor between 1879 and 1890 at the University of Helsinki. In 1890, he became the Principal Director of the Supreme Administrative Board of the Medical Service.

82. Fremdenlisten 1876, 1882, 1888, National Archive of the Richard Wagner Foundation, Wahnfried House, Bayreuth; Fremdenlisten 1891, 1896, 1899, Fredrik Vult von Steijern Wagner Collection, The Royal Library of Sweden, Stockholm. August Fredrik Sundell (1843–1924) worked as a Docent of Physics between 1870 and 1878 and as a Professor between 1878 and 1904 at the University of Helsinki. He made several study trips to different European countries between 1869 and 1887 and obviously participated actively in the local music life. See *Kuka kukin oli,* 497.

83. Fremdenlisten 1884, National Archive of the Richard Wagner Foundation, Wahnfried House, Bayreuth.

84. Fremdenlisten 1876, 1882, National Archive of the Richard Wagner Foundation, Wahnfried House, Bayreuth; Fremdenlisten 1891, 1896, 1899, Fredrik Vult von Steijern Wagner Collection, The Royal Library of Sweden, Stockholm.

85. Künstler der Bayreuther Festspiele 1876–1957, A 2534/III, National Archive of the Richard Wagner Foundation, Wahnfried House, Bayreuth. Johannes Elmblad sang in the festivals during the years 1876–1904, Olive Fremstad in 1896, and Erik Smedes during the years 1899–1906.

86. *Svenska män och kvinnor: Biografisk uppslagsbok* (Stockholm: Bonniers, 1955), 8:446. Vult von Steijern was a contributor to the *Ny Illustrerad Tidning* and a reporter for the paper 1878–81, a reporter for the *Svensk Musiktidning* from 1881, a music critic in the *Dagens Nyheter* from 1885, and finally editor in chief of the paper from 1889.

87. Fremdenlisten 1876, 1882, 1888, National Archive of the Richard Wagner Foundation, Wahnfried House, Bayreuth; Fremdenlisten 1896, Fredrik Vult von Steijern Wagner Collection, The Royal Library of Sweden, Stockholm.

88. *Rigaer Theater- und Tonkünstler-Lexikon,* 205. Heinrich Höhne was from Praemnitz, from the region of Posen (now Poznan in Poland). He acted as a piano teacher at the Riga Music School from 1871 onwards. Besides his teaching, he wrote opera and concert reviews both for the *Rigasche Zeitung* and for the *Zeitung für Stadt und Land.* See also *Rigaer Theater- und Tonkünstler-Lexikon nebst Geschichte des Rigaer Theaters und der Musikalischen Gesellschaft,* ed. Moritz Rudolph (Riga: R. Kymmel, 1890), 100. The Berlin-born Siegert began his career as a singer and chorus master and, despite his busy life, was able to perform (for example in Tallinn) during the 1850s. From 1862 he acted as a conductor and choir leader in Riga.

Siegert also composed music diligently. He composed more than 150 pieces of music, including orchestral works, pieces for piano, and songs both for solo voice and choir. On Siegert's career, see *Rigaer Theater- und Tonkünstler-Lexikon,* 229.

89. Hans-Joachim Nösselt: Das Festspielorchester zu Bayreuth. Verzeichnis und Übersichtstafeln. Richard-Wagner-Archiv 1944. Bd. 1: A–Kad. Signatur A 4966/I, National Archive of the Richard Wagner Foundation, Wahnfried House, Bayreuth.

90. *Rigaer Theater- und Tonkünstler-Lexikon,* 145–46.

91. Fremdenlisten 1882, National Archive of the Richard Wagner Foundation, Wahnfried House, Bayreuth. Zöllner, who was born in Leipzig in 1854, had come to Tartu from Dresden in 1878. Besides his lecturing and teaching of music, he composed brief pieces of music, mainly songs.

92. Zöllner, Heinrich (personal files, I. Fond "Tartu University") Stock 402, Series 3, Item 1810, 1811, The Estonian Historical Archives, Tartu.

93. Fremdenlisten 1876, National Archive of the Richard Wagner Foundation, Wahnfried House, Bayreuth. Musso was born in Livonia in 1857 and studied in Tartu during the years 1876–80. He later studied art in Vienna and also became an owner of a brewery in Tartu. See Musso, Ernst Emil (personal files, I. Fond "Tartu University") Stock 402, Series 2, Item 17387, The Estonian Historical Archives, Tartu. See also *Album Academicum der Kaiserlichen Universität Dorpat* (Tartu: C. Mattiesen, 1889), 724.

94. Fremdenlisten 1888, National Archive of the Richard Wagner Foundation, Wahnfried House, Bayreuth; Fremdenlisten 1896, 1899, Fredrik Vult von Steijern Wagner Collection, The Royal Library of Sweden, Stockholm. See also Inese Bula, "Der Rigaer Deutsch-Baltische Mathematiker Piers Bohl (1865–1921)," *Journal of Baltic Studies,* 24, no. 4 (1993), 319–26.

95. Fremdenlisten 1876, 1882, 1888, National Archive of the Richard Wagner Foundation, Wahnfried House, Bayreuth; Fremdenlisten 1891, 1896, Fredrik Vult von Steijern Wagner Collection, The Royal Library of Sweden, Stockholm.

Chapter 8

1. Frederic Spotts, *Bayreuth. A History of the Wagner Festival* (New Haven, CT: Yale University Press, 1994), 45.

2. Veit Veltzke, *Vom Patron zum Paladin: Wagnervereinigungen im Kaiserreich von der Reichsgründung bis zur Jahrhundertwende* (Ph.D. diss., University of Bochum; Bochum: Brockmeyer, 1987), 136–38.

3. Spotts, *Bayreuth: A History of the Wagner Festival,* 78.

4. Ibid., 78.

5. For further details, see Wilhelm Peterson-Berger, *Richard Wagner som kulturföreteelse. Sju betraktelser* (Stockholm: Ljus, 1913).

6. See, for example, "Bilanz," *Bayreuther Blätter* (8–9, 1884): 228–95.

7. For further details, see *Verzeichniss der Mitglieder des Allgemeinen Richard Wagner-Vereines* (Leipzig, 1885); and *Mitgliederverzeichnis des Allgemeinen Richard Wagner-Vereins* (Leipzig, 1891–94, 1896), Fredrik Vult von Steijern Wagner Collection, The Royal Library of Sweden, Stockholm.

8. *Bayreuther Blätter* (8, 1878): 241–42. Cf. Beitrag zur Vereinsstatistik (A2585–36), Bayreuther Patronat-Verein A2585, National Archive of the Richard Wagner Foundation, Wahnfried House, Bayreuth.

9. Abonnenten-Liste (Hs 223/F/VIII), Wolzogen-Nachlaß (Hs 223), National Archive of the Richard Wagner Foundation, Wahnfried House, Bayreuth.

10. Bayreuther Blätter, Adressen (Hs 223/F/IX), Wolzogen-Nachlaß (Hs 223), National Archive of the Richard Wagner Foundation, Wahnfried House, Bayreuth.

11. Conto-Buch für Bayreuther Blätter (Hs 223/F/V), Quittungen (Hs 223/F), Wolzogen-Nachlaß (Hs 223), National Archive of the Richard Wagner Foundation, Wahnfried House, Bayreuth.

12. *Mitgliederverzeichnis des Allgemeinen Richard Wagner-Vereins für das Jahr 1891* (Leipzig, 1891), Fredrik Vult von Steijern Wagner Collection, The Royal Library of Sweden, Stockholm.

13. Fredrik Vult von Steijern, "Aus dem Briefe eines Schweden über Bayreuth," in *Tannhäuser-Nachklänge. Briefe, Berichte und Betrachtungen über die Aufführungen des "Tannhäuser" in Bayreuth*, 49–53 (Berlin: Freunde der Bayreuther Festspiele, s.a.). In German: "Erst hier ist mir die ganze regenierende Bedeutung dieser Kunst recht klar aufgegangen."

14. Dagböcker 1874–76, Fredrick Vult von Steijern: Dagböcker, 1 kartong (1874–79, 9. vol.), Acc. 1992/92, The Royal Library of Sweden, Stockholm.

15. Dagbok 1877, Fredrick Vult von Steijern: Dagböcker, 1 kartong (1874–79, 9. vol.), Acc. 1992/92, The Royal Library of Sweden, Stockholm.

16. Diary entries on 4, 6, 15, and 18 December 1878, Dagbok 1878, Fredrick Vult von Steijern: Dagböcker, 1 kartong (1874–79, 9. vol.), Acc. 1992/92, The Royal Library of Sweden, Stockholm.

17. Diary entry on 4 April 1884, Dagbok 1884, Fredrick Vult von Steijern: Dagböcker, 2 kartong (1880–89, 10. vol.), Acc. 1992/92, The Royal Library of Sweden, Stockholm.

18. Diary entry on 2 April 1887, Dagbok 1887, Fredrick Vult von Steijern: Dagböcker, 2 kartong (1880–89, 10. vol.), Acc. 1992/92, The Royal Library of Sweden, Stockholm.

19. Diary entries on 15–20 August 1891, Dagbok 1891, Fredrick Vult von Steijern: Dagböcker, 3 kartong (1890–99, 10. vol.), Acc. 1992/92, The Royal Library of Sweden, Stockholm.

20. Diary entry on 21 July 1892, Dagbok 1892, Fredrick Vult von Steijern: Dagböcker, 3 kartong (1890–99, 10. vol.), Acc. 1992/92, The Royal Library of Sweden, Stockholm. In Swedish: "*Parsifal*. Härligt—glömde af allt yttra, blott njutning och dock ej samma hänförelse som förra året. Hvarför vet jag ej, då uppförandet synter mig fullare. . . ."

21. Diary entry on 22 July 1892, Dagbok 1892, Fredrick Vult von Steijern: Dagböcker, 3 kartong (1890–99, 10. vol.), Acc. 1992/92, The Royal Library of Sweden, Stockholm. In Swedish: "Härligt, härligt—denna föreställning rikare än någonsin."

22. Diary entries on 24 July–7 August 1892, Dagbok 1892, Fredrick Vult von Steijern: Dagböcker, 3 kartong (1890–99, 10. vol.), Acc. 1992/92, The Royal Library of Sweden, Stockholm.

23. Diary entries on 20–21 August 1892, Dagbok 1892, Fredrick Vult von Steijern: Dagböcker, 3 kartong (1890–99, 10. vol.), Acc. 1992/92, The Royal Library of

Sweden, Stockholm. In Swedish: ." . . farväl till alla bekanta: Wolzogens, v. Groß, Knieke, Glasenapp, Ashton Ellis m.fl. och sist till Chamberlain, i hvilka vi fått riktiga vänner."

24. Diary entries on 18 July–7 August 1894, Dagbok 1894, Fredrick Vult von Steijern: Dagböcker, 3 kartong (1890–99, 10. vol.), Acc. 1992/92, The Royal Library of Sweden, Stockholm.

25. Diary entry on 21 November 1895, Dagbok 1895, Fredrick Vult von Steijern: Dagböcker, 3 kartong (1890–99, 10. vol.), Acc. 1992/92, The Royal Library of Sweden, Stockholm.

26. Diary entry on 8 October 1895, Dagbok 1895, Fredrick Vult von Steijern: Dagböcker, 3 kartong (1890–99, 10. vol.), Acc. 1992/92, The Royal Library of Sweden, Stockholm.

27. Diary entries on 12–29 October 1895, Dagbok 1895, Fredrick Vult von Steijern: Dagböcker, 3 kartong (1890–99, 10. vol.), Acc. 1992/92, The Royal Library of Sweden, Stockholm.

28. Diary entry on 30 October 1895, Dagbok 1895, Fredrick Vult von Steijern: Dagböcker, 3 kartong (1890–99, 10. vol.), Acc. 1992/92, The Royal Library of Sweden, Stockholm.

29. Diary entry on 17 July 1896, Dagbok 1896, Fredrick Vult von Steijern: Dagböcker, 3 kartong (1890–99, 10. vol.), Acc. 1992/92, The Royal Library of Sweden, Stockholm.

30. Diary entries on 17 July–20 August 1896, Dagbok 1896, Fredrick Vult von Steijern: Dagböcker, 3 kartong (1890–99, 10. vol.), Acc. 1992/92, The Royal Library of Sweden, Stockholm.

31. Diary entry on 9 August 1897, Dagbok 1897, Fredrick Vult von Steijern: Dagböcker, 3 kartong (1890–99, 10. vol.), Acc. 1992/92, The Royal Library of Sweden, Stockholm.

32. Carl Fricdrich Glasenapp, *Richard Wagner als Mensch: Ein Vortrag, gehalten im Wagner-Verein zu Riga.* 3rd printing (Riga, 1890), Fredrik Vult von Steijern Wagner Collection 375, The Royal Library of Sweden, Stockholm.

33. Harald Molander's letter to Henrik Hennings, Helsinki, 10 May 1894, in *Korrespondens rörande Wagnersejouren i Stockholm 1894, Planerade Wagnerföreställningen 1893–95* (F5B), The Archives of the Royal Theaters, Stockholm.

34. Hennings' letter to Molander, Berlin, 4 May 1894, in *Korrespondens rörande Wagnersejouren i Stockholm 1894, Planerade Wagnerföreställningen 1893–95* (F5B), The Archives of the Royal Theaters, Stockholm.

35. Hennings' letter to Molander, Copenhagen, 6 May 1894, Copy of the letter to Mr. Elmblad, Copenhagen, 5 May 1894, in *Korrespondens rörande Wagnersejouren i Stockholm 1894, Planerade Wagnerföreställningen 1893–95* (F5B), The Archives of the Royal Theaters, Stockholm.

36. Molander's letter to Hennings, Helsinki, 10 May 1894, in *Korrespondens rörande Wagnersejouren i Stockholm 1894, Planerade Wagnerföreställningen 1893–95* (F5B), The Archives of the Royal Theaters, Stockholm.

37. Molander's letter to Burén, Helsinki, 10 May 1894, in *Korrespondens rörande Wagnersejouren i Stockholm 1894, Planerade Wagnerföreställningen 1893–95* (F5B), The Archives of the Royal Theaters, Stockholm.

38. In German: "Man vergisst dass man ein Wagnerpublikum—hier—noch nicht geschenkt bekommt sondern mit allen Mitteln erobern mag."

39. Molander's letter to Loewe, Helsinki, 10 May 1894, in *Korrespondens rörande Wagnersejouren i Stockholm 1894, Planerade Wagnerföreställningen 1893–95* (F5B), The Archives of the Royal Theaters, Stockholm.

40. "Anteckningslista till 1sta föreställningen af Walkyrian," in *Korrespondens rörande Wagnersejouren i Stockholm 1894, Planerade Wagnerföreställningen 1893–95* (F5B), The Archives of the Royal Theaters, Stockholm.

41. Karl Flodin and Otto Ehrström, *Richard Faltin och hans samtid* (Helsinki: H. Schildt, 1934), 9, 20–21, 26–27.

42. Ibid., 27–28.

43. Wagner, *Mein Leben*, 479–80, 493, 518.

44. Dahlhaus, "Wagners Stellung in der Musikgeschichte," 82.

45. Franz Brendel, *Grundzüge der Geschichte der Musik*, 5th ed. (Leipzig: Heinrich Matthes, 1861), 59–62.

46. Flodin and Ehrström, *Richard Faltin och hans samtid*, 32–34.

47. Ibid., 35–36.

48. Ibid., 36–37.

49. *Suomen säveltäjiä*, 179.

50. Flodin and Ehrström, *Richard Faltin och hans samtid*, 91–92.

51. Ibid., 208; *Suomen säveltäjiä*, 179.

52. Flodin and Ehrström, *Richard Faltin och hans samtid*, 208–9.

53. Cited in ibid., 209.

54. Cited in ibid., 210.

55. Richard Faltin, "Erinringar från Bayreuth," *Finsk musikrevy* 13 (1906): 237. In fact, in this article, Faltin regards Franciska Ritter as Wagner's sister! This error of his is easy to understand, because Richard and Franciska were almost the same age. Richard Wagner's brother Albert had already been born by 1799, whereas Richard was born in 1813. In his memorial article "En soiré hos Richard Wagner," written a year previously, Faltin, however, correctly calls Franciska Ritter Wagner's niece. For some unknown reason, he came, however, to a different conclusion in the following year. Cf. Faltin, "En soiré hos Richard Wagner," *Finsk musikrevy* 7 (1906): 122. Faltin was bothered about the matter to such an extent that he wrote to the first Wagner biographer, Carl Friedrich Glasenapp, and inquired whether Frau Ritter really was Wagner's sister or possibly his half-sister. On this point, see Richard Faltin's letter to Carl Friedrich Glasenapp, 27 June 1906, Hs 218/A/FIV/1, National Archive of the Richard Wagner Foundation, Wahnfried House, Bayreuth.

56. Cited in Flodin and Ehrström, *Richard Faltin och hans samtid*, 210.

57. Cited in ibid, 211.

58. Faltin, "En soiré hos Richard Wagner," 123.

59. Ibid., 123–25. Despite the fact that the article "En soiré hos Wagner" was published as late as 1905, it is strictly worded following the private letter which was dated in Bayreuth on 27 August 1876.

60. Flodin and Ehrström, *Richard Faltin och hans samtid*, 214–15.

61. *Bayreuther Blätter* (1, 1878): 27.

62. *Bayreuther Blätter* (8, 1878): 241–42. See also "Beitrag zur Vereinsstatistik 1878," Bayreuther Patronat-Verein A 2585, National Archive of the Richard Wagner Foundation, Wahnfried House, Bayreuth.

63. *Bayreuther Blätter* (1, 1878): 27.

64. *Bayreuther Blätter* (3, 1878): 81.

65. *Bayreuther Blätter* (1, 1878): 27; *Bayreuther Blätter* (3, 1878): 81; *Bayreuther Blätter* (10, 1878): 305.

66. Bayreuther Patronat-Verein A 2585–12, National Archive of the Richard Wagner Foundation, Wahnfried House, Bayreuth.

67. "Verzeichniss der ausgegebenen Patronatscheine" A 2585–18, Bayreuther Patronat-Verein, National Archive of the Richard Wagner Foundation, Wahnfried House, Bayreuth.

68. *Bayreuther Blätter* (7, 1881): 215.

69. *Bayreuther Blätter* (5–6, 1882): 191–92.

70. *Bayreuther Blätter* (10–12, 1883): 383.

71. *Bayreuther Blätter* (8–9, 1884): 288–95. The income and expenditure account is dated in Munich on 20 July 1884.

72. Verzeichniss der Mitglieder des Allgemeinen Richard Wagner-Vereines 1885, Fredrik Vult von Steijern Wagner Collection, The Royal Library of Sweden, Stockholm.

73. Verzeichniss der Mitglieder des Allgemeinen Richard Wagner-Vereins für das Jahr 1891, Fredrik Vult von Steijern Wagner Collection, The Royal Library of Sweden, Stockholm.

74. Verzeichnisse der Mitglieder des Allgemeinen Richard Wagner-Vereins für das Jahr 1892–96, Fredrik Vult von Steijern Wagner Collection, The Royal Library of Sweden, Stockholm.

75. Verzeichniss der Mitglieder des Allgemeinen Richard Wagner-Vereins für das Jahr 1892, Fredrik Vult von Steijern Wagner Collection, The Royal Library of Sweden, Stockholm.

76. Verzeichniss der Mitglieder des Allgemeinen Richard Wagner-Vereins für das Jahr 1896, Fredrik Vult von Steijern Wagner Collection, The Royal Library of Sweden, Stockholm.

77. *Suomen säveltäjiä*, 225.

78. Wegelius, *Konstnärsbrev*, 1: 13. This comment is to be found in the preface, written by Otto Andersson.

79. Ibid., 92.

80. Wegelius, *Konstnärsbrev*, 2: 91. In German: "Wer den Dichter will verstehen, muss in Dichters Lande gehen."

81. Karl Flodin, *Martin Wegelius: Levnadsteckning* (Helsinki: The Society of Swedish Literature in Finland), 318–19.

82. Wegelius, *Konstnärsbrev*, 2: 53–54.

83. Ibid., 63–64.

84. Martin Wegelius, *Länsimaiden musiikin historia pääpiirteissään kristinuskon alkuajoista meidän päiviimme*, trans. Axel Törnudd (Helsinki: Holm, 1904), 587.

85. Ibid., 564.

86. Ibid.

87. Ibid., 597.

88. Flodin, *Martin Wegelius*, 482–83.

89. Ibid.

90. Fremdenlisten 1899, Fredrik Vult von Steijern Wagner Collection, The Royal Library of Sweden, Stockholm.

91. Flodin, *Martin Wegelius*, 483.

92. *Rigasche Rundschau* (3 April 1915). The date is given according to the Julian calendar.

93. *Deutschbaltisches biographisches Lexikon*, 246–47.

94. Memorial articles on Carl Friedrich Glasenapp, *Rigaer Tageblatt* (5/18 April 1915); *Rigasche Rundschau* (3 April 1915).

95. *Rigasche Rundschau* (21 September 1907).

96. *Rigasche Zeitung* (18/31 December 1911).

97. Glasenapp's death notice, *Rigasche Zeitung* (3/16 April 1915).

98. This is mentioned in the memorial column in the *Rigasche Rundschau*, see *Rigasche Rundschau* (3 April 1915).

99. "Tannhäuser" in Riga. Aufzeichnungen von Glasenapp, Glasenapp-Nachlaß (Hs 218), National Archive of the Richard Wagner Foundation, Wahnfried House, Bayreuth.

100. For more detail, see Hannu Salmi, *Imagined Germany: Richard Wagner's National Utopia* (New York: Peter Lang, 1999), 185–86.

101. Richard Faltin's letters to Carl Friedrich Glasenapp, 27 June 1906 (Hs 218 A/F IV/1) and 14 July 1906 (Hs 218 A/F IV/2), Glasenapp-Nachlaß, National Archive of the Richard Wagner Foundation, Wahnfried House, Bayreuth.

102. *Bayreuther Blätter* (1, 1878): 27.

103. The lists also mentioned the profession of the guest, see Fremdenlisten 1876, National Archive of the Richard Wagner Foundation, Wahnfried House, Bayreuth. Moritz Rudolph was originally a musician and a music teacher, later he worked as an editor of the *Rigaer Tageblatt*, as a music critic, and as an editor of *Rigaer Theater- und Tonkünstler-Lexikon* (1890).

104. See, e.g., Gustav Engelmann's letters to Glasenapp, 29 August, 15 September, 13 October, 21 October, 6 November, 9 December 1877, Hs 218 A/eXII/2, 4–9, Glasenapp-Nachlaß, National Archive of the Richard Wagner Foundation, Wahnfried House, Bayreuth.

105. Gustav Engelmann's letter to Glasenapp, 2 March 1878 (Hs 218 A/eXII/15), Glasenapp-Nachlaß, National Archive of the Richard Wagner Foundation, Wahnfried House, Bayreuth.

106. *Annals of Opera 1597–1940*, Compiled from the Original Sources by Alfred Loewenberg, with an Introduction by Edward J. Dent (Cambridge: L W. Heffer & Sons, 1943), 519.

107. *Bayreuther Blätter* (3, 1878): 81; *Bayreuther Blätter* (10, 1878): 305.

108. *Rigaer Theater- und Tonkünstler-Lexikon nebst Geschichte des Rigaer Theaters und der Musikalischen Gesellschaft*, ed. Moritz Rudolph (Riga: R. Kymmel, 1890), 201–2.

109. Verziechnis der Mitglieder des Allgemeinen Richard Wagner-Vereines 1885, Fredrik Vult von Steijern Wagner Collection, The Royal Library of Sweden, Stockholm.

110. *Zeitung für Stadt und Land* (4/16 February 1883).

111. Verziechnis der Mitglieder des Allgemeinen Richard Wagner-Vereines 1885, Fredrik Vult von Steijern Wagner Collection, The Royal Library of Sweden, Stockholm.

112. *Album Akademicum der Kaiserlichen Universität Dorpat* (Tartu, 1867), 158.

113. Wilfried Anders was, however, born in Livonia and had studied history, politics and economics at the University of Tartu since 1866. Further details in *Album Akademicum der Kaiserlichen Universität Dorpat* (Tartu, 1867), 325.

114. Verziechnis der Mitglieder des Allgemeinen Richard Wagner-Vereines 1891, Fredrik Vult von Steijern Wagner Collection, The Royal Library of Sweden, Stockholm.

115. Verziechnis der Mitglieder des Allgemeinen Richard Wagner-Vereines 1892, 1893, 1894, Fredrik Vult von Steijern Wagner Collection, The Royal Library of Sweden, Stockholm.

116. Verziechnis der Mitglieder des Allgemeinen Richard Wagner-Vereines 1896, Fredrik Vult von Steijern Wagner Collection, The Royal Library of Sweden, Stockholm.

117. Bernhard Hollander, *Riga im 19. Jahrhundert: Ein Rückblick* (Riga: G. Löffler, 1926), 101.

118. Ibid., 100–102.

119. *Bayreuther Blätter* (6, 1879): 184.

120. *Rigaer Theater- und Tonkünstler-Lexikon*, 55.

121. *Bayreuther Blätter* (1, 1885): 40.

122. *Bayreuther Blätter* (3, 1886): 98.

123. *Bayreuther Blätter* (11, 1886): 380.

124. *Bayreuther Blätter* (1–2, 1887): 63.

125. *Bayreuther Blätter* (4, 1887): 128.

126. *Bayreuther Blätter* (12, 1887): 419.

127. *Bayreuther Blätter* (3, 1884): 95.

128. *Bayreuther Blätter* (7, 1886): 244.

129. Glasenapp, *Richard Wagner als Mensch*, 11, 16, 26–27.

130. *Bayreuther Blätter* (4, 1885): 132.

131. *Bayreuther Blätter* (1, 1886): 38.

132. *Bayreuther Blätter* (11, 1886): 380; *Bayreuther Blätter* (1–2. 1887): 63; *Bayreuther Blätter* (4, 1887): 128.

133. *Bayreuther Blätter* (12, 1887): 419.

134. *Bayreuther Blätter* (1–2, 1887): 63.

Conclusion

1. Richard Faltin, "En soiré hos Richard Wagner," *Finsk musikrevy* 7 (1905): 123. The original quotation is: "Ach! kommen Sie lieber nach Bayreuth. Es freut mich aber sehr, dass es auch dort oben Leute giebt, die meine Musik gern haben."

2. "The Stage of Weimar," *Blackwood's Edinburgh Magazine* (November 1861): 604.

3. *Kikeriki! Humoristisches Volksblatt* (4 March 1875).

4. "Wirkung Wagner'schen Musik auf die 'geistige Gesundheit,'" *Allgemeine Musikalische Zeitung* (8 March 1871). This news was based on a story by the *Neue Freie Presse* earlier in spring 1871.

5. "The World of Weimar," *Blackwood's Edinburgh Magazine* (April 1861): 456.

6. Fredrika Stenhammar's letter to Mrs. Schäfer, 28 May 1853, in Fredrika Stenhammar, *Brev*, ed. Elsa Stenhammar (Uppsala: Geber, 1958), 33–34. In Swedish: "Ni kunna icke göra Er ett begrepp om det."

7. Wilhelm Peterson-Berger, *Richard Wagner som kulturföreteelse: Sju betraktelser* (Stockholm: Ljus, 1913), 88–91.

8. Joseph Horowitz, *Wagner Nights: An American History* (Berkeley: University of California Press), 213–39.

9. Hannu Salmi, *Imagined Germany: Richard Wagner's National Utopia* (New York: Peter Lang, 1999), 194–201 and passim.

10. For more details, see *Evig lycka i Utopia: De inbillade lösningarnas bok*, ed. and trans. Sam J. Lundwall (Stockholm: Lundwall Fakta & fantasi, 1998), 95–97. Lundin's novel was inspired by Kurd Lasswitz's book *Bilder aus der Zukunft*, published in Breslau (Wroclaw) in 1878.

11. Claës Lundin, *Oxygen och Aromasia: Bilder från år 2378* (Stockholm: Seligmann, 1878), 7–8.

Geographical Glossary

German name	English name	Present-day name and country
Bolderaa	Bolderaja	Bolderāja, Latvia
Braunsberg	Braniewo	Braniewo, Poland
Breslau	Wroclaw	Wrocław, Poland
Danzig	Gdansk	Gdańsk, Poland
Dorpat	Tartu	Tartu, Estonia
Dünaburg	Daugavpils	Daugavpils, Latvia
Elbing	Elblag	Elbląg, Poland
Fellin	Viljandi	Viljandi, Estonia
Königsberg	Kaliningrad	Kaliningrad, Russia
Libau	Liepaja	Liepāja, Latvia
Memel	Klaipeda	Klaipėda, Lithuania
Mitau	Jelgava	Jelgava, Latvia
Narwa	Narva	Narva, Estonia
Pernau	Pärnu	Pärnu, Estonia
Pillau	Baltysk	Baltysk, Russia
Posen	Poznan	Poznań, Poland
Reval	Tallinn	Tallinn, Estonia
Stettin	Szczecin	Szczecin, Poland
Tilsit	Sovetsk	Sovetsk, Russia
Wolmar	Valmiera	Valmiera, Latvia

List of Sources

Archival Sources

The Archives of the Royal Theaters (Kungliga teatrarnas arkiv), Stockholm, Sweden
Helmer Key, "Utkast till program för K. teaterns versamhet" A1D:1
"Lohengrin. Polemik mellan Auditor och Spectator, Musikhistoria:
  Kompositörer"
Opera Posters
Opera Programs
Planned Wagner Performance (Planerade Wagnerföreställningen) 1893–95,
  F5B
"Promemoria angående repertoaren för spelåret" 1912–13

The Estonian Historical Archives (Eesti Ajalooarhiiv), Tartu, Estonia
"Dorpat (Tartu) University," personal files (I Fond)
Magistracy of Pärnu (Pernau)

The Latvian State Historical Archives (Latvijas Valsts Vēstures Arhivs), Riga, Latvia
Richard Wagner, personal files (1378 f., 1. apr., 9666 lieta)

The Library of the Estonian Academy of Sciences, the Baltika Collection (Eesti Teaduste Akadeemia Raamatukogu, Baltika), Tallinn, Estonia
Revaler Theater-Almanach 1853, 1860–61

The Library of the Latvian Academy of Sciences, Dept. of Rarities (Latvijas Akadēmiskā bibliotēka, Misina bibliotēka), Riga, Latvia
Rigaer Theater-Almanach 1852, 1855, 1867–68, 1871–72
Theater Posters (Theaterzettel) 1843, 1853, 1855, 1871, 1878, 1889/90,
  1897/98
Music Catalogues (Musikaliekatalogen)

The Library of the Sibelius Academy (Sibelius-Akatemian kirjasto), Helsinki, Finland
Martin Wegelius, "The Unpublished Biography of Wagner"

The Military Archives of Sweden (Krigsarkivet), Stockholm, Sweden
Biographical Cards (Biografikorten)
"Jönköpings regemente, Musikkåren," Serie D 1, Vol. 1
"Livgrenadjärregementet, Musikkåren," Serie D II, Vols. 1 & 2
"Livregementets dragoner, Regementsmusikens notarkiv," Vol. 1694
"Norrlands arilleriregemente, Musikkåren," Serie D 2, Vol. 1
"Regementsmusikens notarkiv," 162b
"Södra Skånska Regementet, Musikkåren," Serie D 1, Vol. 3

The Music Library of Sweden (Statens musikbibliotek), Stockholm, Sweden
Edberg Collection (Edbergska samlingen)
Music Catalogues (Musikaliekataloger)
Wilhelm Bauck's lectures on music history (musikhistoriska föreläsningar)

National Archive of the Richard Wagner Foundation, Wahnfried House (Nationalarchiv der Richard-Wagner-Stiftung), Bayreuth, Germany
> The Artists of the Bayreuth Festival, "Künstler der Bayreuther Festspiele" 1876–1957. Call number: A 2534/III.
> Bayreuther Patronat-Verein (A 2585)
>> "Verzeichnis der ausgegebenen Patronatscheine" (A 2585–18)
> Carl Friedrich Glasenapp Collection (Glasenapp-Nachlaß, Hs 218)
>> "Tannhäuser in Riga. Aufzeichnungen von Glasenapp"
>> Letter from Gustav Engelmann to Glasenapp (Hs 218A/eXII/1–36)
>> Faltin to Glasenapp 1906 (1 letter, 1 postcard, Hs 218 A/FIV)
>> Letter from the editors of *Finsk Musikrevy* to Glasenapp 9 May 1905 (Hs218 A/FXI/1)
>> Letter from the editors of *Finsk Musikrevy* to Glasenapp 15 May 1905 (1 Brief, Hs 218A/FXI/2)
>> Glasenapp's letter to the editors of *Finsk Musikrevy* 12 May 1905 (1 draft, Hs 218/FXI/3)
>> Letter from Armas Jarrnefeld (in fact, Armas Järnefelt!) to Glasenapp 12 April 1903 (1 letter, 2 concert programs, Hs 218 A/JIV)
>> "Reisetagebuch" (Hs 218/K/1)
>> Diaries of Glasenapp (Hs 218/K/19)
> Hans von Wolzogen Collection (Wolzogen-Nachlaß, Hs 223)
>> "Abonnenten-Liste" (Hs 223/F/VIII)
>> "Aufstellung der Korrespondenzen, Abschriften, Entwürfte betreff. Allgemeiner Patronat-Verein zur Pflege und Erhaltung der Bühnenfestspiele zu Bayreuth" (Hs 223/K/III)
>> "Bayreuther Blätter, Adressen" (Hs 223/F/IX)
>> "Conto-Buch für Bayreuther Blätter" (Hs 223/F/V)
>> C. Viktor E. Björkman's letter to Hans von Wolzogen 27 April 1925 (Hs 223/A-2)
>> Richard Faltin, "Eine Soirée bei Richard Wagner" (3 pages, Hs 223/N/2)
>> "Quittungen" (Hs 223/F)
> Hans-Joachim Nösselt, "Das Festspielorchester zu Bayreuth. Verzeichnis und Übersichtstafeln. Richard-Wagner-Archiv 1944." Call number: A 4966/I–II
> "Petition in der Judenfrage an Fürst Bismarck" (Hs 100a)
> Visitor Lists (Fremdenlisten) 1876, 1882, 1884, 1888, 1889, 1891, 1896, 1897, 1899, 1901 (A 2500)

The Royal Library of Sweden (Kungliga biblioteket), Stockholm, Sweden
> Fritz Arlberg Archive (Ep. J. 2)
>> Letters from L. O. Josephson to Fritz Arlberg (32 original letters)
> L. O. Josephson Archive (Ep.J. 5)
>> Letter from Hermann Levi to L. O. Josephson 10 August 1876 (Ep. J. 5:6)
>> Letter from Richard Wagner to L. O. Josephson 17 December 1874 (Ep. J. 5:11)

Letters from J. A. Tichatschek to L. O. Josephson 1866 (5 original letters)
Letter from Fredrik Vult von Steijern to L. O. Josephson (Ep.J. 5:12)
Ellen Key Archive (L 41)
    Cosima Wagner, letter to Ellen Key 1906 (L 41:63)
Karl Valentin Family Archive (L 112)
    Two letters from Bayreuther Festspiele to Karl Valentin 1891 (L 112:1)
    Letters from Andreas Hallén to Karl Valentin 1879–1909 (75 original
        letters)
    Letter from J. A. Tichatschek to Isaac Valentin 1863–66, 3 original letters
        (L 112:4)
Fredrik Vult von Steijern Archive (Acc. 1992/92)
    Diaries 1874–99
Fredrik Vult von Steijern Wagner Collection (Wagnersamling)
    Fremdenliste der Bayreuther Festspiele 1896, 1899
    Verzeichnis der Mitglieder des Allgemeinen Richard Wagner-Vereines
        1885,
    Mitgliederverzeichnis des Allgemeinen Richard Wagner-Vereines
        1891–94, 1896

The Russian State Archive (Gosudarstvennyi Arhiv RF, GARF), Moscow, Russia
    Ministry of Domestic Affairs, Dept. of Secret Police
    Richard Wagner, personal files (F. 109, Op. 3, D. 2266, L. 1–7)

The Sound Archive of the Finnish Broadcasting Company (Suomen Yleisradion äänitearkisto),
Helsinki, Finland
    Fredrik Pacius, Die Loreley (master tape of an opera, recorded in 1959)

The Stockholm City Archive (Stockholms stadsarkiv), Stockholm, Sweden
    Erik af Edholm Collection
    Richard Wagner, letter to Erik af Edholm 30 June 1874
    J. A. Tichatschek, letter to Erik af Edholm 20 July & 22 July 1866

The University of Helsinki Library (Helsingin yliopiston kirjasto), Helsinki, Finland
    Richard Faltin Collection (Coll. 52)
        Letter from Faltin to Olga Faltin 1876
        Letter to Faltin from Wohnungs-Comité in Bayreuth 1899
        Letters to Faltin from Carl Fr. Glasenapp 1906–7 (2 original letters)
        Letters to Faltin from Hans von Wolzogen 1879–97 (3 original letters)
        Letters to Faltin from Verwaltungsrath der Bühnenfestspiele in
            Bayreuth 1878–1901 (8 original letters)
        Letter to Faltin from Hans von Bülow 1885
        Letters to Faltin from Thérèse Hahl 1900–1910 (7 original letters)
    Zacharias Topelius Collection (Coll. 244)
        Letter from Topelius to Thérèse Hahl 1892 (1 draft)
        Letters from Topelius to J. A. Josephson 1852–75 (11 original letters)
        Letters to Topelius from Thérèse Hahl 1886–94 (5 original letters)
        Letters to Topelius from J. A. Josephson 1852–74 (15 original letters)

Newspapers and Journals

Åbo Tidningar, Turku 1821, 1842, 1857.
Åbo Underrättelser, Turku 1869.
Aftonbladet, Stockholm 1865, 1872, 1874, 1876, 1878, 1883, 1887.
Allgemeine Zeitung, Augsburg 1865.
Bayreuther Blätter, Bayreuth 1878–99.
Blackwood's Edinburgh Magazine, Edinburg 1861.
Borgå Bladet, Porvoo 1863.
Dagens Nyheter, Stockholm 1865, 1872, 1874, 1876.
Düna-Zeitung, Riga 1898.
Dörptsche Zeitung, Tartu 1853–54, 1860.
Finlands Allmänna Tidning, Helsinki 1857.
Helsingfors Tidningar, Helsinki 1857.
Hufvudstadsbladet, Helsinki 1865.
Illustrierte Zeitung, Leipzig 1843.
Journal de Saint-Pétersbourg, St. Petersburg 1854.
Libausche Zeitung, Liepaja 1876.
Mitausche Zeitung, Jelgava 1876, 1883.
Musikalisches Wochenblatt, Leipzig 1872.
Neue Zeitung für Stadt und Land, Riga 1876.
Neueste Nachrichten, Munich 1865.
Nya Dagligt Allehanda, Stockholm 1872, 1874, 1876, 1887.
Pernausche Zeitung, Pärnu 1881, 1886.
Post-och inrikes tidningar, Stockholm 1865, 1872.
Revalsche Zeitung, Tallinn 1860–61, 1876.
Revue européenne, Paris 1861.
Rigaer Tageblatt, Riga 1915.
Rigasche Rundschau, Riga 1898, 1907, 1915.
Rigasche Stadtblätter, Riga 1843, 1853–57, 1859–64, 1866–71, 1878, 1889.
Rigasche Zeitung, Riga 1843, 1852–53, 1855, 1857, 1861, 1871–72, 1876, 1878, 1911, 1915.
St. Petersburger Zeitung, St. Petersburg 1853, 1863.
Stockholms Dagblad, Stockholm 1872, 1874.
Suometar, Helsinki 1857.
Svenska Tidningen. Dagligt Allehanda i Stockholm, Stockholm 1857.
Tagespost, Riga 1915.
Zeitung für Stadt und Land, Riga 1871, 1876, 1878, 1883.

Literature and Scores

Aavik, Juhan. *Eesti muusika ajalugu.* Vol 2: *Kunstmuusika.* Stockholm: Estniska Kultursamf., 1969.
Ahtola, Janne. "Thomas Cook & Son—perheyrityksenä maailmankartalle." In *Matkaku-umetta: Matkailun ja turismin historiaa.* With English summaries, edited by Taina Syrjämaa, 39–65. Turku: University of Turku, Department of History, 1994.
Album Akademicum der Kaiserlichen Universität Dorpat. Tartu, 1867.

Album Academicum der Kaiserlichen Universität Dorpat. Tartu: C. Mattiesen, 1889.

Andersson, Greger. "Der Ostseeraum als Musiklandschaft. Musik—Musikinstitutionen—Repertoires im 17. und 18. Jahrhundert. Präsentation eines Forschungsprojekts." In *Balticum: A Coherent Musical Landscape in 16th and 18th Centuries,* edited by Irma Vierimaa, 9–17. Helsinki: University of Helsinki, 1994.

Annals of Opera 1597–1940. Compiled from the Original Sources by Alfred Loewenberg. With an Introduction by Edward J. Dent. Cambridge: W. Heffer & Sons, 1943.

Arro, Elmar. *Geschichte der estnischen Musik.* Vol. 1. Tartu: Akadeemiline kooperatiiv, 1933.

Bacon, Henry. *Oopperan historia.* Helsinki: Otava, 1995.

Bakutyte, Vida. "Musical Life in Vilnius at the Time of Ole Bull's Visit (1841)." In *Nordisk musikkforskerkongress Oslo, 24.–27. juni 1992: Innlegg og referater,* 450–52. Oslo: Det historisk-filosofiske fakultet, Universitet i Oslo, 1992.

Ballstaedt, Andreas, and Tobias Widmaier. *Salonmusik: Zur Geschichte und Funktion einer bürgerlichen Musikpraxis.* Stuttgart: Steiner, 1989.

Baltzer, Eduard. *Unter dem Kreuz des Kriegs: Betrachtungen über die Ergebnisse von 1870–71 in gleichzeitigen Aufzeichnungen von Eduard Baltzer.* Nordhausen: F. Förstemann, 1871.

Bartlett, Rosamund A. "Wagner and Russia: A Study of the Influence of the Music and Ideas of Richard Wagner on the Artistic and Cultural Life of Russia and the Soviet Union 1841–1941." Ph.D. diss., St. Anthony's College (Oxford), 1990.

———. *Wagner and Russia.* Cambridge Studies in Russian Literature. Cambridge: Cambridge University Press, 1995.

Bauck, Wilhelm. *Handbok i musikens historia från äldsta tider intill våra dagar.* Stockholm: Hirsch, 1888.

———. *Handbok i musikens historia från fornverlden intill nutiden: För tonkonstens idkare såväl som för dess vänner i allmänhet.* Stockholm: Hirsch, 1862.

———. *Musik och theater.* Stockholm: Norstedt & S, 1868.

———. *Musikaliskt real-lexikon: Handbok i musikvetenskap för musikstuderande såväl som för tonkonstens vänner i allmänhet.* Stockholm: Hirsch, 1871.

Bauer, Hans-Joachim. *Richard Wagner-Lexikon.* Bergisch Gladbach: Lübbe, 1988.

Bauer, Oswald Georg. *Richard Wagner Goes to the Theatre.* Translated by Stewart Spencer. Bayreuth: Leitung der Bayreuther Festspiele, 1996.

Bayreuth: The Early Years: An Account of the Early Decades of the Wagner Festival As Seen by the Celebrated Visitors & Participants. Compiled, edited, and with an introduction by Robert Hartford. London: Gollancz, 1980.

Bennett, Tony, and Janet Woollacott. *Bond and Beyond: The Political Career of a Popular Hero.* New York: Methuen, 1987.

Bensow, Oscar. *Richard Wagner såsom skapare af musikdramat.* Stockholm: G. Chelius, 1891.

Borchmeyer, Dieter. *Drama and the World of Richard Wagner.* Translated by Daphne Ellis. Princeton, NJ: Princeton University Press, 2003.

Bosse, Heinrich. "The Establishment of the German Theater in 18th Century Riga." *Journal of Baltic Studies* 3 (1989): 207–22.

Braudel, Fernand. *La Méditerranée et le monde méditerranéen à l'époque de Philippe II.* Paris: Colin, 1949.

Braudo, Eugen (Evgenii). "Richard Wagner unter russischer polizeilicher Aufsicht. Aus den Akten der russischen Geheimpolizei." *Die Musik* 10 (1923/24): 748–751.

———. *Vagner v Rossii: Novye materialy k ego biografi.* Petrograd, 1923.

Breğe, Ilona. "Rīgas Pilsētas teātris 1782–1863: Das Rigaer Stadt-Theater 1782–1863." In *No Fītinghofa tēatra līdz Vāgnerzālei: Vom Vietinghoff-Theater bis zum Wagner-Saal.* Riga: Das Deutsche Ku lturinstitut Lettlands, 1992.

Breig, Werner. "Wagners kompositorisches Werk." In *Richard-Wagner-Handbuch,* edited by Ulrich Müller and Peter Wapnewski, 353–470. Stuttgart: Kröner, 1986.

Brendel, Franz. *Grundzüge der Geschichte der Musik.* 5th ed. Leipzig: Heinrich Matthes, 1861.

Brockhaus' Conversations-Lexikon. Supplement zur elften Auflage: Encyklopädische Darstellung der neuesten Zeit nebst Ergänzungen früherer Artikel. Vol. 2. Leipzig: Brockhaus, 1873.

Bula, Inese. "Der Rigaer Deutsch-Baltische Mathematiker Piers Bohl (1865–1921)." *Journal of Baltic Studies* 24, no. 4 (1993): 319–26.

Bussmann, Walter. "Vom H. Römischen Reich deutscher Nation zur Gründung des Deutschen Reiches." In *Handbuch der europäischen Geschichte,* 7 vols., edited by Theodor Schieder, 404–615. Stuttgart: Union Verl., 1981.

Chaves Júnior, Edgard de Brito. *Wagner e o Brasil.* Rio de Janeiro: Emebê, 1976.

Collan-Beaurain, Maria. *Fredrik Pacius: Lefnadsteckning.* Helsinki: Söderström & Co., 1921.

Cygnaeus, Fredrik. *Samlade arbeten III: Literatur-historiska och blandade arbeten.* Helsinki: G. W. Edlund, 1883.

Dahlhaus, Carl. *Richard Wagner's Music Dramas.* Translated by Mary Whittall. Cambridge: Cambridge University Press, 1979.

———. "Wagners Stellung in der Musikgeschichte." In *Richard-Wagner-Handbuch.* Edited by Ulrich Müller and Peter Wapnewski, 60–85. Stuttgart: Kröner, 1986.

Dahlström, Fabian, and Erkki Salmenhaara. *Suomen musiikin historia 1: Ruotsin vallan ajasta romantiikkaan.* Porvoo: WSOY, 1995.

Deutschbaltisches biographisches Lexikon 1710–1960. Edited by Wilhelm Lenz. Cologne: Böhlau, 1970.

DiGaetani, John Louis. *Richard Wagner and the Modern British Novel.* Rutherford, NJ: Fairleigh Dickinson University Press, 1979.

———. "Wagnerian Patterns in the Fiction of Joseph Conrad, D. H. Lawrence, Virginia Woolf, and James Joyce." Ph.D. diss., University of Wisconsin, 1973.

Eberlein, Dorothee. "Zwischen Petersburg und Leipzig. Zur Ausbildung musikalischer Formen in den baltischen Ländern um 1900." In *National Movements in the Baltic Countries during the 19th Century,* edited by Aleksander Loit, 455–60. Stockholm: University of Stockholm, 1985.

Eesti muusika. Vol. 1. Tallinn: Eesti raamat, 1968.

Eesti muusika biograafiline leksikon. Edited by Ela Eelhein, Eha-Pilvi Jõgi, Jüri Kallasmaa, Endel Pajula, Urve Tammjärv, Helgi Tüksamnel, and Tiiu Viires. Tallinn: Valgus, 1990.

Eger, Manfred. "Die Bayreuther Festspiele und die Familie Wagner." In *Richard-Wagner-Handbuch,* edited by Ulrich Müller and Peter Wapnewski, 589–608. Stuttgart: Kröner, 1986.

Eurén, K. E. *Höyrykoneet: Niiden keksintö ja käytäntö.* Hämeenlinna: Eurén, 1863.
Evig lycka i Utopia: De inbillade lösningarnas bok. Edited and translated by Sam J. Lundwall. Stockholm: Lundwall Fakta & fantasi, 1998.
Faltin, Richard. "En soiré hos Richard Wagner." *Finsk musikrevy* 7 (1905): 122–25.
———. "Erinringar från Bayreuth." *Finsk musikrevy* 13 (1906): 236–39.
Filippi, Filippo. *Musica e musicisti: Critiche, biografie ed escursioni.* Milan: Ricordi, 1876.
Flodin, Karl. *Martin Wegelius: Levnadsteckning.* Helsinki: The Society of Swedish Literature in Finland, 1922.
Flodin, Karl, and Otto Ehrström. *Richard Faltin och hans samtid.* Helsinki: H. Schildt, 1934.
Forsgård, Nils Erik. *I det femte insegleets tecken: En studie i den åldrande Zacharias Topelius livs-och historiefilosofi.* Helsinki: The Society of Swedish Literature in Finland, 1998.
Furness, Raymond. *Wagner and Literature.* Manchester: Manchester University Press, 1982.
Gademan, Göran. *Realismen på operan: Regi, spelstil och iscensättningsprinciper på Kungliga Teatern 1860–1882.* Ph.D. diss., University of Stockholm. Stockholm: Stift. för utgivning av teatervetenskapliga studier, 1996.
Glasenapp, Carl Friedrich. *Das Leben Richard Wagners.* 4th ed. Vol. 1 (1813–43). Leipzig: Breitkopf & Härtel, 1905.
———. *Richard Wagner als Mensch: Ein Vortrag, gehalten im Wagner-Verein zu Riga.* 3rd printing. Riga, 1890.
Godlewskaja, Marina M. "Richard Wagner in St. Petersburg." In *Wagner in St. Petersburg.* Edited by Bärbel Hamacher, 13–48. Bayreuth: Bayerische Vereinsbank, 1993.
Gregor-Dellin, Martin. *Richard Wagner: Sein Leben, sein Werk, sein Jahrhundert.* Munich: Piper, 1980.
Grey, Thomas S. "Wagner's *Die Meistersinger* as National Opera (1868–1945)." In *Music and German National Identity,* edited by Celia Applegate and Pamela Potter, 78–104. Chicago: University of Chicago Press, 2002.
Der Große Brockhaus: Handbuch des Wissens in zwanzig Bänden. 15th ed. Leipzig: Brockhaus, 1933.
Gutman, Robert W. *Richard Wagner: The Man, His Mind, and His Music.* New York: Harcourt, Brace & World, 1968.
Hager, Luisa, and Lorenz Seelig. *Markgräfliches Opernhaus Bayreuth: Amtlicher Führer.* Bayreuth: Bayer. Verwaltung der Staatl. Schlösser, Gärten und Seen, 1987.
Hallén, Andreas. *Musikaliska kåserier: Stockholmsminnen från åren 1884–1894.* Stockholm: G. Chelius, 1894.
Hartman, Elwood. *French Literary Wagnerism.* Garland Publications in Comparative Literature. New York: Garland, 1988.
Heikinheimo, Seppo. "Kävikö Wagner Imatralla?" *Helsingin Sanomat* (9 December 1984).
Helasvuo, Veikko. "Martin Wegeliuksen Wagner-elämäkerta." *Musiikkitieto* 11 (1946): 70–71.
Helmer, Axel. *Svensk solosång 1850–1890. 1: En genrehistorisk studie.* Stockholm: Svenskt musikhistoriskt arkiv, 1972.
Hennerberg, C. F. "Carl Wilhelm Bauck." In *Svenskt biografiskt lexikon,* vol. 2, 772–76. Stockholm, 1920.

Herresthal, Harald. "Det borgerlige musikkonsum i Christiania på 1850-talet." In *Nordisk musikkforskerkongress Oslo, 24.–27. juni 1992: Innlegg og referater,* 169–70. Oslo: Det historisk-filosofiske fakultet, Universitet i Oslo, 1992.

Hilleström, Gustaf. *Kungl. Musikaliska Akademien. Matrikel 1771–1971.* Strängnäs: Nordiska Musikförlaget, 1971.

Hinrich, Friedrich. *Richard Wagner und die neuere Musik: Eine kritische Skizze aus der musikalischen Gegenwart.* Halle: Schrödel und Simon, 1854.

Hirn, Sven. *Alati kierueella: Teatterimme varhaisvaiheet vuoteen 1870.* Helsinki: Helsinki University Press, 1998.

———. *Imatra som natursevärdhet till och med 1870: En reselitterär undersökning med lokalhistorisk begränsning.* Helsinki: Finnish Academy of Science and Letters, 1958.

Hohenlohe, Marie zu. *Erinnerungen an Richard Wagner.* Weimar, 1938.

Hollander, Bernhard. *Riga im 19. Jahrhundert: Ein Rückblick.* Riga: G. Löffler, 1926.

Horowitz, Joseph. *Wagner Nights: An American History.* Berkeley: University of California Press, 1994.

Huttunen, Matti. *Modernin musiikinhistoriankirjoituksen synty Suomessa.* English Summary: *The Beginnings of Modern Music History Writing in Finland.* Helsinki: Finnish Musicological Society, 1993.

Jauss, Hans Robert. *Ästhetische Erfahrung und literarische Hermeneutik.* Frankfurt am Main: Suhrkamp, 1982.

Jeanson, Gunnar. *August Söderman: En svensk tondiktares liv och verk.* Stockholm: Bonnier, 1926.

Josephson, Ludvig. *Våra teaterförhållanden: Betraktelser och uppsatser.* Stockholm: Samson & Wallin, 1870.

Josserand, Frank B. "A Study of Richard Wagner's Nationalism." Ph.D. diss., University of Texas, Austin, 1957.

Jung-Kaiser, Ute. *Die Rezeption der Kunst Richard Wagners in Italien.* Regensburg: Bosse, 1974.

Kansojen kirjallisuus. Vol. 7. Porvoo: WSOY, 1976.

Kasemaa, Olavi. "Neue Gesellschaft—Neue Musik." In *National Movements in the Baltic Countries during the 19th Century,* edited by Aleksander Loit, 435–48. Stockholm: University of Stockholm, 1985.

Kastner, Emerich. *Die dramatischen Werke Richard Wagners: Chronologisches Verzeichnis der ersten Aufführungen.* 2nd ed. Leipzig: Breitkopf und Härtel, 1899.

Keudell, Robert von. *Fürst und Fürstin Bismarck: Erinnerungen aus den Jahren 1846 bis 1872.* Berlin: Spemann, 1901.

Kirby, David. *The Baltic World, 1772–1993: Europe's Northern Periphery in an Age of Change.* London: Longman, 1995.

———. *Northern Europe in the Early Modern Period: The Baltic World, 1492–1772.* London: Longman, 1990.

Knif, Henrik. *Gentlemen and Spectators: Studies in Journals, Opera and the Social Scene in Late Stuart London.* Helsinki: Finnish Historical Society, 1995.

Knif, Henrik. "Opera seria—välttämätön ylellisyys. Barokkioopperan suojelijat ja yleisö." *Tiede ja edistys* 1 (1992): 17–26.

Köhler, Joachim. *Wagner's Hitler: The Prophet and His Disciple.* Translated and with an introduction by Ronald Taylor. Oxford: Polity Press, 2000.

Köhler, Ludwig. "Jenseits und Diesseits Wagner." *Signale für die Musikalische Welt* (11 March 1869).

König Ludwig II. und Richard Wagner. Briefwechsel. 5 vols. Edited by Otto Strobel. Karlsruhe: Braun, 1936–39.

Koppen, Erwin. *Dekadenter Wagnerismus: Studien zur europäischen Literatur des Fin de siècle.* Berlin and New York: de Gruyter, 1973.

———. "Der Wagnerismus—Begriff und Phänomen." In *Richard-Wagner-Handbuch,* edited by Ulrich Müller and Peter Wapnewski, 609–24. Stuttgart: Kröner, 1986.

Kroll, Erwin. *Musikstadt Königsberg: Geschichte und Erinnerung.* Freiburg i. Br.: Atlantis, 1966.

Kühnel, Jürgen. "Wagners Schriften." In *Richard-Wagner-Handbuch,* edited by Ulrich Müller and Peter Wapnewski, 471–588. Stuttgart: Kröner, 1986.

Kuka kukin oli—Who Was Who in Finland: Henkilötietoja 1900-luvulla kuolleista julkisuuden suomalaisista. Helsinki: Otava, 1961.

Kuusisto, Taneli. *Musiikkimme eilispäivää.* Porvoo: WSOY, 1965.

Lampila, Hannu-Ilari. *Suomalainen ooppera.* Porvoo: WSOY, 1997.

Lauk, Epp, Inta Brikse, Jonas Bulota, Ainärs Dimants, Sergejs Kruks, Bronius Raguotis, Richards Treijs, and Rems Trofimovs. "A Retrospective Look at the Development of the Media in the Baltics." In *Towards a Civic Society. The Baltic Media's Long Road to Freedom: Perspectives on History, Ethnicity and Journalism,* edited by Svennik Høyer, Epp Lauk, and Peeter Vihalemm, 41–118. Tartu: Baltic Association for Media Research, 1993.

Lehti, Marko. "Suomalaisten Tallinnan-matkailun alkuvaiheet. Tallinna fennomaanien silmin 1800-luvun jälkimmäisellä puoliskolla." In *Matkakuumetta: Matkailun ja turismin historiaa.* With English summaries, edited by Taina Syrjämaa, 94–116. Turku: University of Turku, 1994.

Letters of Richard Wagner: The Burrell Collection. New York: Macmillan, 1950.

Lindenberg, Vita. "Richard Wagners Wirken in Riga." In *Opern und Musikdramen Verdis und Wagners in Dresden: 4. Wissenschaftlicher Konferenz zum Thema 'Dresdner Operntraditionen,'* edited by Günther Stephan, Hans John, and Peter Kaiser, 692–705. Dresden: Hochschule für Musik Carl Maria von Weber, 1988.

Lindgren, Adolf. *Om wagnerismen.* Stockholm: Z. Haeggströms förlagsexp., 1881.

———. "Richard Wagners sträfvanden, i kritisk belysning." *Svensk tidskrift för politik, ekonomi och literatur* (1875): 244–71.

Lithuania. An Encyclopedic Survey. Edited by Johan Zinkus. Vilnius: Encyclopedia publishers, 1986.

Liszt, Franz. *Zwei Stücke aus R. Wagner's Tannhäuser und Lohengrin.* Leipzig: Breitkopf & Härtel, 1853.

Lundin, Claës. *Oxygen och Aromasia: Bilder från år 2378.* Stockholm: Seligmann, 1878.

Lundqvist, Carl Fredrik. *Minnen och anteckningar.* 2 vols. Stockholm: Hugo Gebers, 1908–9.

Magee, Bryan. *The Tristan Chord: Wagner and Philosophy.* New York: Henry Holt and Company, 2000.

Martin, Stoddard. *Wagner to 'The Waste Land': A Study of the Relationship of Wagner to English Literature.* Totowa, NJ: Barnes & Noble Books, 1982.

Martynow, Sergej. "Richard Wagner in Russland. Zum 100. Todestag des Musikdramatikers." *Sowjetunion Heute* 2 (1983): 60–61.

McGrath, William J. "Wagnerianism in Austria: The Regeneration of Culture through the Spirit of Music." Ph.D. diss., University of California, Berkeley, 1965.

Mettig, Constantin. *Geschichte der Stadt Riga.* Riga: Jonck & Poliewsky, 1897.

Mohr, Wilhelm. *Richard Wagner und das Kunstwerk der Zukunft im Lichte der Baireuther Aufführungen.* Cologne, 1876.

Moisala, Pirkko, and Riitta Valkeila. *Musiikin toinen sukupuoli: Naissäveltäjiä keskiajalta nykyaikaan.* Helsinki: Kirjayhtymä, 1994.

Musiken i Sverige: Den nationella identiteten 1810–1920. Edited by Leif Jonsson and Martin Tegen. Stockholm: Fischer, 1992.

Mustakallio, Marja. *"Teen nyt paljon musiikkia": Fanny Henselin (1805–1847) toiminta modernisoituvassa musiikkikulttuurissa.* Turku: Åbo Akademi University Press, 2003.

Naumann, Emil. *Zukunftsmusik und die Musik der Zukunft.* Berlin: C. Habel, 1877.

Neumann, Angelo. *Erinnerungen an Richard Wagner.* 5th ed. Leipzig: L. Staackmann, 1907.

Niitemaa, Vilho, and Kalervo Hovi. *Baltian historia.* 2nd ed. Helsinki: Tammi, 1991.

Nohl, Ludwig. *Allgemeine Musikgeschichte.* Leipzig: Reclam, 1880.

Nohl, Ludwig. *Gluck und Wagner: Über die Entwicklung des Musikdramas.* Munich: Finsterlin, 1870.

Nurmi, Bruno. *Richard Wagner.* Porvoo: WSOY, 1923.

Overhoff, Kurt. *Die Musikdramen Richard Wagners: Eine thematisch-musikalische Interpretation.* 2nd ed. Salzburg: A. Pustet, 1984.

Pappel, Kristel. "Die ersten Aufführungen von Wagners Opern am Revaler Theater." In *Das deutschsprachige Theater im baltischen Raum, 1630–1918*, edited by Laurence P. A. Kitching, 139–44. Frankfurt am Main: Peter Lang, 1997.

Percy, Gösta. "Något om Wagner-traditionen i Sverige." In *Operan 200 år: Jubelboken,* edited by Klas Ralf, 94–104. Stockholm: Prisma, 1973.

Peterson-Berger, Wilhelm. *Richard Wagner som kulturföreteelse: Sju betraktelser.* Stockholm: Ljus, 1913.

Petzet, Detta, and Michael Petzet. *Die Richard Wagner-Bühne Ludwigs II.* Munich: Prestel, 1970.

Pohl, Richard. *Richard Wagner.* Leipzig: Breitkopf & Härtel, 1884.

Poljakowa, Ludmila. "Wagner und Russland." In *Richard Wagner—Leben, Werk und Interpretation: Internationales Kolloquium.* Leipzig: Karl-Marx-Universität, 1983.

Raff, Diether. *A History of Germany: From Medieval Empire to the Present.* Translated by Bruce Little. Oxford: Berg, 1988.

Raff, Joachim. *Die Wagnerfrage.* Braunschweig: Vielveg, 1854.

Ramsay, Anders. *Muistoja lapsen ja hopeahapsen.* Vol. 1, 1836–64. Translated by Antti Nuuttila. Porvoo, WSOY, 1987.

Reval/Tallinn: Porträt einer Ostseestadt. Edited by Erik Thomson. Cologne-Rodenkirchen: Liebig Druck & Verlag, 1979.

Revaler Theater-Almanach mit dem Repertoir der vom 1852 bis März 1853 gegebenen Vorstellungen für Freunde der Schauspielkunst. Edited by Alexander Borosska. Tallinn, 1853.

Richard Wagner an Freunde und Zeitgenossen. Edited by Erich Kloss. Leipzig, 1912.

Richard-Wagner-Handbuch. Edited by Ulrich Müller and Peter Wapnewski. Stuttgart: Kröner, 1986.

Riga und seine Bauten. Riga: Verlag der Buch-und Kunstdruckanstalt der "Rigaer Rageblatt," 1903.

Rigaer Theater-Almanach für das Jahr 1853. Riga, 1852.

Rigaer Theater-Almanach für das Jahr 1856. Edited by A. Herbst and R. Kretschmar. Riga, 1855.

Rigaer Theater-Almanach für das Jahr 1872. Edited by A. Lukan. Riga, 1872.

Rigaer Theater-Almanach für das Jahr 1873. Edited by A. Lukan. Riga, 1872.

Rigaer Theater-und Tonkünstler-Lexikon nebst Geschichte des Rigaer Theaters und der Musikalischen Gesellschaft. Edited by Moritz Rudolph. Riga: R. Kymmel, 1890.

Rose, Paul Lawrence. *Wagner: Race and Revolution.* New Haven, CT: Yale University Press, 1992.

Rose, W. J. "Social Life before the Partitions." In *The Cambridge History of Poland.* Vol. 2. Edited by W. F. Reddaway, J. H. Penson, O. Halecki, and R. Dyboski, 72–87. Cambridge: Cambridge University Press, 1951.

Salmi, Hannu. *"Die Herrlichkeit des deutschen Namens . . .": Die schriftstellerische und politische Tätigkeit Richard Wagners als Gestalter nationaler Identität während der staatlichen Vereinigung Deutschlands.* Turku: University of Turku, 1993.

———. *Imagined Germany: Richard Wagner's National Utopia.* New York: Peter Lang, 1999.

———. *Richard Wagner Suomessa: Suomalaisen Wagner-reseption mahdollisuudet 1800-luvulla.* Oulu: University of Oulu, 1991.

———. " 'Richard Wagner, suuri sävelseppo ja runoilija . . .' Bruno Nurmen Wagner-elämäkerta (1923)." *Synteesi* 1–2 (1991): 92–100.

———. "Sociohistorical Context and the Change of Meanings in Cinema, Especially from the Perspective of Using Filmic Evidence in Historical Studies." In *On the Borderlines of Semiosis: Proceedings from the ISI conference in Imatra, July 1991,* edited by Eero Tarasti, 303–11. Imatra: International Semiotics Institute at Imatra, 1993.

———. "Thüringenistä koilliseen. Richard Wagnerin Tannhäuserin esityshistoriaa Itämeren alueella." *Suomen Wagner-Seuran julkaisu* 6 (1995): 4–9.

Sariola, Petri. "Kävikö Richard Wagner Suomessa?" *Kaleva* (13 December 1995).

Sarjala, Jukka. *Musiikkimaun normitus ja yleinen mielipide: Musiikkikritiikki Helsingin sanomalehdistössä 1860–1888.* Turku: University of Turku, 1994.

Schemann, Ludwig. *Meine Erinnerungen an Richard Wagner.* Stuttgart: F. Frommanns Verlag, 1902.

Schwab, Heinrich W. "Der Ostseeraum. Beobachtungen aus seiner Musikgeschichte und Anregungen zu einem musikhistoriographischen Konzept." In *Nordisk musikkforskerkongress Oslo, 24.–27. juni 1992: Innlegg og referater,* 11–33. Oslo: Det historisk-filosofiske fakultet, Universitet i Oslo, 1992.

Scribe, Eugène. *Hugenotit: Opera viidessä näytöksessä.* Music by Giacomo Meyerbeer. Helsinki: Suomalainen teatteri 1876.

Scribe, Eugène, and G. Delavigne. *Robert af Normandie: Opera i fem akter.* Music by Giacomo Meyerbeer. 7th ed. Stockholm: Albert Bonniers förlag, 1873.

Sessa, Anne Dzamba. *Richard Wagner and the English.* Rutherford, NJ: Fairleigh Dickinson University Press, 1979.

Silvonen, Tauno. "Onko Richard Wagner käynyt Suomessa." *Musiikkitieto* 9–10 (1936): 150–51.

Skrābāns, Raimond: *Izcilie pasaules mūziķi Rigā: Apceres par mūzikas sakariem XIX gadsimtā*. Edited by G. Pupa. Riga: Zinātne, 1993.

Sola, Wäinö. *Wäinö Sola kertoo*. Porvoo: WSOY, 1951.

Spotts, Frederic. *Bayreuth: A History of the Wagner Festival*. New Haven, CT: Yale University Press, 1994.

Statistiline album: Album statistique. Vol. 1. Tallinn: Riigi statistika keskbüroo, 1925.

Stenhammar, Fredrika. *Brev*. Edited by Elsa Stenhammar. Uppsala: Geber, 1958.

Suolahti, Eino E. *Helsingin neljä vuosisataa*. Helsinki: Otava, 1972.

Suomen säveltäjiä. Vol. 1. Edited by Einari Marvia. Porvoo: WSOY, 1965.

Suomen taloushistoria. Vol. 1. Edited by Eino Jutikkala, Yrjö Kaukiainen, and Sven-Erik Åström. Helsinki: Tammi, 1980.

Svenska män och kvinnor: Biografisk uppslagsbok. Vol. 8. Stockholm: Bonniers, 1955.

Tajani, Angelo. *Jacopo Foroni: Från barrikaderna till Kungliga Operan*. Translated by Vibeke Emond. Höör: Två kronors förlag, 2002.

Tappert, Wilhelm. "Perkunos und Lohengrin." *Musikalisches Wochenblatt* 18 (1887): 413.

Tawaststjerna, Erik. *Sibelius*. Vol. 1, 1865–1905. Translated by Robert Layton. London: Faber and Faber, 1976.

Tegen, Martin. "Tre svenska vikingaoperor." *Svensk tidskrift för musikforskning* 42 (1960): 12–75.

Theatralisches Vergißmeinnicht, oder: Letztes Flüstern des Souffleurs. Edited by Christian Müller. Tallinn, 1861.

Tiusanen, Timo. *Teatterimme hahmottuu: Näyttämötaiteemme kehitystie kansanrunoudesta itsenäisyyden ajan alkuun*. Helsinki: Kirjayhtymä, 1969.

Tobies, Harry Herbert. *Das Baltikum: Siebenhundert Jahre Geschehen an der Ostsee*. Berg: VGB, 1994.

Topelius, Zacharias. *Konstnärsbrev: Z. Topelius' brevväxling med författare, konstnärer, skådespelare och musiker*. Vol. 1. Edited by Paul Nyberg. Helsinki: The Society of Swedish Literature in Finland, 1956.

Turbow, Gerald Dale. "Wagnerism in France 1839–1870: A Measure of a Social and Political Trend." Ph.D. diss., University of California, Los Angeles, 1965.

Veltzke, Veit. *Vom Patron zum Paladin: Wagnervereinigungen im Kaiserreich von der Reichsgründung bis zur Jahrhundertwende*. Ph.D. diss., University of Bochum. Bochum: Brockmeyer, 1987.

Voltaire. *Dictionnaire philosophique*. Vol. 2. Gotha: C. G. Ettinger, 1786.

Von Wagner zum Wagnerisme: Musik, Litteratur, Kunst, Politik. Edited by Annegret Fauser and Manuela Schwartz. Leipzig: Leipziger Universitätsverlag, 1999.

Vretblad, P. "Arlberg, Georg Efraim Fritz." In *Svenskt biografiskt lexikon*. Vol. 2, 185–87. Stockholm: Albert Bonniers förlag, 1920.

Vult von Steijern, Fredrik. "Aus dem Briefe eines Schweden über Bayreuth." In *Tannhäuser-Nachklänge. Briefe, Berichte und Betrachtungen über die Aufführungen des "Tannhäuser" in Bayreuth*, 49–53. Berlin: Freunde der Bayreuther Festspiele, s.a.

Wagner: A Documentary Study. Edited by Herbert Barth, Dietrich Mack, and Egon Voss. London: Thames & Hudson, 1975.

Wagner, Cosima. *Diaries*. Vol. 1, 1869–77. Edited and annotated by Martin Gregor-Dellin and Dietrich Mack. Translated by Geoffrey Skelton. London: Collins, 1978.

———. *Die Tagebücher*. 2 vols. Edited and annotated by Martin Gregor-Dellin and Dietrich Mack. Munich: Piper, 1976–77.

Wagner i Catalunya: Antologia de textos i gràfics sobre la influència wagneriana a la nostra cultura. Barcelona: Edicions del Cotal, 1983.

Wagner, Richard. "Ankündigung der Festspiele." In *Sämtliche Schriften und Dichtungen*. 6th ed. Vol. 16, 131–32. Leipzig: Breitkopf & Härtel, 1911–16.

———. *Ausgewählte Schriften*. Leipzig: Verlag Philipp Reclam, 1982.

———. *Bericht an den Deutschen Wagner-Verein über die Umstände und Schicksale, welche die Ausführung des Bühnenfestspieles "Der Ring des Nibelungen" begleiteten*. Leipzig, 1872.

———. *Briefe 1830–1883*. Edited by Werner Otto. Berlin: Henschel, 1986.

———. *Deutsche Kunst und deutsche Politik*. Leipzig, 1868.

———. *Dichtungen und Schriften*. Edited by Dieter Borchmeyer. Frankfurt am Main: Insel Verlag, 1983.

———. *Gesammelte Schriften und Dichtungen*. 10 vols. Leipzig: Siegel's Musikalienhandlung, 1871–83.

———. "The Human Womanly." In *Richard Wagner's Prose Works*. Translated by William Ashton Ellis. Vol. 6, 333–37. London: Kegan Paul, Trench, Trubner & Co., 1896; reprint, Lincoln: University of Nebraska Press, 1994.

———. *Mein Leben*. Edited by Martin Gregor-Dellin. Munich: List, 1976.

———. *My Life*. London: Constable, 1911.

———. "Opera and Drama." *Richard Wagner's Prose Works*. Translated by William Ashton Ellis. Vol. 2, 1–376. London: Kegan Paul, Trench, Trubner & Co., 1893; (reprint, Lincoln: University of Nebraska Press, 1995).

———. "Protest." In *Sämtliche Schriften und Dichtungen*. 6th ed. Vol. 16, 54. Leipzig: Breitkopf & Härtel, 1911–16.

———. *Rienzi, den siste folktribunen: Tragisk opera i fem akter af Richard Wagner*. Stockholm, 1865.

———. *Der Ring des Nibelungen: Ein Bühnenfestspiel für drei Tage und einen Vorabend*. Leipzig: Verlagsbuchhandlung von J. J. Weber, 1863.

———. *Sämtliche Briefe*. Various editors. 14 vols. to date (letters of 1830–62). Leipzig: Deutscher Verlag für Musik, 1967–2000; Wiesbaden: Breitkopf & Härtel, 1999–2003.

———. *Sämtliche Schriften und Dichtungen*. Volks-Ausgabe. 6th ed. 16 vols. Leipzig: Breitkopf & Härtel, 1911–16.

———. *Selected Letters*. Edited and translated by Stewart Spencer and Barry Millington. London: Norton, 1987.

Wagner Werk-Verzeichnis (WWV): Verzeichnis der musikalischen Werke Richard Wagners und ihrer Quellen. Edited by John Deathridge, Martin Geck, and Egon Voss. Mainz: Schott, 1986.

Wagnerism in European Culture and Politics. Edited by David C. Large and William Weber, in collaboration with Anne Dzamba Sessa. Ithaca, NY: Cornell University Press, 1984.

Waris, Heikki. "Helsinkiläisyhteiskunta." In *Helsingin kaupungin historia*. Vol. 3. Part 2, 7–211. Helsinki: City of Helsinki, 1950.

Watson, Derek. *Richard Wagner.* London: Dent, 1979.

Wauters, Karel. *Wagner en Vlaanderen 1844–1914: Cultuurhistorische Studie.* Ghent: Secretariaat van de Koninklijke Academie voor Nederlandse Taal-en Letterkunde, 1983.

Weber, William. "Wagner, Wagnerism, and Musical Idealism." In *Wagnerism in European Culture and Politics,* edited by David C. Large and William Weber, in collaboration with Anne Dzamba Sessa, 28–71. Ithaca, NY: Cornell University Press, 1984.

Wegelius, Martin. *Hufvuddragen af den västerländska musikens historia från den kristna tidens början till våra dagar.* 3 vols. Helsinki: Holm, 1891–93.

———. *Konstnärsbrev.* 2 vols. Edited by Otto Andersson. Helsinki: Söderström, 1918–19.

———. *Länsimaisen musiikin historia pääpiirteissään kristinuskon alkuajoista meidän päiviimme.* Translated by Axel Törnudd. Helsinki: Holm, 1904.

Weiner, Marc A. *Richard Wagner and the Anti-Semitic Imagination.* Lincoln: University of Nebraska Press, 1995.

Westernhagen, Curt von. *Wagner.* 2nd ed. Zürich: Atlantis Verlag, 1979.

Wieck, Friedrich. *Clavier und Gesang: Didaktisches und Polemisches.* Leipzig: F. Whistling, 1853.

Index

Eastman Studies in Music

Wagner and Wagnerism in Nineteenth-Century Sweden, Finland, and the Baltic Provinces

Although Richard Wagner is, of course, a figure of world importance, he and his work have had a particularly distinctive impact within the Baltic Sea region-in Sweden, Finland, and the cities of what are today Poland, Russia, Estonia, Latvia, and Lithuania. This story—or, rather, these overlapping stories—are here told for the first time in all their richness, starting with Wagner's own years as an apprentice conductor in Königsberg (in East Prussia, now the Russian city Kaliningrad) and Riga (Latvia) as well as his eventful concert tour to Russia in 1863.

Wagner and Wagnerism in Nineteenth-Century Sweden, Finland, and the Baltic Provinces explores how Wagner's operas were performed and received in the theaters of Stockholm and other cities of the region and how excerpts from them were arranged for amateur performances in private homes.

Wagner's music and his polemical writings aroused lively discussion around the Baltic, as they did everywhere else in the Western world. Thanks to detailed accounts in newspapers, journals, contemporary literature, and writings of music historians (including some by Sibelius's teacher and friend Martin Wegelius), we are privileged, in Hannu Salmi's book, to "listen in" on these debates, which often deal with crucial questions of national self-determination and of cultural independence from Europe (especially Germany, in this case) and imperial Russia.

Finally, *Wagner and Wagnerism in Nineteenth-Century Sweden, Finland, and the Baltic Provinces* reveals the surprising extent to which music lovers and operagoers from the various countries, many of them women, traveled to Wagner's Bayreuth Festival to attend performances. It also reconstructs the imaginative and patient efforts by which confirmed Wagnerians established Wagner societies in order to promote an understanding of the composer's work. Each country, each city, each local composer and conductor shows a distinctive approach–welcoming, resistant, or some of each—to the challenge of Wagner. In the process, we see music history and cultural history in the making.

"Wagner's connections with Scandinavia and the Baltic countries are more far-reaching than generally supposed, and Hannu Salmi's exhaustively researched study throws fascinating light on the contemporary reception of his works and ideas in that part of the world.
—Barry Millington, Wagner Scholar and author of *Wagner*,
editor of *The Wagner Compendium*, and
co-editor of *Selected Letters of Richard Wagner*

"Hannu Salmi adds significantly to our knowledge, . . . [using] material in languages inaccessible to most readers, and with attention to [Wagner's] effect on domestic music-making and his impact in the opera house. A wide-ranging and highly readable book that fills a genuine gap in Wagner studies, and does so with distinction.
—John Warrack, University of Oxford and
author of *German Opera from the Beginnings to Wagner*